VISIONARY GARDENS

UDO WEILACHER

VISIONARY GARDENS
MODERN LANDSCAPES BY ERNST CRAMER

WITH FOREWORDS BY PETER LATZ
AND ARTHUR RÜEGG

BIRKHÄUSER – PUBLISHERS FOR ARCHITECTURE
BASEL · BERLIN · BOSTON

This work is dedicated to an outstanding Swiss landscape architect who died much too early. He provided the stimulus for this study and was not only a magnificent teacher and mentor for the author, but above all a good friend as well:

Professor Dr.-Ing. Dieter Kienast (1945–1998)

CONTENTS

ARCHITECTONIC GARDEN DESIGN

LANDSCAPE AND GARDEN AS SCULPTURAL SPACES

LIFESCAPES

Foreword by Peter Latz

Udo Weilacher gives an enthusiastic account of visions, as they used to be called. He introduces us to gardens by a highly gifted landscape architect and decribes a typical garden artist's development, his thoughts and the key influences in the course of his life.

He describes a young gardener who takes every possible measure to learn about the world of plants and to apply his knowledge. This means designing perfectly planted gardens as pictures, creating variations on these pictures, blending them into the landscape in order to make them a unique delight. Then we hear about an apparently sudden change: planning is now seen as a rational process. Ever more disciplined structures are invented, images are left to emerge in the eye of the beholder, and gradually gardens are reduced to minimalist sculptures or expressionist objects.

Udo Weilacher does not come up with simple project interpretations. Instead, he meticulously investigates the sources and influences for every phase of his hero's work and his developing personality. He tries to pull together influences that are difficult to grasp, from art and architecture, history and travel geography, from exciting models and exhausting competitions, and he succeeds in doing so.

This book introduces us to four kinds of garden or open space:

Romantic, blossom-filled Ticino gardens, dreams of the good life. Water splashing, flowers tumbling – over walls and pergolas of local stone, summerhouses and teahouses: pictures in a southern light, fixed by a gardener's perfect care.

Places of Modernism or of abstract art, forged from the materials of progress, symbols rather than space. Fascinating sculptures that attracted a great deal of attention at two shows – horticultural shows – precisely because they were not part of the sea of flowers and so appear as irrevocable signs of the future. Like the "Theatre Garden" thrusting into the sky, doubled by water, deeply anchored below.

Lifescapes, practical spaces, made up of geometrical objects and a reduced selection of plants. In harmony with an architecture whose spaces are defined by topography and trees. Grandiose, large-scale works of art for the ubiquitous functions of everyday life. To us, records of faith in the Internationalism of art and architecture.

The logical conclusion: archetypal forms for virtual landscapes, model-like patterns and forms. Their creator: a personality making surprising and amazing turns, perfecting what he has learned and studied, then implementing seemingly sudden but obviously long matured thoughts, which attracted acclaim or hostility within the profession.

The international public is shocked or electrified by the "Theatre Garden" at the IGA in Hamburg, situated somewhere between progressive Scandinavia and the conservative south; the work takes aback established professionals and thrills students and artists who – still today – look for alternatives to the often banal vulgarizations of the over-gardened English Garden.

The ideals of this fascinating carreer could be cast in abstract rules:

The beauty of nature lies in the essence and effect of plants and materials, and in the surrounding view of landscape.

Tension emerges from geometrical clarity, which defines plants and materials, makes them manageable.

Creative work depends upon the totality of garden architecture as tied into new works where it can make its effect.

In the end, the life that Udo Weilacher describes in full detail is reminiscent of another garden architect who is being celebrated at present – Friedrich Ludwig von Sckell: a path from the existence as a young gardener, through training, influence of travel and study, influence of colleagues, building sites, to the mature work of reduction and abstraction, the masterly integration of Baroque and Rococo *joie de vivre* and light-hearted English landscape to form the classical abstraction of an idea of nature. Udo Weilacher does not celebrate Ernst Cramer as an artistic genius, but as someone who continually seeks inspiration and then voluntarily pays the price of being expelled from garden paradise in order to be admitted to the Olympus of art. A garden, for Cramer, is a sculptural space of its own right; the garden iself becomes a work of art. These objects are the Modern vision of the free man: "As in the lucidity of Modern architecture, man senses here that he is at the very centre of this garden space."

IN AN IDEAL WORLD

Foreword by Arthur Rüegg

Undoubtedly space is one of the most valuable things we can treat ourselves to nowadays. Its organization does not merely follow the old maxim: "That which is useful is beautiful too." Architects would like to claim for their work what has been true of landscape architecture from time immemorial: that the house, just like the garden, can be a work of art, capable of embodying its creator's ideas – as well as those of a particular period – as a "condensed image of an ideal world".

House and garden belong together, but their relationship is not a constant one. The pioneers of pre-Modernism – Hermann Muthesius and others – claimed the right to formally emphasize their unity and to shape it with their own resources. Ernst Cramer's early days may have been marked by the "architectonic garden style", but his own practice started from the opposite principle, which established a fundamental difference between house and garden. His extensive œuvre – about a thousand items, which Udo Weilacher makes accessible to us here – precisely traces the change in significance that Swiss gardens have undergone since the late 20s. Cramer was not a garden architecture theorist, but a successful practitioner, although towards the end of his life he did increasingly see himself as an artist. His many works were shaped by professional discourse and also in some ways legitimized by the demand from a wide range of clients.

It is remarkable that in the 30s in Switzerland, the ideal concept of the relationship between house and garden deviated significantly from certain Modern dogmas. At the time, as a result of Le Corbusier's "Five Points of a New Architecture" the roof garden became very important: it was to replace the traditional hipped roof within the new architectural order. In practically all the designs by Le Corbusier and Pierre Jeanneret (and a hundred of their disciples) this architectural element went through almost every possible variation on a "room in the open air". It was always an emphatically artificial garden space, defined by architectural means and often provided with geometrically framed flowerbeds, relating intensively to the outside world via clear-cut apertures. In contrast, the surrounding area served as a kind of foil for the house, in the sense of a Romantic landscape. "A little like in Carpaccio's pictures," Le Corbusier wrote in 1925 on the sketches for the Villa Meyer, and: "The garden is by no means laid out 'à la française', but is a wild copse where you can feel, thanks to the Parc de Saint-James, you are a long way from Paris." As a matter of fact, the house as an architecturally defined artefact was in sharp contrast with a landscape thought to be ideal – a contrast that was to be maintained even in the densely developed quarters of the "Ville radieuse".

The concept of the Swiss "domestic garden" brought house and garden into a more equal relationship. In the Neubühl housing estate, planned and built by a young architects' collective in Wollishofen, Zurich from 1928–32, the gardens of the row houses are strictly zoned in terms of depth, but laterally they are neither separated by conspicuous walls nor by high hedges. Sitting areas in front of the living rooms work as a kind of hinge between indoors and outdoors. The important gardens in this most significant Swiss Modern housing estate were designed by the Zurich landscape architect Gustav Ammann. The reader will repeatedly encounter his views, also articulated in theoretical terms, in this book – an indication that research is urgently needed here! At the 1939 National Exhibition the "garden halls" turned out to be the most interesting features of the section "Our Homes". These covered outdoor areas were intended to provide the most subtle transition possible from the interior to a designed landscape, in a spirit akin to Frank Lloyd Wright's organic architecture. These covered sitting areas were used to reconcile the modern postulate of a close connection between architecture and nature with the demands of a traditional bourgeois existence, a need which probably sprang from a longing for harmony and permanence in difficult times. "Looking out into the garden conveys a feeling that everything here must always have been like this. Everything fits so naturally into the architectural framework," was architect and art historian Peter Meyer's comment at the time. The open garden hall, often with a pitched roof, was reformulated in the 30s as an indispensable element for single-family houses, an element that found a corresponding feature in the drawer-like open balconies of the blocks of flats.

It was not, however, these domestic gardens, characterised by a functional, yet traditional Swiss country style, that sparked Udo Weilacher's interest in Ernst Cramer. Years back, the search for an up-to-date design language for landscape architecture had already led to a rediscovery of Cramer's minimalist "Poet's Garden" of 1959. Those who were out to breathe new life into Swiss garden architecture – above all Dieter Kienast – saw it as a point of reference and as a legitimate descendence of their own aspirations. This work subsequently acquired a kind of cult status among younger Swiss garden architects, and also triggered the present reappraisal of Cramer's œuvre.

Current interest in the "Poet's Garden" has its most obvious roots in the radical quality of the design approach introduced by Ernst Cramer in 1959. At the time, "Die gute Form" had become a matter of prestige and had turned into a style. Ten years of propaganda had passed since Max Bill designed the first exhibition on "Die gute Form" for the Basel Trade Fair in 1949. Swiss interior design, for example, which Cramer encountered at Interbau in Berlin in 1957, was driven mainly by formal severity; after a decade and a half of homeliness and the scent of resin this was evidence of the longing for a different atmosphere. One striking feature, for instance, was a similarity between bookshelves and Concrete images, offering variations on a similar geometrical structure. Upholstery was cut strictly cubically, and wood was often stained black. It was to be anticipated that the shift away from the rustic and the organic would sooner or later take hold of garden architecture. Cramer's powers of expression, however, could not have been anticipated: his sculptural talent was to manifest itself unmistakably from then on.

Today the pyramid shapes of the "Poet's Garden" are certainly not seen in the same way as in Cramer's time. It was to the credit of personalities like Dieter Kienast to reestablish links with the tradition of garden architecture without using traditional elements as mere set-pieces. On the contrary, it was only precise knowledge of the basic conceptual ideas of garden architecture that made it possible to recognize *trouvailles* from all periods, to look at them in a new way and to estimate their value correctly. Thus today's efforts aim to continue a story that has long started. Given this understanding of the profession, the "Poet's Garden" contained the germ of a new landscape architecture that is now once again committed to exchange with neighbouring disciplines – an exchange that architects are increasingly involved in.

It is greatly to Udo Weilacher's credit that he was not content simply to shed light on these current connections: he has ordered and analysed Cramer's complete œuvre and placed it in the context of his times. In so doing, he takes "Cramer's magnificent flower composition" as seriously as Cramer's admiration of Oscar Niemeyer's architecture, which had a crucial influence on the concept of the garden for a modern society in dialogue with modern architecture. The result is an outline of a history of 20th century Swiss garden and landscape architecture which provides exciting insights and suggests starting-points for a wide range of further research.

IN THE POET'S GARDEN
Introduction

The image of Swiss landscape architecture abroad has tended to derive in recent years from the air of semantic austerity surrounding projects by Kienast Vogt Partner, Paolo Bürgi, Georges Descombes, Stefan Rotzler or Weber und Saurer. Dieter Kienast in particular clearly rejected the ecological fundamentalism of the 70s and 80s with his essentially architectonic designs and in both teaching and practice helped young landscape architects in German-speaking Switzerland to find a new self-confidence. But the modern severity of Swiss land-scape architecture – the kind that people like to call "typically Swiss" – is not a new phenomenon. It appears time and again as the opponent of the Alpine naturalism that crops up just as frequently, and is based not least on the "puritanical genetic make-up" and "institutionalized Protestant work ethic" that the Zurich art historian Stanislaus von Moos has ascribed to the country. [1] As early as the 50s, Swiss garden architect Ernst Cramer created a considerable stir internationally with his work, which developed in the tension between naturalism and abstraction. Not just for Dieter Kienast, but also for many other landscape architects, he represented one of the early Modern models.

The conflict between traditional and modern perceptions of landscape design figured even during Ernst Cramer's apprenticeship, which he discharged under the direction of Gustav Ammann with the distinguished Zurich horticultural business Otto Froebels Erben. In the course of the cultural reform movements in Europe in the early 20th century, German architects like Hermann Muthesius, Paul Schultze-Naumburg or Max Läuger campaigned for modern garden architecture that no longer tried to imitate unspoiled nature and landscape, but acknowledged that gardens were the work of man. In Switzerland, the Swiss Werkbund, founded in 1913, was at the forefront of the reform movement. In 1918 it organized an exhibition that in Swiss architectural history is seen as a bridge to Modernism. But the Zurich Werkbund exhibition was also devoted to new trends in garden design. Gustav Ammann, the managing garden architect at Froebels Erben, gave a clear signal with a moderately architectonic garden design for a start in a new direction that he was himself however never able to pursue to fruition. But Ammann was one of the first major influences on Ernst Cramer, and initiated his lifelong search for good design in the garden.

After the First World War gardens had to be used to grow food, and increasingly became cosy re-treats from the hectic everyday world. Therefore more informal, landscape oriented garden design was again in higher demand than architectonic developments, and Cramer's search took him to picturesque Ticino gardens. Like no one else in Switzerland he cultivated the garden as an inhabitable image. He perfected the design of romantic domestic gardens on both sides of the Alps, with magnificent herbaceous planting, rustic pergolas and natural granite stone walls and paving. It was again Gustav Ammann who first recognized that paralysis in the domestic garden style could not be a satisfactory prospect in the long term, and called in 1933 for an end to unconditional adherence to the status quo. In vain. Any remaining, tentative traces of efforts to reform in Swiss garden architecture in the mid 30s were nipped in the bud soon after. Against the background of the threat of German National Socialism, Switzerland turned to national traditional values and rejected the emerging radical Modernism in architecture and garden architecture in no uncertain terms.

It was not until the end of the Second World War that Switzerland started to feel a general urge to shake off traditions, and Cramer had to acknowledge that his rustic garden design had taken him into a cul-de-sac. The Swiss Werkbund was making a vehement effort to encourage moral and aesthetic renewal in all spheres of life, as it felt that Switzerland was marked by isolation caused by the war, and the resulting inner cultural paralysis. In 1944 Ernst Cramer joined the Werkbund; the local Zurich group was directed by the old Bauhaus master Johannes Itten. His deputy, Max Bill, was also a 1944 member, and so were a whole series of other distinguished artists and architects, including Le Corbusier and Alfred Roth. Cramer, constantly on the lookout for design that was appropriate to the day, not only found access to major influential figures in Swiss art, culture and society, but also benefited from the lively cultural-political discourse. The Swiss Werkbund set new guidelines for Swiss culture with its *Die gute Form* programme from 1949, not just for its members.

The Werkbund garden architects, who also included Gustav Ammann, Ernst Baumann and others, wondered whether garden architecture would ever be able to find its way to formal clarity and abstraction and do justice to the modern criteria of "good form". Above all they still felt very much bound by the wishes of their clients. But of much greater weight was the fundamental question of whether it was possible to work with nature and at the same time to represent it abstractly, in the modern sense – without becoming suspected of imitating nature in a reactionary-conservative fashion or being guilty of superficially fashionable decoration.

"It is in the garden that the modernist finds himself stuck. That is where his interpretation of functionalism breaks down. Walls, steps, balustrades and pavements – even hedges and windscreens – are functional features that may be treated as such. Nobody will dispute my statement, however, that most of the gardens that we see is pure decoration for its own sake," was the apposite comment by the Canadian landscape architect Howard Barlington Dunington-Grubb in 1942. *"We need only once glance at the modernist's pitiful attempts out of doors to know that he is stuck. In most cases he has thrown up his hands and done nothing. The few examples where any serious effort has been made are of such severity, or such grotesqueness, as to have little resemblance to anything we should recognize as a garden."[2]*

Most progressive garden architects – and not only in Switzerland – saw no way out of this dilemma, that classical Modernism had already got bogged down in decades before.[3]

In this phase around 1950, Ernst Cramer's marked enthusiasm for experimentation and his openness to current cultural trends proved useful, and so did his talent for unprejudiced collaboration with progressive artists and architects. In his search for *gute Form* he developed the ambition of making an independent and relevant contribution to the culture of his day as an artistically creative garden architect. Intensive application to the principles of modern architecture and art smoothed the Zurich garden architect's path to the renewal of garden design. In particular, architectural innovations in the USA, Finland and Brazil, which had attracted a great deal of attention in Switzerland, served as his reference points. Ernst Cramer's "Poet's Garden" at the G|59 Zurich Horticultural Show not only proved that he had the courage to break with traditional garden architecture, but also revealed his fine instinct for handling earth modelling and modern conceptions of space. It was not the imitation of ideal classical images of unspoiled nature that was central to this masterpiece, but his abstract representation of nature. Cramer gave nature such a timelessly modern expression that attention was drawn to his work even at the Museum of Modern Art in New York, and was specifically honoured in a publication, positioned in between the icons of modern landscape architecture and landscape art.

Today, when landscape architects are looking for a design language that is appropriate for our time and are again paying closer attention to questions of aesthetics, the minimalist "Poet's Garden" is being described as a "sensation" and a "milestone in the history of Swiss garden design" by young garden architects like Rainer Zulauf of Zurich.[4] In those days Cramer did not trigger a movement, but to him the "Poet's Gar-

den", a landmark in modern garden architecture, became a signal for closer co-operation with key figures in modern Swiss architecture. In the late 50s he intensified his search for garden architecture that would harmonize with *Neues Bauen* – and finally found what he was looking for in Brazil. Cramer's radically architectonic, highly controversial "Theatre Garden" for the International Horticultural Show in Hamburg in 1963 was evidence of his enthusiasm for Oscar Niemeyer's architecture and became an interim high point in the search for architectonic garden design.

Seen from today's point of view, the "Poet's Garden" and the "Theatre Garden" were distinguished predecessors of numerous radical projects in the 60s that made Ernst Cramer a model for contemporary landscape architecture. Ultimately his designs not only created the image of "Swiss austerity", they also enrich the design vocabulary of current landscape architecture.

ABANDONING THE ARCHITECTONIC GARDEN STYLE

The architectonic garden style

Criticism of 19th century urban planning included a vigorous rejection of traditional garden architecture. After the turn of the century, the English landscape garden was dismissed as a design model that had had its day, having declined increasingly into a cliché since the great masterpieces created by landscape architects Peter Joseph Lenné and Gustav Meyer. Critics insisted that especially in cities it was essential that architecture rather than landscape be the driving force. Architects in particular started to have a great deal of influence on the development of horticulture all over Europe in the early 20th century. They were proponents of prestigious architectonic gardens, and at the same time they claimed the leading role in garden design for themselves, seeing the "gardeners" as mere helpers. Hermann Muthesius wrote in 1907:

"We absolutely must adhere to the notion that garden and house are an entity whose basic features must be devised by the same mind. They relate to each other in such an intimate way that it is utterly impossible for two people who are alien to each other, the artist and the gardener, to design the house and its surroundings, as has hitherto been the case."[5]

The architect Max Läuger was responsible for the first public park in the architectonic style in Germany in 1909: this was the Gönner Garden in Baden-Baden. Its consistent realization of everything the age was striving for actually managed to elicit an enthusiastic response from the critical garden reformer Leberecht Migge. Even on the small scale of middle-class gardens, it was then customary to aim at the natural depiction of landscape, and the landscape garden style was declining to the level of a picturesque game. The architectonic style, on the other hand, was felt to be acknowledging that gardens are works of man. They were seen as extensions of the house, and consequently an architectonic approach was needed. The aim was to create independent places of sojourn that were clearly structured in formal terms, and prestigious in character. "The art of space in the open air," wrote Marie Louise Gothein in retrospect in 1926, "was soon to be the motto for these modern gardens."[6] This did not just mean that house and garden were to be linked, as in the Renaissance, in other words not just that the exterior lines of the building should be continued in the garden; it entailed consistent spatial divisions in the garden analogous to the ground plan of a house.

Supporters of the traditional Lenné-Meyer school rejected these attempts at reform and fought back in professional publications against "international architectonic clichés," against "unnaturalness" and "fashionable fads".[7] "Mere predominance of geometrical lines, excluding plant life, always seems prestigious, cold, and often empty and lacking in spirit," warned Oskar Mertens, who was teaching horticulture at the time at the school of horticulture in Niederlenz, writing in the official organ of the Swiss Werkbund in 1916. Here he was underlining the sceptical attitude of garden architects to the new, architectonically based trends. But then he came to the conclusion in his article "Über Gartenkunst" (On Garden Art) that the previous century's inclination to imitate landscape had been happily overcome.[8] At the 1918 Werkbund exhibition in Zurich, which is seen in Swiss architectural history as the bridge to Modernism, garden architecture also hesitantly made the change from the landscape to the architectonic style. A firm called Otto Froebels Erben, with its garden architect Gustav Ammann, was one of the participants in this important exhibition. Ammann realized numerous private gardens in the architectonic style with this distinguished Zurich gardening firm, and an apprentice called Ernst Cramer worked on these as well.[9]

Ernst Cramer's early days

Ernst Friedrich Cramer was born on 7 December 1898 in Zurich, at 28 Rämistrasse, to the Zurich businessman Karl Ludwig Cramer and his wife Friederike Cramer-Fleischmann. He was the younger of two sons. The boys lost their father when they were still small and grew up in the rural Sonnenberg district of Zurich with their paternal grandparents, businessman Ludwig Cramer and his wife Karolina Cramer-Nater. The brothers, Karl Gustav Ludwig and Ernst Friedrich, spent their boyhood and their schooldays here. In his years at school from 1905 to 1913, Ernst became very fond of sport and craft activities, developing a particular enthusiasm for drawing. His talents in this field prompted his grandparents to apprentice him in the Zurich gasworks in 1913, to train for a career in technical drawing. But the constraints of the training environment did not suit the boy, and he made a decision that was to have far-reaching consequences a year later, in 1914: he started as an apprentice gardener in the distin-

Garden impression of the 30s, from Ernst Cramer's collection of photographs

guished Zurich gardening firm of Froebels Erben, which was directed by Robert Froebel at the time. Cramer worked enthusiastically in all departments of this large horticultural operation for three years, until he finished his apprenticeship. Entries in his report book from 1916 to

Ernst Friedrich Cramer (right)
and his brother Karl Ludwig
during Cramer's apprenticeship,
in about 1915

1918 show that this apprentice gardener had to address all the gardening and landscaping skills that are still taught today: building paths, constructing dry-stone walls, copse management, site modelling, garden design and so on. Ernst Cramer wrote in his report book under the heading "General points on garden design":

"The artistic design should be linked with the practical requirements. [...] Successful flower cultivation is not the ultimate aim of gardening. The smallest garden is subject to artistic principles. It should present itself to the eye as a whole, before the details assert themselves. Uniformly coherent well-balanced harmony in lines and dimensions."[10]

These entries reflect the contemporary tendency away from the landscape toward the architectonic style in garden design. But current

trends in early 20th century garden architecture were not all that Ernst Cramer learned in the course of his apprenticeship. He also met his first early role model, the Zurich garden architect Gustav Ammann.

Like any good gardening firm at the time, Froebels Erben were not just in the business of realizing gardens from existing plans, they also offered a planning service that managed garden projects from design to completion and maintenance. The strict separation of planning and execution, and the associated distinction between landscape architecture offices and gardening firms, was not established until after the Second World War, at the behest of professional associations, for reasons of market strategy. Otto Froebels Erben had their own company planning office, and this was directed by Gustav Ammann from 1910 to 1934. Ammann was thus responsible for Froebel garden designs for decades, but he also set up his own office in Zurich in 1934, and until his death in 1955 his work there was crucially important in the shaping of Swiss garden architecture. In the first two decades of the 20th century, Ammann, a pupil of the garden reformer Leberecht Migge, the Hamburg garden architect Jacob Ochs and the distinguished German herbaceous plant breeder Karl Foerster, was seen as a progressive advocate of the architectonic garden reform movement. He was one of the first people to place himself deliberately at the side of the architect and give advice as a "consultant garden architect", while most of his professional colleagues tended to object to the architects who interfered in their domain. Richard Neutra, who was also to play an important part in Cramer's life, paid a tribute to his friend and teacher Ammann in December 1954, in the foreword to the book *Blühende Gärten. Landscape Gardens. Jardins en fleurs*:

"Gustav Ammann intensified my understanding that architecture was a production intimately interwoven with nature and the landscape in which it is inserted. [...] The builder of buildings owes a profound debt to the planter of plants, who knows the common language of the two complementary creations, house and garden. Gustav Ammann has taught me some of the the the rich and subtle vocabulary of this language."[11]

Ammann, who was later to acquire an international reputation as a pioneer of garden and landscape design as President of the Federation of Swiss Garden Designers (BSG)[12], Secretary General of the International Federation of Landscape Architects (IFLA) and member of the Swiss Werkbund[13], was – consciously or unconsciously – one of the early key figures in Ernst Cramer's professional career. In Cramer's time as an apprentice, Ammann was not just important to him in questions of plant usage and garden design; and yet no close relationship between the two garden architects ever developed.

As was customary at that time, Ernst Cramer went on his travels for several years after successfully completing his apprenticeship. He worked as a journeyman gardener in Switzerland, Germany and France, here mainly in Paris, from 1918 to 1922. The few sources available mention a job in the Ranft tree nurseries in Basel and work in the horticultural firm run by the botanist and trained gardener Henry Correvon in Geneva. [14] Before being appointed to the Natural History Museum in Paris as a botanist, Correvon had also worked for Froebels Erben in Zurich. He attracted world-wide acclaim when he created the "Jardin Alpin d'Acclimatation Floraire" in Chêne-Bourg near Geneva in 1902. Correvon's outstanding achievements included introducing wild Alpines into garden cultivation, and his commitment to protecting threatened Alpine flora, which was clearly demonstrated in his co-foundation of the Association pour la Protection des Plantes. Correvon is still considered the "inventor" of the Alpine garden, and he successfully propagated the cultivation of Alpine plants on dry stone walls. Cramer and many of his contemporaries shared the enthusiasm that Correvon had triggered for this special kind of wall planting.

After his years of travel, in 1922 and 1923 Ernst Cramer attended Oeschberg Horticultural College in Koppigen, Canton Bern, which was directed by its principal Adolf Erb. The college had been founded in 1920 on the initiative of the Swiss Association of Commercial Gardeners. Given the economic importance of horticulture at the time, the college concentrated mainly on inculcating technical information and skills re-

lating to garden construction. Thus the 1922/23 curriculum contained mainly subjects that conveyed the principles of business administration, and skills concerning fruit and vegetable growing, plant procreation and cultivation, and dendrology. Subjects like geometry, surveying, plan, perspective- and nature-drawing were intended to train garden architecture skills, but teaching in the fields of ornamental plant cultivation and garden design, which would have been particularly interesting to budding garden architects, played a subordinate role at the time. It was not until 1943 that students started to demand these subjects more strongly, and then without success. The college building was not completed until November 1923, and in the mean time various buildings in Koppigen were used to provide the necessary space. [15] Cramer's fellow-students and friends included Robert Bächthold, Albert Müller, Erwin Tschanz, Paul Strebel and Jules Bertschinger. Ernst Cramer, his college reports reveal, impressed particularly with his knowledge of plants, his ability as an artist and draughtsman, and by his achievements in the field of business administration. The last-mentioned area did not continue to number among his strengths as a garden architect in his later professional life. But Cramer did develop his skills as an artist and draughtsman, which he fostered in the photography and modelling courses, to a remarkable extent in subsequent decades.

The garden architect Albert Baumann was responsible for teaching garden technology, den-

Gustav Ammann (right in front, with hat) and his former apprentice Ernst Cramer with their colleagues, in about 1939

drology, plan-drawing, surveying and geometry, and also for the garden design of the new school site, which covered seven hectares. He taught his pupils the fundamentals of garden, cemetery and landscape design. Baumann's major models included the architect Paul Schultze-Naumburg, who had promoted garden design as an architectonic task in his 1902 book *Gärten*. But for Baumann as for Gustav Ammann, the work of the garden architect Leberecht Migge was also an important source of inspiration. It is therefore not surprising that the gardens in the Oeschberg College grounds show clear signs of an architectonically conceived fruit and vegetable garden. The college classes were involved hands-on in the construction of the garden in the early years, and thus learned the principles of the "new style". Contemporary witnesses tell us that Baumann liked using the Goethe quotation "Schreiben muß man wenig, zeichnen viel" (You must write but little, draw a lot). In the plan-drawing course he regularly had his pupils copy historical garden plans, for example the plan of the Versailles gardens, in minute detail, for practice purposes. Ernst Cramer adopted Baumann's motto for himself, and it is said that after this exercise he was even able to draw the Versailles plan from memory. Baumann, who regularly attended lectures in architecture, art history and botany at the Swiss Federal Institute of Technology (ETH) in Zurich, was not merely teaching drawing skills by this method, but was also passing on his knowledge of historical garden art. 30 years later he produced his successful textbook *Neues Planen und Gestalten* (New Planning and Design), which proved to be an important compendium for generations of garden-lovers, gardeners and garden architects.[16] This authoritative work did not only include the grounds of the 20s Horticultural College, but also post-war projects by Cramer as model garden designs. Baumann, unlike Ammann, was not just one of Ernst Cramer's early mentors. Teacher and pupil remained friends

long after Cramer completed his training in Oeschberg.

All that survives from Cramer's time in Oeschberg is a four-sided, hand-written text dating from November 1922. This describes alterations to the old cemetery in the parish of Worb, under the motto "Meine Zeit steht in Deinen Händen" (My time is placed in Your hands).[17] The project description conveys the image of a functionally designed cemetery, spatially structured with poplars, planes and 1.5 to 2.8 metre high hornbeam hedges. The planting suggestions for the graves include the usual range of herbaceous plants, summer flowers, roses and evergreens. But from today's perspective the 24-year-old gardener's suggestion for the design of the central cemetery area was a striking one:

"The whole central section consists of three grave plots separated from each other by hornbeam hedges 2.8 metres high. Each of these plots contains 2 groups of 8 poplars each, including a grave mound planted with evergreens. 8–12 children's graves can be placed here, and grave-slabs are to be used. The 8 poplar columns will create a monumental effect. Low roses are to bloom in the corners of the grave plots."

This kind of grave design, which seems unduly emotional today, was not unusual at the time, and was still to be found in Baumann's 1953 handbook as a possible design alternative. Yet it seems reasonable to conclude that such a pointed, architectonic design of children's graves was a daring suggestion even under the conditions then prevailing.

After completing his training at Oeschberg Horticultural College, Cramer decided to work for five more years, from 1924 to 1929, as a journeyman gardener in gardening firms in Winterthur and in the Schaffhausen municipal gardening department. During that period he got married to Anna Russenberger from Schaffhausen in 1925. In 1929 Cramer took over a gardening firm in Zurich and started to plan gar-

Ernst Cramer (seated left)
at Oeschberg Horticultural College
in Koppigen

Ernst Cramer (standing right)
at a horticultural course

dens independently. He started teaching at the horticultural colleges in Zurich, Wetzikon and Horgen in 1929, the same year his firm was founded. Since there were no expert teachers available at the time, it was more or less compulsory for all Swiss garden architects to teach in a specialist college for a period. Former pupils portray Cramer as a teacher who seldom kept to the prescribed curriculum, but placed most emphasis on his own practical, professional experience. Even then Cramer was acquiring the reputation of a chaotic but committed and imaginative garden architect and teacher.

"What is built must dominate in every case (almost painfully for the eye at the outset), and must seem so strongly and so visibly to be of human design that the vegetation will never be able to suppress it, however luxuriant it becomes. So let us not be afraid of being hard when building gardens, otherwise nature will completely obliterate a language that is all too considerate of her. But, by contrast, we will no longer get around soft elements. This is where the rational and constructive concept fails; its application, transferred to plants, displeased us in the early days of the new architectonic garden, and we who have the landscape garden well behind us as a development cannot now close our eyes and think the result away again. For this touches upon the soul, and this is something we are not prepared to do without in our new gardens.

The cantonal Oeschberg
Horticultural College in Koppigen

The domestic garden style

Cramer realized a whole series of private gardens in the Zurich area from 1929 on, that matched a new ideal of the domestic garden in an almost exemplary fashion. Even in the mid 20s, recollections of the landscape style were gradually creeping back into garden design as the "Wohngartenstil", the domestic garden style. Gustav Ammann was sceptical about this development. "It seems to me that we are starting to move away, gradually but very visibly, from the formal garden, which we thought we had won back."[18] In an essay called "Should we smash form entirely?", the garden architect criticized the way in which garden experts were increasingly using picturesque planting material to break up the formal garden. He therefore demanded:

[...] Let us shape things as we should as human beings, and let us leave the natural process to nature, without anticipation and without deception."[19]
Ammann was still rating architectonic and landscape qualities equally in the garden. But the thrust towards free garden design that had a quality of landscaped openness was becoming increasingly accepted, not least in the discussion about innovations in modern architecture and town planning. Sigfried Giedion's essay *Befreites Wohnen* (Liberated Living)[20] appeared in Zurich in 1929, on the occasion of the 2nd CIAM Congress. Among other things, this spoke out for a move away from closed building volumes aiming at maximum prestige. A series of model housing estates were realized in Stuttgart, Brünn, Basel, Karlsruhe, Zurich, Bres-

lau, Prague and Vienna, based on the principles of Neues Bauen. This would not remain without its consequences for Swiss architecture. Like housing, gardens were to be "liberated" from rigidly architectonic form and shifted towards a landscape form intended to informally embed the crystalline building volume into nature.

A few years later, Gustav Ammann was able to put his ideas about appropriate contemporary garden design, placed between the architectonic garden style and the 'Wohngarten' style, into

style, and abandoned the open planting of large shrubs and trees that was customary at the time, so that free views of the surroundings were not impeded. This achieved a link between garden and landscape, and used the "view from the garden as a space-enhancing experience" as promoted a few years later by Guido Habers, the Munich municipal building director, in his book *Der Wohngarten* (The Domestic Garden).[22] In the interest of openness, the residents had to live without the usual separation of gardens by

The Gönner-Anlage in Baden-Baden, a park in the architectonic garden style by Max Läuger dating from 1909

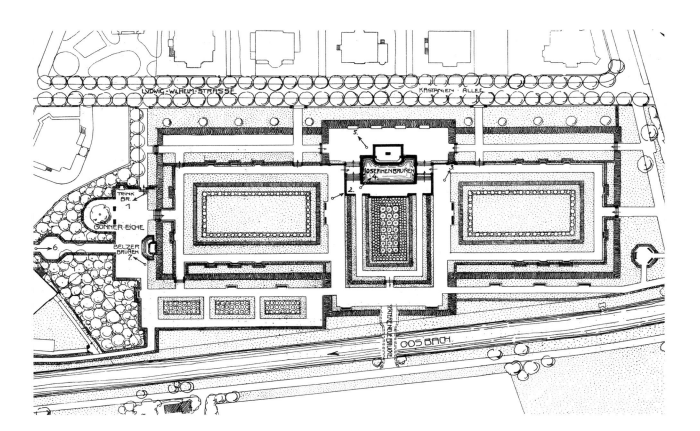

practice when the Neubühl Werkbund housing estate (1930–1932) was built in Wollishofen, Zurich. Unlike other model housing estates at the time of the 1929 economic recession in Europe, Neubühl did not have to meet the requirements of low-income workers, but was designed for the more refined needs of the Swiss middle class. The Neubühl Group, an association of progressive architects including Hans Schmidt, Paul Artaria, Max Ernst Haefeli, Carl Hubacher, Rudolf Steiger, Werner Max Moser and Emil Roth, took its slogan from Sigfried Giedion: "Liberated living. Light, air, openness". Neubühl, with its parallel rows of residential blocks set at right angles to the slope and local thoroughfares and separated by garden zones, was convincing because it offered more views, more intimacy, less noise and more rational access. The estate became the "great demonstration of Neues Bauen in Switzerland".[21]

For the garden zone between the three-storey blocks of flats, Ammann, working with the architects, devised a compelling, uniform green concept based on the architectonic garden

fences and hedges. Only streets and access paths were spatially separated from the rows of flats by rigid hedge-planting. Although scarcely any public attention was paid to Ammann's garden design at the time, it nevertheless signalled a departure from the prestigious architectonic garden and a move towards the useful domestic garden. Gustav Ammann wrote in 1933:

"On the other hand, the architectonic element no longer has to perform the task of exulting, emphasizing broad axes, building up enormous walls, on the contrary, it should be used quite modestly to emphasize the existing tectonic effects on the site or as a contrast with the sculptural and three-dimensional effect of the vegetation. [...] Today the plant is number one in the garden, and sets the tone."[23]

The material privations of the population after the First World War, the economic recession and the need for frugality that this imposed had an effect on the principles of garden design all over Europe. Design ambitions took a back seat to functional criteria. Thus gardens were not there only in the name of self-sufficiency, but also to provide spiritual healing and healthy surroundings. One of the first garden architects to influence the concept of the domestic garden was Harry Maaß of Lübeck. In his successful little book, first published in 1927, with the programmatic title *Dein Garten – Dein Arzt. Fort mit den Gartensorgen* (Your garden, your doctor. No more garden worries)[24], Maaß promoted an economical garden intended to be a "home and a place of healing", the "green homestead":

"Young people can be high-spirited and exuberant in these gardens, and even in the smallest of them there is room to relax your frayed nerves, be it that you are resting between green hedges, in sun or shade – or strengthening your muscles with spade and hoe."[25]

As the extended living space of a house, the new garden type primarily had to meet functional demands. It was intended to be suitable for playing, sunbathing, swimming, gymnastics or practical gardening. In the sixth to eighth editions of his book, Maaß added four new chapters to the catalogue of garden functions and design elements, showing the change of significance of the garden as the European economy consolidated: deck tennis, glass walls, shower pits and allotments. The chapters on "The protective glass walls" and "The garden shower, so important for our green gymnasium"[26] in particular played an important part in one of Ernst Cramer's first exhibition gardens.[27]

For Harry Maaß the functional criteria of garden design were still unambiguously central, and his eye was focused on the inside of the garden. Guido Harbers' book *Der Wohngarten*, however, which appeared in 1933, dealt with "spatial and structural elements", with design principles and with binding the garden into the landscape. The "open-air living-room" as an extension of the house – Maaß had coined these terms as early as 1927 – was certainly spatially separate from the landscape. But at the same time an attempt was made to frame the view beyond the borders of the garden, to

"gain the experience of possessing the whole landscape. Simply as an indication of a greater order, nothing more, the domestic garden, as a work of man, may not detach itself from the landscape in which it is placed, if it is to remain in harmony with its surroundings, which have grown organically."[28]

Harbers promoted design elements that were not to contradict the image provided by the surrounding landscape. For example, linking paths were to be designed essentially unobtrusively, and decorative and paddling pools asymmetrically. Banks and masonry were to be avoided at all costs, while the garden terrace was to be accorded a significant role as a lookout area and sign of the close link between living space and the garden. Harbers included the garden terrace, along with the roof garden, the front garden and all gardens connected with architecture, in the category of "dependent garden spaces".

"Dependent is not a value judgement here, but a distinguishing characteristic. It is intended to define gardens that only acquire value as experiences or living spaces in combination with something built, the house in other words, larger garden retreats and similar structures. Incidentally", added Harbers, as a reservation, *"certainly there are no garden areas that are entirely independent or completely dependent either."[29]*

The connection between house and garden, once close, was gradually loosening.

Domestic garden on a hill,
a 50s design by Ernst Baumann

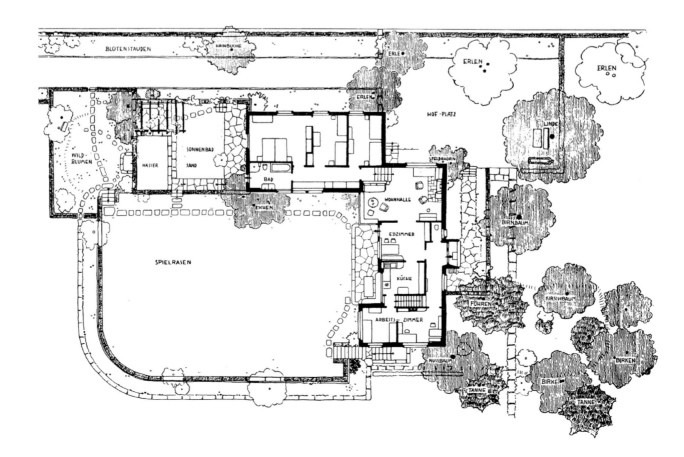

The Zurich Cantonal Horticultural Show, ZÜGA 1933

The Zurich Horticultural Show, ZÜGA, opened on the left bank of Lake Zurich on 24 June 1933. The show took place in difficult economic circumstances, as even Switzerland had not survived the effects of the 1929 world economic crisis entirely unscathed. In fact Switzerland's economy did not slump until a little later, reaching its lowest point in 1935/36, but the writing was already on the wall by 1933. Unemployment was spreading throughout the country, and affected up to 10% of the workforce in subsequent years. So one of ZÜGA's functions was to create jobs, and it did indeed provide employment for 50 to 60 gardeners and other workers for six months. Its other *raison d'être* was to show off the profession's achievements and help it to secure new commissions. The horticultural show was a joint project of the Market Gardeners' Association under the artistic direction of garden architect Gustav Ammann, in cooperation with the architects Karl Egender and Wilhelm Müller. The overall planning was the revised result of a competition between four firms, Otto Froebels Erben, Gebrüder Mertens,

Eugen Fritz & Co. and Paul Schädlich & Co. The exhibition site included the municipal gardening and tree nursery land between the bathing beach and Belvoir Park, and the leased Schneeligut park with its mature trees. The jury was not satisfied with any of the submitted competition projects, and therefore jointly agreed on a revised design by Gustav Ammann. His task was to realize a viable overall concept for the exhibition that would bring temporary exhibition halls, large theme gardens and special gardens created by individual horticultural, tree nursery and plant cultivation firms together as a coherent whole.

Peter Meyer, who had been appointed editor of the influential art and architecture magazine *Das Werk* in 1930, and was known as a committed architecture critic,[30] identified ZÜGA as one of the best Swiss exhibition ventures by any standards during this period.

"It is to the particular credit of this exhibition and its buildings that they reject any overbearing monumentality and anything that smacks merely of advertising with appropriate tact, acknowledging that anything of this kind could have done nothing but harm to the principal feature of the exhibition, its gardens and the charms of its landscape."[31]

Bianca garden on Lake Zurich in Zollikon

General plan of the Zurich Cantonal Horticultural Show ZÜGA in 1933. Number 40 on the plan marks Ernst Cramer's Pool Garden, number 33 Ammann's Colour Garden

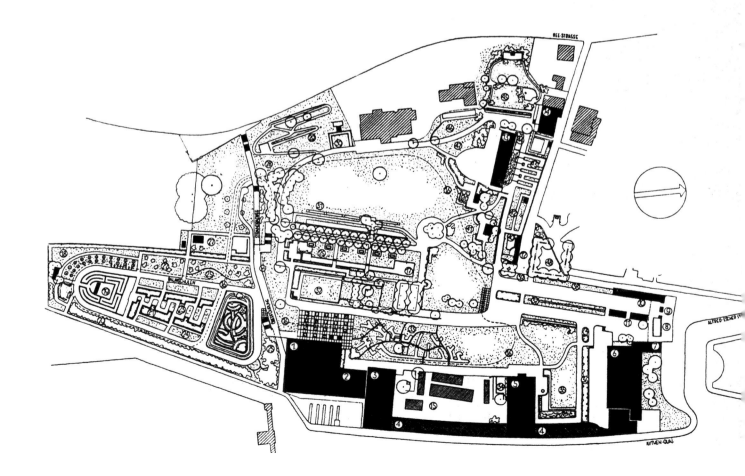

Given the alarm caused by the National Socialists' seizure of power in neighbouring Germany, Swiss architects and garden architects were particularly concerned to reject any sense of monumentality, rigid axiality and schematic imposition of geometrical patterns in the early 30s. Meyer, as an architecture critic, paid particular attention to the ZÜGA buildings:

"The architects, Carl Egender and Wilhelm Müller BSA, working with engineer Kägi of Locher & Co., have built halls that are models of lightness and simplicity, technically almost alarmingly delicate, extremely economical in their use of materials and aesthetic effect, and eminently modern for this reason."[32]

Meyer responded kindly to the garden architecture by and large, but he did also notice an element of solid carefulness that had a certain ponderousness about it. In fact the available

Gustav Ammann's 1933 Colour Garden

photographs of ZÜGA, with some exceptions, confirm his distinction between architectural lightness and solidity in garden architecture. For Camillo Schneider, garden architect and editor of the German specialist magazine *Gartenschönheit*, ZÜGA clearly signalled the end of a period of garden design that was focused on spatial and aesthetic criteria – excessively, in his view.

"The garden of the future will have to be very different in character, doing full justice to the plants as well, and developing artistic quality from the nature of the biological organism."[33]

The formal canon of the ZÜGA gardens was characterized by free lines. In terms of plant selection as well, there were sporadic attempts to resist previous group planting strategies and handle colour and form in the garden more freely. Gustav Ammann undertook a remarkable experiment in this respect. In a prestigious position he created a colour garden that was geometrically organic in form. The form of the garden was considered "wilful" at the time, and sometimes mockingly called the "sixteen-ender" or "octopus".[34] Ammann also looked for new expressive possibilities in the combination of plants, their different blossoms, leaf colours and shapes. Rather like the architects, who were using newly developed substitute materials,[35] Eternit slabs in this case, for cladding the exhibition halls, Ammann, who loved to experiment, used Hürlimann prefabricated concrete bricks to frame the flowerbeds. This choice of material was in stark contrast with the use of natural stone, which was widespread at the time, and was not greeted with enthusiasm by many of his professional colleagues. Ammann replied to his critics, who found such experiments far too bizarre and affected, by saying:

"But there is no point in pillorying this move towards a more open approach as a new fashion or something hypermodern, as individual critics have done. It was just an experiment, like the rose garden and the maze as well. Something as simple as not always sticking with what is already in existence, or even wanting to look for a style, liberating oneself, that should be the precept. And so when one looks at the exhibition plan, perhaps this tangled mass of lines is so strikingly different from the usual order of the past decade that one can rightfully assert that the flexible notion of building and garden is realized in this exhibition for the first time."[36]

While the "garden without a house" had become an idea that Ammann could entertain, many other experts clearly had difficulties with this separation of "autonomous garden spaces". They tried their best to justify both the fact that a house belonging to the garden was missing, and the somewhat fussy design of some gardens as a result of constraints related to exhibition technology, failing to recognize the potential of the new concept.

"And so one can rightly assert," wrote Ammann ten years later, *"that at ZÜGA we had for the first time*

found the realization of a natural, unconstrained and free design, which contributed to making this exhibition so popular and to making its effects visible well beyond the point otherwise reached by such local exhibitions."[37]

Pool Garden

There is no doubt that Peter Meyer had in mind the ZÜGA "special gardens" when he wrote about "solid carefulness" and a certain ponderousness in garden architecture. Here 16 horticultural firms from Zurich and the surrounding area were presenting themselves to the public, including distinguished names like Walter Leder, Gebrüder Mertens, Eugen Fritz & Co., Schädlich & Co., and for the first time Ernst Cramer's fledgling firm. The newcomer had to make do with a little garden plot near the main entrance, with the horticultural show's toilet facilities behind its northern hedge. Cramer chose the "pool garden" as his theme, and produced a copybook combination of glass walls, shower pit, pool, sandpit, a stone garden bench and natural stone paving, following the latest suggestions by Harry Maaß in *Der Garten – Dein Arzt*. Walls of raw glass as sight and wind barriers had been typical elements in his garden designs since 1919. In a 1931 drawing he expressly recommended these walls to protect the garden shower.[38] Cramer took up this idea di-

rectly and separated his pool garden with shower from the adjacent Family Gardens Club garden with a structured glass wall. He combined the shower pit with a shady seating area under an existing maple east of the natural stone pool and a sunbathing area south of it. Two garden chairs and a little round table, a stone bench by the shower and the garden recliner under a sunshade were essential garden furniture at that time, emphasizing the homeliness of the garden. Planting a small number of birches and willows in front of the glass wall and a herba-

The Pool Garden, one of the many special gardens at ZÜGA

The shower in a garden planned by Harry Maaß dating from 1931

ceous border at the edge of the pool played an essentially subordinate role, while including the existing trees and hedges actually determined the character of the spatial organization.

Cramer's contribution was so completely in tune with the current ideal of the domestic garden that it was not mentioned in its own right in the specialist press. Nevertheless, some photographs of the pool garden did appear, which was a sign that the garden architect had succeeded in creating a convincing, atmospheric garden image with few elements.[39] But he also began at a very early stage to make his own photographic record of his work, and the Zurich resident soon came to be recognized by the

The Pool Garden, an inhabitable garden image

The Vogel-Sulzer house and garden in Itschnach

camera that he always carried. Cramer cultivated a photographic view of the garden early on. The garden as an atmospheric image that would make good publicity, and an approach to gardens through photography became increasingly important to him.

We have no way of knowing for certain what influence his work for ZÜGA in 1933 had on Ernst Cramer's professional development, whether he started to be more interested in architecture or the extent to which Ammann's garden experiments with new colour combinations and materials made an impression on him. In any case, Cramer's contribution in 1933 makes it clear that he followed up-to-date gardening principles, influenced by Harry Maaß's writings in particular. In his projects post ZÜGA, which ended on 17 September 1933, Cramer continued to follow the model of the domestic garden, which is not just developed in considerable detail in Guido Harber's book. It was also propagated in 1932 by the German garden architect Otto Valentien in the form of a "Collection of old and new house gardens" with crisp commentaries, entitled *Zeitgemässe Wohn-Gärten* (Contemporary Domestic Gardens).[40]

Early garden images

The Vogel-Sulzer garden in Itschnach

The private garden of the influential Vogel-Sulzer family in Itschnach, dating from 1933,[41] makes it clear in an exemplary fashion how perfectly the Zurich garden architect had mastered the repertoire of domestic garden design. The banker Claus Vogel and his wife Irene Vogel-Sulzer had lived and worked in England for a few years. After they returned in 1927,[42] they purchased an extensive 13 hectare plot with an unobstructed view on a south-facing slope between Itschnach and Zumikon. An architect friend, Professor Dr. William Dunkel, was commissioned to plan a new house by the Vogel-Sulzers. A self-confident client with clear ideas about his own home and the tight economic situation in Switzerland were the reasons why William Dunkel, actually a pioneer of Neues Bauen, could be persuaded to plan a building in the traditional Zurich country house style, contrary to his modern view of architecture. After client and architect had fallen out, the Zurich architect Karl Beer finally completed the courtyard-style complex of buildings to Professor Dunkel's plans. Ernst Cramer, who was already known to the Vogel-Sulzers as a young gardener, was commissioned to design the garden. Apparently original site plans no longer exist, but a collection of photographs[43] taken by Ernst Cramer, and also some magazine articles, which were not written until years after completion, give us some information about the nature of the garden design. A picture of the so-called "tea-house" in the Vogel-Sulzer garden appeared on the title page of the magazine *Schweizer Garten* for the first time in November 1940. But a detailed description of the garden was not published until five years later, presumably by Ernst Cramer himself, under the title "Space and Landscape", in the monthly *Das ideale Heim*.[44] It cannot be ignored that over ten years, including six war years, that, since the garden had been completed, ten years had passed that were not insignificant for Swiss garden architecture in general and Cramer's work

in particular. And yet the 1945 description very precisely matched the ideal notion of the domestic garden developed over a decade earlier: *"It is interesting to observe how in current horticulture the landscape is being drawn into the garden, how the two are becoming interwoven and are trying to dissolve the boundaries between them. In the case of our garden, we were presented with a building complex laid out openly, and the house garden was sent out to meet the landscape from it, as it were. The surroundings and the view always help when designing a garden, and provide important basics, sometimes even defining ones."[45]*

Following Harber's demand that the design of the garden should make it possible to possess the whole landscape as an experience, Cramer rendered the boundary to the surrounding landscape almost invisible, with hedges and forest-like tree plantations. The broad view of the landscape, sometimes framed by trees, then again open, as presented from the garden terrace, shaped the character of the place.

To connect house and garden closely, Cramer built a terrace and a canopy on the garden façade of the house. "When the foundations of the house began to grow, the gardener came", was the caption to a picture in 1945:

"He brought stones, sand, cement. He started his work at the house. His hand built piers and masonry: part of the house, part of the garden. And thus the garden grew out of the house. The same stones in the house and in the garden created the connection, the same character."[46]

The transition from garden to landscape was not made only by polygonal granite slabs and little natural stone walls pointing into the landscape, but was also emphasized by the planting. A variety of display herbaceous plants, mixed with wild herbaceous plants, grew between some of the granite slabs and gradually led into the park-like design of the surrounding area, which seemed to extend to the distant wood, and sometimes even to the next chain of hills. Garden paths made of undressed polygonal slabs led inconspicuously through the garden, then up shallow steps to the tea-house. This is still hidden in a clearing in the restocked wood. It was designed as a simple, romantic garden house with natural stone walls and a slate roof.

"Let us sit on this little wall in the evenings and allow the mysteries of the nearby fir wood to work on us! Let us breathe in and enjoy the peace and nobility of this part of the garden in its simple beauty until the shadows become darker and denser, all the colours grow pale and only the silhouettes of bushes and trees are visible."[47]

Not just the tone of the explanatory text but also the character of the design were determined by romantic images that were to become all the more blatant with the passage of time. In the courtyard, which was treated as a garden in its own right, the texture of the ground was established by paving in alternating colours, and a courtyard fountain, shaded by a gnarled robinia (Robinia tortuosa), formed the central point of attention. Lavish flowers cushions, frothing over the edges of slabs and steps and the tall flowering herbaceous planting rounded off the composition of this domestic garden perfectly.

The romantic character of this garden has largely been retained to this day, despite various structural changes. The growth of the trees has

The Vogel-Sulzer garden: the path up to the edge of the wood through picturesque herbaceous planting

South terrace with a view to the mountains around Lake Zurich

The magnificant herbaceous planting
in the Vogel-Sulzer garden today

Varied herbaceous planting and
carefully worked natural stone

The garden terrace with
herbaceous planting in the 30s

The garden terrace as seen from
the garden six decades ago

run wild today and formerly sunny, open areas of the garden have been transformed into shady, introverted places.

In the 30s, Cramer realized several such prestigious private estates in the romantic domestic garden style, and these were frequently published in specialist magazines. "Taking a look at pictures of gardens …" was the title of one article by Ernst Cramer that was announced in the July issue of *Schweizer Garten* in 1937 [48], and published in the August issue. [49] The programmatic title and the character of the text announcing the article are not just typical of Cramer's design approach, but also of his fundamental dislike of analysing his own work, "[…] for nothing is more difficult for a designer than 'extolling the virtues' of his own creations." Following Albert Baumann's principle "You must write but little, draw a lot" Cramer therefore continued: "So let us leave the why and wherefore for a while and just look at pictures in the next issue."[50] Pictures of gardens always played an important part for Ernst Cramer. By the end of the 40s it was atmospheric, romantic pictures of gardens that attracted his particular attention as a garden architect, but also as an enthusiastic photographer. The article of August 1937 is clear proof of Cramer's interest in the harmony between man and nature that is to show in the realized

The tea-house in the Vogel-Sulzer garden

Draft plans for the design
of the teahouse dating from 1933

changed things considerably, not only the spatial proportions. And the view into the surrounding countryside is not as extensive as it was 60 years ago, not least because hedges and shrubs have not been controlled in their growth. High-maintenance herbaceous planting, which Cramer had placed some distance away from the house, by the tea-house, for example, have

garden image in the combination of house, garden and landscape.

"But let us not just look, let us try to grasp the designer's unambiguous will, which lies in drawing the intimate connection between the garden and the building in clear lines. But for the serious creator of gardens, the garden question is not answered in this direction only. We must strive to in-

clude the surrounding countryside, so that we acquire a real connection with nature."[51]

The fact that the exotic garden picture was sometimes more important for Cramer than the actual connection with the natural surroundings can be seen above all in the sumptuous Schoeller private garden in Erlenbach (1934) and the Bianca garden in Zollikon (1936).[52] Both gardens still occupy an exclusive location directly on the northern, sunny bank of Lake Zurich with a picturesque view of the opposite side of the lake and the Albis hills. The houses for both projects were built in the style of southern Italian villas, which Cramer's garden design adapted to perfectly. As always he included the old stock of trees, thinned it and devised framed views of the surrounding area. But in the Schoeller garden it was above all the broadleaved and palm-like woody plants such as aralias and dragon-trees that helped to establish the picturesque southern character, which Cramer pointed out with pride. He had brought off these southern images perfectly, and at first glance they removed any sense of being in gardens in northern Switzerland.

Even when he was working with simple, unadorned architecture like the houses created by the Aarau architects Richner & Anliker around 1937,[53] the idea of "connecting with nature" was still central for Cramer in his designs. In the ground plans of Cramer's four joint projects with Richner & Anliker in Aarau and Suhr, pub-

lished as "Neuzeitliche Wohnbauten" in 1937, a certain gap was starting to appear between architecture and garden architecture. Cramer held on to his basic principle of opening up the garden to the landscape, and succeeded in making these domestic gardens look bigger. Once more the views of the gardens were determined by striking individual trees and magnificent herbaceous planting, which played around the functional architecture of the houses in a picturesque fashion. It seems as though Cramer continued to design his gardens in the romantic style, following his tried-and-tested recipe for success of the 30s. Even the exterior design for the First Church of Christ Scientist in Zurich by Hans Hofmann and Adolf Kellermüller, dating from 1937/38, shows a certain schematic approach in Cramer's early work. The garden architect reacted to architecture committed to Neues Bauen with perfectly composed, traditional garden images in the domestic garden style. Certainly this solidly conservative design placed Cramer firmly within the trends of a country whose social and political climate, against the background of the threat of war, was dominated by anxiety rather than a delight in experimentation.

The 30s in Switzerland was a decade of contradictions, and not just in terms of architecture and garden architecture.[54] In a spirit of "mental and spiritual national defence", an almost programmatic concept[55] coined by Fed-

Schoeller garden in Erlenbach with grass roof

Italian flair on Lake Zurich

eral Councillor Philipp Etter in 1936, people were increasingly turning their thoughts to original Swiss culture and the traditional ways in which it was expressed. The threat from abroad and the general shift from a crisis economy to a war economy that went hand in hand with it from 1936 increased the desire for autarky in all spheres of life. In architecture, the formally tra-

a technical and organizational basis leads to cultural decline, to the nihilism of naked violence. [...] And after all the collective intentions to make the world a happier place, from the League of Nations to Communism, have failed so miserably, no one will hold it against anyone else if they turn away from collectivism in architecture as well. In any case, this move towards a framework for life secured by tradition is situated on the line of a greater development, and therefore the best of these examples do not seem antiquated, but modern."[56]
The rejection of any kind of pure modernity, clearly evident in the context of the Weißenhofsiedlung in Stuttgart in 1927, was not to be seen merely in terms of a political view of the world, in the sense of national cultural propaganda. The Modern avant-garde apparently failed to build an emotional bridge between the principles of Modern housing construction and the ideas of the general public. Laymen found this new kind of architecture too cool, functional and unemotional. In the early 30s, magazines like *Das ideale Heim* had demanded liberation from traditional ornament and ostentation, but in 1939 the pressure was for liberation from abstract and rigid functionality in the sense of a new comfort. The influential architecture and art critic Meyer on the other hand envisioned a successful symbiosis between Modern and traditional Swiss building, which would finally prove convincing to both experts and the general public.

In garden architecture, the discussion about Modernism and traditionalism was not addressed, or at best to a small extent by Gustav Ammann. In functional terms, the traditional domestic garden continued to meet the demands of Neues Bauen. Attempts, at ZÜGA 1933 for example, to develop a new formal expression for gardens appropriate to Neues Bauen were too hesitant to trigger serious debates. Even before experiments could be started in this direction, in the late 30s the traditional view of domestic garden design had reestablished itself. It concentrated formally on the production of romantic garden designs, adapting to the new living requirements only in functional terms.

ditionalist "Heimatstil" (Traditional Swiss Country Style) was increasingly adopted.
"'Heimatstil' is all the rage," stated Peter Meyer in 1939, *"– what is there behind this unclear and suspicious cliché? A tired regression into the kind of Historicism that the best architects have been fighting for thirty years? By no means, or only exceptionally in minor cases that cannot be considered typical. This trend towards the historic is rooted in the new, entirely modern awareness of the importance of cultural tradition, made more profound by the most recent events, or more precisely an awareness of the legitimacy of culture vis-à-vis things that are arbitrary, unhistorical, technically rational. We see today how loss of individuality on*

The Swiss National Exhibition, Landi 1939

The Vth Swiss National Exhibition, Landi 1939 in Zurich, became a national event of the first rank for Switzerland in the face of the outbreak of the Second World War. From 6 May to 29 October the country presented itself in a thematic show on both banks of Lake Zurich for the first time as an economically and technically progressive, well-fortified state with a strong awareness of its traditions. The architect Armin Meili had been selected to direct the National Exhibition as early as February 1935. His aim was to use the exhibition, particularly in view of the crisis, "[...] to inspire the Swiss with new courage and foreigners with a new sense of esteem for our little land-locked country."[57] Meili rejected the traditional concept of the trade fair and ultimately was able to carry through the thematic organization of the exhibition. Earlier shows had been primarily conceived of as commercially oriented advertising events for the exhibitors. In 1930, social and political themes were central, and the companies involved were subordinate.

The two parts of the exhibition on the right and left banks of Lake Zurich were linked by cable-car, and devoted to different themes. The left bank of the lake, between the Wollishofen shipyard and the Enge harbour, was the site of the "Home and People" section, the commerce and industry pavilions, the cultural sections and the military pavilions. Here the focus was on Switzerland as a modern, economically and technically progressive country, while on the right bank of the lake, attachment to the homeland and its traditions were the guiding themes. Between the Riesbach pier and the Tiefenbrunnen exit stood the agricultural exhibition halls, and on the Zürichhorn lay the so-called "Dörfli", a stereotyped model of a traditional Swiss village.

The difference between the two exhibition parts was also emphasized architecturally. Monumental axiality, a generally popular method for ordering and designing world fairs until then, was out of the question on Lake Zurich by dint of the particular nature of the site alone. While the "Dörfli" presented the traditional Swiss country style, the exhibition pavilions on the left bank of the lake were timber skeleton constructions following the principles of Neues Bauen, and were arranged along the "Höhenstrasse", over 800 metres long, the exhibition's ideological and planning backbone. The principal architect of the National Exhibition, Hans Hofmann, intended this raised structure to control the flow of visitors, but it also served as an attractive viewing promenade and covered passageway as a protection against sun and rain. "The Höhenstrasse," wrote Katharina Medici-Mall in 1996, "was a modern 'promenade architecturale', a Le Corbusier-esque viaduct on pilotis, that made the 'boîte en l'air' popular at a stroke."[58] It is all the more remarkable that Le Corbusier, as the most famous Swiss architect and Modernism's fount of ideas was not involved in Landi 1939 at all.

"The architecture was sweet," wrote Max Frisch cuttingly about Landi,[59] 30 years later, *"that was how we defied the barbaric monumentalism of the Third Reich. Sweet, not a continuation of the Bauhaus, no sign of Le Corbusier. Switzerland unspoiled, and thus as healthy as its cows."*

But Peter Meyer, delighted by the way in which the architecture at Landi 1939 presented itself as a matter of course, saw his desired symbiosis of traditional and modern Swiss building become a reality:

"Thus an exhibition has come into being that is simultaneously Swiss in the best sense and modern in the best sense. Many artists and architects who used to see traditional Swiss values as merely conflicting, a hindrance, realized the value and the special qualities of our nation while working on the Landesausstellung, and traditionally minded circles who saw modern efforts in art and architecture only as a threat to the domestic roots now acknowledge how very much these apparently alien ideas are appropriate to the nature of our country and can contribute to showing the national element in particular, and with what selfless enthusiasm these artists are prepared to serve the concept as a whole."[60]

Poster for the Swiss
National Exhibition of 1939
designed by Alois Carigiet

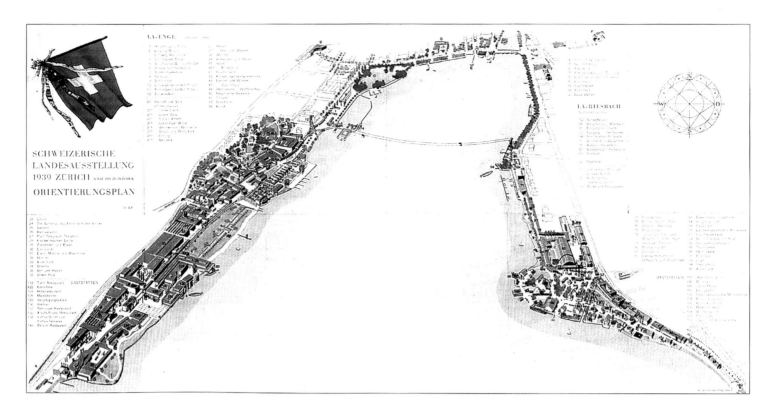

Landi 1939 on the shores
of Lake Zurich, orientation plan

Meyer, probably the most important chronicler of architecture and art in those years, was just as delighted with the contribution made by garden architecture. In a public lecture, he welcomed its liberation from the classical and monumental approach, characterized by architectural regularity:

"On a large scale the garden follows the direction of the architecture, but in detail it complements and contrasts its forms. [...] All good modern buildings, and not least the buildings in the National Exhibition, show that even when forms are purely architectonic, in other words geometrical, a human feeling is created and it is the gardens in particular that make the critical contribution. Given that their markedly open, relaxed design adjoins the buildings, it makes these seem all the more geometrical in contrast, but at the same time it shows that these simple cubes and surfaces behave in a less hostile fashion to organic nature than the classical monumental buildings."[61]

As had already been the case in 1933, Gustav Ammann was put in charge of co-ordinating the garden architecture contributions of 50 different exhibitors. The associations and individual exhibitors reflected the composition of the profession at the time. As well as the general, mixed gardening firms there were garden designers, tree nurseries, herbaceous plants cultivation businesses, pot-plant gardeners, wreath and bouquet makers, the academic branch (schools and research institutions) and the family gardening movement. As six years before, Ammann's goal was again to integrate the garden design in the existing parks as well as the context of city, lake and landscape harmoniously and to make sure he created a relaxed, not unduly dramatic overall composition of architecture and gardens. The two banks of the lake

were designed differently in horticultural terms, to correspond to the architecture. While on the right bank of the lake the preservation of the native countryside and agriculture featured prominently, the gardens on the left bank were more urban in character. The garden designers of this area, including Ernst Graf, Walter Leder, the Mertens brothers, Johannes Schweizer and Ernst Cramer, addressed modern domestic culture in their separate gardens.

The "natural" garden, based on current ideas of domestic gardens and the aesthetic esteem for the unspoiled countryside was expressly made the focal point in 1939. "Here a masterly hand was able to arrange everything that flowered and was green so naturally that one though it had always been like this and – would always have to stay that way," was the Zurich garden architect Walter Leder's enthusiastic comment.[62] Stylistically the Landi gardens in 1939 were little different from the ZÜGA gardens in 1933. Here too Gustav Ammann presented a Colour Garden, but it differed from its predecessor in that it was no longer concerned with "breaking out into greater freedom". In fact, Ammann's colourful garden design at the "Wollishofer Zürichhorn" unfolded rather unspectacularly around Hermann Haller's sculpture. "Don't just always on to what is there," was Ammann's demand in 1933, which he repeated ten years later.[63] But this time there were no signs at all of an experimental treatment of the garden, apart from the unconventional access to the gardens via the popular Schiffli brook and the unusual examples of garden camouflage in the "defence" section. Against the background of the general sense of insecurity, protecting existing achievements was clearly of profound importance to the garden architects as well.

Nevertheless, in his accurate, critical assessment of the Swiss National Exhibition in December 1939, Peter Meyer did write about some striking "Japonisms" that occured in the gardens as well.

"Some of the borrowings in the gardens are a little naïve: the principle of aesthetic balance has been understood – the main thing as far as we are concerned – what has not been understood is the detail, the stepping stones, stone lanterns, groups of stones etc. that have a clear symbolic significance in the East, while we play with them as with formal properties, which would make an educated Asian smile. But taken overall, these "Japonisms" are more than a fashionable curiosity. Present-day Europe is receptive to Eastern Asian ideas and culture much more because to a certain, limited respect it is looking for the same thing itself, and therefore today's architects have a great deal to learn from Japanese models. A feeling for the primary, naturally endowed qualities of materials has never been as highly developed in Europe as it is in the East."[64]

The garden by Eugen Fritz & Co at the Swiss emigrants' pavilion was expressly devoted to the theme of Japan, and Meyer's critical observation was exceptionally apposite. And Gustav Ammann's water courtyard in the "Kleider machen Leute" (Clothes Make the Man) section was one of the features that the architecture critic saw as a "Japonisms". Visitors crossed a lavishly planted pool on circular natural stone slabs, inspired by the stepping stones in Japanese garden pools. Were somewhat clumsy motifs like these indicating the shape of things to come in Swiss garden design? Probably not, as the Japanese garden had long been one of the archetypes of the idealized natural garden.

Hospital Garden

Ernst Cramer contributed a garden design at Landi 1939 in the section called "Vorbeugen und Heilen" (Prevention and Cure). It was more or less ignored by the specialist press, with the exception of a few pictures.[65] Cramer's garden[66] was located on the left bank of Lake

Hospital Garden: relaxing on the deckchairs

Zurich between the "Veska-Spital" and the medical welfare pavilion. "Veska", the Association of Swiss Institutions for Care of the Sick and Sanatoriums, had built a model hospital that showed visitors the whole organization of a large modern hospital at a high level of technical development. The hospital garden, in part of the surrounding open space, functioned as an extend-

hewn natural stone and timbers left in their natural state, using an existing tree as a structural element. A stone sculpture of a pelican was to give an exotic feel to the adjacent pool, framed with polygonal slabs of natural stone. Clay jugs placed around the summerhouse were intended to enrich the whole picture in an atmospheric way. Facing the pelican, at a little distance from the pool, it is possible to make out a sculpture of a small female nude in the photographs. Unlike the rest terrace, this section of the garden did not look so much as if it was there as a matter of course: it was more like a cliché of cosiness. The composition of the sculptures and jugs seemed forced in the photographs and yet was generally admired by the visitors.

Very close to Cramer's garden, Walter Leder designed his contribution outside the pharmaceutical pavilion. In front of a summerhouse under chestnut trees, broad steps led down to the organically shaped bathing pool, which had a sandpit and a shower attached to it. By this time the pool garden had become part of the standard repertoire of Swiss and German garden architecture. A group of cranes by the Zurich sculptor R. Wenning graced one of the adjacent natural stone walls. The little complex was picturesquely framed with lavish herbaceous planting. It is certainly no coincidence that in *Das Werk* of July 1939 Peter Meyer juxtaposed Cramer's simple remedial herb garden and Leder's picturesque garden in a double-page spread.[67] This combination supported his plea for joining the new and the traditional. In comparison with Walter Leder's contribution, Cramer's remedial herb garden, above all the section with the glass screens and reclining chairs, makes a rather functional, matter-of-fact impression. Cramer was reacting appropriately to the functional and formal requirements of the adjacent hospital building, and avoided creating an unduly picturesque image in his garden. The published photographs also confirm that the public were pleased to take up Cramer's offer and use the reclining chairs. Why then did

Hospital Garden: leisure terraces protected from the wind by glass screens

Path paved with slabs to the VESKA hospital

ed rest terrace, fitted with glass screens to keep out the wind as well as reclining chairs, some of them in the shade of old chestnut trees and freely available to visitors. Cramer was familiar with glass screens from the 1933 pool garden. He now worked more freely and architecturally with this element, and placed the L-shaped units in a fan arrangement at the foot of a small modelled embankment. Steps made of natural stone slabs led down to the areas where it was possible to lie down, protected from the wind, and paved with polygonal slabs. The paved areas were flanked with restrained herbaceous planting.

A few paces away from the rest area, around the entrance to the hospital, Cramer developed the motif of a rustic summerhouse built of rough-

he add the rustic part to his garden and not content himself with the simple, almost architectonic style of the rest terraces? It seems as
though he wanted to prove that of course he had
the current repertoire of "natural" residential
garden design completely at his finger-tips. Only the rustic part of Cramer's design appeared
in later publications. It was obviously more to
the taste of the public at the time than the more
austerely designed section of his project.

The Swiss National Exhibition drew over ten million visitors between May and September 1939.
It strengthened Swiss convictions and Swiss
self-confidence at precisely the right moment in
the 30s, as another World War was looming. Un-
derstandably, risky new experiments were not to
be expected under these circumstances. Landi
1939 did not provide any fundamentally new impetus for Swiss garden architecture. It was not
until two years later that hesitant critical voices
started to be raised against everything that was
linear and symmetrical. [68] The exhibition was

in fact a solid, almost dogmatic manifestation
of what had been achieved so far. Cramer was
asserting his position in the profession as a serious garden designer, but his time for sensational innovations had not yet come.

Romantic area in the
Hospital Garden

CULTIVATING THE DOMESTIC GARDEN STYLE

On 2 September 1939, while the Swiss National Exhibition was still running, Switzerland mobilized for war. The country is of course neutral, and so was not directly involved in the events of the war, but it did come to feel the effects of its economic dependence very clearly. Germany cut back on its deliveries of fuel, chemicals, iron and coal, and the building industry suffered considerably. Without coal it was not possible to manufacture cement or smelt iron or make bricks in the usual quantities. A considerable proportion of building machinery and of material available or laboriously produced in the country were needed to erect military facilities. The workforce was called up for military service for months on end. "The years before the war and above all the war years can be called a time of testing, self-criticism, and reflection," Hans Hofmann[69] wrote later, referring to the far-reaching isolation of Switzerland. Nevertheless civilian construction continued in those years, not least to counter the increasing mood of dejection in general and unemployment in particular.

Ernst Cramer spent some of his military service as a border soldier in the Rhine valley near Sargans, and with the auxiliary service camouflage detachment. This was responsible among other things for camouflaging military facilities, which actually secured work for some horticultural businesses, in contrast with other branches of production. Cramer was able to attend to his office every few weeks. He had very few commissions during the war, like all other businesses, but nevertheless moved his office into new premises at Bleicherweg 18 in Zurich in the early years of the war, and even increased his staff. Albert Zulauf, a 19-year-old journeyman gardener from Schaffhausen, advertised for a post as a landscape gardener in 1942, and Cramer took him on. As was the custom at that time, Zulauf had largely organized his own training, and completed an apprenticeship in the Homberger-Rauschenbach family estate horticultural business in Schaffhausen while the war was still on. After that, like many young, active apprentices at that time, he attended Professor Reinhard's botany course at the Zurich School of Arts and Crafts, and also evening classes on design, colour theory, art history and so on. From 1942 to 1945, while he was doing his military service, the young journeyman gardener worked in the field by the month, and then permanently in Cramer's office after the war.

There had been fundamental changes for Cramer's office even in 1938 and 1939. Ernst Cramer, with the then 19-year-old gardener Ernst Racheter, set up his own plant and tree nursery in Suhr. Racheter directed the firm for many years, growing not just herbaceous plants, shrubs and trees, but also carrying out planting work and garden design in his own right. Cramer was not always directly involved in these projects: Racheter worked independently in Suhr, often at his own risk. As it was customary in those days for planning offices to have not just their own gardening firm but also their own nurseries, founding the nursery in Suhr was considered an important stage in the successful enlargement of the Zurich planning office.

Another important change for the office came about when Willi Neukom, a garden architect from Aarau, started to work there in 1939. Neukom, a trained gardener who was 22 years old at the time, had first been employed as a foreman in the building section of Cramer's firm, before starting to work in the Zurich office in 1942. Not only was he a draughtsman with artistic talent, whose unmistakable style was very soon to make its mark on the office's plans and perspective drawings. Neukom also grew to be an outstanding designer and became very skilled at transforming Cramer's casual free-hand sketches into working drawings that could be realized. Thus Cramer was increasingly free to involve himself in creative work and soon left the draughting work to younger colleagues in the office. Willi Neukom was the first in a series of talented colleagues who learned from Ernst Cramer, developed their own style and finally set up successful offices of their own. Neukom shared considerably in the success of Cramer's office until he set up his own office in Zurich in 1951.

The gardener Ernst Surbeck from Oberhallau applied to Cramer in the same year as Albert Zulauf. Cramer obviously wanted to put his business on a more solid footing in 1942. He brought Willi Neukom into the office as a draughtsman, and put the book-keeping into Surbeck's hand, as he had commercial training. Surbeck was soon an important partner, ensuring economic stability, while Cramer never particularly bothered about his firm's financial interests. But occasionally, when Cramer wanted to devote himself to more interesting projects, or his organization became somewhat chaotic again, Surbeck had to take over as site foreman as well.

1943 was a difficult year in Cramer's private life. Anna Cramer-Russenberger, who had been seriously ill for some time, died of cancer in Zurich

Shoreline design in the Forrer-Sulzer garden on Lago Maggiore

that year, at the age of 49. Ernst Cramer knew that he and his 11-year-old daughter Susanna could not be without a wife and a mother for long. He married Gertrud Bürki in 1944, a senior military nurse in the Kurhaus am Alvier, a health resort near Liechtenstein, whom he had already met during his years of military service near Sargans. Gertrud Cramer had some experience in office organization, and occasionally came to Zurich to help out in Cramer's office. She knew about Anna Cramer's terminal illness, and was aware of the difficult situation in which father and daughter now found themselves. Cramer found a steadfast companion in her, who not only looked after the family throughout her life, but also worked in the office with great commitment. Gertrud Cramer devoted herself to organizing the office, working with Ernst Surbeck and the horticultural technician Adolf Dubs, who started work in Cramer's office in December 1944 and was also responsible for invoicing and site transactions at first.

Landscape rules

On the one hand, Swiss landscape architecture went through a serious slump in commissions in the early years of the war, which is also clearly reflected in the specialist magazines of the time. The Swiss Garden Designers' Association (Bund Schweizerischer Gartengestalter; BSG) published mainly projects that dated from before the war and had already been published several times, using titles like *Modern Swiss Domestic Gardens, [70] The Swiss Garden Designers' Association (BSG) shows new work by its members[71]* and *Thoughts about images from new gardens. [72]* Cramer featured in these publications with pictures of the 1939 Landi garden, or with photographs of one or the other private garden. The romantic Vogel-Sulzer garden in Itschnach in particular, [73] with its rustic teahouse on the edge of the wood and the lavish herbaceous planting, was one of Ernst Cramer's most popular show projects in the 40s.

On the other hand, the "time of testing, self-criticism, and reflection" was increasingly used to address the topical theme of landscape design. In a special issue of the *Schweizerische Bauzeitung* in spring 1941, some of the leading members of the BSG addressed the subject of "awareness in landscape design" in some detail: according to Walter Mertens this would increasingly become one of the profession's main concerns. [74] Under the heading "The image of the landscape and the urgency of tending and shaping it", Gustav Ammann formulated what was essentially a statement of principle, and asked some unusually provocative questions, anticipating the subsequent decades of power struggles between planners and designers:

"When dealing with a painting, we are used to the fact that an artist creates it. But a whole group of people, soldiers, farmers, foresters, soil improvers etc. work on the picture presented by our landscape. Today people still have no idea what this undirected work means for the image of our landscape, and how significantly its face will change – certainly not in its favour. [...] For who actually takes responsibility today for these violent interventions and changes of an aesthetic nature, but also relating to climate, biology and hydraulics? The authorities? Is that enough? Is there someone here who really is an authority, who has experience in relation to tending and shaping the image of the landscape, and who does not think only of technical advantages? For what is the nature of these specialists? They are mere technicians, who perfect the landscape idyll mechanically, without seeing it at all, merely from the point of view of reason."[75]

Ammann was not only asking that the interests of landscape, nature and the country be protected, but demanded that landscape design accompany all building projects, and that a planning instrument be created, a set of "landscape regulations" specifically designed to coordinate all interventions in the landscape.

Walter Mertens took Ammann's generalized demands and defined three major fields of work in which garden architects should operate in future:

"1. Opening up existing sections of the countryside as recreation areas for town-dwellers and residents of industrial areas
2. Tending the image of the landscape
3. Involving landscape designers in all enterprises that redesign the face of the landscape"[76]

Mertens paid particular attention to the third point, and divided it into twelve sub-points, in which he included almost all project types, from cemetery design to regional planning, in which garden designers should be involved in the future. This entailed an enormous expansion of the prevailing field of activity, and in time led to a broad spectrum within the profession ranging from garden architecture to landscape design. This expansion of the range of work did not meet with unequivocal enthusiasm in the profession. "The leaders of the groups that have made the greatest inroads into the field of landscape design admit quite openly today: they do not want and cannot permit any more artistic aspects into their work," wrote Professor Hans Schiller, the garden architect and then director of the Institute of Garden Design at the Institute for Horticultural Experimentation and Research in Dahlem, Berlin, as early as 1940. [77] He was fearful for the creative quality of garden architecture in Germany, while his Swiss colleagues, above all Gustav Ammann and Oskar Mertens, [78] tried to dedicate their time in equal intensity to landscape design and garden architecture.

Unlike Mertens, who was sceptical about the new dictates of landscape design, Ammann welcomed the new formal freedom for garden design in principle, and considered the question of whether a garden should be designed regularly or naturally as a mere "matter of the creator's beliefs". But the garden architect saw less latitude in the relationship between landscape and garden. Following the spirit of his statement of principle concerning landscape design to the letter, he insisted that the surrounding landscape be respected when laying out new gardens. Ammann was guided by the profession of the American "landscape architect" and the German "Landschaftsgestalter", and thought it appropriate to create a new profession in Switzerland as well:

"The landscape architect should unite the fields of the civil engineer with those of building and garden architects, whereby urban design principles in the broadest sense and the consideration of the image of the landscape as a whole are applied. This new profession does not only include the purely technical aspects of engineering, the purely constructional aspects of architecture or the purely horticultural, but sees the whole, the landscape and its design."[79]

Thus in 1942 Ammann defined the profession in terms of a very broad range of tasks that would scarcely be manageable from today's point of view; which is today established by the term landscape architect. Cramer remained largely untouched by these new landscape design tendencies. He presented his work in professional magazines in the form of picturesque garden designs. His project list from 1939 to 1944 is made up of a small number of private gardens, including some in Ticino, and the occasional small horticultural show.

of these measures; Sechseläutenplatz in Zurich, one of the most famous public places in the city, was used as a potato field, for example. Grain and potato harvests nation-wide doubled as a consequence, which mitigated the consequences of the trade blockades imposed on food supplies by the belligerent powers.

Against this background, a lavish flower and plant show was seen as a beneficial way of balancing the dictates of utility. The exhibition came as a welcome change for the participating horticultural firms, and was also a good opportunity to advertise the profession. The Swiss Garden Designers' Association contributed an exhibition of plans. A small number of garden designers, including Ernst Baumann, Eugen Fritz & Co. and Ernst Cramer were offered an opportunity to demonstrate their skills in a very restricted space, on the large garden terrace of the Kongresshaus roof. But the critical response in the professional press shows that gardens in the traditional Swiss country style were no longer particularly popular, despite an increase in general national awareness. The architect Karl Egender, who had already had adecisive role at ZÜGA in 1933, complained under the headline "Gardens in the "Traditional Swiss Country Style" of a superfluous accumulation of two many "sweet" garden motifs lacking any convincing effect in terms of space and design.[80]

Autumn in Bloom, 1942

Autumn in Bloom, horticultural and flower show 1942

The "Blühender Herbst" (Autumn in Bloom) horticultural and flower show, which ran from 17–27 September 1942 in the Zurich Kongresshaus, falls into the latter category. The Zurich Master Gardeners' Association planned this exhibition as a colourful demonstration of work by decorative plant specialists, florists and horticultural goods manufacturers, while the so-called "cultivation battle" to ensure food supplies throughout Switzerland was already raging. This emergency strategy was based on an idea by Professor Friedrich Traugott Wahlen that a piece of agricultural land can feed more or less people according to whether arable crops are used first as cattle fodder or instead for the direct benefit of man. The discovery that direct use of food means less energy loss had far-reaching effects on Swiss agriculture and landscape design in view of the supply bottlenecks caused by the war. Cattle breeding and cattle were considerably reduced, while the planting of arable crops was developed as an economic plan. Each plot of land was evaluated according to its suitability for cultivation and recorded in a national production land register. Even parks and green spaces were put under the plough in the course

Roof garden with pergola

There are obvious similarities between Cramer's pergola at the 1939 National Exhibition and the roof garden at the Zurich Kongresshaus in 1942. Once again the garden architect presented a garden with pergola in markedly rustic Ticino style, and with an exotic and lavish array of plants. The support structure of the pergola seemed improvised, and consisted of rough, whitewashed ma-

Ticino romanticism on the roof
of the Zurich Kongresshaus, 1942

Pool in the Kägi garden
with view of Lake Lucerne

sonry. Gnarled branches and a reed mat provided shade as a roof. Paving, paths, simple benches and a fireplace had been constructed from undressed polygonal slabs. To emphasize the southern atmosphere, Cramer used a variety of plants including figs, sunflowers, oleanders and tall ornamental grasses. A few vines grew on simple, sharpened wooden poles, completing the romantic Ticino image. In a small niche in the wall near the pergola there was a fine line drawing of a standing naked couple in a loving embrace, a romantic detail that Cramer photographed himself.[81] But the wilful signature of the work caused particular offence. "CRAMER Gartenarchitekt B.S.G." was written in large, simple brush-strokes on an inside wall of the summerhouse.

"If Cramer's garden is intended to represent Ticino romanticism, then there is certainly some misunderstanding. Ruins were often built in the 90s that Herr Cramer would surely still detest today. Is a sloppy company address a particular recommendation? [...] Such garden jokes should really be called "Nouveautés de Paris'", was Roland von Wyss's comment on Cramer's work.[82]

Cramer had in fact delved courageously but possibly somewhat too deeply into the box of decorative accessories for this garden, and his professional colleagues showed little understanding. Incidentally, his colleague Baumann fared no better with his cosy roof garden. He too received annihilating reviews.

Early Ticino Gardens

But Cramer's "Autumn in Bloom" roof garden is not to be seen as a special case in terms of design. In fact it reflects his enthusiasm for Ticino and the southern romantic garden style, which had already been suggested in earlier projects on Lake Zurich.[83] It is no longer possible to establish precisely how Cramer's first Ticino projects came about in detail. But he certainly found in Ticino what he was always searching for; romantic images and a luxuriant southern splendour as far as plants were concerned. The

romantic mountain and lake landscape with its picturesque villages and smart towns, the mild climate and the Mediterranean vegetation that made Ticino into a popular holiday area also attracted the young Cramer family to the southern edge of the Alps. The young landscape gardener had rented a little holiday home near Ascona as early as the thirties, and enjoyed spending time in the "Casa Biga" with his wife and daughter. He used one room in this house as an office at times, and had evidently acquired a small nursery near Locarno by 1938, which was not only used as a base for building gardens. Cramer was always looking for new ideas, and wanted to cultivate typical decorative plants in Ticino as well for use in northern Swiss gardens, but this did not work out very successfully. Many of the plants were not suited to the climate north of the Alps, and died.

As far as we can ascertain today, Cramer's first Ticino garden projects date from 1941 onwards, one year before "Autumn in Bloom" in Zurich.[84] From this time, the Ticino gardens played an important part for the Cramer office in many respects. Here Cramer could develop his projects with plants that were native to the region and with local building materials, under ideal climatic conditions. And then toward the mid 40s, well-to-do German Swiss and Germans, but also local people who had become

relevant specialist magazines and presented at various exhibitions, did not fail to make an effect. The Ticino garden, with its rustic natural stone masonry, stone steps and paths, exotic plants, pergolas constructed of dressed granite

Design plan for the Kägi garden by the lakeside in Vitznau, 1943

Autumnal mood in the former Kägi garden today

prosperous while working abroad, bought plots of land in the best locations and built villas. This was also the best financial background for creating elaborate gardens, and Cramer consequently gained a great deal of influence in Ticino garden design. His atmospheric images of peacefully romantic gardens, published in the

and unplaned chestnut planks, soon acquired a following north of the Alps as well, and this meant commissions.

The design plans for Cramer's Ticino gardens were usually produced in the Zurich office. In the early years, colleagues like Albert Zulauf and Willi Neukom lived occasionally in the Casa

The picturesque path up to
the villa near the Lake Lucerne

A magnificent backdrop
of trees frames the scene in
the Kägi garden

Biga so that they could direct operations on the
spot. The workforce who realized the projects
were usually local or from nearby Italy. Italian
masons in particular had an excellent reputation for constructing walls and paths in natural
stone.

The Forrer-Sulzer garden in Moscia

Dr. Forrer-Sulzer's garden in Moscia, dating from
1942, [85] and the garden for the Landis country
house in Minusio, dating from 1943, [86] are two
of the early Ticino gardens realized in the area
around Locarno and Ascona. The Forrer-Sulzer
garden was laid out on a wooded slope between
the lakeside road and Lago Maggiore. A three-
storey house was built in natural stone on the
steep, rocky slope. The wall of the house facing
the lake was given a slight convex curve, so that
the sunny view could be better enjoyed. The
façades of the cellar floor and of a small extension were left untreated, thus underlining the
building's strong connection with its natural surroundings. The ground and upper floors of the
house with its traditional tiled roof were plas-
tered in white, which gave the villa a quality of
noble lightness. The site was bordered by high
natural stone walls, some topped with roof-tiles,

while the direct access to the lake was left as a natural rocky shore to as large an extent as possible, but also reinforced with an embankment wall in places. Walls, steps and rocky outcrops complemented each other to form a picturesque ensemble, effectively underlined by the weeping willows that were planted. Paths parallel with the slope and steep flights of steps with traditional granite paving formed the access system for the garden, whose basic spatial structure was determined by the existing trees. Obviously the garden architect wanted to retain much of the natural character of the landscape as he found it, and restricted himself to creating paths, steps, supporting walls and a lawn as a viewing terrace by the lake. Decorative herbaceous planting and elaborate furnishings were largely abandoned in the Forrer-Sulzer garden in favour of adapting to

the landscape and creating a simple domestic garden atmosphere.

Cramer took photographs of individual key features that make it possible to draw conclusions about the atmosphere in the garden and his attitude toward the landscape. The photographs of the garden gate acting as a half-open window, solidly framed in stone, in a wall of trees and shrubs, suggests an intimate, introverted mood. The heavy oak door with its massive bolt still exists. In the 1942 photograph it is half-open, allowing us to sneak a glance into the garden. Cramer's notes on the back of the print point out that when publishing the photograph, attention should be paid to the balanced, soft exposure and its highly "fragrant" character. This makes it clear that he was not trying to achieve a sense of romantic and melancholy gravity. The photographs of the lakeside show picturesque combinations of built and natural elements. Rocks, steps, walls, trees and water combine in the picture to form a harmonious composition. A third key feature is the point of access from the house to the garden: a curved flight of steps leads informally down in the shade of the existing trees to the lawn, and the building withdraws behind the screen of these

Few garden scenes on Lago Maggiore are still reminiscent of the Forrer-Sulzer garden 1942 design

A door in the garden wall as a window in a green screen

Garden steps in the old stock of trees in the Forrer-Sulzer garden

Plan of the Landis garden in Minusio, drawn by Willi Neukom

trees. The Forrer-Sulzer garden as seen in the photographs does not look anything like a gaudily decorated Ticino garden, but draws its life from a natural-looking combination of landscape, garden and house, put together according to the principles of the domestic garden. Bearing in mind Cramer's inclination towards lavish garden compositions, the Moscia project seems strikingly reticent in retrospect.

The Landis garden in Minusio

The garden for the Landis country house was very similar to the "Autumn in Bloom" exhibition garden, and resembled a lavish stage set. It is certainly no coincidence that both projects were published in the same article, indeed on the same page, of the March 1943 issue of *Schweizer Garten*, [87] under the heading "Gardens, landscape and structural matters". The "sketch for Herr L's garden project in Locarno" and the photograph of "Autumn in Bloom" are almost indistinguishable. "But then in Ticino, the whole abundant range of plants should be used, exploiting the climatic advantages," wrote Cramer about the two photographs, and listed a whole series of plants from strawberry bush to eucalyptus that were Mediterranean flora. Cramer also recorded the Landis garden, which was destroyed with the exception of a few fragments of the surrounding walls in the early 80s by the erection of apartments. He took a series of photographs that clearly reflect the character of the garden as its designer saw it.

This project was created on a terraced site on the edge of a little valley in Minusio. The country house, a rustic villa with an L-shaped ground plan and tower-like residential section enclosed the garden on two sides and opened up a view towards the lake. Boundary walls were obviously necessary only on the road side of the garden. The entrance to the site was a simple wrought-iron gate, flanked by a palm. Palms were the leitmotif of the whole garden, whose pergola on the side of the slope, built of granite columns and chestnut timbers, accentuated the view of the landscape. Other important garden motifs were a fountain made of a tree-trunk and above all an open, rustic fireplace in natural stone. One of Cramer's most popular photographic subjects is the seemingly mediterranean view from the veranda of the Ticino mountain landscape. The wrought-iron railings with granite coping and a small sculpture form the foreground, while a palm, the garden fireplace and a few decorative shrubs and grasses make up the

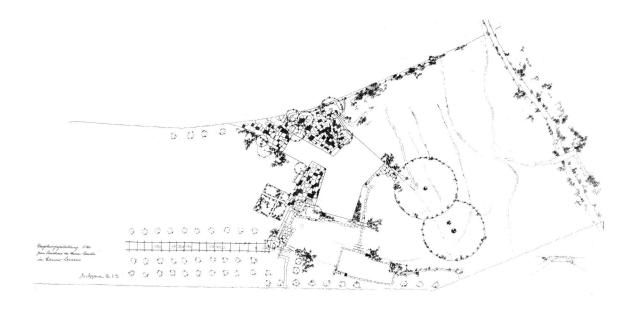

middle ground of the image. A carpet that has been hung up to dry and a chair with a bowl of fruit on it complete the exotic still life. This picture was widely published in the specialist magazines. Cramer's work was of considerable importance in spreading the ideal image of the romantic Ticino garden even then.

Gustav Ammann also published the picture of the Villa Landis in his article "Garden and landscape. Organic garden design and gardens that are alien to the landscape" in 1943 as an example of "local horticulture" in "artistic harmony" with the surrounding landscape. Ammann used the term "bodenständige Gartenkunst" (indigenous, local horticulture), thus recalling an article that he felt had pointed the way ahead. It was by the German garden architect and "Reich landscape advocate" Alwin Seifert, and published in 1929–1930.[88] "Anything alien becomes indigenous, provided that it is in artistic harmony with its surroundings," stated Ammann, invoking Seifert, thus legitimizing the use of foreign plants in local gardens with aesthetic reasons and not on botanical grounds, as had hitherto been the case. But it is not clear whether Ammann was really convinced by Cramer's Ticino garden, as he wrote:

"Here one must consider whether signs of a 'traditional Swiss Country Style' are to be found in today's gardens as well: a certain addiction to an artificially primitive quality and an undue emphasis on craft techniques, false romanticism in using folk ideas from Ticino or Valais, fountains made of tree-trunks and fireplaces inside or outside huts that could be in an Alpine meadow, or in Hollywood."[89]

As though he wanted to present a counterexample, Ammann published a garden – today called "Gustav Ammann Park" – he had himself created, "deliberately with a Ticino atmosphere", in Oerlikon near Zurich. This had none of the accessories found both in his list and in Cramer's garden in Minusio. Ammann preferred the simplicity and harmony he identified as an exemplary quality of Japanese gardens:

"In the 13th century the Japanese people learned the value of elegance and the refinement of simplicity, in connection with a simple way of life and the Zen sect in Buddhism. This will probably be our next aim when creating gardens. Reticence and uniformity are better than undue variety; gradation rather than excessive contrast will go hand in hand with a greater degree of internalization, an inspiration of material qualities. Organic is perhaps the keyword we should keep in mind when creating our new gardens today."[90]

Unlike Ammann, who constantly discussed the theoretical basis of Swiss garden architecture and addressed the relationship with architecture at an early stage, Cramer the practitioner simply published a "short pictorial report" of his work in *Schweizer Garten*. This included not only the Landis garden, but also the Vogel-Sulzer and Landi 1939 gardens, as well as a selection of other private garden projects north of the Alps. Cramer suggested that all the examples were characterized by their "harmonious balance and great empathy", which was also expressed in the plan drawings and perspective sketches. Willi Neukom was already responsible for these in those days, though he was rarely named as author in the particular articles.

In the Landis garden in Minusio

Staged garden image

The Göhner garden in Morcote

One of the most striking projects that was created in Ticino shortly before the end of the war was the Göhner garden in Morcote, on the shores of Lake Lugano. Ernst Göhner acquired a south-facing, steeply sloping plot above the lakeside road and the bathing beach, not far from the picturesque centre of Morcote. He had a villa in the Ticino style built as a holiday home at the top of the slope, with a wonderful view of the lake, and spent a few weeks at a time relaxing here with his wife Amelia. Ernst Cramer was commissioned to design the garden, which was finally realized by a local horticultural firm. Willi Neukom's perspective overall view of the garden, the front door on the lakeside road and the steep path with steps, shaded by a pergola, through the terraced vineyard, shows the proposed design in detail. But it does more than that. In fact the present state of the garden, with the exception of a few changes in the immediate vicinity of the building, still corresponds to the 1944 drawing down to the smallest detail. Today, visitors still enter the garden via a broad flight of steps and through a heavy wooden door at the bottom of the hill, then climb a steep flight of rustically constructed steps in natural stone leading up to the villa, whose palm-shaded terrace is designed as a carefully tended area of flowers and lawn. Even the terrace wall in fired pantiles and a striking wall fountain can be found in Neukom's fine drawing. The Göhner garden, which was realized under the supervision of Frau Göhner in particular, has survived in outstanding condition as one of Ernst Cramer's typical Ticino gardens dating from the 40s. While the view from the garden draws the landscape in visually, a piece of man-made landscape has actually become an important part of the garden. "Vines come up very close to the house," wrote Ernst Surbeck in 1945, "and thus combine the garden created at will with sloping indigenous vineyards that are generations old."[91] The rustic image of the villa garden is still shaped by the great terraced sloping vineyard today.

Neukom's drafting style was characterized by fine, elegant lines, and his pen produced plans as well as atmospheric perspective views. Using fine hatching, Neukom translated Cramer's design sketches into garden plans. These look almost like etchings, and were often jokingly referred to as "muck-scratchings" by the initiated. Neukom took Cramer's ideas and composed artistic and attractive drawings, using loosely grouped trees, shrubs and herbaceous plants, arranged naturalistically, and also irregular paving-stones and long flights of steps. There were no detailed, or even schematic, planting plans. Instead, the idea in the use of the plan drawing was to convince the client of the atmosphere of the garden, and then to stage this on site when the garden was realized. To this end, Cramer always chose the trees from the nurseries himself, usually opting for large, picturesque shapes with bizarre growth or gnarled roots, which the nurseries then delivered to the site. Cramer was less interested in the species of tree than in the way it grew. His enthusiasm for beautifully shaped trees often went so far that he marked too many trees in the nursery and later forgot to have them delivered. A lot of firms had to point out that goods were still to be collected, or delivered items that had been ordered even though the garden was already completely planted. In such cases Cramer showed that he could improvise brilliantly, and either had the trees planted temporarily so that he could later use them in another garden, or he adapted his plans spontaneously on site to the new state of affairs and added the extra trees to the composition.

Cramer adopted a similar approach when designing herbaceous planting. As a rule he instructed Ernst Racheter in Suhr to assemble a certain number of flowering plants for a certain date. Instead of making a precise list of plants, Cramer simply stated that about half the delivery was to consist of large decorative plants. "Cramer's magnificent flower compositions", as they were known, usually consisted of tall, vigorously flowering herbaceous plants like delphiniums, mullein or autumn anemones. This mixture of plants produced its magnificent riot of colour even in the first year, which impressed the client. Then there was the same number of smaller, broad-leaved plants. The garden owners were then to add other summer flowers and bulbs themselves. Ernst Racheter delivered the plants to the site, and then the gardeners started planting, supervised by Cramer. But sometimes Cramer positioned only the large woody plants and shrubs, and left planting the herbaceous beds to one of his staff. Cramer knew his plants very well, but he was usually more inter-

The Göhner garden under construction

Detailed drawing by
Willi Neukom of the Göhner garden
in Morcote on Lake Lugano, 1945

Plan of the Göhner garden

Still intact after over
five decades: the garden steps
in the former Göhner garden

Steps of a deliberately rustic
design in the Göhner garden

The way up to the villa leads
through the vineyard

ested in the pictorial composition than with sitting plants correctly. He left questions of this kind to the gardeners, preferring to see himself as a garden architect and focusing his attention on the artistic design.

Cramer and the Swiss Werkbund

Cramer joined the Swiss Werkbund in 1944, which was not just a sign that he was taking more interest in the cultural trends of the day. The Swiss Werkbund was one of the organizations, not attached to one particular profession, that were seeking creative answers to current problems in Switzerland arising from the isolation caused by the war and the resulting internal cultural paralysis. Besides Cramer, its members in 1944 included the garden architects Gustav Ammann, Ernst Baumann, Eugen Fritz, the Mertens brothers and A. Steinhilber. The local Zurich group was directed by Johannes Itten, the head of the School of Arts and Crafts and the Zurich Museum of Design. His deputy was Max Bill, an architect and sculptor from Zurich, while the managing director of the SWB and architect Egidius Streiff became bursar in Zurich. The 1944 members' list also includes a whole series of distinguished architects and many of what were then the best-known artists and entrepreneurs. Membership gave Cramer access to influential figures in Zurich and Swiss art, culture and society. He also benefited from the active cultural discourse among the members.

The official organ of the Swiss Werkbund (SWB) and the Federation of Swiss Architects (Bund Schweizer Architekten; BSA), the magazine *Das Werk*, had been appearing since 1930, under the direction of Peter Meyer.

"When controversies arose in the early forties, the sole editor Peter Meyer frequently published critical opinions on progressive developments in the fields of architecture and fine art, views rejected by the most advanced groups. In the war years, given the cultural reaction from the north, these views seemed intolerable," was Max Bill's later summary.[92]

Peter Meyer was voted out as editor-in-chief of *Das Werk* in late 1942, and he responded by resigning from the Swiss Werkbund. Beginning in early 1943, the magazine was also published as the official organ of the Swiss Art Association (Schweizerischer Kunstverein; SKV). Under the title *Werk* it was now edited by the architect Alfred Roth and Professor Gotthard Jedlicka. From then on, Max Bill considered that *Werk* was an indispensable, influential source of information and stimulus in Switzerland and abroad. All important current cultural events were recorded and commented on in the magazine. The change of editor, professor of architecture Arthur Rüegg acknowledged later, was particularly important for the continuation of Modernism during the war.[93] The magazine was regular reading matter for Ernst Cramer as well,

at the latest since his joining the Werkbund in 1944. It provided him with some valuable food for thought, and also occasionally offered him the opportunity of publishing his own work. Cramer's membership in the Werkbund was crucially important to the further development of his work.

Early residential and housing estates

The editors tackled the subject of "Planning and building after the war" as early as the January 1944 edition of the magazine *Werk*.[94] People were not only longing for the end of the Second World War, but since the Americans' successful interventions at the latest they were sure that the end was in sight. In January 1944 Alfred Roth spoke about the dawn of an "age of planning", and addressed the tendencies that had been emerging in landscape design since the early 40s:[95]

"The concept of planning is ringing around the whole world. The desires and hopes of a tormented humanity are clinging to it through fear of the uncertainties of the future, through fear of renewed suffering, and because of a feeling that things can no longer continue as they are. Will the coming period of peace be able to realize the longed-for harmonization of different areas of life through useful planning?"[96]

Roth felt not only that regional planning was a key task in the future of Switzerland, but as an architect he turned his attention to housing estate planning in particular. He was convinced that the synthesis of architecture and planning would be able to enhance both the functional organization of estate activities and also their artistic quality. The first issue of *Plan. Schweizerische Zeitschrift für Landes-, Regional- und Ortsplanung*, from 1944 the official organ of the Swiss Regional Planning Association, also represented a clear signal for planning efforts in the post-war period. Unlike Alfred Roth's plea, which was probably also the view of the Swiss Werkbund, there was scarcely any mention of artistic concerns in *Plan* 1/1944.

Cramer's increased commitment to the design of open spaces in housing projects from the mid 40s can to a considerable extent be seen to relate to this changed perception of landscape and the opening up of new fields of work associated with it. "CRAMER ZURICH garden architect B.S.G. advises, plans, builds gardens for housing estates" was the text of an advertisement in the magazine *Das Wohnen* for February 1944.[97] Ernst Cramer was involved in several co-operative housing estate projects for the first time that year. He thus benefited from the "second heyday" of housing construction, which came about because of the commitment of public funds and the foresight of Ernst Göhner. This phase marked the garden architecture office's entry into a field of work that was to play an important role for Cramer until the mid seventies.

Since the turn of the century, the amount of housing available in Zurich had increased more than the population growth would actually have required. Nevertheless, a stubborn housing shortage persisted in city and canton for a long period. It became clear that increases or decreases in population were not the sole factors affecting the housing market. In fact, changed living conditions and higher life expectancy were the key to the permanent lack of housing. To counter this, the Federal Government decided in 1942 to fund the construction of social housing through private developers and charitable organizations. The most important developers in the construction of housing estates in Switzerland after the First World War had been co-operative housing associations: there were 45 such housing associations in Zurich alone after 1918. By 1945 there were 36 more, and during the Second World War it was mainly public money that sustained construction activity with targeted funding programmes, under the difficult conditions of the war economy. The city of Zurich alone supported the building of 3343 dwellings in the first campaign in 1942. [98] After October 1945, housing construction was also supported for fiscal reasons as a job creation measure. This gave the co-operative housing associations the opportunity, provided they were not building expressly middle-class housing, to claim considerable sums of public money, according to the guidelines for social housing construction. 4223 dwellings were built in Zurich as a result of this second campaign between October 1945 and the end of 1947. [99]

Finally, Ernst Göhner, whose private garden in Morcote had been designed by Ernst Cramer in the mid 40s, was one of the leading private Swiss developers during the Second World War. The fact that he had laid in stocks of building materials at the right time – cement was rationed from 1942, for example – enabled this window manufacturer and building contractor to become one of the country's biggest builders, despite the shortage of materials. Following the motto "Building sites against defeatism", Göhner constructed about a sixth of the buildings in the country in the years 1939 to 1942 and 1944/45. [100]

Open spaces Wasserwerkstrasse housing estate in Zurich

One of the first of these construction projects involving Cramer's office was the housing estate on Wasserwerkstrasse, [101] built by the Zurich architects Max Aeschlimann and Armin Baumgartner. [102] The estate was built in two phases, in 1945 and 1946 for one of Zurich's oldest housing co-operatives, the federal government employees' housing co-operative, founded in 1910. One important requirement for building the estate was its central position in the city near Wipkingen station, where numerous federal government employees worked. The southwest-facing, sloping site met basic conditions,

and offered sufficient space to build an estate according to "modern thinking", as the 1944 explanatory notes put it:

"*In consideration of the strips of green planned by the municipal authorities along the banks of the Limmat, the rows of houses were placed at right angles to the adjacent streets, to correspond with modern thinking about access to residential areas. This siting made it possible to create coherent green areas 25 to 26 metres wide between the rows of houses, which will form an agreeable extension of the projected green zone on the riverbank. At the same time, this has achieved a good level of sunlight and access to views for all the dwellings, and the view is also kept open to pedestrians on Imfeldstrasse and for the subsequent buildings above this street. In the interest of admitting more sunlight to the principal living spaces, the rows of houses have been shifted slightly off the north-south line. To adapt to the terrain, which slopes steeply to the south-west, the individual houses are staggered both in height and ground plan, which gives the building masses a welcome articulation and sense of variety. In this way, it was possible to achieve a spacious development with large, coherent green areas, and also a rational opening up and exploitation of this valuable building land. As compensation for giving up any use of the attic and basement storeys for dwellings, and with a view to fitting the building project into the urban pattern well, the building authorities gave the required exceptional permission for building together at the rear, and abandoned the observance of multiple length distances vis-à-vis the building lines.*" [103]

This broken-up building scheme with communal play and garden areas corresponded to the current model of "organic urban planning" that had been the principal guideline for post-war urban planning. In parallel with developments in

General plan of the Wasserwerkstrasse housing estate in Zurich

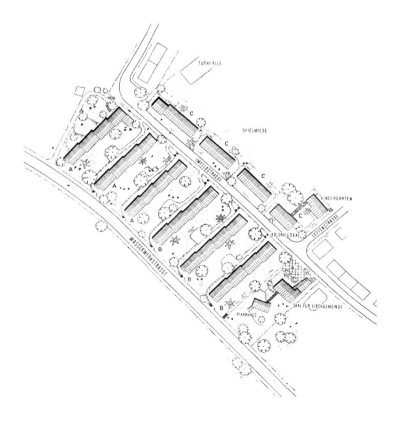

architecture, urban planners were also distancing themselves from the modern approaches that had been in evidence even in the early 30s in the Neubühl Werkbund housing estate, and keeping to traditional design features. Thus diversity, variety and "naturalness" were considered to be the ideals in garden and landscape design, which, according to Hans Hofmann in his inaugural lecture at the ETH in Zurich in May 1942, had to bring nature back into the towns.

"For this we need wide, very wide street profiles, and we need large distances between buildings, to meet the hygiene requirements. But now these wide spaces allow us to bring nature back into our towns more than we have done up to now. This allows trees to be planted in great abundance, not creating rigid avenues of trees, but following the landscape character that we use for our current garden design."[104]

Cramer's design for the outside areas precisely met Hans Hofmann's requirements: the same design elements as in Ernst Cramer's private gardens, in other words polygonal paving stones, openly planted individual trees, natural stone steps and walls, and also mixed hedge planting characterized the gardens of the Wasserwerkstrasse housing estate. Even "Cramer's magnificent flower compositions" were featured, and completed the picturesque image of the gardens, framed by the four-storey blocks of flats. To prevent the estate from resembling monotonous mass housing, the gardens were subdivided into smaller spatial units by means of open hedge and tree planting. Fences were abandoned completely.

"The housing estate is within the scope of the human eye, and avoids the impression of mass accommodation. It appeals to people as individuals

Street view of the Wasserwerkstrasse housing estate in Zurich

and makes them feel that they are at home and domiciled," acknowledged Hans Volkart, professor at the University of Stuttgart, in his book *Schweizer Architektur*, published in 1951.[105]

The material shortages of the war years meant that supporting walls and steps could no longer be used to deal with differences in height, and so these were compensated for by appropriate modelling of the site. After the war, this method, which had been developed out of necessity, was seen as a successful strategy that pointed a better way for tying estates into the surrounding landscape.[106] Cramer achieved precise site modelling in each of the four long garden spaces between the rows of buildings on Wasserwerkstrasse. In this way, each building was provided with a flat, usable lawn. Areas for drying washing and structures for beating carpets were standard features, as were the tree-shaded sandpits in each of the five gardens. Cramer designed each of the sandpits, which were framed with natural stone slabs, differently, so that there was a little variety here as well. This estate has retained the same image to this day: its internal appearance suggests a location within the open countryside rather than in the middle of a city. The impression of inner-city uniformity was to be avoided at all costs, and a sense of "massing" was to be resisted. At the same time, foreign visitors admired the impressive uniformity of the Swiss estates,[107] which was achieved not least by the consistent breaking up of the outdoor design.

The co-operative housing estate in Wasserwerkstrasse can be seen as a representative example of the many other construction projects Cramer was involved in in the 40s and early 50s. Despite different sites, and different building and estate forms – mixed development gained general acceptance in the late 40s –, garden architects held on to the model of the domestic garden that was open to the landscape for years, and transposed the traditional design principles of the private garden to the scale of the housing estate. In the course of the next few years, above all in the phase of enormous growth in the post-war period, garden designers were paying full attention to the "physical and mental hygiene of city-dwellers" and to "humanizing" the city. Green areas were allotted the role of "neutralizers" amidst teeming housing complexes. In his article "Housing construction and green areas" of March 1950, Willy Rotzler, an art historian and assistant at the Zurich Museum of Design, summed up the key principles for the design of open spaces in housing estates, drawing on his experience of projects by Cramer, later Cramer & Surbeck, among others, to support his arguments. Rotzler mentioned the Bühlacker estate in Buchs, Bellerivestrasse in Zurich and Schmockergut in Steffisburg, then also turned to the Wasserwerkstrasse project and commented appositely:

"There is no denying it: all our efforts to increase and improve green spaces contain a certain ro-

mantic longing for something that is lost, the romantic dream of a life amid unspoiled nature from which we have largely been alienated by modern life. Romanticism as such is neither good nor evil; the only question is how we indulge in it. Living in green space is not the worst form of flight from the inhospitality of everyday life and work in towns."[108]

Openly structured green spaces in the landscape style

Children's play areas on the terraced sloping site

Switzerland experienced a great sense of relief at the end of the Second World War in May 1945, though it was muted to some extent by the fact that large parts of Europe had been destroyed. The greatest concern was to rebuild Europe, and the country committed herself actively to a wide range of aid activities in neighbouring areas. At the same time, after its involuntary encapsulation, Switzerland tried to strengthen her contacts with foreign countries and with her sister democracies. Denmark, Sweden and Finland, but mostly the United States played a considerable part in rebuilding Europe and also acted as an important role model for architecture and urban planning.[109] The exhibition "USA baut" (USA Builds), which ran from 9 September to 7 October 1945 in the Zurich Museum of Design, was one of the first events of its kind. The director of the museum, Johannes Itten, created a remarkable demonstration of the new start. This presentation of American architecture did not just make people feel confirmed in their own progressive tendencies. Modern American architecture, above all the work of Frank Lloyd Wright, served as an example for a whole series of progressive architects. Wright not only built, he preached democracy, and also set standards in American landscape architecture. Swiss garden architects did not remain untouched by these new models.

Cramer & Surbeck

From 1942 onwards, Ernst Surbeck was responsible for the financial consolidation of Ernst Cramer's Zurich office. Cramer himself sometimes forgot to sort out the financial arrangements for planned projects when speaking to the clients, and would suddenly send the astonished client an invoice when he was short of money. Surbeck made sure that the books were properly kept, and efficiently directed the general project and office organization.[110] After a few years of successful work for the Cramer office, Ernst Surbeck expressed the wish to leave the firm and set up his own office. Cramer, however, valued Surbeck's support as a colleague, and offered him an equal partnership from 1945. Surbeck accepted the offer.[111] This step was enormously important for the great success of Ernst Cramer's work in the first postwar boom.

As early as January 1945, Ernst Surbeck wrote an article in the specialist magazine *Schweizer Garten* about Ernst Cramer's work in the preceding years.[112] Entirely in the spirit of his artistic and visually creative partner, Surbeck presented garden designs in the form of perspective sketches, in an article called "The garden seen from a draughtsman's point of view". All twelve drawings, including the ones on the cover of the magazine, were created by Willi Neukom's pen, even though his name was not mentioned in the article. Neukom's drawings captured the romantic mood of the planned private gardens with effortless ease, and helped the clients to gain a better impression of their future gardens. This would not have been possible with plans alone. Surbeck emphasized these correlations in his article, but between the lines also gave some insight into the design principles that Cramer was pursuing in the 40s.

Although natural garden design unquestioningly prevailed, Cramer did see the creation of a garden as an architectural task, as a meaningful spatial outdoor extension of the built accomodation. Plants were the garden designer's main building material, and were to complement the architecture formally and spatially. But Surbeck's article also stressed the creative, almost decorative aspects of Cramer's work: impressively shaped trunks and elegant decorative grasses provided accents, groups of trees drew the eye into the landscape like a stage set, objects that might spoil the view were masked by the broad crowns of trees, and slender Lombardy poplars set in counterpoint. The gardens had acquired the character of habitable ideal images. It is no coincidence that a third of the drawings depicted gardens in Ticino, which were formally scarcely distinguishable from gardens north of the Alps any more. Cramer's firm had taken part in the annual Fiera Lugano since 1944. They were the only horticultural business represented, exhibiting their southern-looking domestic garden paradises as temporary installations. Presence at this fair gained the garden architect a large number of contracts in Ticino. Albert Zulauf was responsible for directing most of the projects there on site from 1945 to 1947. Willi Neukom travelled to Ticino regularly to visit new projects with Zulauf, or Cramer himself would spend several days in Ticino to bring himself up to date about the progress of work on the various building sites. Sometimes the programme consisted of visiting tree nurseries and choosing suitable plant material. This could easily take up a whole weekend. Not all the projects planned by Ernst Cramer were realized by his own horticultural business. Sometimes local firms were appointed to put the plans into prac-

Fountain with "Akrobaten" (Acrobats) sculpture by Uli Schoop for the Dorf primary school in Suhr of c. 1954

tice, or clients used their established right and commissioned the work from firms that had worked for them before.

Cramer & Surbeck had been working for some time in Ticino with a reliable gardener who ran a good horticultural business and his own tree nursery in Cadempino. Arnoldo Manni was an

excellent plantsman and later a distinguished cultivator of azaleas as well. He met Ernst Cramer at a horticultural exhibition in Zurich. Cramer & Surbeck joined up with Manni around 1947, and founded the firm of Manni – Cramer & Surbeck. The partners regularly showed at the Fiera Lugano under this company name, and realized some of the best Ticino gardens in subsequent years. This was not the only reason why 1947 was an important year for Cramer: it also marked the successful launch into the post-war phase of growth. The 1947 advertising slogan read: "Cramer & Surbeck, Gartenarchitekten BSG SWB. Zurich, Suhr, Lugano. We design and realize gardens all over Switzerland."

Where is horticulture now?

In the February 1945 issue of *Schweizer Garten*,[113] Gustav Ammann, in response to an article by Georgine Oeri,[114] asked the question: "Is the 'natural' a substitute for form?" He followed her in that "naturalness" had let to a dismissal of formalistic garden design in the mid 30s, but he wanted the quality of "natural" to be applied not only to vegetation, but to architecture as well. Against the background of her interest in art history, Georgine Oeri had defined "naturalness" as an "untransformed, undesigned copy of reality", in contrast to formalism

and stylization. Ammann went one step further and acknowledged that "naturalness" had in turn become a style itself, and threatened to end up as formalism. Cramer's projects were already showing symptoms of this, and Ammann prophesied:

"The 'naturalness' that we are creating is probably valuable as a necessary transition, but it will not survive in the long run. But the emerging counter-movement will by no means lead to artificial canals without any bends. Rather, in Georgine Oeri's view, it is emerging only because of a retrospective metaphysical connection that is being generally experienced and acknowledged through conviction, and which does not seem impossible after these world events."

This prophecy was not just evidence of the great upheaval that the Second World War had caused in all spheres of life. It suggested the readiness to make a fresh start. Ammann's example of a "natural" garden, which he wanted to use to demonstrate the new trend, had geometrically organized paths, rectangular natural stone slabs and a tentative opening up of the garden space in favour of a clearly bordered lawn, hesitantly hinting at imminent innovations in garden design. Ammann was giving the house – a low building with "all mod cons" and large windows, admitting a great deal of light, reaching to floor level on the ground floor – an essentially moderately traditional domestic garden. From today's point of view it would be placed somewhere between the traditional Swiss country style and modern garden architecture.

One year later, Ernst Cramer published his first article in *Werk*. Called "Where do we stand in horticulture today?"[115], it is one of his few articles on theoretical principles. The essay clarified his view of his work and suggested a change of course in his thinking as a garden architect, even though the illustrations imply that he was clinging on to traditions: the photographs of the Vogel-Sulzer garden in Itschnach[116] were published yet again, complemented by Willi Neukom's typical drawings of a small domestic garden project in the Canton of Lucerne.

Cramer defined the garden architect as a creative artist who, like all architects, sculptors and painters, should have the right inclinations and talents. This avowal matches Cramer's intuitive approach to his work. At the same time, and this was a new component, he emphasized the need to create order and to plan deliberately, as this was the only way to achieve results that could be assessed practically. The need to plan and to create order runs like a thread through all spheres of life, including art, after the Second World War. In fact Alfred Roth had announced the "planning age" as early as 1944.[117] And even a year before that, Georg Schmidt had written in an interesting appreciation of an exhibition on abstract and surrealist art in Switzerland:

"There is a power at work in all three forms of non-representational art that is particularly strong in

our day, and this is no coincidence: rational and geometric constructivism shows the desire for order, for the sensible use of strengths and for overcoming things that are chaotic, senseless and devoid of function."[118]

Cramer was still a long way from rational and geometric constructivism, although he did know Max Bill from the Zurich Werkbund group, and was soon to come into contact, at a horticultural show, with one of those iconic works whose predecessors were also acknowledged by Georg Schmidt in his article: Bill's "Kontinuität" (Continuity). Nevertheless it is clear how the garden architect's thinking had been lastingly affected by the events of the war, and in which direction the new ideas were pushing. As well as a thorough theoretical and practical knowledge of the profession, Cramer's treatise required the garden architect to have a well-developed sense of colour, form and proportion, knowledge of social conditions and an ability to empathize with the life-style and needs of the future users of the garden. Even at that time, Cramer was markedly characterized by this sensibility. His unobtrusive negotiating skills and his gift for addressing each of his client's wishes creatively gave him a good reputation and elicited numerous interesting commissions.

In 1946, Cramer still saw every garden as an "independent garden space", as Guido Harbers had put it.[119] But he also emphasized new factors that affected decisions, namely the influence of the environment and landscape. The Swiss landscape in particular, with all its different regions, climatic conditions and building traditions, was pointed out by Cramer in his article. He also stressed the value of using materials appropriate to the location. The man who even a few years earlier had tried to export Ticino plants, materials and garden design elements into German-speaking Switzerland, stated in 1946 that any attempt at transplanting place-specific motifs was inevitably condemned to failure: "For example, we will never be able to make a Ticino pergola look natural in our gardens north of the Alps."[120] Cramer was interested in plain, unfussy design and site-specific plant selection, and he emphasized the gardener's obligations to landscape architecture and nature. Hedges and tree-lined avenues that had formerly been cut geometrically were now to be replaced with groups of trees and plants growing freely. House, garden and landscape were to form an unpretentious unit by means of decorative and architectural plant use, and thus do justice to the human need for harmony.

It is only by comparing Ammann's ideal garden design of February 1945 and Cramer & Surbeck's garden plan in the theoretical article of March 1946 that it becomes clear how strongly Cramer was formally bound to the traditional domestic garden type. Stressing regional qualities certainly hampered uninhibited imitation of Ticino garden images north of the Alps, but it also harboured the danger of pre-

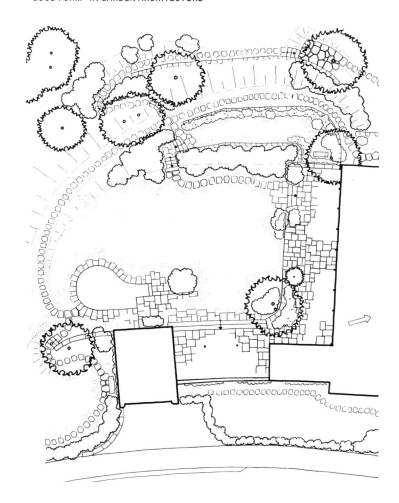

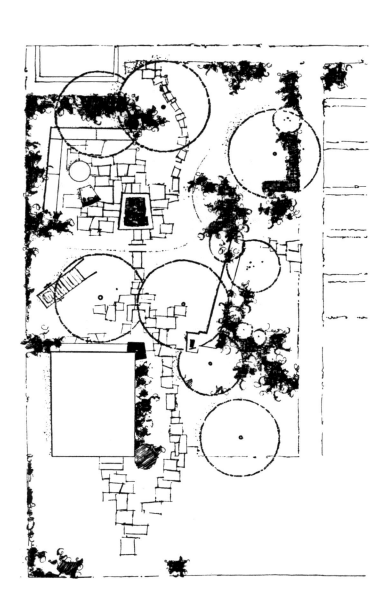

venting new and innovative ideas. Hans Jakob Barth, who started work in Cramer's office and horticultural business as a young gardener – and also a talented draughtsman – in 1946, described his experiences in this period in great detail in an article called "Gardens like bouquets of flowers" in 1987. [121] Cramer's intuitive drive in matters of design, his high esteem for impeccable craftsmanship, and his efforts to design garden images in three dimensions are clearly expressed in Barth's description of the period between 1946 and 1951:

"He created pictures, that was his strength. He was best at exhibition gardens. For Cramer planning was an intuitive process, not consciously rational, but quite irrational, almost instinctive."[122]

The Zurich Cantonal Agriculture and Trade Exhibition, ZÜKA 1947

The fear that the war-related depression would lead to an economic crisis in the country proved groundless. On the contrary. The demand for goods in war-damaged Europe was so great that exports from Switzerland, whose infrastructure had remained intact, rose in leaps and bounds. As part of the economic boom, the city of Zurich regained its importance as a commercial and cultural centre. To manifest this position, cantonal trade and agriculture circles and the Swiss Animal Breeders' Association decided in 1945 to stage the Zurich Cantonal Agriculture

and Trade Exhibition, ZÜKA from 23 August to 19 October 1947. Architect Hans Fischli was to direct the exhibition. He had been involved in Landi 1939 as Hans Hofmann's assistant where he had built the "Palais des attractions" and the "Children's Paradise". Fritz Haggenmacher, as the ZÜKA garden architect, working with the City of Zurich's Horticultural Department, was responsible for co-ordinating contributions by garden architects. Once again part of the right bank of Lake Zurich was made available to participants to present their disciplines. Expectations of this first large show of agricultural and commercial achievement since the war were running high, not least because the public remembered the success of "Landi 39". Like Landi, ZÜKA was arranged thematically, but in terms of the exhibition architecture Hans Fischli did not want to copy the Landi style. Any comparison with the Landi was bound to suffer from the fact that far less money was available. Many critics also felt that it was ill-advised to hold an exhibition of this kind in view of the flourishing economy, the labour shortage and the lack of materials. They turned out to be right to an extent, as the exhibition was a financial fiasco, for which people wanted to blame Hans Fischli. In fact, given full order books, the exhibitors had to force themselves to take part. But some did also see, after years of isolation and a generally burgeoning interest in goods imported from abroad, that it was necessary to present themselves to their national public as a productive industry.

Cramer & Surbeck's garden tent at the Zurich Cantonal Agricultural and Trade Exhibition ZÜKA in 1947 in a drawing by Willi Neukom and ...

In the October 1947 issue of *Werk-Chronik*, the exhibition – with the exception of the interior design section – was judged positively, and the sensible spatial organization of the individual agricultural and forestry sections was praised.[123] Horticulture was presented on the lawns of the arboretum in special gardens, with the aim of placing the plants themselves "at the centre of horticultural creativity, in all their infinite form and colour". Most of the horticultural businesses went along with this conventional aim, and showed picturesque gardens and "the most captivating floral experiences", as one enthusiastic commentator put it in *Schweizer Garten*.[124] Peter Meyer's comments on the garden designers' achievements were much more critical and, as usual, to the point:

"Another set of very dubious items are the various pieces of garden 'architecture' erected by the exhibitors: summerhouses, arbours, pergolas etc. Some of these look like ruins badly preserved with cement, others are actual collections of minerals. These structures look as cardboard as theatre sets in all their frantic attempts to be natural, overloaded with every conceivable show of sincerity, antiquity and other tomfoolery that is unbearable to look at after a fortnight. Certainly it is all right to

have some playful elements in a garden, but I am afraid that the producers and consumers mean us to take this sort of 'Traditional Swiss Country Style' (for both furniture and architecture) seriously, and are blurring the borders between exhibition and reality."[125]

Light-weight construction for a garden tent

Criticism of the garden design was also heard from within the ranks of the profession:

"Here, with one exception to which I will return, I miss a sense of the bold step that is necessary if something new is to be shown. A new idea, a new form in structural terms and quite particularly a new idea for the infinite abundance of different forms and colours of the plant material. [...] Here I return to the one garden that has something new to show me and certainly many other visitors as well. Relating to the dark group of firs, the artist has successfully used stone slabs to emphasize the horizontal that shifts quite directly into the wide expanse of lawn. And in the middle of this expanse he has placed a tent surrounded by slabs that in all its amazing simplicity becomes the centre of the whole design. Quite light planting with herbaceous material and bamboo enhances the good impression and allows the eye to rove freely in all directions."[126]

... in reality

Roland von Wyss, who had tersely dismissed Cramer's contribution to the 1942 "Autumn in Bloom" exhibition as a failure, was now calling Cramer an "artist"![127]

In contrast with the rustic summerhouse in the Ticino style of 1942, Cramer's current exhibi-

Surbeck's Zurich office from 1947 to 1949, had to stay on the spot for the duration of the exhibition to advise the public about the correct way to use these plants and to take orders.

But the visitors were particularly impressed by the garden tent. Five round poles 3.5 metres long and two horizontal poles of the same length made up the main support structure of the tent, which was 3.5 metres wide and about 7 metres long. A white, rectangular awning was fixed on top to form a roof. Five long, light laths prevented the tent canvas from sagging. A substructure of eight light bamboo poles served to attach the fabric side walls, used to protect the rear half of the tent from the wind and from being overlooked. A simple deckchair and a wooden chair invited visitors to linger. Cramer's structure conveyed a new sense of open lightness that was fervently longed for after the difficult war period and the withdrawal into constricting isolation. Hans Fischli's timber architecture also emphasized the provisional, improvised element as a design factor in and of itself. *"Above all, there are a lot of rooms at Züka and relatively few 'façades'"*, Werk reported. *"The sense of fresh improvisation and deliberate emphasis on things that are temporary, the harmony of fresh timber, of colours and canvas, of grass and lake, will create the real exhibition atmosphere for many people."[129]*

In 1948, Max Bill added in his positive assessment of the exhibition: "The use of simple, often primitive timber structures protected the overall effect from any false emotion."[130] The garden architects were not prepared for the frequent requests to buy the Cramer & Surbeck

View from Cramer's garden tent

Garden tent by Cramer & Surbeck at the Aargau Horticultural Show

tion garden was convincing in its elegant lightness. It bore scarcely any resemblance with the unrestrained romanticism of his previous gardens. Cramer had recognized that it would not make sense to try to use Ticino motifs north of the Alps. On top of it, the public had got fed up with looking at pergolas made of chestnut timbers and granite columns, garden fireplaces and garden halls. Instead of slabs of Ticnino granite, Cramer used rough, undressed sandstone slabs in rectangular shapes for the slightly raised area in his garden. Of course "Cramer's magnificent flower composition" was much in evidence in the selection of plants used, but this time it was accentuated by decorative long-leaved grasses and bamboos. Even in Willi Neukom's design drawing the planting had underlined the elegance of the garden.[128] Potted ficus, lagerstroemia and rodgersia, bizarre, southern-looking objects, caught the eye, and a selection of marsh plants was presented in pools. Cramer & Surbeck did not merely want to demonstrate their design skills, but – and this was the main commercial purpose – they also wanted to sell herbaceous plants. Albert Zulauf, who worked in Cramer &

marquee. "This tent gave Cramer a different, a modern name, because it was something totally new," Albert Zulauf pointed out about fifty years later.[131]

Emboldened by the success of his Zurich exhibition garden, Ernst Cramer decided to present a tent at the Aargau Horticultural Show

AGA[132] in September of the same year. This one was considerably smaller, was made up of three round timber poles and a circular, reinforced sheet metal roof suspended between the poles, with occasional supports. Ernst Bolliger, as Cramer & Surbeck's head gardener in Suhr,

"Kontinuität" (Max Bill)

Max Bill's sculpture "Kontinuität" (Continuity) was one of the exemplary individual projects, along with Cramer & Surbeck's garden design, that was appreciated individually with selected photographs in *Werk*'s report on the 1947 exhi-

made sure that the surrounding area was correctly provided with natural stone paving and pools of water. But the Aargau tent looked forced in its structure, with strange proportions, an unusual circular shape and striped curtains wafting around to close it off. It was considerably less convincing than its Zurich predecessor, and this showed clearly in contemporary reviews in the specialist press. [133] But the ZÜKA design set new standards and for the first time secured recognition from architects for Cramer.

bition. The sculpture was about three metres high, was made of reinforced plaster with a limewash rendering, and formed a broad, winding band. Bill had been interested in sculpturally interpreting a mathematically derived, non-representational formal world since the 30s, and first presented "Kontinuität's" forerunner – the "Unendliche Schleife" (Infinite Loop), based on the principle of the Moebius strip – at the Triennale di Milano. When Hans Fischli, deliberately setting a confrontational course to traditional ideas about art, invited his Werkbund colleague, the artist Max Bill, to exhibit a temporary sculpture in a location of his choice as part of ZÜKA,

Max Bill's "Kontinuität" (Continuity), photograph by Ernst Cramer

Bill decided to show "Kontinuität" on a lawn by the lake in the arboretum, with an old weeping beech as an impressive backdrop. He placed the work unconventionally on a group of erratic blocks that he had found in the upper Sihl valley. He arranged other erratics as accents on the rest of the lawn.

"The placement of this sculpture in the park on the right bank of the lake in Zurich is an almost ideal solution. The lawn extends horizontally, the trees tower up vertically, the stones instil the idea of the circle. The shape of Bill's sculpture contains the circle, and, as a mediation and transition from the horizontal to the vertical, a diagonal element. It confronts the inorganic "decomposition forms" of the stones and the organic forms of growth of the trees with the spiritual form of human composition."[134]

"Kontinuität" was atmospherically illuminated at night, and was generally admired, even among garden architects, who tended to embrace more traditional ideas:

"Scupltural forms that are beautiful not in comparison with something already familiar to us, but because of the rules inherent in them and the rhythm they create, form a harmonious contrast with their surroundings. The attempt was first made at 'Züka' to show a modern sculpture of this kind in public, built into its surroundings, and the positive response shows that it is possible to prove in practice the theoretical correctness of a thesis that had hitherto been thought extreme."[135]

The confidence signalled in the title of the work, the hopeful faith in continuity, certainly helped to make the modern sculpture more acceptable after the shock of the world war. Furthermore, Bill's work was an invitation to engage in a visual and spatial experiment, seemingly simple at first, that the artist had been addressing for some time: representing an infinite space in infinite movement. It is certainly no coincidence that Max Bill published a photograph in *Werk* in 1948 showing both Cramer's marquee and his sculpture.[136] It was possible for people to sit on the shady seat of the marquee and let their undisturbed eye wander across to the white sculpture, allowing the mysterious object to have its effect while they were completely relaxed. Cramer's collection of photographs taken at the time includes a whole series of shots of the same motif. One photograph[137] shows "Kontinuität" as an elegant unique object and makes it clear how greatly Cramer, who had been called an "artist" himself for the first time, was interested in this remarkable icon of concrete art.[138]

Only Peter Meyer, whose dislike of art for art's sake was already well known,[139] sharply criticized Bill's sculpture as a modernistic artefact that could have nothing at all to say to the general public, even using the wrong title for the work:

"Max Bill's "Unendliche Schleife", positioned in an exemplary fashion, makes a not inconsiderable impact. It is the purest of art-pour-l'art events, as, entirely lost in itself, it revels in its winding forms with all its plaster whiteness. Decades ago, when petrified neckties of this nature appeared as abstract decoration at the Milan Triennale, they were more loosely tied – now the style seems to have shifted into its late phase, in which the tighter and more complicated knot is transparent only to the specialist without closer study."

But there were others who had difficulty with abstract art, as is proved by the fact that "Kontinuität" was destroyed by unknown individuals on the night of the "Sechseläuten" festival in April 1948. Given the fact that the sculpture was temporary anyway, the local press merely reprimanded this vandalism as a kind of boyish prank. But the incident provoked a considerable level of protest in distinguished international artistists' circles, precisely because it called to mind the Nazis' campaigns to destroy so-called "degenerate art".

Modern romanticism

At first the positive examples shown at ZÜKA 1947, in terms of both art and garden design, had little tangible effect on Swiss garden architecture in subsequent years. The October 1948 issue of *Schweizer Garten* did devote itself in great detail to the theme of "Small-scale architecture and sculpture in domestic gardens",[140] but there was scarcely any sign of the new ideas that Roland von Wyss had already adumbrated the year before. This is partially explicable by the fact that garden architecture was never a métier in which new trends and tendencies could be quickly implemented. It takes years for gardens to reach a certain stage of maturity, for the vegetation to make its full impact and for the influence of a creative innovation to be fully assessed. But the suspicion of innovations were on other grounds in 1948. Klaus Leder's article on "Sculpture in the garden"[141] clearly reflected the prejudice against modern art in gardens. He called free sculpture, and here we should remember Peter Meyer's comments on "Kontinuität", pure art for art's sake, and saw it as an element dominating space. He preferred "functional sculpture" for domestic gardens. It should adapt itself entirely to the surroundings in style and position, and be kept on a modest scale. Figurative sculptures in the form of female figures, deer, fish, foxes or foals were consequently preferable subjects. The discrepancy between the current artistic output of the Zurich group of concrete artists and the work that was becoming customary as art in gardens could not have been greater. Most of the illustrations used by Gustav Ammann, Klaus Leder and Mathias Jenny to accompany their articles in October 1948 dated from the war or pre-war years. Attempts to depart from the rustic style could be discerned at best in photographs of gardens by Ernst Baumann, above all in the architectural character of his wooden pergolas. Cramer &

Surbeck also featured prominently in *Schweizer Garten* in October 1948 with a whole series of pictures and a Neukom drawing.

At the latest since his success at ZÜKA 1947, Cramer was considered a major and influential figure in Swiss garden architecture, which is confirmed not least by the rapid increase in the number of commissions in and around 1947.[142] Intensified contact with contemporary architects, including Barth & Zaugg of Olten and Schönenwerd, the Zurich architects Max G. Sütterlin, André Bosshard, Ernst Schindler and Max Kopp was characteristic of this upturn, and was recorded in a series of publications in the magazines *Das ideale Heim* and *Werk*. An article called "The new unity of house and garden"[143] made it clear how well Cramer was able to adapt his style to the particular architecture and the client's wishes.

The Hegner garden in Feldmeilen

This last point was demonstrated most tellingly in the design for the Hegner home in Feldmeilen.[144] The client, Wolfgang E. Hegner, was co-owner of Siber Hegner & Co., a global business, founded in Japan in 1865, that traded in the Far East. The Zurich architect André Bosshard built a country house at the client's request on the shores of Lake Zurich. The style was modelled on East Asian buildings, an approach that was by no means usual at the time. To accompany this architecture with its simple, Japanese-looking timber-frame structure, Cramer composed a garden that was to enhance the Far Eastern atmosphere with its assortment of decorative grasses, bamboo and rhododendrons, but also Japanese maple and pines. A small, organically shaped garden pool in concrete, accentuated by picturesque blocks of rock, rustic stepping-stones and pampas grass, completed the image of Cramer's garden, this time in a style that was supposedly Far Eastern. But Cramer's garden in Feldmeilen had little in common with Japanese gardens. Cramer had no detailed knowledge of Japanese garden art at the time, and worked instead with motifs that Peter Meyer had already branded as "Japonisms" at Landi 1939.[145]

Roth roof garden in Lyss near Berne

In the 1948 issue of *Schweizer Garten,* Cramer & Surbeck presented numerous photographs of naturalistic and romantic gardens that had already been published. But they also included a project devoted to a new theme that had so far seldom been addressed in Swiss horticulture: the roof garden. At the time, roof gardens were not part of the usual repertoire of garden architecture. They were generally seen as a novelty, even though Le Corbusier had made the idea acceptable in architecture decades before. Cramer & Surbeck had realized the published roof garden along with a boccia alley on the second floor of a watch factory for the industrialist Peter Roth in Lyss near Bern.[146] It was quite

clear that this project, just as in the case of the 1942 "Autumn in Bloom" project,[147] was a domestic garden applied to the roof that could have been realized just as well at ground level. For the same reason, the photographs taken at the time did not even reveal that the garden was located on a roof. The chosen plants, including gnarled koelreuterias and aralias and the familiar combination of flowering herbaceous plants,

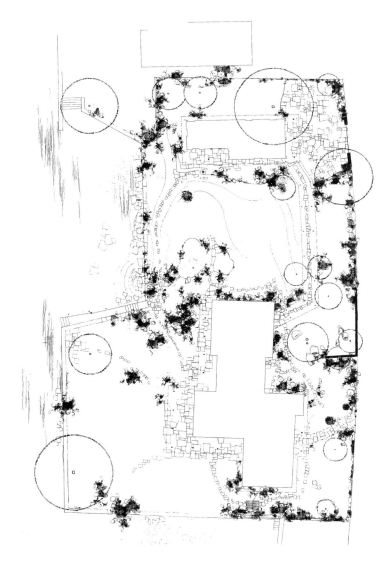

Plan for the Hegner garden in Feldmeilen by Cramer & Surbeck

Pseudo-Japanese garden pond on the shores of Lake Zurich

suggested a traditional approach, just as the circular fountain basin, garden fireplace, natural stone walls and granite slabs. The free design of the pergola on the other hand did hint at a new formal language. The roof garden pergola was a simple timber structure using planed strips of squared timber resting on slender steel supports. A light grille made of narrow wooden laths, cut in a free, organic-architectural form rested on top. A narrow band enclosed the edges of the grille and underlined the wilful, amorphous shape, which became completely emancipated from the support structure. A pergola in the garden for Dr. Spälti[148] in Küsnacht near Zurich was constructed in a similar way. Here the garden architects had not put a band around the grille, which made for a more open, less restricted, almost fragmentary impression.[149]

Cramer also designed the fountain in the Roth roof garden with a new finesse. He installed a water supply in the shading grille, and allowed the water to flow from above into a shallow hanging bowl, from which the water splashed down into the pond. It is characteristic of Ernst Cramer's inventiveness that he experimented with new details. However, he did not yet know how to handle the actual potential of a roof garden at the time.

These first signs at the level of detail were hesitant in comparison with tendencies that had been in the wind the previous year. Gustav Ammann, usually known for his demanding tone, seemed to be withdrawing from the affair almost apologetically in his leading article in October 1948:

Roth roof garden drawn
in pencil on transparent paper

Perspective drawing of
the roof garden

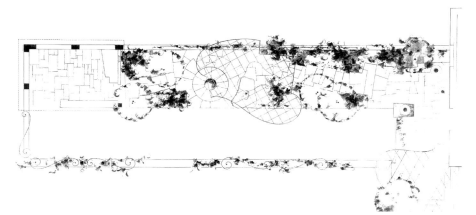

"When we try to examine closely the gardens that have been created here in our materialistic epoch that is committed to rationalization and functionalism, we see to our astonishment that these gardens do not reflect these ideas at all, but a modern romanticism and freedom, a diversity in contrast with our daily life. It is as though people today want to find everything in a garden that they are not able to realize in as they go about their other business; they are running away from themselves and expressing a state of 'paradise', if I might put it in that way. Here it would be completely wrong to reproach the garden designers with being the very people who are living in another world and imposing their own ideas on the owners of the gardens. They are merely an instrument playing the notes that people want to hear."[150]

Most garden architects saw themselves less as interpreters than as their client's mere instruments. This was a key cause of discrepancies between the delight in experiment exuded by the exhibitions, and the hesitant implementation of innovations in everyday projects. Ammann's stance, adopted by most garden designers over decades, was by no means beneficial to the further development of garden architecture.

Roth roof garden in Lyss

Pergola in the Spälti garden
in Küsnacht dating from 1948

"Good Form" as a model

In the post-war period, "Die gute Form" – The Good Form – was probably the key campaign programme seeking to enhance society's sense of cultural responsibility and to proclaim an aesthetically binding model for all spheres of life. Max Bill, whose name is inextricably linked with "Die gute Form", summed up in 1976:

"The achievement of the so-called concrete artists, to devise various possible systematic processes for objectifying artistic expression, is also the special contribution that Switzerland has made in the field of fine art in the post-war period, and from it has arisen something that has established the main direction for modern aesthetics within information theory (Max Bense: Ästhetica). Not just developments in Switzerland, also those in Italy, Germany and South America, but above all American tendencies like Op Art and Minimal Art, can be traced back to the 'Zurich Concrete Artists' as forerunners, even in places where people like to suppress the fact for chauvinistic reasons. It is often asserted that concrete art has evaded an examination of time and people. But its commitment is not to representational images but to principles, i.e. to the attempt to create models for developing the environment and society."[151]

With financial support from the Federal Ministry of the Interior, the Swiss Werkbund used the Mustermesse – the annual trade fair in Basel, MUBA 1949 – to put on a special show called "Die gute Form", to demonstrate the Werkbund's educational and reform aims. The director of the local group in Basel had already suggested a "special show about quality at the Mustermesse", and this idea was greeted with great interest by Theodor Brogle, the director of the fair.[152] Brogle had identified the structural changes that were taking place within the world economy, and felt that it was necessary for reasons of marketing strategy to gain more recognition for Swiss production internationally. Swiss consumer goods were to be made competitive on the world market through a high standard of "form-creating quality work".[153] Max Bill was commissioned to design and realize the special exhibit. In his keynote speech in October 1948, entitled "Beauty from function and as function", he stressed the necessity for careful design in all spheres of life, "from pins to home furniture and equipment, designed in the spirit of a beauty that is developed from function and fulfils a function of its own through its beauty."[145] Bill's primary aim in the design of the 1949 special exhibit was to raise the general level of culture. He was assisted by a small committee, whose members were the Central President of the Swiss Werkbund, Hans Finsler, Director von Grünigen, Egidius Streiff, Alfred Roth (President) and Alfred Altherr (Central Secretary of the Swiss Werkbund). Bill divided the exhibition into four thematic areas that covered practically every aspect of life: 1. Forms from nature, science, art and technology;

2. Forms from planning and architecture; 3. Forms from the domestic sphere and 4. Forms from various pieces of equipment and transport technology. Most of the formally well-designed objects selected by the Swiss Werkbund, from the salt cellar to the grinding machine, were presented in the form of photographs. This part of the show later toured Europe and helped to disseminate the Swiss Werkbund's ideas. Max Bill's work as a sculptor was not just represented in the exhibition by a photograph of "Kontinuität". There was also by a version of his sculpture "Rhythmus im Raum" (Rhythm in Space), which had previously been shown in granite on the Aussenalster in Hamburg, and provided a three-dimensional logo for the 1949 exhibition. A few years later, Bill defined the absolute value that he attached to the concept of form and the forms that he preferred:

"The crucial motive that leads to good product design is of a moral and aesthetic nature: we are against the idea of someone selling something that we do not like to an unsuspecting person for the money that he has earned by his honest work, with the result that the whole level of culture is lowered. We do not agree with a state of affairs that leads to so much ugliness. We know that this kind of ugliness on a small scale leads to ugliness on a large scale. We know that in every place where something has to be covered up, some form of decoration is applied – today usually streamlined simplification and simultaneous distension/puffed up –, be it in everyday objects, or in government – on both small and large scales. We do not like this new or old type of decoration, we do not want it. We resist it with the idea of "gute Form", from the smallest object to the city."[155]

These statements express Max Bill's view of the world, but also the way in which the Werkbund positioned itself. It saw itself as an authority of moral and aesthetic control that not only wanted to set standards for creative production, but ultimately intended to define moral standards as well. From today's point of view, it is permissible to question the extent to which these claims of almost missionary fervour could have been fulfilled and stood up to new ideals. In creating the mark of quality "Die gute Form", first introduced in 1949 and awarded annually from 1952 to formally perfected products, the Swiss Werkbund was formulating a design standard by which its own members, with Ernst Cramer among them, were to be measured for two decades.

"Examining these design problems, which are to an extent demonstrated in crystalline form, does not only apply to the production of consumer goods, but is also an existential question of the first order for the further development of architecture. Unless these questions are addressed positively -but certainly not in the spirit of linking architecture with mural painting and sculpture as a decorative accessory –, then architecture, just like the production of consumer goods, will at best remain at the level of satisfying primitive needs, or lose itself in historicist or artistic games."[156]

Analogous to these statements about the qualitative future development of architecture, the Werkbund garden architects had sooner or later to address the question, whether they liked it or not, of whether garden architecture could ever live up to the criteria of "Die gute Form". The Werkbund was aiming for design that was good both functionally and aesthetically. But garden architecture was still much too committed to the "Landi style", which "Die gute Form" rejected most resolutely. Gustav Ammann had described, almost with a note of resignation, the role of garden architects as "merely an instrument playing the notes that people want to hear". This self-perception by garden architects was a flagrant contradiction of the demand for moral and aesthetic leadership that the Werkbund had formulated. Cramer's 1947 exhibition garden may have been on the way to formal clarity and abstraction in garden architecture, but in his everyday projects he achieved these qualities only with great difficulty, if at all.

Schools

After private gardens and outdoor areas in housing estates, designs for schools were among Cramer & Surbeck's most frequent projects. The increase in population, and even more changing attitudes toward education and the associated new teaching methods and curricula meant that increasing numbers of new schools had to be built after the Second World War, above all primary schools. The large school buildings of earlier decades were replaced by decentralized, small schools with limited numbers of pupils, reducing the distance that children had to travel to school. In addition, in accordance with the teaching of Heinrich Pestalozzi, a goal was to make the transition from a protected home to life at school as easy as possible, especially for the reception classes, by creating small, almost intimate schools with few classrooms. The new school buildings shifted from the centres of towns and villages to their peripheries, seeking links with the countryside and, as in the housing estates, a salutary contact with nature. Consequently the crucial distinction between the old and the new schools lay in a sophisticated approach to the design of the outdoor areas.

In 1950 the young American architect G. E. Kidder Smith, in his influential book *Switzerland Builds – Its native and modern Architecture*, produced a glowing report for Swiss architecture in general and for school building in particular. He identified four important aspects that he felt would also be especially interesting for American architects:

"The first is the incorporation of covered play areas. The second, which is practically a trademark, is the universal presence of mural and sculpture. The third is the great care which the Swiss lavish in (a) placing their schools to take greatest possible

advantage of natural planting and landscaping; (b) developing and planting additional gardens, trees and green areas. Finally, it is axiomatic in planning Swiss schools to have a south-easterly orientation for all general purpose classrooms in elementary, primary and secondary grades. No lower schools have corridor-divided classrooms, with some facing one direction and others the opposite. All pupils thus have sun and light throughout the entire school day."[157]

The bare, often gravel-covered school yard, was a thing of the past. A well-drained, tarred or paved yard for break-times, a grassy area to play on, the school garden and the gymnastics area were all current outdoor components as important as the covered play area for use in breaks. A fountain had been a typical element in Swiss schools yards from time immemorial, and it was to remain one of the key features in future as well, along with the artworks mentioned by Kidder Smith. In comparison with Scandinavian and American models, Swiss schools were still essentially traditional from an architectural

ground plan. In his article, Surbeck stressed the intention of making the school a homely and friendly place, to be achieved by using benches, shady, indigenous individual trees and "harmoniously laid strips of slabs" in the granolithic topping. The severely geometrical form had given way to something freer and more informal, stated Surbeck.

Outdoor areas for the Im Gut school in Zurich

The outdoor areas of the Im Gut school in Zurich, built in 1949 by the architect Christian Trippel, were also designed on traditional lines by Cramer & Surbeck, even though the school, unlike its counterpart in Rüti, was sited on the outskirts of Zurich rather than in the countryside, and the school building was based on a considerably more severe, rectangular ground plan. The three-storey school building was built as a reinforced concrete skeleton construction. Because the terrain was originally high in clay and peat, the building is still supported by 170 reinforced concrete piles that only reach firm

Design plan for the outdoor spaces of the Rüti school building in Zurich by Cramer & Surbeck, 1949

A Classrooms
B Wing with caretaker's dwelling
C Singing room
D Cloakrooms
E Gymnasium
F Vine hut
1 Playground
2 Botanical Garden
3 Lawn and decorative shrubs
4 Fountain
5 Caretaker's garden
6 Grass play area
7 Outdoor gym
8 Play apparatus
9 Pole vaulting
10 Climbing frame
11 Entrance to apparatus room
12 Side entrance
13 Sandpit
14 Swing pit
15 Existing copse

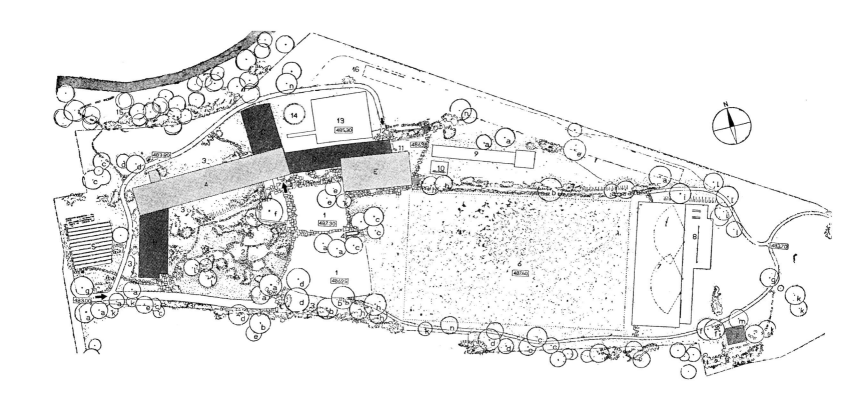

point of view. Garden designers were therefore compelled to choose traditional forms when planning school grounds, following the current style for domestic gardens.

The new school in Rüti in the Canton of Zurich, built by the architect Edwin Bosshard of Winterthur in 1949, shows clearly that Cramer was still pursuing traditional design lines in those years. Ernst Surbeck reported on the planned project in the June 1949 issue of Werk, in an article called "On garden design for schools".[158] As can be seen in the garden plan published here, the whole complex is designed on a free, informal

ground at a depth of 12 metres. Beside the 15 classrooms, the primary school building had a whole series of specialist and craft rooms. It was definitely not one of the smaller school buildings. Hans Volkart included the project in his collection of pioneering examples of Swiss architecture, Schweizer Architektur, and pointed out the apparent contrast between lucidly structured, modern architecture and relaxed, traditional garden design.[159]

The decisive design elements in the school complex included a picturesque group of pines, a fountain and a kidney-shaped concrete pool. In earlier projects Cramer had still been concerned to clad the edges of his pools with natural stone to make them look rustic. This time he left the concrete as a visible building material in the garden, stressing the artificial nature of the design.

Another important design element was the large animal sculpture, two entwining giraffes in shell limestone called "Group of Giraffes", by the sculptor Arnold d'Altri.[160] The project records do not show any collaboration on the design between Cramer and d'Altri, although the two had known each other since ZÜKA 1947. The artist had shown two female figures in sandstone there. The illustrations strongly suggest that the sculpture was an afterthought. Albert Zulauf, who left the Cramer & Surbeck team in 1949 and moved on to the Mertens und Nussbaumer garden architecture practice, pointed out that sculptures by Arnold d'Altri were a novelty at the time and that Willi Neukom, who was a friend of the artist, had arranged the collaboration.[161] Clearly the school projects were a welcome opportunity for co-operating with some of the leading sculptors of the day.

A school project in Suhr, that had already started in 1950, was to offer a chance for a remarkable, indeed pioneering collaboration.[162] But first, profound organizational changes needed to be made in the Cramer & Surbeck practice. They would not be without far-reaching consequences for Cramer's career.

Ernst Cramer in his office in
Kappelergasse in Zurich in about 1950

Design plan for the Im Gut school
in Zurich 1949

Cramer & Surbeck split up

Ernst Surbeck played a considerable part in the commercial success of the Cramer practice, later Cramer & Surbeck, even though he had little influence on the planning and design work. Between 1945 and 1950 the number of projects realized each year reached a volume that was to be equalled later only with difficulty. The practice had moved as early as 1947 from Bleicherweg into larger premises in Kreuzplatz. In 1949 it moved to Seefeldstrasse 128, and since the early 40s also had offices in Kappelergasse. The branches in Ticino and in Suhr flourished, and the number of employees in the office and in the horticultural business was correspondingly high, 30 in all. But success came at a price, not just in terms of Cramer's private life. There was little time for the family, and this particularly affected Cramer's sons, Thomas and Hans-Ulrich, born in 1947 and 1948. In addition, his relationship with his partner was not without tensions. Increasing success led to constant arguments about who had come up with which new ideas. When Ernst Surbeck, who was said to have a lav-

ish life-style, was accused of irregularities in book-keeping, the partnership was dissolved. An entry in the Canton of Zurich company register dated 10 July 1950 shows that Ernst Cramer was again sole director of the firm.[163]

Surbeck's departure had an impact: his efficient business management had given the employees a feeling of security. Shortly afterwards, Hans Jakob Barth, Willi Neukom and other employees, including the site managers Max Schoch and Ernst Bolliger, left the firm as well. Neukom, who had played a considerable part in the success of Cramer and of Cramer & Surbeck since 1939, resigned in 1951 and founded his own garden architecture and landscape design studio in Zurich, and it soon acquired great renown. Willi Neukom had not just been responsible for the quality of the project plan drawing. As a garden architect enthusiastic about art and architecture, he had provided valuable and stimulating input for the work of Cramer's practice for years.

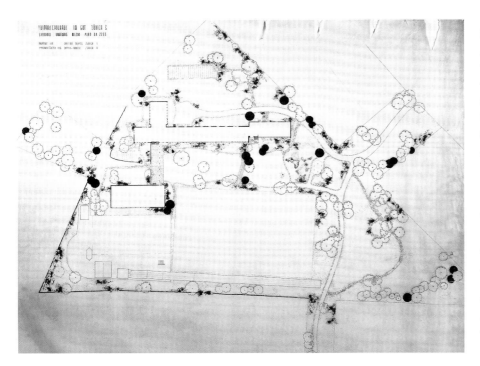

The split was a crucial turning-point for the development of the Zurich garden architecture practice, not least in terms of the rapid decline in the number of commissions between 1950 and 1953. From 1950 to 1952, business management was in the hands of a specially engaged employee. After his failure, Gertrud Cramer took over again, assisted by a garden architect called Wolf Hunziker. Hunziker, trained as a herbaceous gardener, had joined Ernst Cramer's practice in 1949, recommended by the head of the Oeschberg College of Horticulture, Albert Baumann, and stayed until 1956. Cramer, who got on well with his former teacher, often went to the horticultural college to look for young and talented employees. Wolf Hunziker, who was 22 at the time, started work at a monthly salary of about 400 Swiss francs. Cramer usually engaged his new staff for a probationary year, and only then fixed a salary. Cramer first sent them to do practical work in the Suhr plant and tree nursery, as an introduction to the work. A move into the Zurich office was then possible. Hunziker was quickly promoted to be the draughtsman whose job it was to translate Cramer's sketches into plans that could be implemented. Hunziker reported later[164] that Cramer was fairly ruthless in his criticism at first, and taught his employees that a design did not always have to begin with meeting functional needs, but could also start by developing a successful form.

Karl Pappa joined the garden architecture practice in 1950. He was another important employ-ee who was to remain with Cramer until 1973. The practice's situation was starting to stabilize around 1953, and the staff could be gradually expanded again. But Willi Neukom's departure at the latest marked the beginning of the new phase for the practice, and this showed in the nature of the projects.

Discovering geometry

Outdoor areas for the Dorf primary school in Suhr

At first glance, there is nothing spectacular about the project for the Dorf primary school in Suhr. On closer inspection, however, it is clearly one of the first in which we can see signs of a new, more abstract formal language in Cramer's work. Cramer had already worked successfully with the Aargau architects Richner & Anliker a few years previously. The work was also made easier by the fact that Cramer's horticultural business and tree nursery were based in Suhr. A school yard and the public outdoor spaces were to be designed for the new school. Additionally, the Untervogtshaus, the historic residence of the deputy governor, now the local museum, bordered the school yard, which was at a slightly higher level. The area around this building was also to be designed. Cramer started on the first drawings for the project in November 1950,[165] using a traditional design repertoire: open herbaceous and tree planting, benches, a fountain, and an asphalt school yard, articulated with bands of natural stone

Design for the Dorf school house in Suhr dating from 10 July 1952

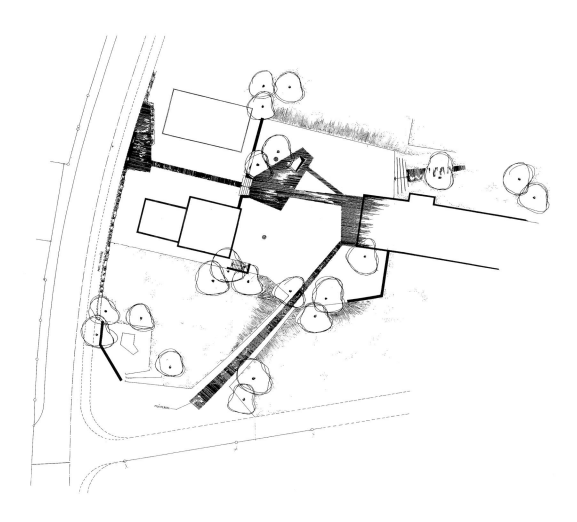

slabs. While the area around the school and the museum were designed according to design principles current at the time, the garden architect came up with a new formal idea for the school yard: he linked the Untervogtshaus and the school building using a pentagonal square, and experimented in the drawings with straight bands of pavement, constructed with geometrical precision, to articulate its surface. The bands were to formally connect the covered playground with the stairs leading down to the museum and with the adjacent Trammstrasse. A second connecting line, which is clear on a plan dated July 1952, [166] linked the covered playground to the nearby road junction via the main entrance.

Finally, in the course of the design process, Cramer developed a central triangle consisting of bands of paving slabs in the surface of the school yard. The corners of the triangle were fixed by the covered play area, the steps down to the museum and a fountain. These paving stones are still in place today, set in the asphalt surface of the school yard. It was not unusual at the time to use natural paving stones to give structure to asphalted areas. All that was new was the strictly geometrical derivation of the large-scale basic form. Additionally, the garden architect playfully built small, isolated geometrical forms into the surface of the playground, relating to geometrical theorems. They are intended to illustrate the mathematical syllabus. As well as triangular, square and circular shapes, there was also a combined figure of a triangle and three squares, showing Pythagoras' theorem. This was the first time that the triangle as a basic figure cropped up in Cramer's work. From now on it occurred regularly in his designs. The uncomplicated, clear handling of lines, based on the principles of geometrical construction, was to play a central role in future.

The collaboration with the sculptor Max Ulrich Schoop, who had been commissioned to provide a fountain figure for the school, turned out to be a particular source of inspiration. Cramer had got to know Schoop's work at ZÜKA 1947, in the form of the sculpture "Störche im Anflug" (Storks in Flight). This was a composition consisting of two birds in abstract form, hovering harmoniously one above the other. Schoop's bronze sculpture "Akrobaten" (Acrobats) in Suhr also emphasized the elegant rhythms of moving bodies. Three athletic acrobats, supporting each other using their hands and feet, make up a finely balanced, symmetrical joint figure. The recumbent acrobat's legs, which are stretched upwards, and the arms of the second athlete, which are supported on them, form a two-dimensional parallelogram. The legs of the second and third athletes form a three-dimensional X, floating in space. Because of the geometrical precision of its basic structure and the movement of the depicted athletes, the group of figures is in a state of dynamic tension. One feels compelled to look at the sculpture from all angles to see how the perception of proportions, perspectives and three-dimensional geometry changes.

Schoop had almost completed his artistic design when Ernst Cramer was still in the process of developing the fountain basin that was to accompany it. The sculpture was to be placed at its centre. [167] "The fountain's shape and concept reflect the balancing qualities of the figure", was Cramer's comment on his four design drawings, which were published in *Schweizer Garten* in 1953. Three of the drawings, all part of the first draft, show a shallow, circular basin set on three thin legs. A second variant, however, although closer to the traditional image of a solid stone fountain, was responding to the sculpture's basic geometric structure. The basic

Fountain trough for the Suhr school building, variant 1

Fountain trough for the Suhr school building, variant 2

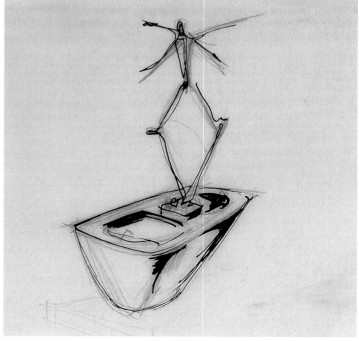

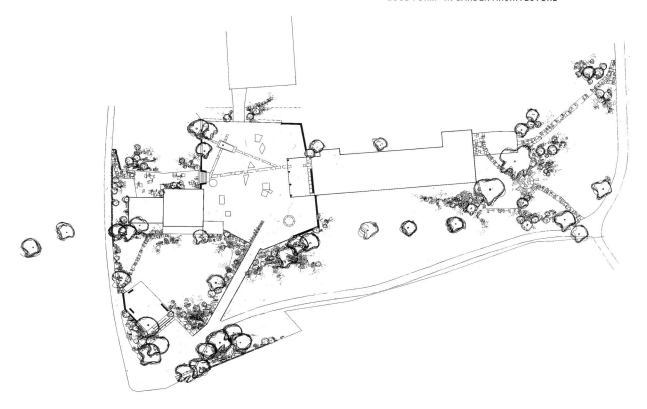

shape of the cut stone was a trapezohedron. Although nothing was said about the materials, in the first variant it is possible to recognize one of the Eternit asbestos cement shells being developed at the time at the Kunstgewerbeschule in Zurich, following the design principles of "Die gute Form". In November 1953, after an appropriate contract had been agreed on with the Suhr local authority for the design of the outdoor areas, another concept was finally realized.

The fountain basin, a solid concrete basin with the usual natural stone cladding and three inlets, can still be seen at one of the corners of the great triangle in the school yard today. Anyone leaving the school building through the main entrance and the covered play area is led directly to the fountain by a line of paving stones. The impression given on approaching the basin and coming up to the sculpture head on is that the ground plan of the basin is rectangular. It is only on by walking around the fountain that you realize that the ground plan is not a rectangle but a trapezium, with its narrow side facing the school entrance. The positioning of the trapezoid basin produces an optical illusion from a distance, which is dispelled only as you come closer. In this way Cramer's design was responding to the three-dimensional geometrical puzzle picture that Schoop had staged with his acrobats, and complemented the multi-dimensional ensemble: sculpture and the design of the surrounding area form an attractive design unit that is more than the sum of its parts.

In this project, Cramer seems to have tasted the joys of geometrical precision and of games with perception for the first time. He had, however, already given clear proof of his delight in exper-

Design plan for the school yard
and the outdoor spaces of the Dorf
school building in Suhr

"Akrobaten" (The Acrobats) by Uli Schoop

The fountain at the Dorf school
in Suhr today

imentation and openness to modern trends in architecture and garden architecture only a few years earlier in Zurich.

The fountain at the Dorf school
in Suhr today

Who's afraid of experiments?

The Kunstgewerbeschule and the Kunstgewerbemuseum in Zurich, now the Museum of Design, were considered a centre for avant-garde currents in art and culture in the 50s. Johannes Itten, who directed the museum and the school from 1938 to 1954, was not only interested in contemporary international trends, but also in critical study of the past. For the year 1952, he planned an exhibition called "Um 1900" (Around 1900), which was to address the applied arts products of the Jugendstil movement for the first time in Switzerland. Itten's intention was to shift the Jugendstil creations, which had fallen into disfavour as formalistic playthings, back into the correct light. He wanted to reveal their creative power and show how valuable the applied arts production had been for the renewal of the arts at the turn of the century.

Temporary display planting for Willy Guhl

The designer Willy Guhl, who had been appointed by Itten to teach interior design at the Kunstgewerbeschule in 1941, was commissioned to design the exhibition at the Kunstgewerbemuseum. Some time before, the Eternit company of Niederurnen had approached the Kunstgewerbeschule to ask whether it would be possible to design new plant containers and window boxes using their asbestos cement. When Itten passed this enquiry on to the appropriate specialist teachers at the school, no one felt it would be possible to achieve workable results with the material. It was thought that it could not be

modelled, and the job was rejected. Willy Guhl, however, was interested and contacted Eternit AG on Itten's behalf. When Guhl had developed a series of models with his class, and the Niederurnen people had agreed to produce the first prototypes, the designer came up with the idea of presenting the new products as part of the planned exhibition. It was felt that this would forge an interesting link between past and present. Itten, as director, accepted the suggestion that the Eternit containers should be shown on the lawn in front of the museum, under the entrance roof, in the foyer, on the steps to the lecture theatre and outside the lecture theatre. Eternit delivered all the prototypes to Zurich and Willy Guhl looked for an expert to plant these innovative containers. As the museum and the school were municipal institutions, at the time the Zurich Municipal Gardening Department would have been contractually obliged to provide floral decorations for exhibitions. But when Guhl explained his request, the job was turned down in no uncertain terms, with the justification that no one could reasonably be asked to plant anything in containers like that. Traditionalist ideas of garden design were obviously not only widespread, but irreconcilable with modern design approaches, but Willy Guhl did not give up. He issued a written invitation to a whole series of florists and garden designers to a meeting about the planned project, then negotiated in interviews on an hourly basis, but was turned down by everyone. Only the owner of a florist's shop in Wollishofen was prepared to take the job on if another gardener or florist could be found. Shortly after this a garden architect responded to Willy Guhl's invitation, asked to see the plant containers in the cellar of the Kunstgewerbeschule, responded enthusiastically to the new creations and spontaneously declared that he was prepared to be involved. But, Ernst Cramer explained to the amazement of the designer, he would not be needing another comrade-in-arms. [168]

Two days before the exhibition opened there were still no plants in the containers and Willy Guhl telephoned Cramer nervously to ask what was going on. Cramer reassuringly said that he would be doing the planting the following day; everything had been prepared. On the day before the exhibition opened Cramer and two of his employees delivered the plants and started on the design. Guhl was enthusiastic about the elegance and beauty of the plant arrangements, above all about the innovative compositions using decorative grasses and branches. As it was impossible to keep the cut flowers in the summer heat for long, Cramer came every other day and mounted completely new arrangements. Guhl tells us that Cramer did not require a fee for his work.

Eternit AG later produced seven different models, including the classic flower spindle and free form plant containers, in series or as individual pieces. In a specialist article written in 1952,

Willy Rotzler, the curator of the Zurich Kunstgewerbemuseum, praised the initiative as a successful example of the way in which collaboration between designers and industry could develop products that met the criteria of "Die gute Form".[169] This exhibition marked the beginning of a long and successful association between Willy Guhl and Eternit AG. Ernst Cramer too was commissioned with a project by the Niederurnen company a few years later as a result of this successful project. In October 1953 the architects Haefeli, Moser and Steiger were commissioned to build a new headquarters for Eternit AG in Niederurnen. Cramer was appointed as garden architect.

In his first collaboration with Willy Guhl, the Zurich garden architect did not just prove his delight in experimenting and his openness toward new ideas and "Die gute Form". He also recognized the need to develop a new kind of formal expression for garden architecture, and felt confirmed in his efforts to simplify his profession's formal language. His enthusiasm for Guhl's elegant Eternit containers and their pioneering 50s formal language indicates the change in Cramer's conception of form. Once again Cramer's innovative thinking had come to the fore on the occasion of an exhibition. Seen against this background, the Suhr school yard project described above, completed in 1954, can be considered the first successful step on the road to developing a new formal language for garden architecture viable on an everyday basis. Cramer had almost succeeded in making a connection with current developments in architecture and art.

Against this background, Cramer's statement of his position called "Gärtnerische Planungen" (Horticultural Planning) can be seen as programmatic.[170] Using only a few pages of text and some plans, Cramer set out the new direction of his design, which he saw as being closely related to innovations in architecture, interior design, and furniture and product design, true to "Die gute Form" programme. Cramer saw sources of inspiration particularly in the new conception of function and material. He called upon garden architecture, whose new approach he felt was "still very much in suspense", to forge a link with architecture by developing simple, beautiful forms. Cramer demonstrated what he meant with plans and drawings of new projects in Ticino and German-speaking Switzerland, including the design sketches for the fountain at the school in Suhr described above. The influence of the new design guidelines was clearly discernible in almost all the illustrations, especially the plan and perspective drawing of the spa park with dance-floor in Thun,[171] even if there was no denying the traditional picturesque style in one project or another. Cramer's projected new bandstand for Thun was a cast shell element. Its simple, modernistic form established a clear link with current architectural trends.

"The published ground plans are a convincing record of how the thought processes undertaken have been realized in practice," Cramer confidently wrote. *"Attention should be drawn to the clean lucidity of the approach, which is expressed by handling the lines in an uncomplicated way. Despite the surprising simplicity of the basic line there is enough refinement in the precisely balanced proportions to give the project as a whole the personal note of a garden world that is closely bound up with nature. [...] It would be desirable to see the ground formation increasingly used as a design element"[172]*

Here Cramer is for the first time expressly addressing formal use of land movements. This was something that he was soon to control in a masterly fashion. It gained him an international reputation and later brought him close to Land Art.

Willy Guhl (left) and Ernst Cramer with
Eternit asbestos cement plant container

At the latest since splitting up with Ernst Surbeck and Willi Neukom in 1950/51, Ernst Cramer struck out in a new direction and achieved a remarkable breakthrough in the second half of the 50s. As always, Cramer accomplished this very pragmatically, rather than through the application of theory. If one considers his creative development to this point, several important influences can be identified that led to the striking transformation in his style. The break with Ernst Surbeck, and the radical changes in the Zurich office that this triggered were certainly an occasion to analyse and rethink his position. Cramer's ability to recognize young talents and integrate them into his practice was equally crucial to the success of his work and the freshness of his garden designs. But the reasons for the design change in Cramer's work were more complex. None of these tangible causes would have led to an innovative thrust in Cramer's work, had he himself not been very keen on experimentation and always restlessly on the lookout for something new.

The fresh start after the war in Europe and Switzerland was marked by a great will to reform, and this was generally the crucial factor for comprehensive innovation. The Swiss Werkbund was one of the most important protagonists of moral and aesthetic renewal in all spheres of life. Its "Die gute Form" (The Good Form) programme established new guidelines for Swiss culture, and not just for Werkbund members, which included Ernst Cramer. Additional factors were Cramer's pronounced interest in contemporary architecture and art, and a greater degree of co-operation with architects and artists who were attentively following the international cultural developments of post-war Modernism themselves at that time. This considerably influenced Cramer's garden architecture. The international influence was to become even more marked in the 50s.

Swiss garden architecture
in an international perspective

The image that Swiss garden architecture enjoyed in neighbouring countries in the 50s can be elicited from the first travel reports that appeared in the pertinent specialist publications after the end of the war. The whole country seemed like a well-tended garden to visitors from abroad, and was impressive not just because man's influence on the landscape was so benign and the picturesque gardens were so pleasing. People also liked the fact that there were no fences, and the associated impression of open, natural domestic landscapes in the housing estates. In comparison with neighbouring countries, garden architecture in Switzerland was generally more highly thought of, and this was often attributed to the country's high standard of living. Every new building was given a garden as a matter of course, intended to informally extend and complement the living space. The ideal image of the domestic landscape as promoted by Guido Harbers and Otto Valentien had obviously been realized in an exemplary fashion here. [173] Although architectural motifs like walls, pergolas, pools and seating areas seemed essential in Swiss gardens, the austere line of formal design was relinquished in favour of a comfortable and natural-looking atmosphere.

The reporting travellers particularly appreciated the conservative approach adopted by Swiss garden architecture and its immunity to new, fashionable ideas. Garden architect Walter Leder stressed the following points to his interested guests from abroad:

"[...] that his country is averse to all dogmas, specialist fads and principles; that things are not the same in Switzerland as they are in Germany, where someone demonstrates something or other, and everyone else has to do and think the same for the next ten years. Herr Leder, who has attended congresses and exhibitions all over Europe since the war, explained that Switzerland certainly has something to show, but that Sweden, the most socialized country in Europe, is far superior to Switzerland in anything to do with green areas."[174]

Swedish gardens, and this is confirmed by other noted garden architects of the day, [175] were more compellingly simple and regular in form and colour than their Swiss counterparts. Modern, simple garden and building forms were used considerably more as a matter of course there than in other European countries. Rather similarly to the Swiss, the Scandinavians were sceptical about fashionable influences, above all when they originated in overpowering neighbouring countries. The idea of preserving one's own identity and political neutrality was also expressed in a resistant and stable design culture. Sweden, but also Denmark and Finland were significant models not only in garden architecture, but in contemporary architecture as well. Post-war Modernism in the United States and Brazil also shifted into the centre of interest in the 50s, as will be discussed in more detail.

The use of concrete in Swiss gardens was a source of some astonishment. Young garden ar-

"Theatre Garden" at the International Horticultural Show IGA 1963 in Hamburg, at night

chitecture students from Weihenstephan, on a trip through Switzerland in 1951, were amazed to report:

"Placing a little concrete wall in a public garden, unrendered, with the traces of the shuttering still on it, would cost you your reputation and your job in Germany. Are the Swiss a different kind of human being? Are they poorer? On the contrary! Astonishing sums of money are spent on designing playgrounds, school grounds and public parks. [...] And so Switzerland is in fact setting a good example with its unprejudiced use of concrete, and I think that more attention should be paid to the possibility of using it in Germany."[176]

But concrete was not used in anything like the unprejudiced way that the visitors had perceived. Hitherto, and this was to remain the case for a few more years, natural stone had been preferred without reservation in garden design. When concrete was used in private gardens for pools or walls, it was clad in natural stone. It was only in public places, where natural stone cladding would have been too expensive, that concrete walls with shuttering marks were left untreated and just covered on top with slabs of natural stone. In domestic gardens, which had to fulfil a compensatory function as places of romantic retreat, exposed concrete was obviously considered disturbing. Even Eternit – asbestos cement – was scarcely tolerated in gardens; one has only to think of Willy Guhl's experience with his new plant containers.[177] In the 50s, Cramer not only discovered the thrill of asbestos cement, but increasingly worked with exposed concrete in his gardens. Numerous contemporary publications show that this was by no means taken for granted yet, and that architecture had a great part to play in the introduction of the artificial stone to gardens. For example, in January 1953 the magazine *Garten und Landschaft* devoted an issue to the relationship between new architecture and new gardens. Hans Jakob Barth, a former employee of Ernst Cramer's, put in a plea for a more positive attitude to this material in his article "Concrete slabs in the garden?", mentioning the lower price, the way in which it could be worked simply and rapidly, and honesty in handling modern materials as arguments for using concrete in the garden.[178] Still, he could not help mentioning the unnaturalness of concrete slabs and their stereotyped shape as disadvantages. However, above all because of the significance of concrete in recent architecture, he thought it appropriate to make increasing use of the material in gardens. In the same issue, Otto Valentien pointed out that steel, glass and concrete had a long tradition in garden architecture and stressed that these building materials suited the period. The garden architect also saw an opportunity in the new architecture for a different and new kind of relationship between house and garden.

"The new architecture has made it possible for us gardeners to link the interior and the exterior more effectively. The wall between the house and the garden has lost its character as a division and is now imaginary."[179]

But despite all his recognition of the high standard of Swiss gardens, Valentien did criticize a tendency to overload and overemphasize motifs, and the inclination towards false romanticism.[180]

Valentien was not alone in this criticism of the state of development in Swiss garden architecture, but it was not the only field characterized by stagnation in the early 50s. Swiss architects too were displeased with a certain level of smugness in their country. As editor-in-chief of *Werk*, Alfred Roth, writing an article called "An up-to-date view of architecture" in 1951, not only addressed the state of development of international architecture, but also drew up a critical balance-sheet of the Swiss situation:

"But unfortunately post-war development is also afflicted with certain concomitants that are no less displeasing. Prosperity has become affluence, security carelessness and peace self-satisfaction, in all a far from pleasing situation from a cultural point of view. [...] The traditional Swiss country style fashion, that cross between Hollywood and Berchtesgaden, is still flourishing, and is an unmistakable expression of everything that is not in order in Switzerland's current intellectual and cultural life."[181]

Roth did not content himself with providing a general critique of the general intellectual climate in Switzerland. He criticized architecture in particular for a lack of commitment to crucial questions in housing provision, a confusion of simplicity and triviality, a tendency towards graphic cosmetics in building, the lack of an open commitment to beauty, and a mistaken conservationist movement that was unable to shake off traditional clichés and exclusively promoted the traditional Swiss country style. It was clear that in the post-war boom, architecture's previous fundamental aims, working toward a moral and aesthetic renewal of Swiss society, had come to be of secondary importance. Comparisons with Scandinavian, American and Brazilian architecture in particular, with Roth finding the last-named country particularly progressive, brought home the rigour of his criticism of the situation at home all the more acutely to his readers. Distinguished colleagues, Roth admitted decades later, called for his dismissal as architectural editor, but ultimately this was not supported by a majority of Werkbund members.[182] But this was by no means the end of the clash between the traditionalists and the Moderns, which marked the sense of radical change in the architectural schools, above all the ETH, the Federal Institute of Technology in Zurich.

A few years later, but all the more severely, the writer and architect Max Frisch attacked the same target as Alfred Roth, under the title "Cum grano salis". When Frisch returned from a year's study in the USA funded by the Rockefeller Foundation, he lectured to the local Zurich group of

the Federation of Swiss Architects. He was critical of the state of Swiss architecture, as his recent experience abroad was fresh in his mind.
Alfred Roth published the revised version of his
lecture in the October 1953 issue of *Werk*, thus
also supporting his own critique of architecture. [183] Frisch too deplored the dominant traditional Swiss country style and a creeping
sense of boredom and monotony, resulting from
compulsive attempts at compromise in architecture and a lack of courage,
*"[...] never even simply wanting anything radical,
never mind actually doing it. Someone returning
home (liberated for a while from the familiarity that
lulls our sense of judgement to sleep) is somewhat
depressed when confronted with our domestic architecture again, astonished by the country's
sense of self-satisfaction; the myth of compromise, the escape into detail, the dictatorship of
the mediocre, the cult of the pretty, the striking
nostalgia for the day before yesterday, and the dan-
gerous opinion that democracy is something that
cannot change – certainly, none of this is covered
by architects' liability."[184]*
Anyone who was looking for something new in
architecture and garden architecture – and
Ernst Cramer was always on the lookout for
something new – pursued developments in
Scandinavia, but above all those in the USA and
Brazil with interest. In Zurich, Johannes Itten,
as director of the Museum of Design, made sure
that international architecture remained in the
centre of interest by means of the exhibitions
that he mounted. In the late 40s and early 50s,
exhibitions on Alvar Aalto (1948), on Swedish
architecture and design (1949), on Frank Lloyd
Wright (1951), on American school buildings
("Das neue Schulhaus" 1954), and on modern
building in Brazil ("Brasilien baut" 1954) attracted a great deal of attention. Alfred Roth felt
that the USA was able to grasp its pioneering
role in the Modern Movement with both hands
because it lacked a strong tradition of its own,
was open to new developments, and was home
to an architectural élite made up of the best the
world had to offer. He also sensed that the crucial stimulating factor for modern Brazilian architecture was Le Corbusier's influence. [185]
Sigfried Giedion too ascribed the remarkable
development of modern architecture in Brazil
mainly to Le Corbusier's visit in 1936. He also
attributed the range of development of Brazilian architecture to the open-mindedness of
clients, the government and other authorities. [186]
Werk addressed modern architecture and art in
Brazil comprehensively for the first time in August 1953. Sigfried Giedion painted a revealing
portrait of the country and its leading architects, who had proved that they had risen to the
standards of European and American architecture at the latest with the Ministry of Education
and Health building in Rio de Janeiro, started in
1936 and completed in 1941. A young Brazilian
garden architect had also been involved in this

project. He still enjoys an almost legendary reputation in his home country today, and is undoubtedly one of the most glittering personalities in 20th century international garden architecture: Roberto Burle Marx.
*"Brazil also has a landscape architect, the painter
Roberto Burle Marx,"* wrote Giedion in 1953, and
stressed Marx's exemplary qualities: *"After modern
landscape architects have done all their complicated fiddling around with plants sunk in stone
slabs or growing in a complete muddle, Roberto
Burle Marx's gardens show a parallel with the simplification that is such a striking feature of Brazilian buildings."[187]*
This was clearly the first time that a tribute was
paid to the Brazilian garden architect in the Swiss
specialist press, and it came from one of Modernism's most distinguished historians of art
and architecture. Only a few pages later, Giedion
dedicated another section solely to the Brazilian
architect, underlining his importance for modern
garden architecture. At the same time, Giedion
was criticizing the way in which contemporary
Swiss garden architecture seemed to be completely at a loss for words or ideas, and asked in
vain for distinguished exponents of the subject.
*"I would unhesitatingly include the painter and
garden architect Roberto Burle Marx of Rio de
Janeiro among the few new creative forces. He is
an artist who understands the language of plants.
[...] His secret is that he knows how to handle
plant colours and places them in his lawns in
large, kidney-shaped beds, or at least always
framed by free curves. [...] He uses them as an abstract painter uses colour: clear, freely demarcated
areas of colour are brought into a relationship with
each other, freely placed in large areas."[188]*
And it is quite true that Burle Marx, who studied
painting, sculpture and architecture in Germany
from 1928 and then from 1930 at the Escola Na-
cional de Belas Artes in Rio, drew inspiration for
his garden designs from modern painting, the
work of Georges Braque, for example.[189]
Many of his spectacular garden plans came into
being on canvas and were then transferred to
the garden. This created a particularly graphic
impact when seen from above.
Roberto Burle Marx's work was of particular interest to many garden architects until well into
the 70s, because of its combination of artistic
and horticultural qualities. His work, which he
presented in a touring exhibition in the 50s,
quickly attracted a great deal of attention in the
USA, England and Germany as well. Even though,
since Leberecht Migge at the latest, landscape architecture had not been regarded as a free artistic discipline, but at best as applied art, it was obvious that hope of a renaissance of classical landscape architecture had never been abandoned.
Burle Marx was so interesting not least because
to many people he represented the garden architect of genius, a figure that had long been missed.
In addition, over decades the abstract and
painterly style seemed most appropriate for
modern architecture, and was occasionally even

expressly promoted in the specialist press as something worth imitating. [190]

Such powerful simplicity, obviously modelled on modern, abstract painting, was in demand by progressive architects and soon became a characteristic of Ernst Cramer's radical experiments as well. His work as a garden architect started to be compared with abstract art a few years later, and was praised by Hans Fischli on the basis of similar criteria to those applied to Burle Marx by Sigfried Giedion. [191] It has not been proved beyond doubt that Ernst Cramer first took notice of Burle Marx in 1953, but it is very probable. After the exhibition "Brasilien baut" (Brazil builds) was shown in the Zurich Museum of Design in 1954, an exhibition called "Roberto Burle Marx" was mounted in the same venue two years later. This exhibition prompted Hans Curjel to ask to what extent Burle Marx's design methods could by applied to local landscapes. [192] In 1960 at the latest, Cramer had the opportunity of admiring Roberto Burle Marx's work in Brazil with his own eyes, and three years later he met the charismatic artist at the International Horticultural Exhibition in Hamburg. Cramer was still familiar with progressive foreign tendencies only from the specialist press, and knew the garden architects at best from international congresses held in Switzerland. But by the end of the decade the Zurich garden architect was keen to travel to distant countries.

The general shift into a new phase of garden architecture was supported by the publication of a number of new books. In Switzerland, books like *Neues Planen und Gestalten* by Albert Baumann, 1953, [193] and Gustav Ammann's *Blühende Gärten / Landscape Gardens/Jardins en fleurs*, 1955, [194] but also Ernst Baumann's *Neue Gärten*, [195] published in the same year as Ammann's book, rapidly acquired the status of standard works.

Albert Baumann, as a "teacher and architect in Oeschberg", as the title had it, unlike the other two authors, was particularly concerned to present practicable, functional design suggestions in textbook form. His *Neues Planen und Gestalten* provided his students, but also professionals in Switzerland, with a kind of reference work that for the first time offered systematic, easily understood instructions on how to design streets and paths, walls and terraces, gardens, public parks and cemeteries, and did more than leave interested people astonished with beautiful photographs of model garden creations. He did not go into technical details or address questions about construction, but instead preferred to emphasize how the design elements he showed related to models from the history of garden design and promoted connecting aesthetics with function. Following his motto "A picture says more than a thousand words", Baumann published a large number of schematic drawings, in which he systematically explained different possible solutions for various garden

Neues Planen und Gestalten

für Haus und Garten

VERLAG AG. BUCHDRUCKEREI B. FISCHER, MÜNSINGEN

Albert Baumann's standard work *Neues Planen und Gestalten* with a photograph of Ernst Cramer's Bianca garden in Zollikon as title picture

design fields, for example designing paths and steps. He was also concerned to use photographs of realized gardens in order to point to model designs. The book was soon on garden designers' shelves as a standard work.

Projects by his former pupil Ernst Cramer, drawn above all from the traditional and picturesque phase of work up to 1953, were Baumann's preferred source of model solutions. But a small number of these drawings and perspective views do already show Cramer's new line. Baumann commented on them with appropriate benevolence, identifying a "bold game with geometrically shifted lines" or a "solution for masters who are confident of their design skills". [196] Cramer's reputation as a garden architect benefited in no small measure from the fact that so many of his projects played a key part in this compendium, and a photograph of his 1936 Bianca private garden in Zollikon was even used as the title picture.

In contrast to Albert Baumann's book, Cramer's projects did not play a part in the publications by Gustav Ammann and Ernst Baumann. Neither was intended to be a textbook, but instead reflected the self-positioning of garden architecture and an awakening interest in new design dimensions. In *Neue Gärten. New Gardens*, Ernst Baumann, also a former Oeschberg student, presented nothing but his own private garden projects in the current domestic garden style. He structured his collection according to landscape situations – garden in a town, on a slope, by the lake, on a hill and so on – and recorded them in the form of general plans, simple explanatory texts and sketches. Baumann's marked interest in garden plants is striking. However, he did not present them merely in their function as shapers of space, using schematic planting plans, aerial photographs and atmospheric garden pictures. On the contrary, a large number of greatly enlarged images of individual blossoms, stages of fruit and leaf structures are evidence of detailed interest in the botanical context and positive immersion in fascinating plant details.

"Whether it is 'the traditional Swiss country style' or quarrystone masonry à la Wright and Corbusier, both fulfil the same need, to which the modern travelling, rambling and camping movement also owes its existence: escaping at least for a short time and as a kind of gesture from the technical world and its radical alienation from nature. But this need finds its purest and as it were its most legitimate expression in the horticulture of our day," wrote Peter Meyer in his introduction to *Neue*

Neutra clearly gained a great deal of crucial impetus for his work from his master, and later often designed the gardens for his buildings himself. Against this background it is easy to understand why in the chapter on the "Country house garden", which occupies the largest part of the book, Ammann devoted a separate, concluding section to the subject of "Californian gardens" and Richard Neutra's projects. [199] Unlike the other private Californian gardens in Ammann's book, most of them by the garden architects Lawrence Halprin and Osmundson & Stanley, the gardens Neutra designed himself show a modern and yet an essentially traditional relationship with landscape and garden.

"A building forms a stark contrast with organic

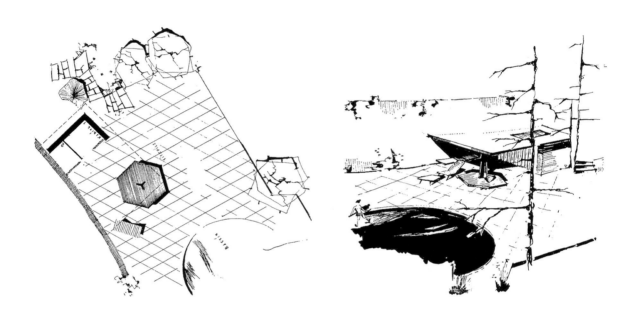

Gärten. [197] If Baumann's domestic gardens were places for withdrawal into domestic privacy, his much enlarged photographs were not only a sign of enthusiasm about the aesthetics of nature, but at the same time a withdrawal into the fascinating world of the microcosm of plants.

Gustav Ammann took the opposite path: instead of withdrawing into the realm of botany, he enticed his readers away on garden journeys through Japan, Europe and the USA. The very fact that his book was published in three languages is a claim to open-mindedness, and this is clearly reinforced by a foreword that Richard Neutra had written as early as 1954. Thus in the very first pages of the book, Ammann was stressing his interest in Modern architecture and his close contact with one of the most famous exponents of this style. Neutra and Ammann had been friends since 1918, when the young architect worked as an apprentice to Froebel's Erben for a while. During this time he met his wife Dione, the eldest daughter of the Zurich Municipal Architect Alfred Niedermann. [198] Rather like Ernst Cramer, who had become apprenticed to Ammann only a few years earlier than Neutra,

things as given by nature, whether we like it or not," the architect explained later. *"We are subject to its influence, until it has fallen into ruins and returns to nature as an ivy-covered ruin." [200]*

Neutra, an enthusiastic garden- and naturelover, wanted to have natural gardens into which he could fit the clear mass of his buildings. For this reason he developed garden ground plans that – if one were not aware of the influence of the Mediterranean climate and the typical nature of the appropriate fauna – would scarcely be distinguishable in formal terms from current garden ground plans by European garden architects. Entirely in the spirit of his mentor Frank Lloyd Wright, in whose office he worked for a few years, he anchored his country houses harmoniously into the landscape and was greatly concerned with the close relationship between interior and exterior. For this reason he did not just emphasize horizontals architecturally, in order to underline the relationship with the ground, but liked to break up the outside walls with large panes of glass reaching to ground level.

Gardens by Lawrence Halprin, but also by Osmundson & Stanley, were unlike Neutra's gardens in that they were based on geometrical

Examples from Baumann's book: "Solution for masters of design"

garden design and biomorphic basic forms in the lawns and planted areas, garden walls and pools. Already in the 30s, a group of progressive garden architects in California had come together and tried to develop a new language for garden architecture that was more appropriate to its day. This search gained its impetus not just from developments in modern art and architecture, but above all from the rapid social changes that were taking place in the USA. The United States too experienced an enormous economic boom after the end of the war. The American garden architect Peter Walker explained the significant post-war change as follows: "What actually brought Modernism into landscape architecture in the United States was not revolution but evolution: gradual, profound changes in the lives of the American middle classes."[201] Thomas Church, James Rose, Dan Kiley and Garrett Eckbo were the chief exponents of the new Southern Californian garden architecture. They too developed a new formal language in landscape architecture, with its basic geometrical elements drawn from the Cubist and Surrealist movements in art. Before Lawrence Halprin set up his own practice in 1949, he had worked for Thomas Church in San Francisco, and his own projects had soon won him the same fame as his older colleagues. The contrast between biomorphic and geometrical elements was not the only striking feature of illustrations of Halprin's projects. In addition, large rocks, placed to look like an arid landscape, clearly show the influence of Japanese garden design.

Ammann's introductory comments on the Californian gardens clearly revealed his preference for Neutra's informal, natural style. Like Neutra he also put in a plea for preserving a naturally relaxed quality in garden design. But in his explanations of why modern Californian gardens were different, he did not refer to new movements in international architecture and landscape architecture.

"In our gardens we try to capture the whole abundance and variety of the surrounding landscape and the indigenous vegetation, and then to handle it in a way that is perhaps somewhat emotional and picturesque. But the American designers show only small, closely demarcated, indeed firmly framed details from nature, grouping them around the openly placed buildings with a great sense of control and taste. Just as we decorate our rooms with framed pictures, to give the space atmosphere and character, the American designers adorn their gardens with 'oases', with neatly assembled elements, rocks and plants, which they relate to the architecture very closely. This sort of garden design is somewhat alien to us and arises from the fact that the climate is very dry from May to October."[202]

The sunny climate of California was certainly helpful for establishing large and luxuriant gardens, but it was by no means the crucial factor for the new trends in form and content of gar-

den design. But despite his slight uncertainty about the reasons for the new tendencies, Ammann was certainly particularly impressed by the clear, functional and generous design of American gardens in contrast with the picturesque designs of his home country.[203] Ultimately it was this very simplicity that Ammann had always admired in Japanese gardens, to which he devoted an entire section in the introduction to his book. Although he seemed to recognize the signs of the times, Gustav Ammann was obviously not yet quite certain where the development of modern garden architecture was going to lead. He sensed the potential of the burgeoning new connection between modern art, modern architecture and the new landscape architecture, which he had helped to initiate. Tragically, Gustav Ammann was not to see his important book completed. The man who was perhaps the most influential and openminded Swiss horticultural thinker of his day died unexpectedly on 23 March 1955 from the consequences of an operation.[204]

The 5th Congress of the International Federation of Landscape Architects (IFLA) took place at the ETH in Zurich from 20 to 24 August 1956. It was organized by the Federation of Swiss Garden Architects (Bund Schweizer Gartenarchitekten; BSG). Walter Leder was then acting president of this association, which had been founded in Cambridge as early as 1948; he resigned his office when his term ended in 1956. The IFLA committee elected René Pechère of Brussels, a landscape architect and co-founder of IFLA, to be the new president for the next two years. Under the general title "Landscape in the Life of Our Time", over 250 participants and guests from 25 countries addressed the themes of "Urban Landscape", "Industrial Landscape", "Agricultural Landscape" and "Natural Landscape". Addressing the first two themes was a clear sign of the violent changes taking place in post-war society, that were proving such a challenge to landscape architects – not only in terms of integrating into the landscape areas of post-war reconstruction, rapidly growing housing estates and industrial complexes. In their lectures, experts like Daniel Collin from Paris, Sylvia Crowe from England, Georg Boye from Copenhagen and Erich Kühn from Aachen examined the acute urban planning problems posed by post-war rebuilding. Joane Pim from Johannesburg, Heinrich Wiepking-Jürgensmann from Hanover and Leon Zach from the USA reported on conceiving new industrial landscapes. The IFLA Congress had more visitors that ever before and promoted an international exchange of views on current developments in landscape architecture. In this context, Ernst Cramer's work attracted particular attention from abroad for the first time.

As part of the IFLA context, and in the same general theme "Landscape in Modern Life", an exhibition was shown in the Helmhaus in Zurich and the ETH in which IFLA members presented plans, photographs and models of their work. This exhibition, in which Ernst Cramer showed his projects as well, was devised as a touring exhibition and was intended to be shown in Cologne and at the Milan Triennale in the following year, then later in Portugal, Canada and the United States. The publishing house *Das ideale Heim* published a *Domestic Garden* special issue [205] on the occasion of the congress. It was designed by Willi Neukom and Fred Eicher and showed projects by members of the Association of Swiss Garden Architects. Presumably the examples were the same as the ones in the exhibition. Examples of gardens by major Swiss garden architects, including work by the late general secretary of IFLA, Gustav Ammann, whose son Peter Ammann had taken over the horticultural firm, were published in this special issue. Most of the photographs and garden plans showed the traditional domestic garden style, and even Cramer was unable to resist publishing some of his "classics", including the Vogel-Sulzer garden in Itschnach (1933) and the garden for Annie Bodmer-Abegg in Riesbach, Zurich (1951), along with the pseudo-Asiatic Hegner garden in Feldmeilen. But there were two new garden plans in which Cramer clearly demonstrated his "new line", with its characteristic geometrical ground plan figurations.

Leisure garden for Riwisa in Hägglingen

The general plan for a small leisure garden from 1956 for the Riwisa plastics factory in Hägglingen, Canton Aargau, was particularly striking. The small plot, approximately L-shaped, had an area of about 400 square metres and was located between the modern glass façades of two factory buildings. Cramer designed a garden characterized by triangular areas, but most particularly by a distinctive pool, an equilateral triangle with sides seven metres long. The garden's space was structured by a combination of trimmed hedges, walls and steps. Large square concrete slabs were aligned or offset as paving, underlining the functional character of the terrace area. Once again Cramer used 70 by 70 centimetre concrete slabs, but this time in a relatively small garden. Cramer's courage in working on a generous scale in small gardens was admired particularly by his younger colleagues. In Hägglingen, following his "Guidelines for the Client", the garden architect once more played with the contrast between built and planted areas, between the artificial and the natural, and complemented the austere layout with free planting of herbaceous and woody plants, shown in plan graphics that were close to Willi Neukom's drawing style. The garden no longer exists, but the 1956 plan very clearly reveals the exciting dialogue between built austerity and natural informality. In this garden, Cramer literally took the formal play with triangles to a climax, even though the garden plot did not provide any compelling reason to do so. Modern

form was decisive. The garden's unusual character was further underlined by the fact that Cramer apparently used light red paving slabs in the garden. Cramer drew a great deal of public attention with the radical quality of such designs, not least of Gerda Gollwitzer, the noted landscape architect and editor-in-chief of the German specialist magazine *Garten und Landschaft*.

The striking plan for the Riwisa garden crops up again as a record of Cramer's unusual approach in a short article called "Swiss Garden Talk" in the December 1956 issue of *Garten und Landschaft*. [206] The article is in the form of the first and only published interview with Cramer. What makes the short text particularly interesting is Gerda Gollwitzer's attempt to find out very directly why Ernst Cramer's work had developed in this new way. The occasion for the interview and the visit to Cramer's practice were the IFLA Congress in Zurich and the exhibition of contemporary garden design. Projects that had attracted particular attention here were those "that were very different from the usual image of Swiss garden design. These were the work of the Swiss garden architect Ernst Cramer," explained Gerda Gollwitzer in the opening notes to her observations. She identified Cramer's designs, along with recent work by Willi Neukom and Gunnar Martinsson, as further indications that garden architecture was undergoing a change.

But let us look first at the interview with Ernst Cramer:

"*G: When we visited your office we saw some very good work dating from earlier years. But these*

General plan dating from 1956 for the garden of an industrial business in the Canton of Aargau

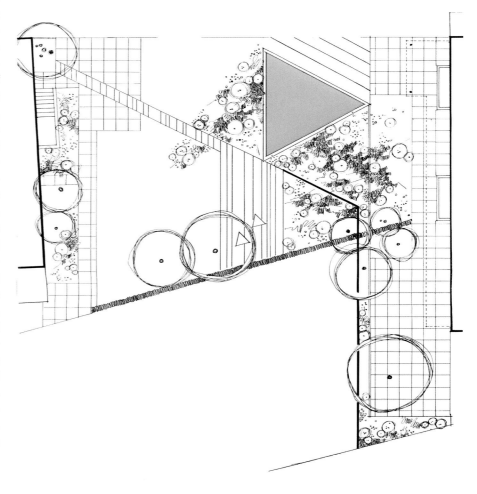

school grounds (Untermoos, Zurich)[207] show quite a different approach. Here the garden no longer forms an attractive and informal contrast with the buildings, as in other Swiss gardens, and also in your earlier work. Here you pick up the proportions and lines of the building and continue them across the rest of the site. How did you come to develop like this?

C: The lines of good contemporary architecture, derived from function and purpose, demand the same clarity in their surroundings as well. The 'attractive and informal contrast' that you speak of often ran counter to the purpose of the complex, as has been proved by many examples of designs for the areas around public buildings in particular. It has been shown over and over again that the beauty of a garden is not reduced by the clarity and functional nature of its lines. I think that it is also unnecessary to emphasize that the garden is more likely to be in a state of unity with good architecture the more it tries to realize its purpose-derived forms in the surrounding area as well.

G: I have noticed that you use mainly concrete and artificial stone in your gardens. Is there a deeper meaning to this?

C: Paving made up of entirely regular forms is best suited to my way of designing gardens. Additionally, a slab covering can be used much more effectively if it has the smoothest possible surface. Natural stone paving with these qualities is so expensive that too little money remains for important parts of the garden. Artificial stone and concrete can be made in the desired form at a much more reasonable price, the surface is impeccably smooth and if the paving is used properly it fits in with the garden and the architecture perfectly.

G: We too are now using artificial stone slabs a great deal for paving paths and squares, but they are usually rectangular slabs of different sizes. You seem to prefer square slabs of the same size, with the joints running continuously?

C: Square slabs with continuous joints on both sides fit in best with my approach. We can get them here in very high quality, in all sizes and in a wide range of colours, down to a grey that is almost black.

G: Does your approach to gardens affect the planting as well?

C: The planting makes it possible to emphasize the lines of the garden's ground plan by adapting the edges of the planting to these lines. Or you might wish to relieve the severity of a ground plan built up on clearly architectural lines, and the plants are the best medium for achieving this. There have been outstanding examples of both ways in the history of garden design, and I use both ways myself. But you have to think precisely and carefully in order to choose the right one.

G: We are often surprised that it is sometimes precisely modern architects who are entirely clear in their approach to architecture who have a very romantic attitude toward garden design. How do Swiss architects, and above all clients, react to this?

C: There are still all sorts of different views about this here as well. But there are a whole series of young, good architects with modern ideas who do see the sense in our garden design principles, and I work very well with them. The number who see this as the right approach is by no means low today. This is clear simply from the fact that many clients view it positively as well. And it is ultimately only in this way that we can realize what we are trying to do."[208]

Essentially this interview underlines how important Modern architecture was as a model for Cramer, and his interest in trying to find an appropriate response in terms of garden design. Only a few weeks before the interview was published, in October 1956, Richard Neutra was invited to Zurich and Basel as a visiting lecturer. This attracted a great deal of public attention, and certainly Ernst Cramer was not left unimpressed. Cramer's essentially functionalist arguments for the use of concrete slabs seem to have a hint of tokenism about them at first. But it is also possible to see them against the background of the Werkbund's efforts to promote beauty through function and as function, which Max Bill had earlier defined.[209] Gollwitzer was obviously unable to get to the bottom of the complex reasons behind Cramer's rethinking of his approach to design.

In the mid 50s, Cramer was concerned above all to very pragmatically develop an up-to-date, modern language for garden architecture. The 58-year-old obviously shared this need with some younger garden architects. If one studies the special issue *Wohngarten* published on the occasion of the 1956 IFLA congress a little more carefully, it is striking that in their designs Willi Neukom and Ernst Graf were starting to handle lines in the new and modern way as well. Fred Eicher, a trained gardener and former student of Hermann Mattern in Kassel worked in Ernst Graf's office in those years and helped out his friend Willi Neukom from time to time. Eicher remembers the unease felt by the few progressive colleagues about the fact that the materials, shapes and plants used in garden architecture were absolutely always the same.[210] Apparently his boss, Ernst Graf, also needed to be patiently persuaded to move with the times in terms of architectural trends and to adopt a new creative line. Occasionally, Eicher admits, there was scarcely any evidence of the modern nature of the plan drawing in the garden as actually realized, but the new line simply sold better. Eicher too was stimulated to rethink by the young, modern architects' recent work – he was personally interested in Leo Hafner's architecture at the time.[211] After setting up his own practice in 1962, he successfully collaborated with the architect's practice in Zug. Willi Neukom was obviously seized by a similar interest in Modernism, and in Eicher's opinion had learned from Ernst Cramer that great things were possible even in small gardens.

Garden for the Wilhadi Tower, Bremen (Gunnar Martinsson)

It is clear from some comments made by Gerda Gollwitzer in the introduction to her interview with Ernst Cramer that laborious rethinking in garden architecture was not confined to Switzerland. She referred to a heated argument within the Association of Young Garden Architects.[212] This public debate about modern garden architecture attracted a great deal of attention in the profession and pointedly characterized how difficult it was for European garden architecture to implement the new direction. In August 1955 the Horticultural Department of the City of Bremen in Germany had announced a competition for the members of the Association of Young Garden Architects, and 35 participants entered. A new small park with areas for resting and play facilities was to be designed for a ruined site in the rebuilding area of Bremen's western suburbs, by the ruins of the war-damaged Wilhadi Church. It was not the 1st prize, but the 2nd prize, awarded to the 31-year-old Swedish garden architect Gunnar Martinsson, that unleashed waves of outrage among experts.

Only a year earlier, Martinsson had submitted an uncontroversial, traditional design for a domestic garden competition run by the Arbeitskreis junger Gartenarchitekten that was denied the first prize only because it exceeded the prescribed construction budget.[213] In the same period as Cramer, the Swedish garden architect had significantly revised his design style, and was now working in a similar way to Cramer, using very few, but all the more powerful design devices. For merely formal reasons, he used modern, equilateral triangles and intersecting paths to design the striking little park by the Wilhadi Church. In its report, the jury praised the modern use of emphatic contrasts. But soon after the competition results were published, outraged colleagues were asking:

"Has this second prize anything at all to do with 20th century garden design? [...] It is extremely risky to award a prize to anything like this. An abstract painting by Picasso or Mondrian is similar. It is a composition, but scarcely a design. Things like this rub off! Have we now come to a 'crossroads' with our design?"[214]

It would also have been possible to make a comparison with Modern gardens in the 20s in France, where Gabriel Guévrékian, for example, had caused a sensation with the striking triangular geometry in his "Jardin d'eau et de lumière" at the Paris "Exposition des Arts Décoratifs et Industriels Modernes" in 1925.[215] But the reference to Mondrian and Picasso was not made at random, even though in this particular case Martinsson was relating more to developments in modern architecture. In fact, an exhibition covering the entire oeuvre of Piet Mondrian, who had died in New York in 1944, was touring major European cities in 1955 and was most highly acclaimed. The exhibition came to

the Zurich Kunsthaus in late May, and was received with great enthusiasm, particularly among progressive circles of artists, architects and designers.[216] Many saw Mondrian as a modern artist who had followed in an exemplary fashion and without concessions the vocation imposed upon him by the spirit of his age. Was it possible to develop modern garden architecture with a similar lack of concessions? Ernst Cramer tried, and later referred to the Dutch artist as a preferred comparison when describing his own work as a garden designer.[217]

Gunnar Martinsson, whom Ernst Cramer was to meet and get on well with a few years later, defended his competition entry for the Wilhadi Tower garden entirely in the spirit of his older Swiss colleague. He expressed a desire for a modern formal language, modern materials, clear contrasts and by relating to contemporary architecture. Here the Swedish garden architect referred to the Central President of the Swiss Werkbund, Hans Finsler, quoting him in 1956:

"There are two clearly discernible approaches in architecture today. One is characterized by emphasizing horizontal and vertical lines, by right angles and cubes, and often by circles, cylinders and spheres. Technical products like reinforced concrete, steel and glass are particularly highly esteemed. Earlier exponents of this approach include, among others, Gropius, Mies van der Rohe and Le Corbusier. The other approach prefers abstract organic forms that cannot be constructed. Natural materials are used: timber, stone, bricks. Earlier exponents of this approach are Frank Lloyd Wright and Alvar Aalto."[218]

Martinsson also identified both approaches in international garden design and referred in particular to exemplary garden architecture in the USA, Mexico and Brazil, while he felt that Europe had a great deal of catching up to do.

"I think that, like the architects, we too need these two modes of expression, and I think that we, as young members of the profession, must now get garden design moving. The aim is not a specific type of garden, but gardens that share the formal language with the buildings that they are supposed to be associated with."[219]

Gunnar Martinsson not only made a similar

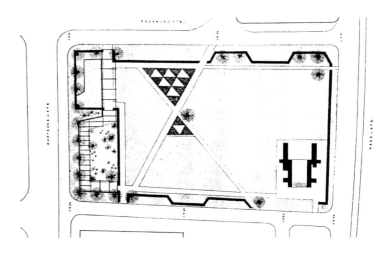

Competition design for the Garden for the Wilhadi Tower in Bremen by Gunnar Martinsson, 1956

change in his style at the same time as Ernst Cramer, but also gave the same reasons as his Zurich colleague. Here it is once again clear that individual and personal motives were not the main cause of the radical change in Cramer's work. The transformation in garden architecture was happening on an international scale, stimulated by modern art and architecture, even though the majority of garden architects were resistant to giving up traditions that they had grown attached to.

Cramer's "new line"

Aware of the general discontent among architecture critics and garden architects regarding the lacking power of renewal in Swiss architecture and garden architecture and aware of current international trends, Ernst Cramer continued to specifically develop his new creative line in the 50s. With a growing volume of commissions after 1954 and a new team in his office, he increasingly had the opportunity, next to the traditional design commissions, to realize the new geometrical formal language in a variety of projects. His good contacts with notable Swiss industrialists, for example in the clock- and watch-making industry in the Canton of Solothurn, led to the realization of large scale projects that were often developed over a period of years before finally being realized. Specialist articles were often published only at a project's completion, and many plans and sketches are not clearly dated. Therefore it is often not possible today to identify either the precise moment at which Cramer developed new ideas, nor the events that would have influenced his choice of solution.

Idyllic scene with view of the Menzingen Seminary for Female Teachers

The school site on a south-facing slope

Open space design for the Bernarda Seminary for Female Teachers in Menzingen

Cramer's collaborations with distinguished architects, for example with Haefeli, Moser, Steiger on the new Eternit AG headquarters in Niederurnen from 1953, contributed to the fact that he was increasingly consulted in architectural circles. Also in 1953, the progressive Zug architects' practice of Hafner and Wiederkehr, working with architects Hanns A. Brütsch and Alois Stadler, was commissioned to prepare project studies for the new building for the Seminary for Female Teach-

ers in Menzingen. Cramer was asked to plan and realize the extensive outdoor areas. The new Bernarda training establishment for female teachers was intended to accommodate about 275 students and was built on a terrace of land near the little town of Menzingen for the convent of the same name. The educational centre acquired its name from Mother Bernarda Heimgartner, who had founded the religious community with the Capuchin father Theodosius Florentini in 1844. The architects submitted preliminary studies to their clients in autumn 1953, and work on the extensive complex, consisting of a seven-storey residential building, a refectory, the actual school building, a chapel, a theatre and a gymnasium, began in summer 1955. The new Bernarda Seminary in Menzingen was festively inaugurated on 26 November 1958 [220] after a building period of three years. All the buildings were linked by covered, partially glazed connecting passages, and its modern architectural approach reflected the current model for American school buildings. Cramer's first task was to model the soil excavated during the building process in such a way that it would successfully adapt to the surrounding terrain. Instead of shaping the site naturalistically, Cramer opted for a precise geometrical topography. The central open space of the complex, bordered by the gymnasium, school building, dining-hall, residential section and linking halls, is still a large, almost square sports- and play field today. Gardens intended for teaching, with rainwater collection pools and compost facilities, were placed on the northern edge of the site, separated from the sports field

only by a glazed corridor. Cramer designed the triangular, south-west facing section of the site, located between the school building and the theatre, as a lawn with seats, so that people could spend time in the open air, and he established a terraced study garden on the adjacent slope. He developed a magnificently coloured display of herbaceous planting between the long, 70 centimetre wide steps made of concrete slabs, which still proves an atmospheric accompaniment to one's lingering enjoyment of the view. Cramer used the distinctive lines provided by wide slab steps as shading to emphasize the horizontal element of the landscape, thus creating a close link with the horizontal articulation of the surrounding buildings, as is shown clearly in Peter Ammon's photographs taken at the time. [221] Even years later, experts were still citing the interplay between the severe lines of the terraced area and the loose naturalness of the herbaceous planting as an interesting attempt to link architecture and garden. Neither the austere formal language nor the combination of materials were customary at the time. [222] Another powerful feature was the way in which Cramer restricted himself to the simplest of resources even when designing the seats. He used rectangular concrete slabs 3.5 metres long, 75 centimetres wide and 26 centimetres thick, setting them in such a way that a strip of shadow eight centimetres wide gave the impression that the heavy blocks were floating above the lawn. Along the driveway that led on to the site, Cramer created some seating. At the same time, he managed to use a massive ex-

posed concrete bench almost 40 metres long both to accommodate the height difference on the site and to separate the visitors' car-park from the garden.

The overall appearance of the open spaces corresponded to Cramer's new line and was based strictly on right angles, particularly in the layout of the paths. Cramer wanted to respond to the clarity of Modern architecture down to the last detail of his design, and therefore restricted himself to a small range of materials for the outside areas as well. All the paths were designed using heavy, square concrete slabs. The 70 by 70 centimetre slab format was not only difficult to handle, but not in general demand, and had to be commissioned specially from the manufacturers, according to contemporary witnesses. Cramer's intention in using this slab format, which he preferred from the mid 50s onwards, was to convey a modern spaciousness in garden design that had nothing in common with traditional intricacy. There was one exception to the selection of materials for the paving, but it was all the more remarkable for that: the 1100 square metre entrance courtyard. Its dimensions, about 30 by 36 metres, had been conceived by the architects to relate to the proportions of the adjacent, six-storey convent. From the first perspective sketches onwards, the façade of the residential section was accentuated by strong horizontal articulation. The highly contrasting striped effect was produced by the solid, unarticulated parapets and the open corridors behind them with continuous bands of windows. When designing the entrance courtyard, Cramer responded with

General plan of the Menzingen seminary

A Convent
B Refectory and kitchen
C Capel and theatre
D School
E Gymnasium
F Connecting hall, sides glazed
G Connecting hall, sides open
H Old institute
J Grass play area
K Car park
L Drive
M Yard
N Service drive
O Teaching garden
P Study garden
Q Old institute yard
R Wall for sitting
S Seats

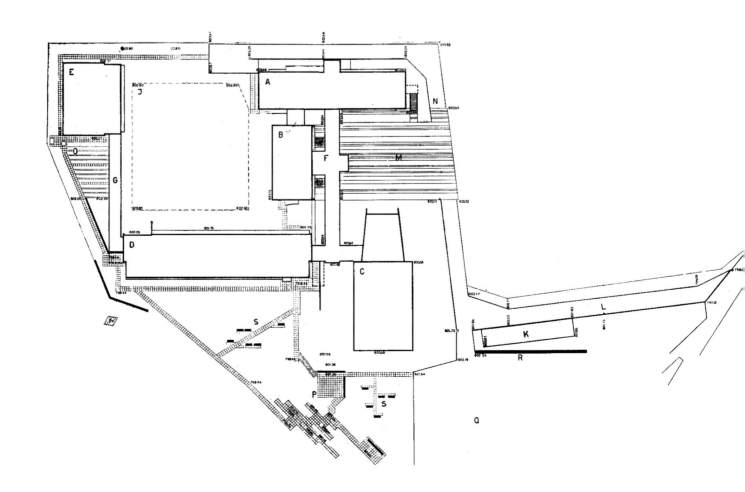

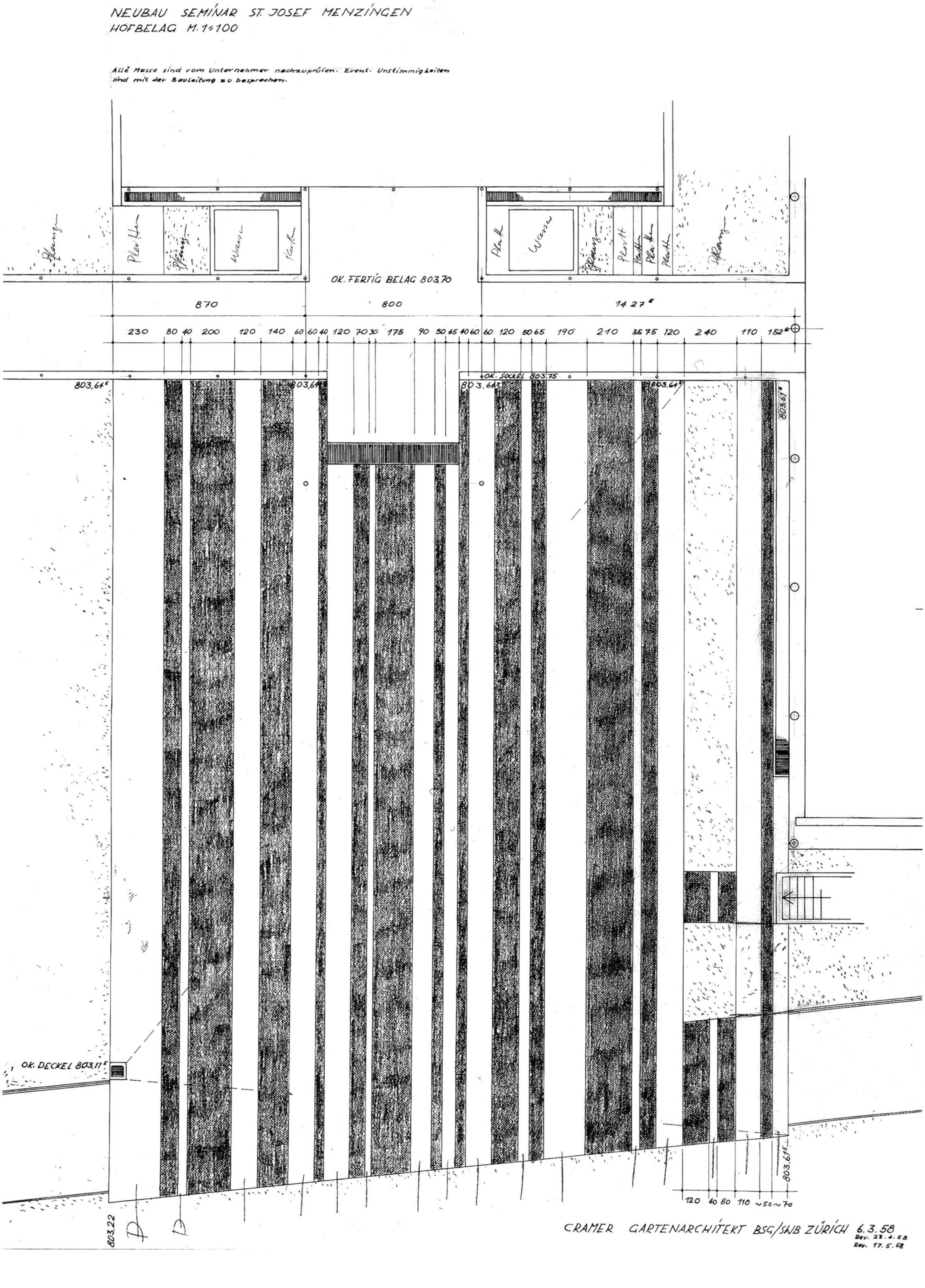

NEUBAU SEMINAR ST. JOSEF MENZINGEN
HOFBELAG M. 1:100

Alle Masse sind vom Unternehmer nachzuprüfen. Event. Unstimmigkeiten
sind mit der Bauleitung zu besprechen.

OK. FERTIG BELAG 803.70

870   800   14 27

230 80 40 200 120 140 60 60 40 120 70 30 175 90 50 65 40 60 60 120 50 65 190 210 35 75 120 240 110 152

803,64   803,64   OK. SOCKEL 803.75   803,64
                                803.64   803,64

OK. DECKEL 803.11

120 40 80 110 ~50~70

803.22

CRAMER GARTENARCHITEKT BSG/SWB ZÜRICH 6.3.58
Dev. 23.4.58
Rev. 17.5.58

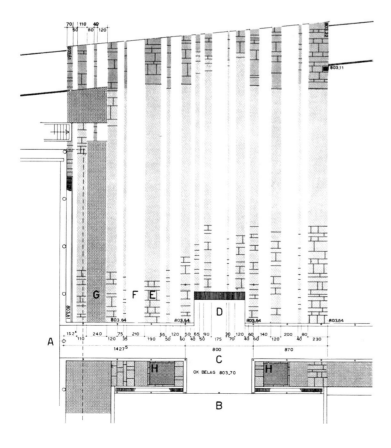

Light natural stone slabs and dark
asphalt in a modern striped pattern
at the Menzingen seminary

Working plan for the entrance courtyard

Opposite page: preliminary design for the
striped carpet at the Menzingen seminary

The garden steps in Menzingen
as a horticultural companion piece
to the modern architecture

Today the view of the residential wing
of the seminary has become blocked by
excessive plant growth

equally strong contrasts. His striped paving was made up of light Bernardine quartzite and black asphalt. Rather than repeating the regularity and proportions of the façade on the courtyard floor, and responding in an unduly superficial manner, Cramer used stripes of different widths, creating an austere and yet lively floor pattern. Here he abandoned concrete slabs, and by his choice of natural stone created a very subtle contrast between the exterior and the architecture.

Cramer's carpet of stripes was 30 metres wide overall and related to the dimensions of the refectory as well. It ran towards the main entrance of the building and the connecting hall, and continued consistently in the narrow space between the ambulatory and the refectory. Here Cramer enlivened the striped pattern by transforming some of the stripes into reflecting pools or planted areas. The reflecting pools and the almost directly adjacent, highly polished paving inside the glazed entrance hall gave the ensemble the unusual atmosphere of a hall of mirrors flooded with light. The inner courtyards acquired a lively atmosphere from varied herbaceous and floral planting and strikingly shaped trees, although the garden architect was running the risk of overfilling the restricted spaces. Cramer had already cautiously tried using a

geometrically conceived combination of asphalt and natural stone in the Dorf school in Suhr. He returned to the idea in Menzingen only a few years later, but more powerfully and convincingly this time. The striped carpet, its side edges emphasized with flanking planting along the length of the building, seemed almost like an abstract painting, and never failed to make

its visual effect either from the point of view of pedestrians or from the upper storeys of the convent. Unfortunately, it is no longer possible to experience the unique effect made by the courtyard design. The striking pattern was recently covered with an unbroken layer of asphalt. Apparently the area had become too expensive to maintain.

Inspired by the courtyard, the architects decided to create an interplay between the natural and the artificial in the buildings as well, and had the garden architect's firm provide stone cladding for the chapel. Rocks up to three cubic metres in size had appeared during the excavations, and these were split and used to clad the outer walls of the chapel – with the cut surfaces on the outside – in a cyclopean arrangement. This was not a new architectural technique, but it tended to be used rarely because of the associated cost. The architects were familiar with the attraction of natural stone from modern American projects, and in Menzingen combined the rustic appearance of the split stone with the modern mass of the building. Cramer was certainly also familiar with the traditional method of building walls with split natural stone in northern Europe, and applied this knowledge in Menzingen to give the chapel a lively appearance with its reddish, grey and earth-coloured stone. This made the chapel look as though it were linked more closely with the ground, but also provided a marked contrast with the adjacent white theatre building with its slat-like, windowless façades. The design dialectic created between the chapel and the theatre was not as subtle as the striped concept for the courtyard, it was very striking instead. Visitors were fascinated by the sight, which was rather unusual at the time. The project as a whole attracted a great deal of attention from architects and garden architects alike. [223]

In this project with Hafner and Wiederkehr, Cramer was able to show how he imagined a successful, modern dialogue between architec-

Powerful concrete elements still determine the character of the Menzingen complex

Simple seating elements in the gardens

Drawing of a gnarled tree in the courtyard of the Menzingen Seminary for Female Teachers

Gardens between the refectory and the glazed linking corridor

ments in determining form. [...] There are two groups of design elements that have to be treated very differently in the modern garden. On the one hand we have the elements relating to construction, in other words the hard elements; these have to be added to the ground plan of the building in clear, uncompromising forms. We like to declare our faith in works that are shaped by human hands and placed in nature nowadays. They should emerge crystal clear, and not lose themselves in nature in a spirit of false romanticism. On the other hand we are permitted to use plants in all their naturalness as a means of introducing variety in the right place. These two insights bring us to solutions in the ground plan that automatically do justice to the architectural principles of repose and movement."[224]

The design for the open spaces for the Bernarda seminary is built consistently from the "Guidelines for the Client" quoted above. But the period between the first designs for this project and its completion a few years later was filled with significant events and projects that proved to be of lasting influence not only on the result of his work in Menzingen, but on Cramer's further career and the extent to which he was known outside Switzerland as well.

Garden for Am Bohlgutsch House in Zug

Fritz Stucky of Zug, who had founded the Stucky and Meuli practice with the building technician Rudolf Meuli in 1956, was one of the "young, good architects with modern ideas" whom Ernst Cramer preferred to work with in those days. Fritz Stucky had started to study architecture at the ETH in Zurich in 1949, and like many of his fellow students had sensed the blatant discrepancy between the traditional view of architecture that his professors were teaching and the pioneering feats in Modern international architecture. These were discussed by Sigfried Giedion, for example, in his visiting lectures at the ETH, much to the annoyance of his colleagues. Like Giedion, who had been at Harvard as early as 1938 at the invitation of Walter Gropius, Fritz Stucky was also looking for a chance to study in the USA, and did indeed find one. He was accepted by Frank Lloyd Wright's distinguished Taliesin school for apprentice training in architecture in Wisconsin in 1950, on the recommendation of Professor Werner Max Moser, himself one of the first students at the Taliesin Fellowship, founded in 1932. After intensive study, associated with practical project experience in Taliesin West, studies at the University of Washington in Seattle, and a working visit to Mexico City, Stucky returned to Switzerland in 1955, where he soon set up his own architect's practice, given the boom in building and commerce that was already on the horizon. In 1956, Ernst Cramer was involved as a garden architect in one of Stucky and Meuli's very first building projects, the Am Bohlgutsch House in Zug, although his influence as a designer could scarcely be discerned in the finished product. A

ture and garden design. "Close co-operation between client, architect and garden designer is always worthwhile in this respect, but at the same time the work becomes more uniform and perfect as a whole," wrote Cramer in a key article in the mid 50s:

"The outstanding characteristic of modern design technique lies in the direct development of the garden from the building, with the functional requirements of what is designed as the key ele-

building land and increasing building costs. The architects were therefore interested from the outset in high-density building, especially on sloping sites. Cramer was soon confronted with new garden design questions in the context of some remarkable subsequent projects. In the case of this first project, resistance from conservationists and experts with a conservative cast of mind obviously proved a considerable obstacle and was overcome only with difficulty, as shown clearly by comments in the specialist press. In January 1957, the editors of *Bauen + Wohnen* published the project not just for this reason, but also to combat mistrust of Modern architecture by colleagues in central Switzerland. [225]

Am Bohlgutsch house in Zug
by Stucky and Meuli 1956

modern building containing three dwellings – a one-bedroom flat, a three-and-a-half bedroom flat and a house with a separate entrance and a large roof-garden terrace – was built on a plot about 1100 square metes in size on a steep northern slope above the old town of Zug. Stucky and Meuli had seen that it was necessary to achieve higher utilization factors in the face of a growing population, limited reserves of

Simply designed garden plan for
the Am Bohlgutsch house in Zug

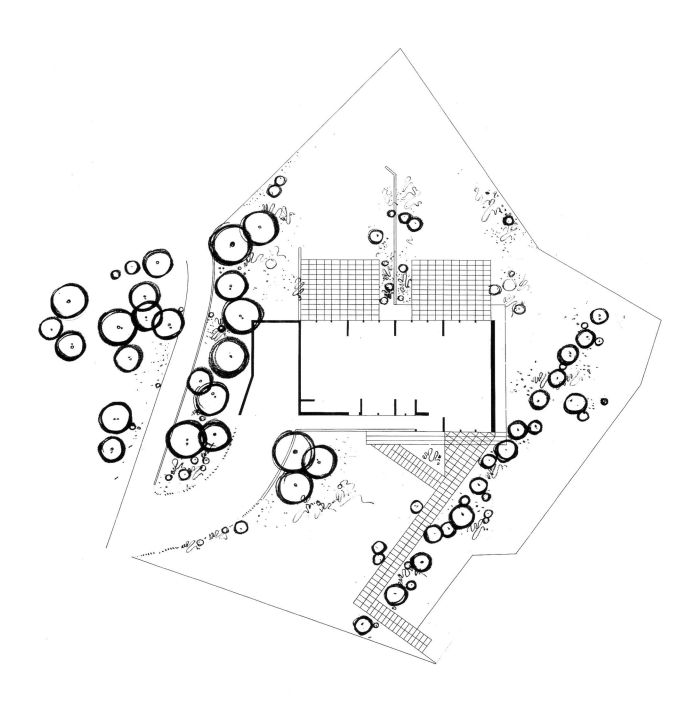

Interbau Berlin 1957

The Internationale Bauausstellung – International Building Exhibition – in the Hansaviertel in Berlin 1957, was one of the most important events to have a lasting effect on Ernst Cramer's interest in modern architecture. In about 1946, Hans Scharoun, the first Municipal Director of Building in the post-war administration, and his colleagues developed a plan for rebuilding the ruined city of Berlin. It did not involve reconstructing dense historical urban structures, but was aiming at an open, green urban landscape following the principles of the Charter of Athens. This so-called "Collective Plan" defined the modern guidelines of the Berlin land use plan passed in 1950. Most of the housing estates drawing on modern ideas were built on the outskirts of the city, and there were few opportunities for restructuring formerly heavily built-up inner-city areas. Thus rebuilding the Hansa district, over 75 per cent of which had been destroyed in night air-raids on 22 and 23 November 1943, was considered a particular challenge. This site between the Spree and the Tiergarten offered a chance of proving that the urban planning ideal of an open, green city was viable. In political terms, the Hansaviertel was a unique opportunity to demonstrate that West

The urban planning competition entry submitted by the Berlin architects Gerhard Jobst, Willy Kreuer and Wilhelm Schliesser in December 1953, which won first prize, gave a first impression of the future character of the quarter. The prize-winning design consisted of rows and slabs of uniformly designed multi-storey buildings of different lengths and heights. They were placed in an open landscape designed like a park, with a seamless transition to the Tiergarten. The informal, open placing of the buildings followed certain basic principles. One of the aims was to use a chain of high-rise slabs to screen off the adjacent roads and the S-Bahn elevated train line. A second motif was clearly opening the housing complex on to the park, as signalled by the open, semicircular placing of two groups of buildings around central park areas that extended from the Tiergarten into the residential area.

The design followed the model of the articulated and open city as promoted in influential books by Hans Bernhard Reichow in 1948[226] and Göderitz, Rainer and Hoffmann in 1957[227]. The key feature of this model was the idea of a green "spatial continuum", accentuated by individual buildings that were added in as "urban dominants". Jobst, Kreuer and Schliesser's competition entry was not originally intended to form the basis for a building exhibition, which was decided upon on 3 August 1953 and was originally to have taken place in 1956. It therefore had to be amended substantially to accommodate the demands of the exhibition project. The "Aktiengesellschaft für den Aufbau des Hansaviertels" was set up in late 1954 to handle the technical, commercial, legal and financial organization of the building exhibition, and the "Internationale Bauausstellung Berlin GmbH" was established to organize the exhibition. In addition, a "Steering Committee" was set up under the President of the Federation of German Architects (Bund Deutscher Architekten), Otto Bartning, whose role was to solve design problems, but also to choose the architects who were to be invited.

"Architecture and green areas were on a par in the urban design concept of the green and open city that Interbau intended to demonstrate, programmatically and to the highest possible standard. It was clear that the idea of open, fluent spaces could take shape only by using the resources of garden design, and that landscape architects should be involved as equal partners from the outset."[228]

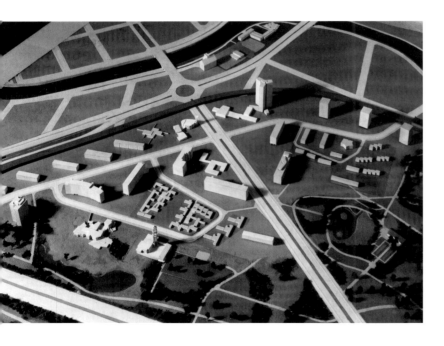

Hansaviertel Berlin, model

Berlin had the will to rebuild and to create a modern inner-city residential project with international participation. The garden historians' dream not of rebuilding the quarter, but extending the Tiergarten down to the Spree, as Peter Joseph Lenné had once intended, was rapidly abandoned because the cost of land was too high and the were too many objections in urban planning terms. Instead, the town planners aimed to closely link the park and the newly designed district.

Walter Rossow, a Berlin garden architect and chairman of the German Werkbund, was a member of the Steering Committee from the beginning of the building exhibition. His younger colleague Helmut Bournot was responsible for coordinating the open space planning, and dealt with the site supervision of the landscape architecture. He underlined the importance of involving garden architecture in drawing up the general plan, and wrote in retrospect:

"The majority of the building architects felt at first that they had to design the green planning as well. But long arguments and discussions persuaded a large number of those architects that collaborating with garden and landscape architects is to be welcomed not just for reasons of aesthetics and design, but also on financial grounds. No building will be erected in the Hansaviertel without the position and the height of the terrain having being checked or fixed by garden architects. [...] One has to have experienced the nerve-racking and yet ultimately successful discussions and negotiations between building and garden architects, between officials and free-lance garden architects, if one is to get anywhere near assessing the consequences of the events in the Hansaviertel."[229]

In August 1954 the Steering Committee started to choose internationally distinguished architects who were to realize the total of 34 building projects in the Hansaviertel. By 1955 the list of 53 participants was fixed. The most eminent names included: Le Corbusier from Paris, Walter Gropius from Cambridge, Massachusetts, Oscar Niemeyer from Rio de Janeiro, Alvar Aalto from Helsinki, Arne Jacobsen and Kay Fisker from Copenhagen, Pierre Vago from Paris, Egon Eiermann from Karlsruhe, Johannes Hendrik van den Broek and Jacob Berend Bakema from Rotterdam, Max Taut, Hans Scharoun and Wassili Luckhardt from Berlin, Luciano Baldessari from Milan, Sep Ruf from Munich and Otto Heinrich Senn from Basel, one of Switzerland's foremost Modern architects. Then came ten distinguished garden architects: Herta Hammerbacher from Berlin, Wilhelm Hübotter from Hanover, Edvard Jacobson from Karlstad, Gustav Lüttge from Hamburg, Hermann Mattern from Kassel, René Pechère from Brussels, Pietro Porcinai from Florence, Carl Theodor Sørensen from Copenhagen, Otto Valentien from Stuttgart and Ernst Cramer from Zurich. His experiments with garden architecture were made public outside Switzerland only gradually, and were therefore not internationally known in 1954. But his good relations with progressive Swiss architects, his membership in the Swiss Werkbund and his contacts with IFLA and leading garden architects in Europe must have had a part to play.

Gardens for five atrium houses in the Hansaviertel in Berlin

For the purposes of landscape architecture, the Hansaviertel exhibition site was divided into five areas, each with more or less uniform building types. A team of two garden architects was responsible for designing each area. Ernst Cramer had the pleasure of working with a German colleague of about his own age, whose work he had admired for a long time: Otto Valentien. Cramer and Valentien, who were both known above all for their successful domestic garden design, were allotted area II. This was directly adjacent to the Tiergarten, and was covered like a carpet with mainly single-storey atrium houses. These low buildings, a few of which had two storeys, had intimate domestic gardens and were designed by ten architects, including Eduard Ludwig, Arne Jacobsen and Sep Ruf. Area II also included the Kaiser Friedrich Memorial Church (building no. 22), built by the Berlin architect Ludwig Lemmer, and a three-storey residential building with exhibition and commercial facilities (building no. 25) by Paul Baumgarten, also from Berlin. The official Interbau exhibition catalogue names Ernst Cramer and Otto Valentien jointly as the garden architects responsible for all the objects in their area. But Cramer's list of work mentions only the gardens for the five single-family houses by Eduard Ludwig and the areas outside the Kaiser Friedrich Memorial Church. As only these two projects are documented in the garden architect's estate, it is to be assumed that Ernst Cramer was mainly responsible for design and execution in these places only, while all the other projects were created under the direction of Otto Valentien.

The single-storey atrium houses represented a modern building type reminiscent of elegant American bungalows, while at the same time taking into account the post-war need for privacy. Their architect, Professor Eduard Ludwig, had studied at the Dessau Bauhaus from 1928 to 1932, and taught at the Hochschule für Bildende Künste in Berlin; he had achieved international fame mainly for his Airlift Memorial at Berlin's

Draughtsman's study by Cramer's office for the design of the entrance area to the Kaiser Friedrich Memorial Church in Hansaviertel, Berlin

General view of Eduard Ludwig atrium houses

Tempelhof airport in 1951. The five buildings west of the Händelallee were the only single-family houses that were completed when Inter-bau opened. There was a range of variants, with areas between 128 and 200 square metres, each with a little garage. All the buildings, whether they had a standard, U-shaped or L-shaped

leading through the lawn to a triangular paved area, a small garden niche. This was evidence of Cramer's delight in playing with ground plan geometry, though in a somewhat hesitant form. The furniture was dealt with as austerely as the gardens' ground plans. There was coloured gar-den furniture in the style of the times to set a few

Perspective drawing by Cramer's office for one of the Interbau Berlin atrium gardens

Intimate living and garden space

ground plan, had been erected at reasonable cost, using a unit building method with storey-high porous concrete slabs and with no cellars. The outer walls were clad with asbestos cement slabs with a glazed, coloured surface. The gar-den courtyards were also enclosed in storey-high asbestos sheet piling, so that no one could look in from the outside. But on the inside, the large windows of the living rooms and bedrooms faced south on to the garden courtyard. The courtyards are intimate open-air living rooms; the park landscape of the adjacent Tiergarten impinges on them from the outside at best in the form of individual trees or overhanging crowns of trees. At the time visitors, and also residents, were delighted, as they still are at the time of writing, with the ease with which these ground-level living areas could be used, the chance to spend time in the enclosed garden undisturbed and the close spatial relationship between gar-den and house. Even today the atrium buildings seem entirely inaccessible from the outside.

When designing the little inner courtyards, Cramer was concerned above all to create a close link between the functional architecture and the garden. Square concrete slabs, arranged in a grid pattern, and simply designed pergolas complet-ed the ground plan of each building. Small, care-fully tended lawns were laid like green carpets, and complemented only with sparsely placed decorative grasses and herbaceous plants. In on-ly one garden the design broke the strict right an-gles of the overall complex with a diagonal path

cheerful accents, but beyond this there was noth-ing but a few round, square or triangular asbestos cement plant containers. Of course the familiar flower spindle had to be there, and so did Willy Guhl's well-known beach chair, that he had devel-oped in 1954.

These gardens typically reflected Cramer's new approach to design. They matched the current image of the modern domestic garden, and fol-lowed Helmut Bournot's intention of remaining true to modern, functional design and prevent-ing anything that smacked of "landscape ro-manticism" in the Hansaviertel. [230] Architec-ture and garden complemented each other for-mally and functionally in such a way that it was impossible for outsiders to discern whether the architect or the garden architect had been in charge of the project as a whole. The symbiosis of house and garden was perfect and very in-conspicuous for precisely that reason – essen-tially just as inconspicuous as the garden de-sign for the Kaiser Friedrich Memorial Church, which, unlike the domestic gardens, was scarce-ly mentioned in specialist publications.

In this sense, Interbau 1957 was certainly not ex-perimental terrain in which Ernst Cramer could implement his own garden design innovations. And the other garden architects involved did not have spectacular innovations in mind either. Rather, their intention was to work closely with the architects to demonstrate the unity of house and garden, city and landscape, architecture and nature as skilfully as possible, in the spirit of the official theme "Man in the green metropolis". Lightness, cheerfulness, homeliness, festiveness, colourfulness and a sense of security were intended to set the atmosphere of the Hansaviertel, the "City of Today". The actual innovation from the point of view of the landscape architects was that the usable green spaces played such an important part in establishing the structure. Walter Rossow summed up the central task by saying that "in the 'City of Tomorrow' green areas will be the framework for the urban structure of the city", and argued that the natural order of the landscape should be the basis for planning the city and the countryside. All building was to be subject to this law. "In the heart of the city, in the

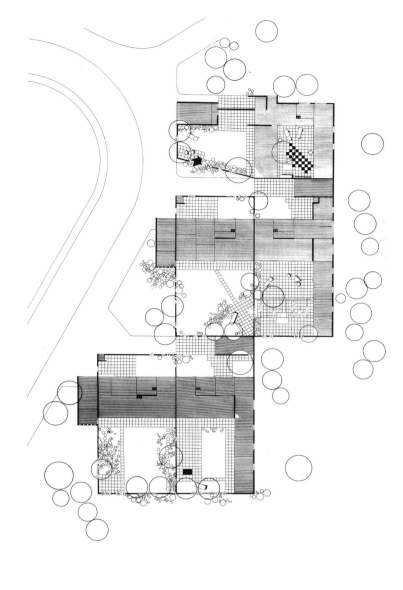

Garden plan for the atrium houses dating from April 1958

centre, green areas designed in the most intensive way, that are in the best sense at the centre of landscape architecture, should largely predominate."[231] Thus garden design, seen as nature staged according to purely aesthetic criteria, played scarcely any part at Interbau. Instead, every detail of the design, from the pattern of the slabs to the pergola, met functional requirements first and foremost. The fine arts made their presence felt in isolated cases.

Outdoor areas for the Klopstockstrasse children's day-care centre in Berlin (Hermann Mattern, René Pechère)

And yet there are landscape architecture projects in the Hansaviertel that are revealing in terms of garden design and Ernst Cramer's further work. The October 1957 issue of the specialist magazine *Garten und Landschaft*, dedicated to Interbau Berlin, shows the astonishing design plan for the outdoor areas of the children's day-care centre in Klopstockstrasse (building 6). [232] It includes the building's striking ground plan, composed of hexagons, which was to have been realized by the Stuttgart architect Günther Wilhelm. Hermann Mattern and René Pechère designed a garden for the immediate vicinity. They divided the space into smaller units by modelling the site three-dimensionally. The garden architects, borrowing

Garden for an atrium house by Eduard Ludwig framed by Eternit asbestos cement walls

View from the living room into the garden space

The Canadian sumac, a popular focal point in Cramer's gardens

Diagonal concrete slab path in the atrium garden

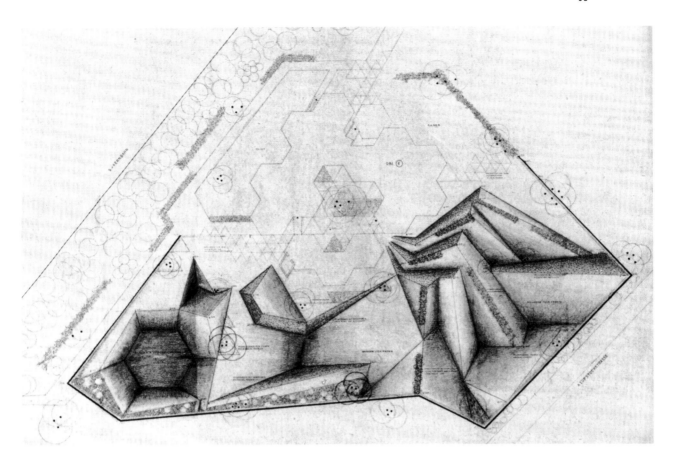

Planning around the children's day-care centre (building 6) in the Hansaviertel by Hermann Mattern and René Pechère

from the honeycomb ground plan of the architecture, did not want to pile up naturalistic mounds of earth, but tried to create an artificial landscape made up of geometrically shaped bodies of soil. These grassy mounds would have screened the kindergarten off from the street and would have playfully kept the children "in the desired state of lively movement" on the off-set, sloping surfaces, as the garden architects explained. [223] They intended to emphasize individual areas on the mounds, but also some striking lines, with the appropriately austere use of roses and herbaceous plants, while small groups of trees would have quietly emphasized other spots. The project was not realized in this form, but was built later as a flat-roofed building in two parts on square ground plans, to a simpler design by the Tiergarten district building department. Instead of the severely geometrical mounds, the large play-garden was modelled with small, landscape-like mounds and troughs. The original design is remarkable in contrast because its abstractly shaped mounds anticipate a motif that Cramer applied in a masterly fashion barely two years later when designing his "Poet's Garden". [234] The Mattern and Pechère design clearly represents the attempt to represent landscape abstractly, in the classical Modern tradition, rather than to imitate it naturalistically. We do not know whether Cramer had discovered the attractions of this design strategy as early as 1957. Two-dimensional form was still the crucial design feature of his work at this time, in geometrically conceived paving and pools, for example. He had yet to explore the third dimension of design.

A key figure: Oscar Niemeyer

Not just the opportunity to exchange ideas and work directly with the leading European garden architects of the day – forging friendships that lasted for a long time in some cases – made Interbau 1957 such a key experience for Ernst Cramer. What excited him above all was the close encounter with international Modern architecture and its distinguished exponents. [235] Otto Senn in particular, whose architecture very clearly showed the influence of Frank Lloyd Wright, was a master of the vocabulary of Modernism and like his Werkbund colleague Cramer, was engaged in a radical search for the truth of form well into old age. [236] Ernst Cramer designed the garden for the architect's house in Zofingen in the year after Interbau, [237] and it is to be assumed that Senn appreciated the Zurich garden architect's radical approach to form. But Cramer must have been particularly fascinated by the architecture of Oscar Niemeyer, whom the French magazine *l'architecture d'aujourd'hui* considered to be one of the most interesting participants in Interbau. [238] The seven-storey block of flats that Niemeyer built in the Hansaviertel was more than an example of modern Brazilian architecture; to many people interested in architecture it represented a vision of the planned new capital, Brasilia.

Oscar Niemeyer was unmistakably basing the design of his Berlin building on Le Corbusier's exemplary Unité d'Habitation, already built by the old master of Modern architecture in Marseilles between 1947 and 1952. The South American architect had personally met Le Corbusier, who was thirty years older, in 1936 when Le Corbusier was visiting Brazil to give decisive advice and support to Lúcio Costa and his team in planning the new Ministry of Health and Education in Rio de Janeiro, considered a model project. Niemeyer was part of the Brazilian architectural team at the time, as were his famous colleague Affonso E. Reidy, the young garden architect Roberto Burle Marx and others. Le Corbusier was the young Brazilian's role model. Like Le Corbusier's Unité d'Habitation, Niemeyer's Berlin block was also supported by piers, the so-called pilotis, though the Brazilian made them V-shaped. The large communal area on the fifth floor, known as the "Contorno", and the striking light slits in the otherwise windowless concrete walls of the topmost storey – without going any further into the details of the architecture – are other analogous features. The building's fundamental idea of "making the living-cells that are fitted together in a building into a community"[239] is further clear evidence that Le Corbusier served as the model. But many other details are rightly cited to show that this was very much a design by Niemeyer in his own right.[240] It was at that time that Niemeyer started to distance himself from Le Corbusier's functionalist architecture, which he considered outdated.

The Niemeyer building[241] housed a highly acclaimed special foreign exhibition that made a guest appearance in the Zurich building department only six months later. It was this exhibition that really whetted Cramer's curiosity. It was called "Brasilia – the city of tomorrow becomes reality", and exhibited five of a total of 26 competition entries for the overall planning of the new Brazilian capital. The urban planning competition, which created a world-wide sensation, had been announced in September 1956 and was judged with Oscar Niemeyer as a key figure in March 1957, only a few months before the opening of Interbau Berlin. Lúcio Costa's design won the competition, and was to be built within a period of only three years. At the time of the exhibition in the Hansaviertel, the Brasilia building operation was already fully under way. Lúcio Costa's overall architectural design suggestions corresponded so precisely with the conception of his former pupil Oscar Niemeyer that the latter found ideal conditions for realizing his own architectural ideas and became along with Costa, the most important architect for the capital city project. In Europe, the realization of a grandiose architectural Utopia, "the most radical implementation of what generally came to be known as the Charter of Athens or as Le Corbusier-esque ideas," was followed with fascination.[242] Le Corbusier himself stated in 1962: "It is very simple to design bold architectural forms in Brazil, because the people find them easy to accept and understand; in Europe our creations meet with a great deal more resistance."[243] And so Brasilia was not just of general interest to Cramer as a symbol of the

dawn of a new age. Rather, it was the simple, bold forms that Le Corbusier mentioned that obviously excited the garden architect and made him especially interested in Niemeyer's architecture.

From the mid 50s on, the Brazilian changed his view of architecture and not only distanced himself from Le Corbusier but increasingly earned himself the reproach of photogenic and spectacular formalism.

"Generally speaking," wrote art historian Alexander Fils, "Niemeyer's architecture has to be defined as very artistic, if not in fact affected. In his case, functional and structural aspects are dominated by aesthetics. He referred to European architecture, by which he meant the Bauhaus, as cold and geometrical, while wanting to give his own architecture a sculpturally expressive quality."[244]

Some of the most vehement criticism came from Switzerland, where monumentality in principle was viewed with particular suspicion, and this annoyed Niemeyer a great deal. Max Bill warned in Rio in 1954: "Architecture in your country is running the risk of falling into the dire condition of being anti-socially academic."[245] The expressive quality of this architecture was bound to displease the vigorous advocate of "Die gute Form", if only for the reason that he saw in it the very tendency towards streamlined simplification combined with distension that he had rejected years before as a new and meaningless kind of decoration.[246] His criticism, which by no means all architectural experts in Switzerland agreed with,[247] was apparently not enough to diminish Cramer's fundamental interest. References to the expressive components of Niemeyer's architecture recur in his late work. But for the time being Cramer remained wedded to a "cold geometrical" formal language.

Villas and terraced buildings

Cramer drank in the ideas and inspirations of Interbau 1957, and was only waiting for a suitable occasion to put this new approach into practice. The fact that he had been involved in the acclaimed exhibition reinforced his reputation among architects and professional colleagues in Switzerland, and this had a discernible effect on the firm's order-book. Former project partners like Fritz Stucky confirm that Ernst Cramer took a certain pride in telling them in passing about his interesting sojourns in Berlin.[248] He was involved in various housing projects with Stucky and Meuli in 1957 and 1958, but also worked with Eduard del Fabro and Bruno Gerosa on the "Im Feld" school building project in Wetzikon, and advised Hafner and Wiederkehr about their Darius hotel project in Teheran, though this was never realized because of the political upheaval in Iran. Cramer, in collaboration with the young architects Ruth and Edi Lanners and Res Wahlen, took part in the competition for the Altstetten cemetery in Zurich in 1957. The team earned 4th place, while Fred Eicher, Ernst Graf, Hans Hubacher and Ernst Studer won and finally also realized the remarkable Eichbühl cemetery. All the archi-

the Gimmenen country house on Lake Zug for the Brunner-Gyr family. Cramer proved his worth as an experienced partner in projects like these, knowing how to respond both to the architects' requirements and to the occupants' needs, even with traditional materials like polygonal granite

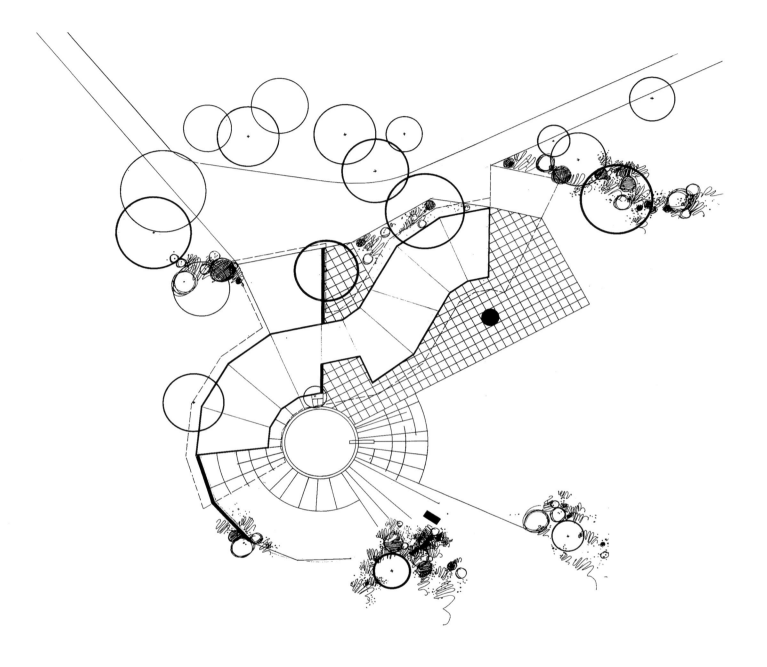

Ground plan of the Gimmenen country house on Lake Zug

tects that Ernst Cramer worked with in these years had in common the fact that they were guided by international Modern architecture. Cramer approached the projects in the same way that he had his Interbau work in Berlin. His garden designs complemented the severe architectural concepts, without ostentatiously pushing into the foreground. For him as ever the client's wish and not an urge to realize himself as a creative force was decisive.

Garden for the Gimmenen country house on Lake Zug
Among the first commissions in which the Stucky and Meuli architectural practice were able to use their modern vocabulary were prestigious villas for progressively thinking clients like

slabs and decorative planting. To meet the client's request for a lot of sun and a view of the lake, the architects had devised a ground plan made up of thirteen identical trapezoid segments assembled to form a long building organized around the centres of three circles. The supporting structure was made up of similar, far cantilevering concrete frame elements and the wall and window sections were executed in wood, giving the single-storey house an elegant look despite its considerable size. Stucky's interest in the building style of Frank Lloyd Wright showed unmistakably in the expressive quality of the flat-roofed building, the balanced use of concrete and natural stone and the close relationship between landscape and architecture. [249]

Cramer added a garden with a simple ground plan immediately adjacent to the building. This adapted formally to the curved line of the building and created some natural highlights at very few carefully chosen points, for example by the entrance to the house, with lavish herbaceous and tree planting and large erratic stones. Cramer's preliminary designs show that he originally intended to manage without natural stone slabs and use concrete slabs for the terrace. A large round pool was to mark the centre of the circular living section in the open air. Bands of slabs radiating from this would have structured part of the garden. It is not clear why this design was finally rejected, but it seems reasonable to suppose that both the client and the architect preferred to follow American models. The dialogue between architecture and nature in the form of landscape-like gardens was crucially important in Wright's work. Cramer's design had far too brusquely rejected natural garden design. The pool was in fact realized, and like the lavish terraces and steps it responded to the striking, geometrically structured ground plan of the house. But instead of a grid of concrete paving-stones, the old, tried-and-tested granite slabs in polygonal units were laid. This certainly did not fit in with Cramer's latest ideas, but did no harm to the elegance of the complex. The rest of the garden flowed gradually and naturally from a carefully tended lawn accentuated with individual trees into the adjacent orchard.

Green areas for an estate of terraced buildings in Zug

But it was the houses on terraces that Stucky and Meuli planned and realized all over Switzerland that became a kind of trade mark for the Zug architects' practice. The first complex of this kind was built in Zug in 1958, in collaboration with Ernst Cramer.

"A subject of enormous concern for the building authorities," wrote Fritz Stucky about the state of affairs at the beginning of the project, *"was the ultra-rapid increase in the population before the 'pill downturn'. The Zug building director [...] already had his 'inner eye' on a town of 20,000 inhabi-*

tants on the north shore of Lake Zug. Thus the available building land had to be exploited better, with higher utilization figures. For this reason we were faced with the question: how can one build much more densely without reducing the standard of living. How can all the demands made on a large single-family house be met in a housing development, for example."[250]

The few remaining building plots in Zug, almost all of which were located on steep slopes, forced the architects to think about building reasonably priced, dense houses on slopes with inclines of up to 80 per cent. The approach was similar to building stairs: concrete side pieces were built into the slope and prevented from sliding by a solid block of garages at the bottom. The individual dwellings were placed on top of the side pieces like block-steps, thus obviating the need for expensive retaining walls and elaborate building to compensate for the slope. As each owner only had to purchase a narrow strip of land, and the majority of the dwelling was placed on top of the next owner's, building costs could be kept to a minimum. Each of the houses, like a storey in a block, was equipped with an autonomous infrastructure. This made it possible to fit solid floors between the dwellings to provide the desired sound insulation. "The balconies are placed diagonally, so that even the large terraces cannot be overlooked from above, and the 80 centimetre wide parapets are designed as plant troughs," explained Fritz Stucky.[251] 25 houses on terraces were built in Zug, and the architect maintains that they could be realized only because the building authorities were so receptive to new architectural concepts.

It was Cramer's task to provide the basic planting

The large pool in the garden
of the country house

American bungalow architecture
by Stucky and Meuli in Gimmenen

for the complex. He suggested regular grid-like planting with juniper, which was intended to structure the whole roofscape, while the detailed design was left to the individual residents. For this type of building, the garden design element was not as important as being open to progressive urban planning ideas, and Cramer used this quality to recommend himself for interesting subsequent projects, like Walter Jonas's ntra Houses, for example. [252] Given the building boom in the 50s and 60s, triggered by the growth in population, the decreasing number of residents per dwelling, the rising demand for land brought about by prosperity and property speculation, innovative housing projects, rationalization, standardization and industrialization of the building industry became more and more important. For Cramer too, questions regarding the treatment of the landscape and the design of the open spaces for the new housing estates became increasingly important in the coming years.

The First Swiss Horticultural Show G | 59

An invitation to the First Swiss Horticultural Show G|59 on the shores of Lake Zurich was a good opportunity for Ernst Cramer to implement his modern garden design ideas in a striking fashion. At last, once again at a show, he found the scope he needed to explore new design approaches that ran counter to the functional constraints of everyday life, and against the principles of the bourgeois garden ideal.

From the point of view of Swiss garden architects, Germany was the "classical horticultural show country" in the late 50s. Germany had had a National Horticultural Show every two years since 1951. Large cities in particular – for example the City of Essen in 1959 – liked to use these temporary shows in the post-war period as an engine for refurbishing war-damaged districts in the town and on the outskirts, and for creating new parks, and recreation areas just outside the city. The cities' most important partner in setting up the garden shows was the Central Association of German Vegetable and Fruit Growing and Horticulture, which was principally interested in advertising its profession by presenting model garden design and a large number of plant varieties, rather than establishing new, permanent parks. Switzerland had been largely spared from war damage, and felt no need for large horticultural and building exhibitions, like Interbau Berlin, to refurbish whole districts. Temporary, usually cantonal shows were thus the rule. The First Swiss Horticultural Show too was conceived for one summer only, to demonstrate the performance of the Swiss horticultural industry. What was realized under the direction of the Swiss Association of Master Gardeners on 150,000 square metres of existing parks and gardens was above all an "industrial show of domestic horticulture "[253]. It made no marked influence on the debate about future urban development, but had all the more impact on modern Swiss garden architecture. The Zürichhorn on the right bank and Belvoir Park on the left bank of the lake were the main show sites, and their magnificent stocks of trees gave the show a spectacular spatial quality. The Schneeligut, the Mythenquai and the Enge Harbour, which were connected by pedestrian bridges, linked Belvoir Park with the lake like stepping-stones. Special boats plied between the show sites on the two shores of the lake, but there was also – as at Landi 1939 – a sensational cableway, conceived by the Zurich engineer Max Walt. The large, elegant pylons for the cableway on the banks of the lake were seen by many visitors as the key visual image of the show, and as a built expression of the Bauhaus maxim "form follows function". The pylons could be seen from a considerable distance, and against the landscape backdrop they symbolized the spirit of the show as pointedly as the striking G|59 poster, designed by graphic artist Franz Fässler. He placed a rich green circle behind the image of a single lime leaf, and put in the abbreviated formula for the exhibition, "G|59" in austere white lettering. *"The visitor who translated 'G|59' as 'Graphics 1959' has obviously picked out a certain key feature of the show, as its gardens reveal a line, a line*

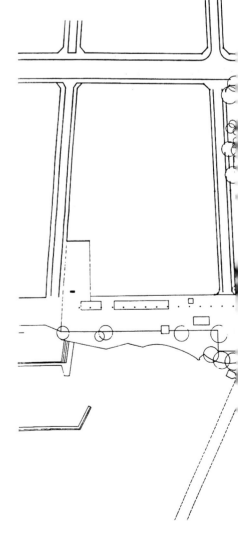

that makes a clear distinction between things that are growing and things that have been built, between the outward appearance of the plant as a natural creature and the building as a human creation," was the journalist Emil Steiner's apposite comment.[254]

The same modern relationship between things built and things grown also characterized the buildings at G|59, for which the architects

Werner Stücheli and Paul R. Kohlbrunner were responsible. Their low pavilions and restaurants, usually in white or the colour of the materials, fitted in inconspicuously with the overall concept of the grounds. Following the model of elegant bungalows by modern American architects – many people felt clearly reminded of Richard Neutra[255] – their large window surfaces and seating terraces opened on to all the diversity of form and colour in the surrounding gardens and parks in a most enjoyable way.

Pierre Zbinden, the horticultural inspector for the City of Zurich, was responsible for the grounds as a whole, but it was decided that two teams of experienced garden architects should be commissioned with the right and left banks respectively. Walter and Klaus Leder of Zurich were responsible for designing the left bank, working with Johannes Schweizer of Basel. Responsibility for the concept of the right bank was handed over to their younger colleagues Ernst Baumann and Willi Neukom, both members of the Swiss Werkbund. This was a great challenge and a unique opportunity for Willi Neukom in particular, who was running his own small practice in Zurich at that time, and he seized it with both hands. The team had about 12 million Swiss francs to spend on designing

Title page of the official
exhibition catalogue for G|59

The First Swiss National Garden
Show G|59, general plan of the right bank
of the lake Zurich with the Poet's Garden

1 Seefeldquai entrance
2 Earthmound/Poet's Garden (D)
3 Fountain
4 Bellerive cableway station
5 Kiosk
6 Special show
7 Hornbach entrance
8 Tombola kiosk
9 Park café
10 Rotunda
11 Greenhouses
12 Exhibition hall
13 Exhibition restaurant
14 Jardin d'amour
15 Phlosopher's Garden
16 Nymphs' Pool

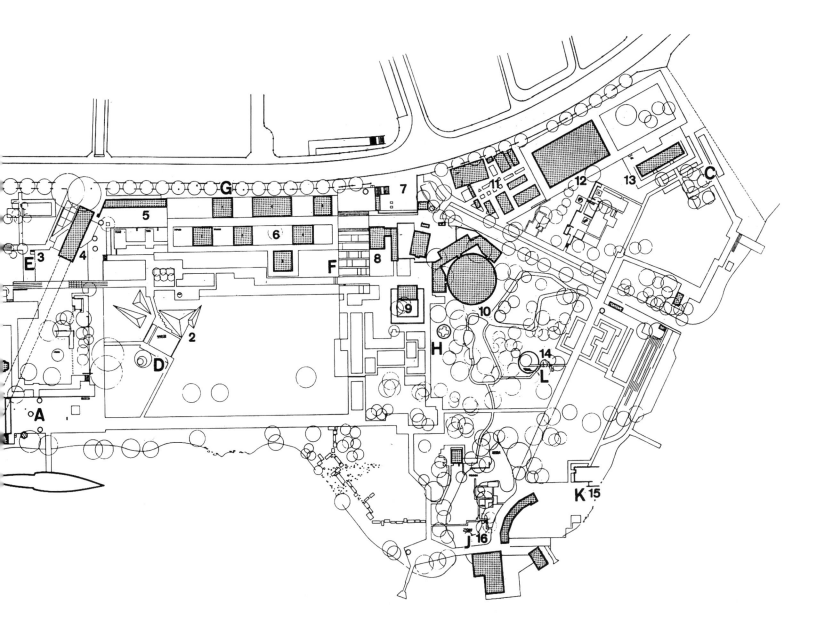

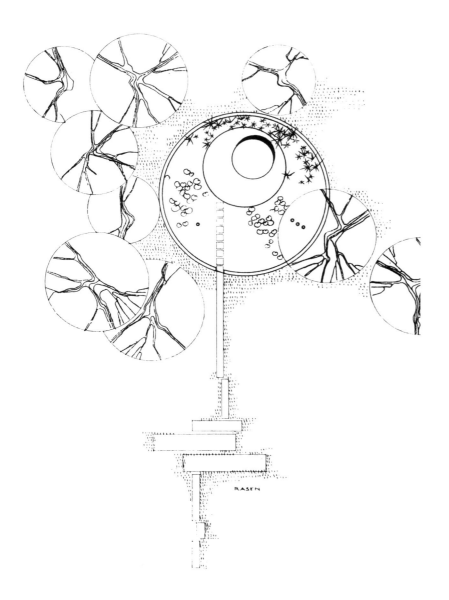

the right bank. Only a few months were available to build the whole grounds, as SAFFA, the major Swiss Women's Labour Exhibition on the same site did not end until autumn 1958 and G|59 was to open already on 25 April of the following year. While Leder and Schweizer realized essentially moderate modern motifs in their area, and adapted their design for paths and gardens to the landscape character of Belvoir Park, Neukom and Baumann had a little more scope on the Zürichhorn. Even on the plan they set the Modern style of the right bank by laying out their paths on a strictly orthogonal pattern. [256] Gerda Gollwitzer wrote from a German point of view:

"This is not just a demonstration of how we design our gardens today, but also of how our garden design might develop further [...] This applies above all to the east shore, where a team from the younger generation had been in action. Their inventive and individual motifs constantly fuelled lively arguments, above all because of the somewhat demanding names they chose ('The Poet's Garden' – 'The Philosopher's Garden' – 'Jardin d'amour') were rather shocking at first."[257]

"Romantic themes," ran Neukom's explanation, "were chosen deliberately to be given a kind of modern interpretation by the use of contemporary building materials like concrete, glass, shaped bricks. They are certain to make a direct statement and immediate effect given the ascetic simplifica-

Plan of the Jardin d'amour
by Willi Neukom, 1959

Jardin d'amour

*tion of form, which is restricted to essentials. The
meaning should ultimately be discernible in their
formal expression."[258]*

Willi Neukom, once the driving creative force in
the Cramer & Surbeck practice, had drawn attention to himself through his interest in new
trends in international garden architecture even
in the years before G | 59. He had written articles
in *Bauen + Wohnen* called "Garden variations"
and "New gardens and garden projects" in 1956
and 1957, turning against traditional domestic
garden design, which he suspected of imitating
nature.

*"Efforts by some to look for other paths and to gain
recognition for more sharply defined design principles have not been very successful to date. But
surely this can only be a question of time,"*
Neukom hoped in 1956, *"as developments in architecture, the influence from abroad, the lavish
gardens created by a designer like Burle Marx in
South America, and then Japanese garden culture,
with its extraordinary vivid intensity, even though
we Europeans rarely if ever grasp its essence fully,
provide us with food for thought."[259]*

As well as his own projects, Neukom presented
work by Ernst Graf and Fred Eicher, who wanted
to introduce more austere lines into gardens. A
year later, modern garden designs by Eywin
Langkilde and Ingwer Ingwersen in Denmark,
and gardens by Mien Ruys in Holland were central to his interests. But he paid most attention
to the work of Roberto Burle Marx in Rio de
Janeiro and San Salvador.[260] Neukom admired the austere abstract composition of
these gardens, but also the dynamic vigour of
their forms. When developing the general plan
for G | 59, he and Baumann opted for austere ba-
sic structuring for the general organization and
lines of the paths, while the meditative Japanese mood, for instance, was to make its presence felt in special gardens. Neukom wanted to
leave "enough scope for realizing concrete or
abstract design possibilities" to the individual
designers[261] at G | 59. At the same time it was
crucially important to him to do justice to the
Werkbund's fundamental demands for "Die gute
Form":

*"The path of looking for simplicity, authenticity
and forcefulness, which can be recognized in the
consistency of the lines of the paths, in the fact
that excessive clichés in fitting in the individual
gardens have been abandoned, in the retention of
coherent areas that are as large as possible, still
seems to us [...] even today, after the exhibition
has closed, to be the right one,"[262]* the garden
architect stated in November 1959.

"Jardin d'amour" (Willi Neukom)

The first model photographs of the "Poet's Garden" and the "Jardin d'amour" were published
during the preparations for G | 59, when nothing
had been said about Ernst Cramer's participation in the show. [263] Neukom was responsible
for both projects, but ultimately of the two projects he realized only the "Jardin d'amour", and
described the concept of his little garden in detail in *Garten und Landschaft*:

*"There is nothing new about the theme itself, it
has just been dusted off a little and presented in a
new way. A form had to be found that is connected
as closely as possible to human life, a form that
makes a contemplative effect. The circle as a symbol of attachment and completeness is a primal
artistic element, undoubtedly originating in myth.
Everything in the Jardin d'amour was arranged eccentrically, the individual elements are set off
against each other purely, peacefully and lucidly,
each effective as such and yet part of a whole.
The rising trunks of the old trees outside the garden are just as much part of the concept as the*

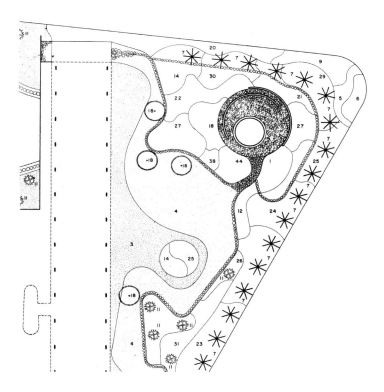

*slight hollow in which the whole thing is set. Step-
ping-stones lead neatly across the water, which is
enlivened by water-lilies, to a large round slab that
– as the actual centre of the garden – is crowned
with a jewel, a broken glass sphere.
The planting, water lilies and bulrushes, was complemented by two-metre high cyperus and some
sugar-cane plants. A little water feature and goldfish sufficiently enliven the scene in a way that is
natural in the changing light of evening.
The only attribute from earlier days is the entrance
gate, but its playfulness refers precisely to the spiritual location, which is intended to encourage
meditation here ..."[264]*

Plan of the garden at the Da Lagoa
hospital in Rio de Janeiro by Roberto
Burle Marx, 1955–1957

Access to the garden, which was enclosed by a circular, exposed concrete wall, was via a straight path of concrete slabs, continued inside the enclosing wall by round stepping-stones. These stepping-stones, which protruded only a little way above the surface of the water, were a popular motif at G|59, which was used effectively both in the "Crystal Garden" and in Baumann and Neukom's "Nymphs' Pool". In this way the garden designers were clearly taking up the Japanese garden design tradition, without – as had become customary at most German horticultural shows – imitating Japanese gardens in every detail.

The Jardin d'amour was one of the more unusual gardens at G|59. Experts saw it as a peripheral piece of garden design, because it seemed to visitors less like a traditional garden than an abstract artistic composition. When looking for similarly conceived earlier projects or sources of inspiration in 20th century garden history, one quickly comes across a French project dating from 1925 and a Brazilian garden dating from 1957. Roberto Burle Marx, whose work Neukom thought particularly highly of, created a small, abstract garden for Oscar Niemeyer's Da Logao hospital in Rio de Janeiro between 1955 and 1957. The most important part of this garden was a circular seating area, partly enclosed by a concrete wall, with a pool placed off-centre within it. The formal similarity between the two projects in plan is amazing, even though their final forms differed in reality. The main elements in Burle Marx's garden were the screening wall, a long curved bench and the planted pool. But the central element of the Jardin d'amour was the glass sphere. This was in turn clearly reminiscent of an even earlier modern garden designed by Gabriel Guévrékian for the 1925 "Exposition des Arts Décoratifs et Industriels Modernes" in Paris: the often-published "Jardin d'eau et de lumière", which was built on a triangular ground plan. The central eye-catching feature in this garden was also a coloured glass sphere, surrounded by pools and a semi-transparent wall. In parallel with the Cubist painting of the garden, which served as a model for the design, the planted areas were framed geometrically and really seemed as though they had been painted, as a result of the severe planting with ground cover and herbaceous plants with uniform, intensely coloured blossom. [265]

Guévrékian was an architect and artist and – rather like Burle Marx – used plants just like glass and concrete as material for creating his Cubist painting. But Neukom, as a garden architect, had too much respect for the nature of plants to be able to use them as radically as that. The Jardin d'amour had difficulty in measuring up to the demand for modern design in accordance with the principles of "Die gute Form" that Neukom had himself formulated for the show. The radical nature of the formal abstraction still hinted at in the model and the plan of

Jardin d'eau et de lumière
by Gabriel Guévrékian, 1925

the garden were abandoned almost completely at the realization stage in favour of decorative arrangements. The powerful effect that Neukom had expected of the confrontation between "ascetic simplification of form" and "romantic themes" did not materialize because the young garden designer seems ultimately to have lacked the self-confidence or the courage to re-

strict himself consistently to essentials. Neukom himself admitted some insecurities in retrospect. [266] The enclosing wall, the wrought-iron entrance gate, the round stepping stones, the water feature and the goldfish were unduly traditional elements of bourgeois garden design and provided too much of a distraction from the essentials. Had not Willi Neukom expressly demanded that "excessive clichés" should be abandoned? Additionally, the garden ran counter to the principal postulates of classical Modernism in its view of space, use of materials, and in its detailing. Neukom was also unable to find his way out of the classical dilemma that had already ensnared Moderns in the garden, and so ultimately the "Jardin d'amour" remained a compromise between modern art and bourgeois garden architecture.

Poet's Garden

It is difficult to see why Ernst Cramer was not substantially involved in planning G|59 from the outset, but was merely a member of the "Plan and Photography Show Commission" – even though he was one of the most influential Swiss garden architects and an important representative of the new line of garden design. One of the reasons must have been that Cramer always preferred to develop his own projects and was never publicly known as an organizational talent. In addition, garden architects with large, flourishing businesses in times of a booming economy have never been particularly interested in taking on extensive, and often badly paid organizational tasks like these. Matters of this kind had been significant even at ZÜKA 1947. [267] The garden architect Walter Frischknecht, who was employed by Ernst Baumann at the time and worked on the planning for G|59 in this capacity, described how, one day during the preparations, Willi Neukom and Ernst Baumann agreed that Ernst Cramer too should contribute to the exhibition.[268] Neukom apparently already had an idea how to involve Cramer, and commissioned the 61-year-old Zurich garden architect to design the "Poet's Garden" near the Bellerive cable car station, in the northern half of the large open lawn.

A preliminary design by Willi Neukom, consisting of four naturalistically shaped mounds of earth, provided Cramer with the first design idea, and clearly constituted the basic idea for the garden. Neukom had built a model of the complex which shows an abstract sculpture on a plinth and a large glass sculpture on two crossed bands of paving stones between the mounds of earth.[269] It was part of the horticultural show's programme and according to Neukom an "educational duty" [270] to present selected works by well-known Swiss sculptors to the public. An overall plan of the show published in October 1959, apparently a preliminary design,

area, in such a way that the centre lines of the two large pyramids and the long axis of the pool pointed exactly north. Thus the garden architect deliberately detached the ensemble from the system of order that applied to the rest of the horticultural show and anchored it in a universal reference system.

Three straight connecting paths led at different angles from the central pool to the nearest footpaths. If the garden as realized is compared with the two draft plans in Ernst Cramer's estate,[273] it is immediately striking that originally only two footpaths were planned, leading away from the pool at right angles. The later adjustments were probably made for purely functional reasons, and are obviously compromise solutions, as they are appropriate neither to the needs of pure form nor to those of pure function. Even shorter connecting paths would have been possible in terms of function. And if form had been the crucial criterion, then the northern path would have had to be abandoned along with the angled direction taken by the second path. But these adjustments do seem to have been the

shows three long mounds at the proposed spot, with two short paths leading into them at right angles.[271] This principle fitted in with Neukom and Baumann's general concept of the exhibition. The mounds of earth clearly adapted to the overall orthogonal structure in their position parallel with the lake shore. *Bauen + Wohnen* published a general plan of the right bank of the lake in the same month in their *Chronik*, recording the exact position of the garden and its topography.[272] The position had not changed fundamentally, but the character of the garden was obviously completely different from Willi Neukom's preliminary design, even on the plan. The latter was definitely lacking the radical quality that Cramer so admired in visions of Modern architecture and art. So Cramer changed the naturalistic miniature landscape with its four round mounds of earth into an abstract composition of four differently sized earth pyramids and a stepped sphere of earth, placed around a large rectangular pool. Cramer arranged the whole complex, about 2,500 square metres in

only compromises that Ernst Cramer allowed. Apart from them, he realized his garden in an uncompromisingly modern and radical way that put all the other garden architecture projects at G|59 completely in the shade.

Of course the garden architect wanted to find a response as to how to create a place in very restricted space that would emanate something like poetic calm in the middle of this colourful flower shower, already popularly known as the "Flower Landi". It was also for this reason that Cramer decided on the greatest possible contrast with the rest of the horticultural show when designing his Poet's Garden, completely abandoning the usual repertoire of forms and materials.

Even if they ever existed, no plans have survived of the Poet's Garden that give precise measurements, so all technical construction details of the garden have to be reconstructed from the first two draft plans and from photographs of the garden as realized.[274] The earlier draft plan, drawn in pencil on tracing paper, differs

Preliminary design for the
Poet's Garden by Willi Neukom, 1958

from the revised draft, prepared in Indian ink and coloured adhesive foil on transparent paper, in a few details, but they are interesting ones. Both plans, which resemble abstract collages because of the schematic nature of their formal composition, show the four three-sided pyramids of earth, anchored in the orthogonal basic grid of the garden by the direction of as least one base line. Only the smallest pyramid – not shown correctly as a section figure in either of the plans, but simply placed schematically – was directly adjacent to the largest body of soil and shifted almost imperceptibly off the east-west axis. [275] This basic arrangement once more clearly shows Cramer's interest in handling triangular geometries, which he had already tried out consistently in other projects. [276] But now for the first time he dared taking a triangle into the third dimension and built pyramids two, 2.8, three and four metres high. The fifth body of earth, a stepped, asymmetrical truncated cone with an overall height of three metres and a base diameter of about eleven metres, appears in the same place on both plans, somewhat to the side of the group of pyramids. In the preliminary

mounds of earth, measuring about 17 by 20 metres, was never planned as one continuous area to be walked on, but was conceived from the outset as a shallow, reflecting pool of water. Cramer knew that the mounds of earth would be reflected in the surface of the water and would thus seem considerably larger. In fact, many contemporary witnesses felt that the pyramids were much higher, and were surprised to find out that the tallest was only four and not eight metres high. The fact that the diagonal sides of the pyramids made a precise estimate difficult because of their perspective effect further strengthened this mistaken impression and increased the effect of the artificial landscape. The central pool, later built at the size of 12 by 19 metres, was originally intended to be somewhat wider, and would have been divided into two small strips and a larger area of water by two continuous bands of slabs. The only path across the pool was finally divided into individual stepping stones, which emphasized the coherence of the area of water just as much as did the fact that it was not further subdivided. Cramer intended from the outset to create all the paved areas and paths exclusively with simple concrete slabs 50 by 100 centimetres in size. Not a single one of these slabs, neither those in the paved area nor those in the two-metres-wide paths, was to have been allowed to break out of the grid. Both drafts kept strictly to this requirement, but there were certain deviations in the realized version. One of the two paths that were originally planned was shifted slightly for functional reasons and the slabs had to be cut to the right shape at the central connection. The second path was detached from the grid in that the direction in which the slabs ran was changed slightly and its point of origin moved slightly towards the north. A third, diagonal path was added and its direction adapted to the base line of the nearest pyramid by the staggered arrangement of its slabs. Here too the slabs had to be adapted. If Cramer's sensitivity to functional requirements, his undogmatic attitude and his disinclination to be academic showed in this project, then it was in the design of the paths. Some may have wanted to see a more radical attitude in this detail, in the interest of a powerful and succinct result, but being radical for its own sake was not Cramer's objective.

Cramer added some crucial details in terms of modern furnishings to the revised draft and to the later executed version. He had two types of prefabricated concrete cable and shaft cladding piled on top of each other at various points in the central paved area in such a way that they produced simple seats, 30 and 40 centimetres high. The piled-up packages were up to 4.5 metres long and were arranged so strictly within the orthogonal grid that they looked almost like abstract pieces on a large chessboard. And in fact these elements were not really very important as seats, as visitors to the show had far

Design plan for the Poet's Garden, variant in pencil on transparent paper

draft its tip was still leaning out of the ensemble. But finally conceived and realized, the upper truncated cone leaned outwards ambivalently, but with the tip leaning inwards again. In the first draft the body of earth was still linked to the pool by an eccentrically placed, straight path or a wall. This idea was not pursued further, however. The truncated cone formed the counterpoint with the pyramid ensemble. It had hitherto appeared in Cramer's projects only as a simple, two-dimensional circular form.

It is significant that the central area between the

more comfortable, portable seating freely available all over the show site, also at the Poet's Garden. The alienating use of cable coverings was an open commitment to the mass produced prefabricated product in concrete, whose use in garden design was taboo. But Cramer was also using these elements to establish a three-dimensional internal structure that organized the open space between the mounds of earth. Another design element in the ensemble that could be interpreted as an ironic comment on the colourful "Flower Landi" was a round concrete plant container, densely planted with red geraniums. The red geraniums, a traditional balcony plant and by no means an exquisite rarity found only at horticultural shows, formed the single

striking dab of colour in the abstract ensemble. They entered into a dialogue of contrasts with another unique feature of the garden: an abstract sculpture by the young artist Bernhard Luginbühl.

In 1959 the 30-year-old sculptor from Bern was still unknown and fighting for recognition for his work. His first work in steel, a bull that the highly individual, self-taught artist had created in 1949, caused some surprise and displeasure among the public. *Werk* wrote as late as in 1960: *"The age of steel, concrete and glass is still unable to make us any more friendly with the fact that sculptors use iron rather that marble and bronze, and a welding torch rather than a chisel and a graving tool. There is still a great deal of prejudice*

Design plan for the Poet's Garden, variant in adhesive foil on transparent paper

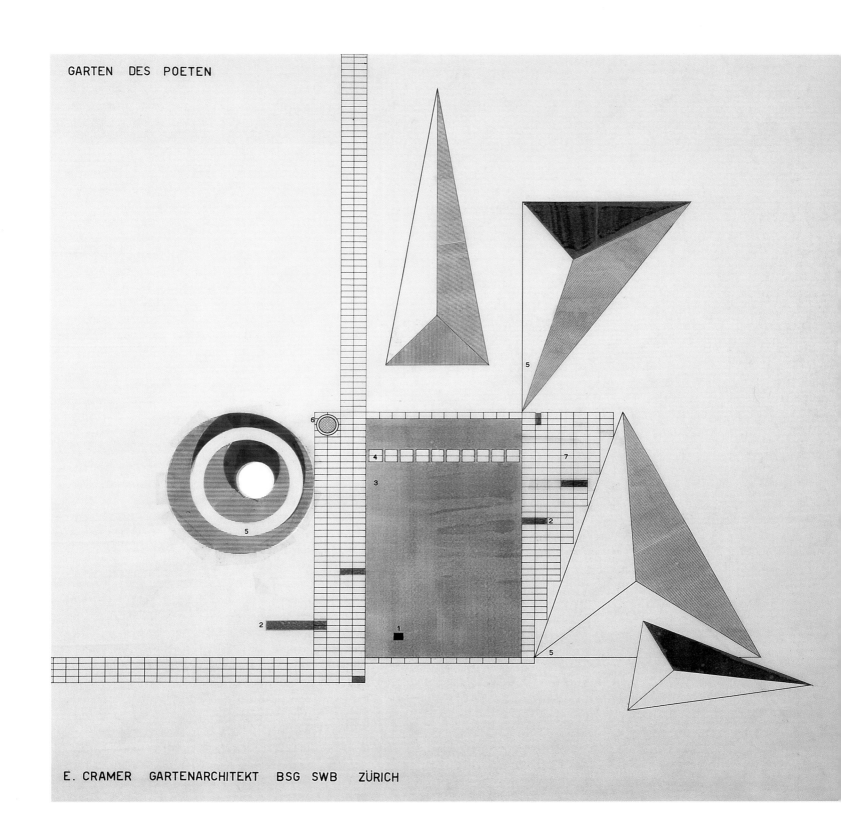

GARTEN DES POETEN

E. CRAMER   GARTENARCHITEKT   BSG   SWB   ZÜRICH

against iron as an artistic material. *The sculptural artist is not a sculptor any more, but a shaper of images.*" And the author wrote in the same place about Luginbühl's most recent, abstract iron sculptures: "*One particular advantage of Luginbühl's sculpture is its clear, unambiguous formal order. [...] His forms do not live in isolation, but in dialogue with air and light, which they penetrate and fill at the same time. Born of the contemporary sense of bold constructive thinking, his three-dimensional forms are able to grow beyond the random and acquire a monumental expressive quality*

Construction work in the Poet's Garden

A precise ensemble of mounds of earth, constructed without a precise working plan

Building the mounds presented new challenges for the gardeners as well

that – especially in the case of free sculpture – imposes itself on the surroundings and complements it."[277]

The artist had sculpted almost exclusively in iron since 1953, and he finally helped to make this medium very successful in the 60s. By 1964 Luginbühl had created a series of ensembles that were characterized by the aggressive wrestling with iron energy and mass, packed into abstract forms. The series with the programmatic title "Aggression" was one of the first sets of abstract iron sculptures created between 1955 and 1962. These slender sculptures were often several metres high, and stood on small, thin legs supporting a large iron band with a concave incision. The sweeping gesture of this element was physically restricted by the rear vertical element and the horizontal incision at the apex, but the generous circular movement, once it had been initiated, seemed to continue dynamically in the space.

Cramer placed one of the works from this series in the southern-most area of his reflecting pool, anchoring it on a little concrete cube. The sculpture accentuated the vertical dimension at a particular point in the spatial structure, and also, because of its top-heaviness and the sweeping dynamic gesture, formed an effective contrast with the heavy, earth-bound quality of the pyramids. From the point of view of a nearby observer the iron sculpture formed an elegant link between heaven and earth, which was further elongated by the reflection in the surface of the water, and thus enhanced even more. The position of the sculpture was consequently chosen so that the visitor approached it on the longest of the three paths from the west. In addition, Cramer moved the sculpture as far away from the pyramids as possible, so that the sculpture, which was already about three metres high, appeared taller than the four metre high pyramid in the background. Only in this way was "Aggression" able to make the maximum impact in the open air.

This way of handling "art in green spaces"[278] fitted in precisely with the views of art historian Willy Rotzler, curator of the Zurich Museum of Design at the time. Rotzler not only supported Cramer's project, but helped him to choose the sculpture. Rotzler, as chairman of the Commission for Artistic Decoration and Graphics, was the person principally responsible for choosing works of art for G|59. He defended Cramer's venture against objections made by sceptical garden experts by declaring without more ado the Poet's Garden to be a work of art.[279] Rotzler's intention was to "educate the general public artistically and morally", by confronting them with works by young modern artists. He was strictly against the misuse of a work of sculpture as a substitute for a natural experience, in other words against any superficial imitation of nature:

"*We are pursuing different aims when we set up works of sculpture in green spaces, i.e. sculptures*

The large pyramid, reflected in the pool

of bodies or of structures that create space, that human beings have shaped according to their will. We are enticed towards tying natural form and artistic form into a dialogue that is profitable to pursue and listen to. Sculpture can shape green space, can introduce it invitingly, and can open it up to people who are approaching it. It can be the centre of a green space, a demanding mid-point towards which the green space develops, a crystallization point where all forces are concentrated. But sculpture can also mark the boundaries of a green space by commanding distance; it can explain the various lines of movement within a garden landscape that are perhaps penetrating each other, and it can, especially in wide-open spaces, serve as a scale, a tangible orientation mark in space, making it easier for people to master and experience that space."[280]

When Cramer was looking for a sculpture for the central pool and asked his advice, Rotzler recommended choosing a work by the young Luginbühl from the collection in the Museum of Design. According to contemporary witnesses, Cramer decided on "Aggression" because it came closest to his ideas of modern, dynamic art.[281] There was no contact between Luginbühl and Cramer, who was thirty years older, and the artist confirms this. Apart from Lugin-

Piles of prefabricated concrete
elements structure the area

Picnic in the Poet's Garden

One of the rare colour photographs
of the Poet's Garden

The double pyramid in the Poet's Garden

The concrete slab path crosses
the water surface

Ernst Cramer in his Poet's Garden

Lüginbühl's sculpture "Aggression" in the Poet's Garden, a link between heaven and earth

Cramer's garden and Luginbühl's sculpture seemed enigmatic to many visitors

bühl, a number of other artists with whom Cramer had already worked were represented at G|59, including Arnold D'Altri, Max Bill and Ulrich Schoop. Cramer's responsiveness to work by a young, unknown artist and the prominent integration of the controversial sculpture into his *Gesamtkunstwerk* is particularly remarkable against this background. But the modern art was not greeted with great enthusiasm by most exhibition visitors, and Willi Neukom, who was also a member of the commission chaired by Willy Rotzler, summed up somewhat disappointedly:

"But even the number of voices that have been raised quite loudly against the sculptures, which were selected from the most recent body of work by the best-known Swiss sculptors, show that the majority of the public rejected them. Thus the educational aim seems questionable, and so does the expectation that spectators will make an effort to get to know the background of the artistic statement."[282]

And Ernst Cramer's Poet's Garden was anything but easily accessible garden design for most of the unsuspecting visitors. And Cramer had used archetypal forms that were perfectly familiar. Of course Cramer was aware of the cultural and historical predecessors of his earth structures, for example the pyramids of Ancient Egypt or

Fürst Hermann von Pückler-Muskau's tumuli, and deliberately transformed the earth pyramid form for his own purposes. An article about "Fürst Pückler's tumulus in the park at Branitz" was actually published in *Garten und Landschaft* during the planning phase for G|59,[283] and former employees of Cramer's report that a photograph of these fascinating earth pyramids hung on the wall of Cramer's office for a long time. While the Pückler pyramids borrowed a great deal from the ancient Egyptian tombs in terms of both proportion and function, Cramer worked with pyramid forms made up of three unequal sides, and intended to be understood only as structural works of art. The garden architect was not interested in building tumuli that could have been interpreted as tombs. Rather, Cramer was concerned to represent nature and landscape abstractly, and so visitors looked away over his artificial earthworks to the moraine hill on the opposite bank of Lake Zurich, which had been formed by the convulsive forces of nature in the Ice Age.

Cramer was aware of the power of "pure" abstraction from his study of abstract art, and knew that he was unlikely to meet with a high level of understanding from his professional colleagues, who were still mainly inclined to draw on the picturesque imitation of nature for their garden design.[284] And indeed, criticism was not slow to come, based at first on the somewhat superficial assertion that a garden without plants – evidently the geraniums were not enough – could hardly be called a garden. In rare cases this criticism was not just whispered behind people's hands, but voiced in the specialist press:

"Is it really possible to talk about these mounds covered with sparse grass and the area of water entirely without plants as a garden?" asked Heini Mathys in his article about Cramer's work, which was otherwise very positive. *"There is no doubt that this sight evokes profound and genuine feelings of displeasure for a gardener, who is concerned first and foremost with purveying plants. In this respect the Poet's Garden is certainly not a good advertisement. Producing horticulturalists feel betrayed by the 'poet'. But this almost desert-like lack of plants – the bald hills are reminiscent of the empty, erosion-threatened interior of Sicily – does once*

before in the open air. You prove that given an ingenious mind and precise use of the craft, it is not absolutely necessary to use this valuable material soil in a way as the forces nature do. You do not create an imitation of a natural event, but you create a work in a way that we abstract painters and sculptors have been trying to achieve by concrete means for years.

I have looked at your creation from all sides, from close up and from a distance, with all my critical faculties engaged. Your work drew me into the very midst of itself, and above the pool and around it I had a sense of quietness that can be experienced only in a designed space or then on the lonely heights.

Yours sincerely.

Hans Fischli"[289]

Fischli came across the Poet's Garden at precisely the moment that he was moving into his sculptural phase, and looking for three-dimensional forms of abstraction. After studying design theory at the Dessau Bauhaus in 1928/29 under Josef Albers, Paul Klee, Wassily Kandinsky and Oskar Schlemmer, the search for a poetic abstraction of reality played an important part even in his early work as a painter.[290] Between 1929 and 1930, when Rudolf Steiger sent him into the Alps of the Valais as a building site supervisor, Fischli discovered a fascination with landscape that was to last throughout his life:

"When I was sent to the Valais to build [the Bella Lui sanatorium], to Montana, where the mountains are enormously beautiful, the landscape suddenly

Bridges cross gravelled
areas on the slab path

again show how courageous he is as a designer, prepared to pursue his own, highly individual paths."[285]

Emil Steiner, a journalist and in later years a friend and admirer of Ernst Cramer, could not conceal his scepticism about the Poet's Garden either and called it "much more a matter of the mind than of the heart". From a gardening point of view, he particularily criticized the use of plants as an inadequate solution, and as too easy to destroy.[286] The edges of the pyramids, which had not been additionally stabilized on the inside, were not specially reinforced and quickly eroded through use. Children in particular liked to storm the mounds and slide down the sides. This garden laid the foundation for Cramer's persisting reputation for not being a connoisseur of plants, and never having really bothered about the needs of vegetation because he was too interested in formal refinement.

Mathys put things in a nutshell at the end of his article with a quotation from Gottfried Benn, and referred admiringly to Cramer's work as the "most courageous garden ideaof the year."

"Man stepped out of nature. His aim, perhaps only his transition, in any case his existential task, was no longer natural nature, but processed nature, stylized nature – art."[287]

The distinguished architect, painter and sculptor Hans Fischli, director of the Zurich School of Design and the Museum of Design from 1954 to 1961, also subscribed to this opinion. He was impressed by the Poet's Garden and wrote a letter to Cramer, whom he had known personally at least since ZÜKA 1947, on 26 August 1959:[288]

"My dear Herr Cramer,

It was not until last week, well rested after my summer holidays, that I made my big critical tour of G59, after hearing a great deal of praise and blame from many quarters. Since this visit I have felt very strongly that I wanted to write to you, dear Herr Cramer, that I find your design almost the only example that attempts to show and indeed does show that the most important role of every major exhibition is to discover something new and to show it to the visitors. It seems to me that there are far too many repeats at G59, or that previous good examples have merely been taken over superficially. But you bring us a completely new landscape, you create a sense of space that I have never felt

became important to me and when I had finished work, or on Sunday, when I had nothing to do on the site, I drew sections of the landscape, the other side of the valley, or I tried to make something that represents the mountains, like rocks or snowfields [...]"[291]

The search for an artistic language for the abstraction of nature led Fischli to create an increasing number of geometrical compositions, and at the same time to increase the relief texture of the surface of his pictures. At first, in the very late 40s, he mixed sand and gravel into the

The lake pyramid in Branitz park by
Fürst Hermann von Pückler-Muskau, 1855

Isamu Noguchi: Sculpture to be seen
from Mars. Sand model (destroyed), 1947

Robert Smithson: Untitled. 1963–1964

paint, but shortly after that, around 1953, he
produced his first strictly geometrical relief images.

*"The architect has started to get involved. I paint-
ed in the office, and so my colleagues were very interested in what I was up to there. And one of my
colleagues was a quite wonderful specialist in
form, in fact I told him he was the Golden Section
in person. He drew reliefs for me of the panels,
which I no longer put down parallel with each other, in other words not at the same level any more,
but in a three-dimensional relation; I thrust into
space with the image, I staggered the individual
panels and allowed the ground, which was continuous underneath, to make an effect as well."[292]*
In the late 50s, after he had thoroughly investi-
gated the possibilities of painting and decided
he was mature enough, Fischli made a serious
start on sculpture. His work in natural stone dating from that time, mainly in basalt, granite,
marble and limestone, is evidence of his fascination with abstraction and geometrical purity.
But the sculptures always remained objects
withdrawn into themselves, to be looked at from
the outside, or were merely miniature landscapes that viewers could walk into in their
imagination, but that scarcely afforded a modern experience of space. This would never be entirely satisfactory for an architect of the Neues
Bauen movement like Hans Fischli.
Ernst Cramer on the other hand had created a
spatial promenade sculpture that met the criteria of the classical-modern view of space and

formal language in an ideal way. Here the first crucial dimension is the modern, non-hierarchical view of space that Hans Fischli called a unique sense of space. Structured, finite space was seen as a bourgeois scheme for creating order, and Modernism countered this with the concept of infinitely flowing space. The space that Cramer created between the bodies of earth could only be seized by moving in it oneself. There was no clearly defined viewing point and no clear sense of a boundary between the garden and its surroundings, and neither was there a rigid pattern imposed by right angles or symmetry. Secondly, the Poet's Garden's open organization of space and ground plan made it a transparent structure, in the figurative sense, as defined by Robert Slutzky and Colin Rowe. [121] Cramer decided not to screen his garden off from the outside, even allowing the individual spaces between the mounds of earth to relate to a variety of reference systems. Furthermore, Cramer's mounds correspond formally with the postulate of geometrical purity, a key concept of Modernism. Cramer had reduced the natural forms to their essentials and with one exception, which could almost be called ironic – the red geraniums – he decided to do without the decorative planting that is usual in garden architecture. Finally Cramer preferred modern, mass-produced prefabricated concrete units to build his garden, above all for the paved areas and seats. This was seen as a clear commitment to the machine age, and as a departure from bourgeois garden design in the eyes of the art historians. Here we find the spirit of Modernism as described by Max Bill with reference to Concrete art:

"Concrete art is in its particular qualities something that is independent. Its existence is equal to that of natural phenomena. It should be the expression of the human mind, intended for the human mind, and is said to have the sharpness of focus and the lack of ambiguity, indeed the perfection that can be expected from works of the human mind."[294]

Against this background it is easy to understand why Fischli was so enthusiastic about the Poet's Garden. It was an expression of the human mind in this sense, and therefore had nothing to do either with imitating nature or with bourgeois ideas of a romantic garden. For many architects and artists this modern garden seemed to be the long-desired breakthrough in garden architecture, which as a discipline was finally contributing to the Werkbund's discussions about "Die gute Form".

Cramer's garden could be interpreted simultaneously as an independent work of art, an abstract interpretation of landscape and an architectural ensemble – but was it still a garden? Certainly Heini Mathys discerned a certain triumph of the garden over art, and wrote:

"We stand fascinated before a new formal world; for what we see is – if I may put it like this – abstract art in the garden! And wherever you look it is

possible to realize, and this is as astonishing as it is delightful, that this 'Modernism' in combination with the living materials of the gardener has led to much more convincing solutions than is usual on the artist's canvas."[295]

People still wonder on what theoretical basis Ernst Cramer developed his radically abstract, modern Poet's Garden. Was he deeply familiar with the theories of modern art or the principles of the Bauhaus? Is it possible that he was directly guided by some of his contemporaries' visionary landscape projects like Alberto Giacometti's 1930 "Project for a square", Isamu Noguchi's 1940 "Sculptured Playground" or his utopian "Sculpture to be seen from Mars" dat-

Isamu Noguchi and his model for the Contoured Playground project, 1941

Alberto Giacometti: Model for a Square. 1931. Plaster. 18 x 26 x 16 centimetres

ing from 1947? The first two projects had already been published in 1954 by Carola Giedion-Welcker in her influential book *Plastik des XX. Jahrhunderts. Volumen- und Raumgestaltung* in Zurich.[296] It is not possible to answer these questions satisfactorily, as Ernst Cramer never put anything in writing about the background to his work on the G|59 project. This pragmatist, who took such delight in experimentation, was not very interested in theoretical analysis. Most of the indications that have already been discussed suggest that Cramer knew how to creatively interpret a series of actual requirements for the project. And so his work was certainly based more on an intuitive and rational approach than on a theoretical and philosophical concept. But the Poet's Garden was definitely not the random result of a mysterious inspiration: it was the high point to date in the search for an up-to-date mode of expression in modern garden architecture. In this work, Cramer concentrated his hoard of experience and all the enthusiasm that he had accumulated through close contacts with the most recent vi-

published in her collection. But it is also possible that the American became aware of Ernst Cramer's work through her first husband, the Basel architect Rudolf Mock.[298] Mock, a graduate of the ETH in Zurich and a Taliesin student, practised his profession in the USA but remained in close contact with his home country. He had been friendly with Otto Senn since they had co-operated successfully on the Parkhaus Zossen apartment building in Basel in 1934–35, and was aware of Ernst Cramer's extraordinary garden architecture. Elizabeth Kassler placed Cramer's Poet's Garden, "not so much a garden as a sculpture to walk through",[299] somewhere between the icons of early landscape art and modern landscape design.

Only a few years later, American Earth Art, also called Land Art in Europe, scored some major successes with spectacular works of landscape art. As a result, people liked to call Ernst Cramer a "pioneer of Land Art".[300] Although there are superficial formal similarities between Cramer's work and the avant-garde landscape

On the right of the picture is the container with geraniums – a provocation, or just for fun?

sions in modern architecture, and it brought him world-wide acclaim.

The Poet's Garden was levelled at the end of the show on 11 October 1959, but only a few years later the Museum of Modern Art in New York paid tribute to Cramer's work. The distinguished American art historian Elizabeth B. Kassler published a collection of influential international garden projects entitled *Modern Gardens and the Landscape* in 1964, in an attempt to get to the bottom of the question about the modern relationship between nature and art. It is likely that the art historian's attention was drawn to the Swiss garden architect by the International Horticultural Show IGA in Hamburg in 1963.[297] Along with Ernst Cramer, this show involved other leading garden architects of the day, including Roberto Burle Marx, Pietro Porcinai, Eywin Langkilde, whom Kassler also

projects of the 60s in the USA, it is no more appropriate to call the Zurich landscape architect's work Land Art than it would be to call Michael Heizer's "Earthworks", for example, landscape architecture. These correlations will be discussed in greater detail later in the book. But the mere fact that Cramer deliberately incorporated a sculpture by another artist in his garden may be the first indication of the striking difference between Land Art and landscape architecture. Heizer, for example, would never have dreamed of placing a sculpture in his "Double Negative". That would have run completely counter to the work. Land Art was never interested in placing sculptures in the landscape, it intended to use the landscape to create sculptures. Cramer's garden could be seen as a sculpted piece of landscape in the spirit of Land Art, but by placing the iron sculpture in it he made it clear that he did not see his garden as an independent, non-functional work of art, not as a promenade sculpture, but as an abstract, three-dimensional structure in which a sculpture could easily be presented if one

wished. Cramer was expressly looking for a sculpture that would round off his work as an ensemble, as a *Gesamtkunstwerk*. His intention was to create usable, highly aesthetic spaces. He did not start to make purely artistic and aesthetic demands on his own work until years later. And yet Cramer's Poet's Garden is a landmark in the history of 20th century European garden architecture and has influenced the work of many landscape architects down to the present day.

Poet's Garden with view of Lake Zurich

Mondrian as a model?

Blözen Cemetery in Pratteln

Radical simplicity was the order of the day for the Blözen Cemetery in Pratteln competition entry in spring 1959, which Ernst Cramer had developed with the Basel architects Wurster und Huggel. [301] The Pratteln local authority had invited four architects' practices to design a cemetery with 5000 grave plots, a funeral chapel to seat 350 people and a mortuary, to be built on an area of high ground east of the town. The jury, which included Fred Eicher, Richard Arioli and Willi Neukom, was impressed by the unpretentious approach taken by the design submitted by Cramer and the Basel architects, praising the use of the simplest possible design elements in particular. The reticent placing of trees and shrubs, and the fact that the site was not screened off from the open countryside on the south-western side, a device that Cramer used deliberately to retain the spacious nature of the terrain, was almost a little too radical for the jurors. Nevertheless the committee of experts decided in April 1959 that the project should be realized in the following years.

Already shortly after its completion in 1962 the complex became one of Cramer's show projects, recording his progressive thought on the subject of cemeteries as well. Even today, although Cramer edged the whole cemetery with trees as required and some sections were changed later independently of the basic concept, the radical, right-angled basic structure and the highlights provided by tree planting in the inner area create an impression of spaciousness, reminiscent of Scandinavian models. The austere lucidity of the architecture finds its equivalent in the landscape architecture, with its simple seating and lighting elements in concrete, the paths designed in asphalt and in parts with large-format concrete paving slabs, and an impressive 60-metre long pool in the centre of the complex. As in the project for the female teachers' seminary in Menzingen, which had been completed shortly before the cemetery competition got under way, here too the uniform character of the complex

Plan of Blözen cemetery
in Pratteln near Basel, an exemplary
project by Ernst Cramer

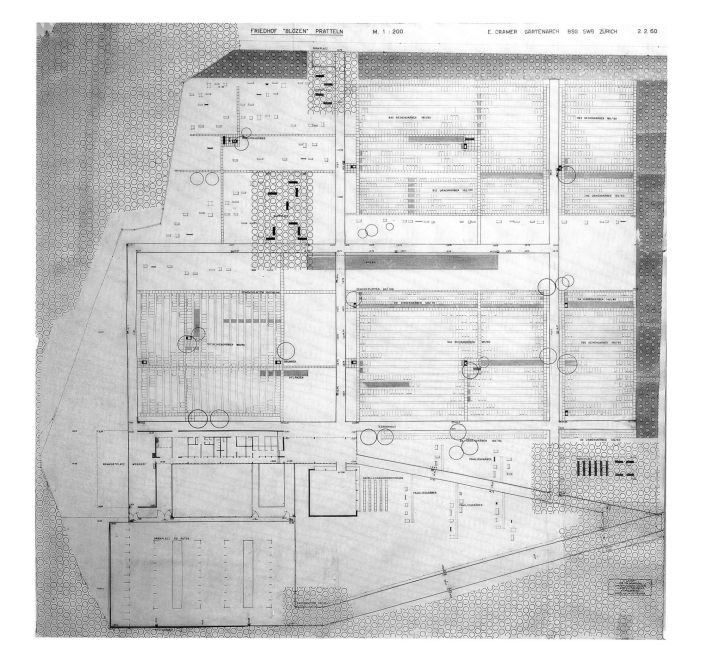

shows how successfully architects and garden architect had worked together.

In 1961 Ernst Cramer developed a design idea for the two entrance gates to the cemetery – one for the drive and one for pedestrians – which is particular evidence of his enthusiasm for abstract painting. He occasionally experimented boldly, drawing new inspiration from modern art for his projects, and this applies to the design of these gateways as well. In fact, they were not built in accordance with the design ideas, but careful examination of the designs identifies the fundamental problems which the garden architect confronted when handling artistic models.

Six designs in coloured and black felt pen show variants for the compartmentalization of the cemetery gates' tubular steel frame structures, which were 1.1 metres high and 6 and 3 metres wide respectively. The main frames of the two-leaved gates were to be welded from rectangular 8 centimetres wide and 4 centimetres high. These frames would have been subdivided with rectangular elements with slightly smaller dimensions, into which fine transverse bars 20 millimetres thick were to be fitted. All the steel parts were to be painted with black artificial resin enamel. Cramer designed an almost symmetrical subdivision for the main gate, with a simple cross rising through full height of the frame in the middle. This image resulted when the gate was closed, by the double, vertical steel members on the rabbet, which were not connected with the rest of the steelwork in the centre, while the gate's straight handles formed the horizontal beam of the cross. In the coloured preliminary designs this horizontal beam consciously deviated from the prescribed grid, a device intended to emphasize the cross. This accent was given up in the June 1961 construction plan.

In the areas to the right and left of the central cross, individual rectangular fields in different positions and proportions were to be filled in with thick, deep-red and dark-blue panes of raw glass. In all the six variants that Cramer developed for the design of the double gates, only between four

and six different fields were intended to be glazed. The tension in the graphic image was created by the break with symmetry achieved by filling different, mainly long, narrow or approximately square fields with one of the two primary colours in each case. With one exception, the ratio between the different coloured fields was 2:3 or 2:4, with the predominant colour always used in the narrow compartments.

All six designs are strikingly reminiscent of Piet Mondrian's neo-plastic painting. Perhaps Ernst Cramer, on his way from naturalism to abstraction, recognized certain parallels with the work of the Dutch artist, which was also shaped by a consistent search for the elemental. But written

Compelling ecclesiastical architecture by the Basel architects Wurster und Huggel

Expressively matched: the chapel and the adjacent open space with simple concrete benches

A long shallow pool emphasizes the generous scale of the complex

The competition model – programmatic reduction to the simplest possible design

Coloured sketches
à la Mondrian for the large entrance
gate of Blözen cemetery

A variant for the small gate

Construction drawing
for the gates

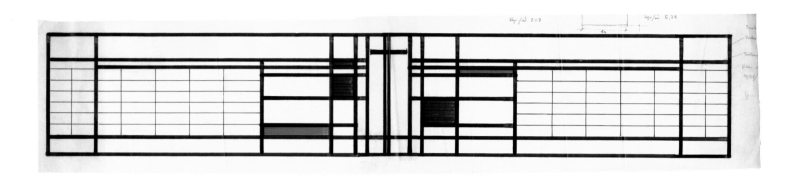

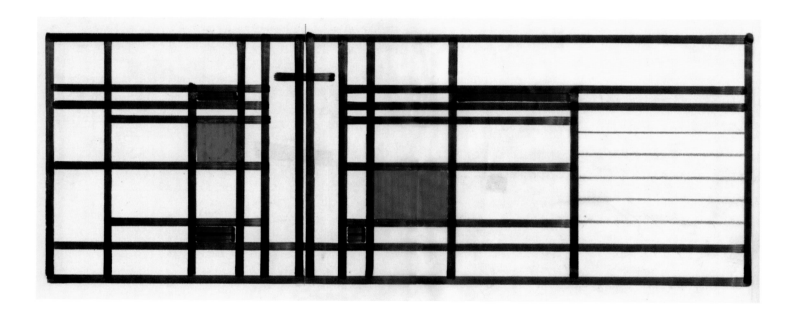

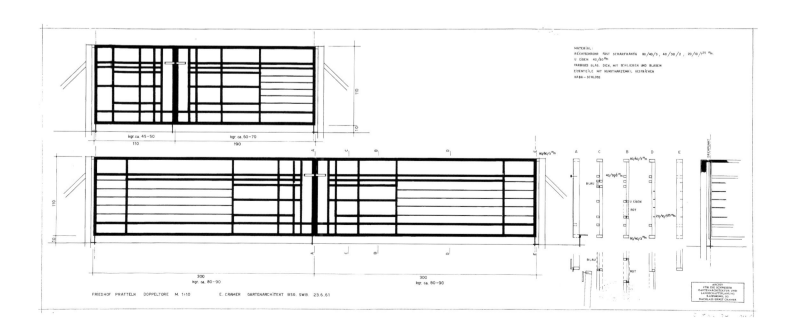

evidence of interest in Mondrian does not appear until a decade later, when Cramer was passing on his knowledge about garden design to students at the Athenaeum Ecole d'Architecture in Lausanne.[302] There Cramer defined the phenomena of pure form as the source of creative power, and stated: "I am thinking above all of Mondrian's creative methods."[303] The work of this painter, who had died in 1944, still highly controversial during his lifetime, was generally accepted by the late 50s. This gave rise to the temptation to exploit the artist's formal resources without considering their underlying meanings. Even in the furniture industry, angular shapes with subdivisions in the manner of Mondrian were by no means revolutionary any longer, but seen as appropriate to the times.

Cramer's design "à la Mondrian" reveals precisely the problems of formalism that art historians[304] had been discussing a few years earlier. He was simply basing his design on the artist's formal language, and had no reservations about building Christian symbolism into his design. This had nothing to do with taking his vocabulary back to an elemental level, and the question is whether Cramer, when he talked about "Mondrian's creative methods" a decade later, had found a more appropriate understanding of modern painting.

So the 1963 designs should be seen at most as proof of Cramer's purely formal interest in Concrete Art, but show no signs of an in-depth analysis of the theoretical basis of modern art. On the contrary, they suggest a degree of uncertainty in interpreting modern painting. This source of inspiration scarcely influenced other projects, even though contemporary critical witnesses like to assert that Cramer increasingly perceived himself as in artist after his success at IGA 63, and neglected his craft as a garden architect.[305] But there is absolutely no doubt that Cramer continued to be interested above all in modern architecture. Transferring basic architectural principles to garden design was far less fraught with difficulty for him, as both disciplines were concerned with handling three-dimensional spaces that were also intended to be functional.

Cramer in Brasilia

Neither Cramer's interest in modern architecture nor his delight in experimentation diminished after his sensational success in 1959, quite the contrary. In the year after the horticultural show, which brought a remarkable increase in new commissions for his office, Ernst Cramer did something that he had been wanting to do for a long time. At the age of 62, he set off on his first major trip overseas; his destination: Brazil. Earlier chapters have shown why Cramer was impressed by Brasilia and Niemeyer's architecture.[306] Exhibitions in the Zurich Museum of Design, detailed articles in *Werk*, Sigfried

Giedion's appeal to Swiss garden architects to follow the example of Burle Marx, his encounter with Oscar Niemeyer's architecture in Berlin, and not least the interest taken by younger colleagues like Willi Neukom in Brazilian garden architecture[307] had been firing Cramer's desire to travel ever since the early 50s. And his resolve may have been further stiffened by the fact that Mary Vieira, a distinguished Brazilian artist, took part in G|59. She had lived in Switzerland

Brasilia in a photograph by Ernst Cramer, 1960

since 1951, and not only showed her Concrete granite sculpture "Upright Cross" on Lake Zurich, but created "powerful pieces of non-functional architecture"[308] for the new capital city, Brasilia, as Willy Rotzler wrote. On his own, Cramer set off on a journey that in retrospect was to turn out to be one of his most important.

We do not know how long the trip to Brazil lasted, nor the exact route that Cramer took. In Cramer's estate there is not even any written evidence of the precise year in which the journey was made. But the photographs that Cramer took on the journey suggest that he must have been in Brazil in 1960.[309] The cities the garden architect visited include São Paulo, Santos, Belo Horizonte, Rio de Janeiro and Brasilia. The new capital had only been ceremoniously inaugurated in April 1960. Apart from the usual tourist highlights of this trip, Cramer was of course particularly interested in modern architecture, above all in Oscar Niemeyer's elegant buildings. Cramer's collection of photographs includes pictures of the Ministry of Education and Health in Rio de Janeiro,[310] the Montreal office building and the elegant high-rise block for the Companhia PanAmericano (Copan) in São Paulo, and also the Mineiro da Produçao bank in Belo Horizonte. There is no doubt that the visit to Brasilia was the highlight of the journey for Ernst Cramer. This can be seen from the number of photographs that

Cramer took himself or bought to supplement his own. Niemeyer's most important and impressive buildings that were complete by 1960 in Brasilia included the Palácio da Alvorada, the president's residence with chapel, the first residential blocks of the Superquadras, the Palácio do Planalto, the eleven ministry blocks, the Brasilia Palace Hotel and the impressive, central complex of buildings for the Congresso National. Brasilia cathedral was still under construction at the time. Thus, alongside the images of the buildings mentioned above, Cramer's photographs show the striking, ecclesiastical building, planned in the shape of a crown, and its 21 buttresses as a shell.

With its monumental buildings, which particularly around 1960 still stood like lonely symbols in the wide, open plateau against a red background, Brasilia seemed like a composition of modern art, a landscape of promenade sculptures. "Brasilia [was] built as a monument, more durable even than bronze,"[311] was Umberto Eco's apposite identification of this characteristic. The iconic symbolism and monumental quality of the individual buildings and also of the ground plan of the city as a whole were intended to achieve one of President Juscelino Kubitschek's government's main aims: the memorable image of a modern capital was to rapidly take root in the consciousness of the whole population and to facilitate the identification with the new national centre. Alexander Fils shows how successful this concept was in his revealing book about Brasilia, where he also cites advertising around the world. The ads not only used the name of the new capital, but also striking architectural shapes and images to market a whole range of products more efficiently – from ties to aeroplanes.[312]

Niemeyer's most significant forms, and Cramer was enthusiastic about these as well, included the trapezoid columns on the Palácio da Alvorada and the somewhat modified version on the Palácio do Planalto.

"I did not want to use the usual cylindrical or rectangular columns, which would have been a lot simpler and cheaper," explained Niemeyer, *"but I wanted to find another form that even if it ran counter to certain functionalist demands would give the buildings their character, lend them a greater sense of lightness, in that I built them as floating forms, or supported lightly on the ground. [...] Forms that were intended to surprise and to make an emotional impact and that should take visitors away – even if it was only for moments – from the difficult and sometimes insuperable problems with which life torments all human beings."[313]*

It was from these predominantly aesthetic ideas that Niemeyer independently developed the columns, set almost like sails, that soon became a symbol of democracy in Brazil and a kind of unmistakable trademark for Niemeyer. These expressive elements were a clear sign that Niemeyer had turned away from the dogma of classical, right-angled Modernism, and regularly earned him the reproach from his critics – remember the severe warning from Max Bill[314] – that he was inclined to produce decorative architecture. There is clear evidence that the garden architect from Zurich was also stimulated by these forms, having specially bought a slide of the Palácio da Alvorada, with its bold, sail-like columns mirrored in the water of the great reflecting pool. Ernst Cramer must have been aware of his Zurich Werkbund colleague's severe criticism of this formal language. But as he moved between the two worlds himself, torn between his constraint to be more functional and his enthusiasm about formal matters, Niemeyer's simple aesthetic solutions must have seemed like a successful combination of both worlds. It was not until the early 70s, when Cramer had exhausted the possibilities of architectural orthogonality in garden and landscape architecture, that he openly devoted himself to expressive qualities in his work and created some of his most remarkable late projects, in parts borrowing directly from the form of Niemeyer's columns.[315]

In contrast, the ensemble of buildings for the National Congress works largely according to the postulates of classical-modern views of space and ground plan organization. The high-rise section called "Annex I" in particular, consisting of two slabs, dominates the monumental axis of Brasilia even from a distance, and was from the outset another of Brazil's symbolic, world-famous architectural monuments. The low parliament building extends transversely across the whole axis, which is about 200 metres wide. It also bridges the geometrically modelled grassed hollow at the striking drop in the terrain formed by the monumental axis, thus effectively forming an artificial horizon. The fact that both chambers of parliament, the Senate and the Chamber of Deputies, are housed in this low building, is announced by two striking sculptural elements on the roof. The dome of the Senate, a white hemisphere, resembles an abstract mountain, while the Chamber of Deputies, as its formal counterpart, is designed as a white dish, also hemispherical. The approximately 90 metre high building, containing the offices for the senators and deputies, is slightly shifted in plan, at right angles to the parliament building; Niemeyer was absolutely determined that no building should be placed across the monumental axis where it would have blocked the view of the surrounding landscape. The high-rise building, conceived as an H-shape in both plan and elevation, looks like a monolith that has been split down the middle because of the uniform green of its windows and the white marble cladding on the narrow sides. It stands in a large, rectangular pool, an artificial lake. The reflection of Annex I further reinforces the building's impressive effect. Formally, the whole ensemble works like a large sculptural theatre piece, a surrealist stage set with an artificial roofscape

shaping the horizontal and a powerful monolith stressing the vertical. The real landscape with the picturesque clouds in the sky that are typical of this region forms an atmospheric background to this architectural sculpture that seems to stretch to infinity.

The photographs that Cramer took in 1960 are not the only evidence of his enthusiasm about this kind of sculptural treatment of landscape and architecture. It is possible that despite the obvious differences in scale and use of materials he recognized the conceptual parallels between his Poet's Garden, a piece of abstractly represented landscape, and the artificial roofscape of the parliament building in Brasilia. Certainly for the garden architect one of the most fascinating aspects of this work was the bold handling of geometrically pure architectural bodies in the wide open space of the landscape. Barely a year later Cramer developed the concept for a second abstract exhibition garden, and people were quick to notice its formal relationship with Niemeyer's congress building.[316]

It is very noticeable that Cramer's photographic record of his trip to Brazil does not contain a single example of work by the distinguished Brazilian garden architect Roberto Burle Marx, least of all from Brasilia. Although the landscape "flowed" generously through the urban structure of Brasilia, according to the Modernist ideal, garden architecture had scarcely any part to play in the new capital in the early stages. Burle Marx was world famous by then, but even he was not allotted any projects. Burle Marx himself felt that political reasons and an uncomfortable relationship with President Kubitschek were the reasons for this.[317] It was not until 1961, when the central axis of Brasilia and the zoo-botanical park were being designed, that he was consulted. But even if Cramer couldn't find any of Burle Marx's work in Brasilia in 1960, he would have been expected to visit one of the many garden projects in other cities. He could not have overlooked the garden design for the Ministry of Education and Health in Rio de Janeiro, completed in 1943, which Cramer is known to have visited and photographed.[318] And so the conclusion is obvious that Burle Marx's biomorphically designed gardens did not provide the stimuli that Ernst Cramer was looking for in the early 60s. It was not until the end of the decade, after Cramer had met his Brazilian colleague in person in Hamburg, that biomorphic forms started to appear in his designs.

So there is no doubt that Cramer's interest in and enthusiasm for modern architecture were central to his 1960 Brazilian trip. He drew on the impressions gained on this journey until the end of his life. It was a successful prelude to a series of further excursions to Asia, the Far East, Northern and Eastern Europe.

Brasilia Palace Hotel, photograph by Ernst Cramer, 1960

Palácio da Alvorada, Brasilia, c. 1960

National Congress in Brasilia at night, c. 1960

National Congress in Brasilia, c. 1960

An architectonic land sculpture

Military cemetery at the Passo la Futa, Italy
(Dieter Oesterlen, Walter Rossow)

While Ernst Cramer was in Brazil, Gertrud Cramer and the garden architect Fritz Dové looked after the organizational side of the practice in Scheuchzerstrasse. Karl Pappa, who Cramer was particularly close to, was responsible for the planning and design side of the projects. Heinz Rimensberger, who had worked in Cramer's office since 1955, dealt mainly with site supervision. Fritz Dové had been employed in the office on the business side since 1958, as commissions had been rapidly on the increase at least since 1959, and Cramer was still inclined to lose sight of his company's financial and organizational needs in the euphoria of new projects. A whole series of large-scale projects that often ran for years were now under way, including housing estates, school grounds, cemeteries, business premises and private gardens. In the same year as G|59 Cramer won the major competition for the new Blözen cemetery in Pratteln with an austere, almost minimalist design with the architects Wurster and Huggel of Basel, and this was executed in subsequent years. [319] He was also still realizing a series of projects in Ticino, and according to Fritz Dové once even entertained the idea of setting up a new branch in Milan, next to

Military cemetery
on the Passo la Futa

the two others in Suhr and Bellach; Frau Cramer had the wisdom, foresight and experience to veto this. [320] Cramer apparently wanted an office in northern Italy to make it possible to give better attention to the Ticino projects and also to new and in part very extensive commissions in Italy. These included one for the German military cemetery on the Futa pass from 1961. This project, the largest war cemetery in Italy, was not completed until 1967 and was highly significant for Cramer, even though he was not responsible for the design, but definitely for the implementation of the project.

Architect Dieter Oesterlen of Hanover and landscape architect Walter Rossow of Berlin were commissioned to plan this cemetery by the National Federation for the Care of German War Cemeteries (Volksbund Deutsche Kriegsgräberfürsorge e.V.). It was to be built on an area of about 100,000 square metres on an eminence near the Passo la Futa between Bologna and Florence, at an elevation of about 950 metres. Helmut Bournot, who had already directed the open space planning for Interbau 1957 in Berlin, [321] where he also held a professorship, was brought in to support his colleague Rossow. Constructing a German cemetery of this size as a memorial to over 30,000 who died in the Second World War in Italy was not only a logistical problem, but also required a great deal of political sensitivity. It was self-evident that the project had to be executed by drawing on the local workforce. In addition, Oesterlen and his team were looking for a German-speaking firm to carry out the work that was based nearer to the site, knew how things were done in Italy and would guarantee a certain neutrality. Rossow and Bournot knew Cramer from Interbau 1957 and valued his long years of project experience. They also knew that he regularly employed Italian workers, and not just in Ticino. Helmut Bournot succeeded in convincing Ernst Cramer that the commission was extremely attractive in every respect, and had something left to offer even on the design side. And so Cramer decided to accept the offer and put Fritz Dové in charge of the site without more ado. Ermes Cescon, an experienced Italian foreman from the Modena region, who had been working for Cramer for a long time and had realized the Poet's Garden among other projects, was to be employed on the large site in his usual capacity.

The basic concept was based on the idea of developing the structure from the landscape and allowing a natural stone wall two kilometres long to spiral from the cemetery entrance to the top of the hill. The wall was intended to terrace the site and also to include, both constructively and conceptually, the most important cemetery buildings, above all the information centre and the memorial. The height of the wall rises rapidly from half a metre to two metres, and is accompanied by a path. This spiral path, with numerous branches and three narrow flights of connecting steps arranged radially around the hilltop, provides access to the whole cemetery with its 75 fields of graves. The grave fields contain tilted granite slabs arranged on a grid pattern, with the names of the dead engraved on them. At the highest point of the complex, the wall itself becomes higher still, forming the enclosing wall for the court of honour, under which are the crypt and the comrades' tomb, and ends in a steep spire 16 metres high, pointing up to infinity. An abstract mosaic in black, grey and white natural stone, designed by the artist Helmut Lander of Darmstadt, symbolizes a lightning flash striking the top of the tower and spreading over the court of honour. At this point it becomes clear that this hybrid structure of

Rainwater is collected in circular
cisterns along the stepped path

The central stepped path of the
military cemetery on the Passo La Futa
leads up to the tower

The consistent extensive
planting still determines the
cemetery's character today

Schematic general plan

The pointed tower at the end of the spiral

The spiral wall ends in a tower
with cladding designed by the sculptor
Helmut Lander

landscape architecture, architecture and sculpture is an abstract symbol intended to convey a soldier's path through life.

A crucial feature of the homogeneous character of the complex as a whole was the uniformity of the building materials and the absence of elaborate planting. The natural stone walls were built largely of light-coloured sandstone from the nearby Fiorentino valley. The extensive areas of grass were conceived as low-maintenance meadows, with individual trees to provide accents at very few points. As the natural stone walls decisively shaped the appearance of the complex as a whole, Cramer was very concerned that they should be precisely executed, which did not originally fit in with Oesterlen and Lander's intentions. According to the sculptor, they were looking rather for rustic masonry of the kind used in vineyards. But Ernst Cramer's rustic days were over, and he was possibly also aware of the design problems that would have resulted at the point of transition to the court of honour, which required high precision in its execution. Two different techniques for building the wall would have made it very difficult to achieve uniformity for the complex and continuity for the spiral. The retaining wall climbs up the

slope in long and short offset straights, but the joints were to be absolutely horizontal. The coping stones for the wall thus had to be cut in a wedge shape, to make the top continuous, without a stepped effect. Ernst Cramer instructed his colleagues appropriately and together with Fritz Dové was able to rely on Ermes Cescon as a reliable foreman. Cescon also had the difficult task in the early stages of teaching the largely untrained local workforce how to use a spirit level and stone-cutting tools. Ultimately he not only managed to have the work carried out to a very high standard, but, on the side, he also improved the infrastructure for the inhabitants of the neighbouring communities. [322]

Stone crosses protruding vertically from the sloping surface of the wall were fitted into the walls at regular intervals. Unlike the wishes of their client, the architects were opposed to a large central cross at the highest point of the cemetery, and reached a successful compromise with the crosses in the wall. Oesterlen and his team were also against the request by the Volksbund Deutsche Kriegsgräberfürsorge e.V. for flagpoles. Any kind of national, monumental drama was to be avoided. Nevertheless a flagpole was erected and the German flag flown after the project was completed. [323] Apart from these minor disagreements everyone involved worked together smoothly. After about five years under construction and a great deal of movement to other graves, the new cemetery was consecrated on 18 June 1969 and is one of the most impressive monuments of its kind in Europe today.

But the cemetery on the Futa Pass was not immune to the general criticism levelled at controversial war cemeteries, which were often unduly stylized as memorials to heroes. Some of Ernst Cramer's colleagues referred to the project polemically as a "Germanic siege castle", as a "battle for Rome in natural stone", and asked the entirely justified question of why there should be so much movement between graves to reunite the soldiers in their units 25 years after their violent death, instead of letting them be buried as civilians. [324] Both Fritz Dové and his later colleague Christofer Eriksson admitted that they found the idea of revering heroes questionable, but felt that the responsibility for the design lies with the managing team of ar-

A masterpiece of craftsmanship: masonry by Ermes Cescon for the military cemetery on the Passo la Futa

The outer boundary of the cemetery with stone slabs set vertically

chitect and landscape architect. [325] At least, unlike in other war cemeteries of the day, eagerly mounted with artillery, statues of fighting soldiers and similar objects in celebration of heroism, the architect on the Futa Pass had been determined "not to use any emotion or drama in the usual form, and to represent the implacable fate that had been suffered rather than a glorification of war."[326] There is no record of any personal statements by Ernst Cramer, but comments by other contemporary witnesses suggest that the project must have been important to him. On the one hand, a project on this scale, executed with eminent partners, carried a certain element of prestige. On the other hand, Cramer's prior development suggests that he was fascinated by the project's abstract, artistic and architectural treatment of the landscape situation, without being particularly bothered about the ideological significance of the cemetery. To him, the crucial feature was the conceptual and formal simplicity of the complex, whose effect was further enhanced by the dialogue with the characteristics of the landscape, the conscious play with the view of the surrounding Apennine mountains.

Helmut Lander's sculpture in the court of honour

combining his old infatuation with modern principles.

Some of the most interesting projects were created with the architect Emil Siegfried Oberholzer, who built a series of prestigious villas and residential complexes on Lago Maggiore. These included the Terra del Sole complex in Ascona, the Hochstrasser villa in Moscia, the Neeff villa in Galliate near Varese and the Hischmann villa in Brione. Oberholzer, whose teachers included Hans Hofmann and Fritz Hess at the ETH in Zurich, favoured a solid, functional approach that was anchored in the culture of the region without lapsing into the popular traditional Swiss country style. With the exception of his own modern house on the steep banks of a Ticino river, all his other buildings related stylistically to the plain, traditional structures of Sotoceneri farmhouses. Tiled hipped roofs, galleries with round arches, round

Private gardens between tradition and modernity

Most of the commissions during the period of growth in the early 60s were for private gardens. And it is these gardens in particular that show us how much Cramer adapted his designs to his clients' functional and formal wishes and to the nature of the architecture involved. Rather than asserting his new ideas about modern garden architecture at any price, he found ways to build the new principles affecting spatial organization, sight lines and paths and the basic formal structure into his work. Cramer's attempts to combine tradition and modernity are especially vividly demonstrated in the Ticino gardens of this period. In a region where most well-to-do owners of country houses essentially still wanted a rural villa in a wild romantic landscape, it was particularly tempting to create popular, traditional garden architecture as before. Cramer had discovered his genuine love of picturesque and naturalistic garden design in Ticino, [327] and was now faced with the difficult task of

Access to the Hischmann villa with view of Lago Maggiore

Hischmann garden in Brione

granite columns and white-rendered outside walls were the typical features of the houses for which Cramer designed the gardens.

Hischmann garden in Brione

Planning work on the Hischmann villa garden on a sunny sloping site above Brione started in 1961, and was commissioned by a German industrialist. The two-storey building went up on a terraced plot with retaining walls in natural stone in 1963. A path made of rectangular-cut granite slabs still links the lower garden entrance on the access road with the villa, which is higher up. The façades of the garage on the street side and the small rustic summerhouse on the upper garden terrace were designed in the same natural stone as the retaining walls and the path. Cramer took particular care over the line of the paths and treatment of the sloping site. But in contrast with his 30s and 40s projects, he did not use polygonal slabs, nor did he build steps that looked like rustic improvisations. He used a model to find the best line for the path and the optimal combination of ramps

Now surrounded by luxuriant
vegetation: the former Hischmann garden

A draughtsman's view of the sloping
Hischmann garden

and steps needed to get to the house comfortably. [328] Even today, although the vegetation, consisting of pines, palms and flowering woody plants, has become very rampant, the dramatic quality of the line of the paths can be clearly experienced. Cramer took visitors from terrace to terrace in straight, gently rising stages, and made sure that there was a view of the countryside or a contained garden situation at the end of each section of the path. These were intended to mark changes of direction and act as a reward for the climb. Visitors pass through various spatial strata formed by precisely placed backdrops of trees and shrubs. It is only on reaching the topmost supporting wall that care-

Spirig garden in Olten

The extent of Cramer's expressive flexibility and sensitive response contrasting styles of architecture can be seen in two private gardens that were created at about the same time north of the Alps in Aarau and Olten. The Zug practice of Stucky and Meuli was responsible for the new Spirig house in Olten, on which work started in 1961. The clients engaged the practised team of architect and landscape architect because they were impressed by the Gimmenen country house on Lake Zug. [329]

The Olten terrain sloped slightly and had to be massively banked up to create a flat, usable garden and building site. According to Fritz Stucky, Cramer took advantage of this measure to create a shallow, biomorphically shaped lake, fed by a small brook, on the plot of about 40,000 square metres. The basic idea was to place the bungalow-like house, in the style of Stucky's teacher Frank Lloyd Wright, on the edge of the lake in such a way that an impressive spatial experience was created, closely relating to the landscape. One wing of the large, low house was intended for the children, one for the parents and one for general living. The floor of the living wing, which had large glass façades, was set only 50 centimetres above the water level of the lake, which came right up to the large terrace. Viewing the lake from such a low angle produced an effect of generous, open space, further enhanced by planting an extensive lawn in the background. An elegant peninsula planted with grasses and thrusting out into the lake caught the eye in the middle ground, while Cramer accentuated the horizon with large Lombardy poplars. Dense planting of trees and shrubs on gently modulated mounds effectively framed the space at the sides, and provided the neces-

Palms and pines provide highlights on the viewing terrace of the Hirschmann garden

View across the terrace and the new lake in the Spirig garden in Olten

Spirig garden with modern bungalow

fully designed wide steps lead to the main terrace of the property.

There is no longer any sign here of the ostentatiously rustic quality of earlier gardens. Instead, the contrast between nature and the basic architectural structure has a crucial part to play. Cramer had succeeded in writing these components in his Futa Pass project, which was being worked on at the same time. Clarity and simplicity in the spatial and formal conception also determined the design of the large garden terrace. Cramer used carefully placed single trees to create accents, to conduct a dialogue between architecture and nature or to frame the magnificent view. A large, central rectangular lawn constitutes the main area for spending time in the garden, and lends the whole complex a certain spaciousness that was maintained until a swimming pool was installed later. Even in this subsequent addition in the mid 70s, Cramer adapted his design to the character of the existing garden, and stuck to simple geometric structures for of the paths.

The big willow and the elegant
roof form of the Spirig house

Paving detail in the Spirig garden

sary protection against being overlooked. Cramer himself, according to the client, sought out individual, well-grown solitaire trees, including large willows and beeches, meant to enter into a dialogue with the lake and the architecture. All the paving around the house and in the garden was executed in sawn, rectangular, shell limestone slabs, with special plans drawn for the joint lines. [330] The whole complex, when completed, presented the ideal image of an elegant, spacious garden, deliberately made to resemble modern Californian examples.

Schmidlin garden in Aarau

Cramer was much more daring in his designs for the little gardens for the Geiser and Schmidlin houses in Aarau in 1961. Years later, *Schöner Wohnen* was still writing about these gardens: "*Someone imagining a beautiful garden is certainly not likely to think of concrete. On the contrary – this hard, grey, artificially produced stone material seems to many people to be the epitome of the 'unnatural'. They accept concrete as a necessary evil for the construction of roads, houses, bridges and industrial buildings, but concrete is 'taboo' for them in gardens. Two Swiss architects, H. Geiser and J. Schmidlin of Aarau, were courageous enough to break this taboo: they commissioned the garden architect Ernst Cramer to design gardens for their houses in which concrete plays a dominant role; as a material for paddling pools, terrace floors, walls to sit on, roofing for seating area, protection against the sun and for privacy. The photographs show that these gardens are not 'concrete' showpieces but living, green open-air spaces [...]."[331]*

The Schmidlin garden in particular has not only been preserved in the professional photographs by Evelyn Hagenbeck and Werner Erne, but is still largely in its original state at the time of writing, a striking example of a small, modern domestic garden.

Josef Schmidlin, who ran an architectural practice with Hans Geiser, was one of three clients who were jointly building on a series of plots in Aarau. All parties involved were interested in keeping a certain sense of spaciousness despite the building density involved, and avoid

Plan of the Schmidlin garden in Aarau

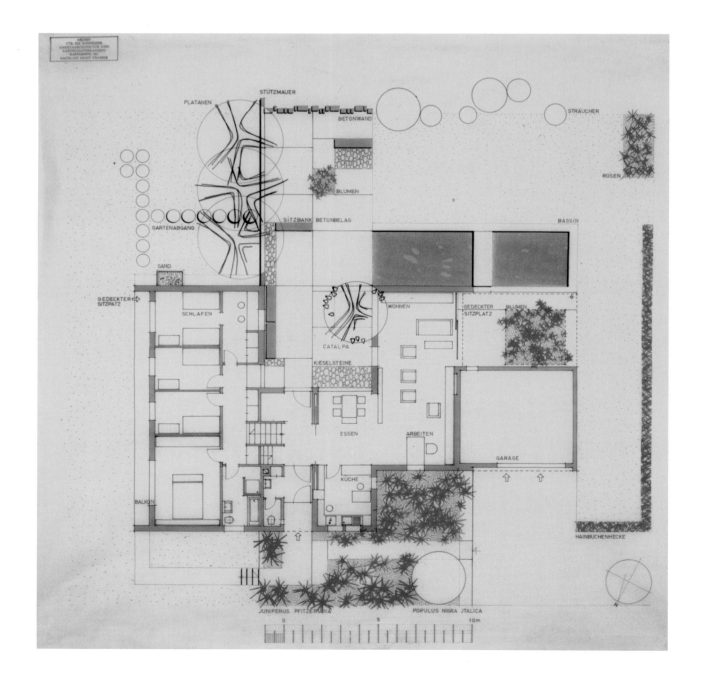

blocking the view of the sky. For this reason they decided to build the three detached houses on neighbouring plots as modern low constructions. The fact that modern architects like Richard Neutra were among Geiser and Schmidlin's models is clear from the elegant buildings, which were kept very simple, but also from the attitude of the client, Josef Schmidlin.[332] His interest coincided with Ernst Cramer's views, who reported enthusiastically about his experiences in Brazil and his current project on the Futa Pass. He had started working with the architects years before, after being introduced by Ernst Racheter. In the early stages, Geiser and Schmidlin always designed the gardens for their buildings themselves. It was not customary to especially employ a garden architect at the time, and for many clients it was too expensive. If Geiser and Schmidlin did occasionally need a gardener, they frequently turned to Racheter, who ran his gardening business and tree nursery in nearby Suhr. Cramer took on the garden design for Josef Schmidlin's very first commission, the Amsler-Merz house in Aarau in 1953, and even then surprised everyone involved with a project that did not fit in with the usual 50s garden image.[333] Subsequently Geiser and Schmidlin consulted him on a regular basis.

"There are two ways of making a relatively small plot look large: either you bring all the areas together to make them look spacious, [...] or you use

rigorous structuring to create a lot of different 'spaces' that constantly offer new and surprising perspectives," was Josef Schmidlin's retrospective view of his strategy for designing his own garden.[334]

It was important to him to recreate the austere architectural lines of his house in the garden as well, in order to emphasize the close connection between house and garden. Here Schmidlin's approach differed from the approach of his Modern models, like Richard Neutra, for example, who preferred to create a contrast between

crystalline architecture and surroundings that had been designed in a natural way.

Cramer treated the commission similarly to his job for Interbau Berlin, where he had created intimate courtyard gardens for Eduard Ludwig's low buildings. In Aarau he modelled his garden design so closely on the material and expressive qualities of the buildings that ultimately he created an indivisible unity of house and garden. But this certainly did not in any way detract from the strong identity of the garden, quite the contrary. The garden architect underlined the closed nature of the façades on the building's north-facing entrance by restricting the access with juniper bushes, and framing the western border of the plot with a trimmed hornbeam hedge. Only initiated visitors know that it is easy to get into the south-facing garden by walking on the lawn along the hornbeam hedge. Although it looks at first as though it is sealing the garden off hermetically, in fact the hedge precisely marks the edge of the space, like an L-shaped screen. Another boundary-marking element, also conceived as a free-standing screen, is a sculpturally designed concrete wall at the south end of the garden. To give privacy, Cramer assembled a wall about six metres in length from individually prepared stelae of exposed concrete with differing, rectangular cross-sections. The individual stelae protrude to varying

Children playing in the Schmidlin garden

A domestic garden made of concrete with decorative planting

Schmidlin garden, impression
dating from the 60s

View from the dining room
to the garden courtyard

Two windows on to the sky:
the framed view upwards and the
reflecting pool on the ground

Abstract design in the
modern style of the 60s

extents, and there are wide gaps between the elements, producing a charming, artistic play of light and shade. Seen through the large dining-room window, this wall concludes a garden area that seems rather like an atrium, which Cramer highlighted and shaded with a single, hand-picked trumpet tree. He went to the tree nursery specially, and took a model of the house with him, to be sure of finding the right tree with an appropriate character. To emphasize the depth of this stage-like space, two solid exposed concrete blocks about two metres long were placed across the line of view at different distances. They could also be used as seats. A third block, four metres long, was placed opposite the catalpa tree to provide seating inside the courtyard, which was enclosed on three sides. This central recreational area, with an area of about 90 square metres, was paved with large concrete slabs cast on site, with some rectangular gaps. These were planted either with decorative herbaceous plants or filled with large pebbles.

In close co-operation with the architect, with minimal resources and the simplest possible raw materials, Cramer had created a small garden that produced the effect of an abstract stage set. Later photographs by Werner Erne, in which the children of the family are 'playing' the venue, and the scene is complemented by modern garden furniture like Willy Guhl's garden chair, emphasize the theatrical and at the same time sculptural character of the space.

The area for a large 30-square-metre unplanted pool was created by superimposing the ground plan of the house and the layout of the garden courtyard. The first of the two short benches in the adjacent courtyard marks both the width of the pool and the dimensions of its concrete edge. The pool, placed on the south-west façade of the house, is for children to play in, and also reflects light on to the wall of the house and into the adjacent garden seating area by the living-room. At the same time, the water separates the recreation area by the house from the central lawn. A simple concrete bridge leads across the reflecting pool to the seating area. Here the architect cut a large, unglazed aperture of

about three by three metres in the roof, supported by columns and providing a framed view of the sky. It also lights a decorative flowerbed, also square, below. Plane trees had been among Ernst Cramer's favourites for use in gardens since the early 60s, because they have attractive bark, grow well and tolerate being cut to a remarkable extent. They could be trimmed into any shape without difficulty. And so the whole L-shaped garden space is bordered on the east side by a row of three plane trees, which Cramer intended to have cut into a green, box-shaped screen. Behind this screen is a place for drying washing and the children's sand-pit, at the foot of a little embankment. This area is partly shad-

Willy Guhl's beach chair in the Schmidlin garden today

ed by the house and thus protected from the rain. Circular steps and slabs made of concrete lead down into this less prestigious, more functional part of the garden.

The Schmidlin garden is one of the rare private garden projects in which Cramer was able to implement his accumulated wealth of experience and his new ideas purposefully in a modern domestic landscape, not least because he was co-operating successfully with a like-minded architect. This was the first time that he used concrete as a material with a consistency that had previously been possible at best in exhibition gardens like the Poet's Garden. Some elements of the successful 1959 exhibition garden, like

The central garden space, over three decades after it was created

Pool and garden seating area in the 60s

the shallow reflecting pool, the sculptural plac-ing of the seating elements and the bridge, as well as the way in which the concrete surface was broken up with individual gravel fields and the extremely small number of herbaceous plants, placed all the more precisely, were used again here. In fact, this garden, above all in the court-yard area, was like a sculpturally designed land-scape for living in, of the kind that Cramer had experienced shortly before on an urban scale in Brasilia. Only in his "Theatre Garden" in Ham-burg in 1963 would he implement the idea of a garden as an abstract stage design even more radically.[335] It is therefore no coincidence that the magazine *Schöner Wohnen* presented the exhibition garden and the Schmidlin garden in the same article.[336] But Cramer never in-tended to design a non-functional sculpture; he had far too much respect for the occupants and too strong a sense of function. Even when the clients decided that the unplanted pool was too unecological in the late 70s and turned it into a marsh garden, Cramer did comment that "you have destroyed my garden",[337] but accepted the clients' desire to have their own design ideas and remained on friendly terms with them. Cramer had proved with this garden that it was entirely possible, using modern materials and an abstract formal language, to create an archi-tectonic garden that was worth living in and that did not fall into the bourgeois cliché of a pictur-esque domestic garden.

Modern residential landscapes – Utopia and reality

The scope of tasks that Ernst Cramer and his practice dealt with in the boom of the early 60s was very large. From cemeteries to play-grounds, from urban designs to private gar-dens, they increasingly handled projects that unlike those of earlier decades often ran for years and had to be worked on all at the same time. This did not inhibit Cramer's delight in ex-perimentation in any way, and so alongside quite concrete jobs, like designing small private gardens and large housing estates, he also em-barked on visionary experimental projects like Walter Jonas's gigantic Intra Houses.

Landscape design for Walter Jonas's Intrapolis

Faced with the ultra-rapid growth of cities and an enormous increase in mobility, voices were increasingly raised in the heady atmosphere of the early 60s, that called for a fresh start, pre-dicting that growth was limited, as well as criti-cizing the wear and tear on the countryside and the deterioration of the quality of life in the in-ner cities. At the same time, since the Sputnik launch in 1957 and the first manned space flight in 1961, humanity seemed to have devel-oped unlimited technical capabilities that would make it possible to solve the impending problems. Many architects and town planners who felt compelled to look for creative solutions to the problems of humanity, developed fantas-tic and sometimes absurd projects for the city of the future, which grew increasingly detached from the surface of the earth and in extreme cases could have been realized in space. Many of these visions, collected in the 1986 exhibi-tion catalogue *Vision der Moderne. Das Prinzip Konstruktion*,[338] showed a more or less marked hostility to cities, and inclined romanti-cally towards escapism. The visionary Intra House project by the German painter and graphic artist Walter Jonas, who lived in Switzerland, was one of these Utopias.[339]

"The enormous increase in present-day mass set-tlement conceals enormous dangers," wrote Wal-ter Jonas in 1962, when he first published his proj-ect. *"Loss of individuality with all its human and political consequences. [...] Putting psychological and physical health at risk. Modern cities are in-creasingly like threatening jungles emitting poi-sonous odours. Traffic also demands its victims. The mass settlements of today can also be com-pared with cancerous growths."[340]*

As an alternative to the "battlefields of the modern struggle for existence",[341] the artist, working alone at first, and then with like-minded architects, engineers, landscape architects and patrons, developed the idea of a funnel-shaped building up to 100 metres high, intended to ac-commodate 2000 people. Three gigantic struc-tures of this kind would have linked up to form the basic unit of the future "Intrapolis". Unlike a traditional city they would have taken up very lit-tle land, which the artist felt would not only pro-tect the countryside but also make it possible for traffic to flow more freely and less danger-ously on the ground. Pedestrians on the other hand were to have been able to move around safely mainly on the upper edges of the cones, which would have incorporated some garden de-sign on connecting bridges between the build-ings and in the central green areas on the floors of the individual funnels.

"What is Intrapolis? The word Intrapolis com-bines the concepts of Introversion and Polis. In-trapolis is a project that could make it possible to live humanely, even in a highly technical world," wrote Walter Jonas, and compared life inside the cone with traditional urban models of classical antiquity, the Middle Ages, American Indian settlements and prehistoric life forms, in which communities were always grouped around a central, public square.[342] In fact, the urban and architectural types cited were far more aesthetically and socially complex than would have been possible in the great concrete funnels, and the supposedly visionary concept of the Intra Houses was based essentially on an idealized, traditional idea of the city as a cen-tral entity, a harmonious unit. These contradic-tions in Walter Jonas's arguments were criti-cized not only by subsequent generations,[343] but also by the artist's contemporaries like Lu-cius Burckhardt, for example:

"Let us freely admit why: as programmatic accommodation for a metropolitan and mobile population the interior of the funnel houses seemed too much like a village to us, too neighbourly, too cosy. And as a recreational landscape for this same population we found the world between the funnels too technical, workshop-like and constructivist. Now Walter Jonas has redrawn his idea with architect Franz Steinbrüchel and engineer Rudolf Kaltenstadler, and taken a some of the sting out of our criticism."[344]

Ever since Walter Jonas had introduced his concept to the Zurich "Club Bel' Etage", an association of alternatively thinking architects and engineers, in 1960, Franz Steinbrüchel and Rudolf Kaltenstadler had been supporters of the Intrapolis idea and had helped to develop it. Hans A. Wyss was a member of this circle as well, and his Zurich Origo publishing house printed a book called *Das INTRA-HAUS*[345] in 1962. This included contributions by Jonas, Steinbrüchel and Kaltenstadler, and also by the physician Dr. Klaus Laemmel, and the garden architect Ernst Cramer. It is not possible to ascertain in full how Cramer and Jonas came to work together. But the garden architect's inter-

est in visionary ideas and his delight in experimentation must have been just as well-known as his practical experience with urban planning projects at Interbau Berlin[346] and his work on the first Swiss housing estates built on terraces[347] by Stucky and Meuli. The artist and the garden architect also shared a fascination with Brazil, which Jonas had visited as early as 1958. He had collected some important impressions there that led him to develop the Intrapolis project. But unlike Cramer, Jonas saw the building of new towns in Brazil as a threat, as in his eyes the impenetrable thickets of the felled Brazilian jungle were simply being replaced by another, an architectural thicket.[348] And yet the forms that Jonas chose for his new cities spoke the same, architecturally daring language as Oscar Niemeyer's buildings. For example, the external slatted structure of the funnels was reminiscent of the façade of the elegant high-rise building for the Companhia PanAmericano (Copan) in São Paulo. A frequently published perspective view of Intrapolis, drawn by Franz Steinbrüchel, showed funnel-shaped structures standing amidst their surroundings on pilotis.[349] Formally these looked like mushrooms

Intra Houses by Walter Jonas, model

shooting up in the countryside, which was certainly conducive to the image of being close to nature – which would be called "ecology" today. But essentially the urban planning concept of the project was based on the ideal image of classical Modernism, which saw high-rise build-

Intrapolis, consisting of
a group of funnel houses

ings as "crystals" that would "grow" among untouched nature.

Ernst Cramer wrote a chapter called "Building and nature" for Jonas's little book, in which he shared the artist's fears that in the long term the countryside would suffer greatly from the growth of the cities. Primarily interested in matters of form, Cramer recognized:

"The view of the Intrahouse in natural surroundings certainly shows clearly how much influence man has on nature, but here we are dealing with an honest contrast between building and nature. This solution, which creates the natural and the built in pure form, or allows them to continue to exist, shows us a way that not only opens up new paths architecturally, but has the essential characteristic of admitting dense settlement in a landscape without having to destroy it."[350]

In his plan, Cramer confined himself to a rather trivial landscape design intended to fit in harmoniously with the existing landscape. This conscious creative reticence was the only means at his disposal to retain the contrast between nature and building that he valued so highly. All the dwellings inside the funnel buildings were to have gardens designed like the ones Ernst Cramer had already conceived for other buildings on terraces in earlier years. And so the Intrapolis idea scarcely offered the landscape architect any opportunity for real innovation. We are compelled to conclude that he was enthusiastic both about the un-Swiss boldness of the idea as such and about the purity of the architectural form, and decided to work on the absurd project for these reasons. Something that had hitherto only seemed possible in Brazil in terms of sensational architecture and breath-taking urban planning had suddenly become conceivable for Switzerland as well. Ernst Cramer was pleased with the idea of being part of this exciting development, but it remained a Utopia.

The striking Im Wilerfeld play area
mound of earth in the shade of the fully-
grown plane trees

Despite support by wealthy patrons and more than one attempt at building, first on a private plot in Gockhausen near Zurich and then in 1964 at the EXPO in Lausanne, a prototype Intra House was never realized. Disputes about land ownership in the former case and planning errors in the latter prevented the funnels from being built. Even so, the models of the Intra Houses appeared in numerous international exhibitions. Then in 1970, when the Intra House project was examined in terms of its technical and commercial feasibility for the Federal German Building Ministry, and the German Tenants' Federation planned to built 10 Intrapolis units in the towns of Wulfen, Haltern and Freiburg im Breisgau, it seemed that the vision was very close to being realized. But his time lack of financial strength on the part of the company commissioned put an end to the dream. As faith in the power of technology to solve environmental problems disappeared, and scepticism about the sense and purpose of architectural megastructures increased, in the 70s interest in projects like the Intra House disappeared as well.

Open spaces for the Wilerfeld housing estate in Olten

Ernst Cramer found it considerably easier to deal with urban projects back on the earth's surface, rather than Jonas's visions. As the ideal of the garden city had had its day in Switzerland by the early 60s because of an increased shortage of building land and rising land prices, large estates with blocks of flats were being built even in the smaller towns.

"There was an enormous change of scale in the 50s and 60s; and this was especially true for a small country that was 'reporting back', after the constraints of the war, from building that adapted to the landscape and the 'city as a village' to unconditional Modernism and the 'world as a city'."[351]

In this atmosphere it was easier than it had been for Cramer to put new ideas in open space design into practice, even though or perhaps because his clients were now making heavier demands in terms of function that in terms of the way the town looked. Two estate projects show especially clearly how Cramer tried to draw on his experience from the Poet's Garden and his impressions gained in the encounter with mod-

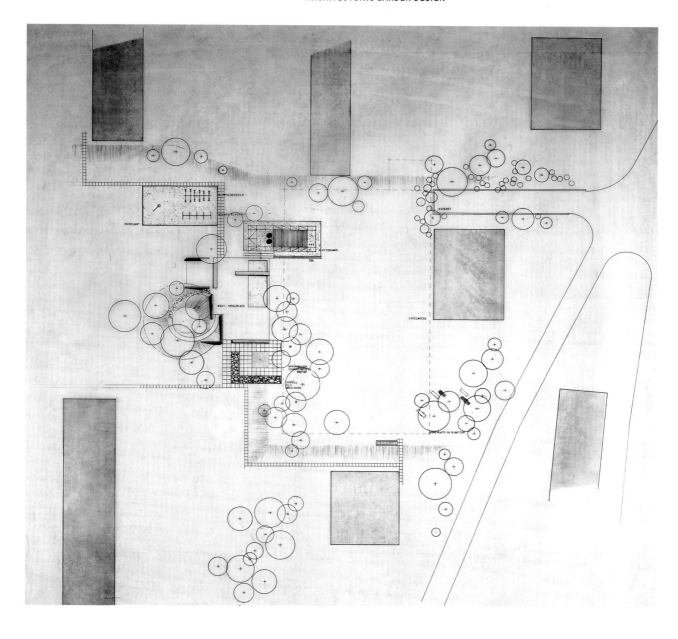

ern architecture when designing public open spaces. Both projects, which were realized in about the same period between 1960 and 1963, can be seen as forerunners to the spectacular Theatre Garden in 1963[352] or as a kind of "missing link" between the Poet's Garden and the Hamburg project.

The architects Hermann Frey, W. Hächler and P. Schmidli of Olten built six-storey straight-line blocks and a twelve storey high-rise building in the Wilerfeld district as the result of a competition, and fitted an underground car-park between the free-standing buildings. Cramer was commissioned to design a playground on top of the underground structure; the design was to include the large ventilation shafts from the car-park – two concrete tubes about four metres high. Ernst Cramer and Hermann Frey knew each other from the time when the garden architect had designed a private garden in Zurich for Frey's former practice partner, the Zurich architect Ernst Schindler, in 1946. The two architects, who ceased to be partners in 1947 after about ten years, sought to achieve a synthesis between modern ideas and functional and economic demands, and Frey obviously remained

committed to this basic idea for the Wilerfeld housing estate as well.

Cramer's aim was to use the playground "to create a combination that is able to hold its own against these large blocks, both formally and in terms of size."[353] In its austere and architectural basic concept, but also in the way materials and elements like walls, seating and bridges are handled, the playground is today still clearly reminiscent of the Schmidlin private garden in Aarau. The orthogonal paths and the squares, with the exception of the central asphalted area, are paved with large-format slabs measuring one by one metre. An L-shaped band made of coarse boulders lends structure to the area, and so does a square trough in small block pavement, edged with concrete slabs, which was formerly used as a shower basin. Sandy areas surrounding the play apparatus provide the necessary protection against falls. A concrete beam about ten metres long and one metre wide spans the large central sandpit, serving as a bridge that is very similar to the simple bridge structure in the Schmidlin garden as well.

The most striking elements of the abstract play landscape, which was to be shaded by plane

Plan of the playground for the Im Wilerfeld housing estate in Olten

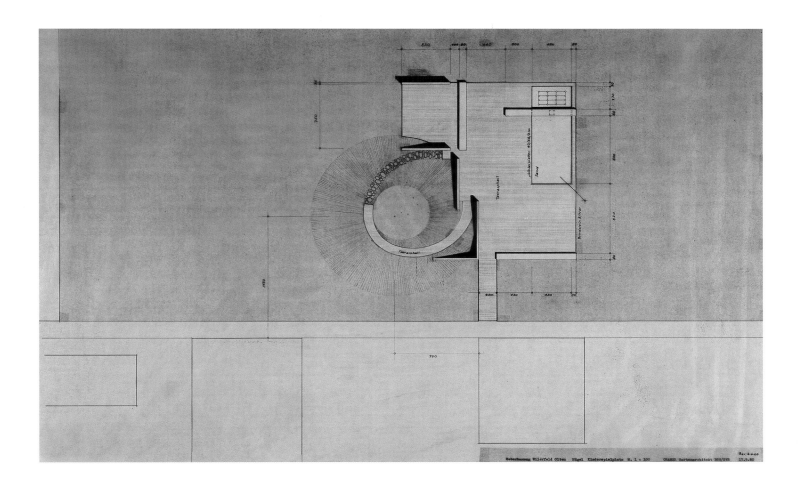

The playground of the Im Wilerfeld
housing estate as of about 1963

The play hill, framed by shear walls

Detailed plan of the playground with
play hill and free-standing shear walls

Climbing- and play-frames
around the ventilation shafts

View from the hill to the climbing
frame. The corner between the shear
walls is now closed

trees, were a large climbing frame and a grassy mound about four metres high. The climbing frame was about three metres high, six metres wide and 16 metres long. The tubular construction was built around the two ventilation shafts from the underground car-park in such a way

that they looked almost like the funnels of an ocean liner. This impression was further enhanced by the rings painted on the tubes. Cramer fixed a fibre-glass reinforced polyester sheet at a height of 1.9 metres, to serve, with the appropriate railings, as a deck and to provide protection from rain and sun for the area below. A few wall elements were fixed to extend the possibilities for play in the climbing frame. In comparison with the nearby sandy area, which still contains swings and seesaws, the climbing frame looked rather unconventional, and offered primarily a three-dimensional framework that could be played in a number of ways.

Unlike the climbing frame, the large grassy mound has survived to the present day. It is conical, planted with a very few trees and framed on two sides by an L-shaped wall and two freestanding concrete slabs about two metres high. A simple path, oval in plan, leads between the walls and up the truncated cone, and then down again on the other side. Part of the "mountain path", as Cramer called it, was asphalted, and linked up directly with the central asphalted area, while the rest of the path from the top of the hill downwards was paved with natural stone. Even on the plan the ensemble of the basic geometrical forms of circle, oval and straight lines looked like an abstract constructivist painting. [354] In reality it turned out to be a Cubist-Constructivist sculpture, revealing a skilful interplay between elemental spatial definition using free-standing walls and landscape abstraction. Cramer was obviously drawing on his experience with the Poet's Garden when he decided to present a mountain abstractly, and combined this strategy with the modern architectural concept of fluent, non-hierarchical space. Cramer, who was always greatly concerned about use and function, was relieved that the project had a clearly defined programme. This discharged him from the obligation to justify his essentially landscape-art and aesthetics based intervention theoretically. Neither was it necessary here to implement a genuine element of art as in the Poet's Garden, to avert the suspicion that the garden architect intended to create art himself. This was the first project in which Cramer had successfully harnessed the landscape art impetus that he had consistently developed at horticultural shows, and used it in his everyday work. After his resounding success at G|59, architects no longer expected Cramer to come up with purely functional designs, but with usable open spaces in up-to-date language, matched to architecture's new character and lines.

Open space design for the Badenerstrasse residential colony in Zurich

Cramer owed the commission for the Badenerstrasse residential colony in Zurich to his contact with Alice Schoch-Bockhorn, whose private garden in Zollikon he had designed in 1957. Frau Schoch-Bockhorn was the wife a Zurich gravel contractor who invested her money, among other things, in building new housing estates intended to provide affordable housing for people in the middle and lower income brackets. In about 1960 she commissioned the Zurich architect Alfred Heinrich Furrer to build a new estate in Zurich and

Cramer used very little of the usual play apparatus in his design, and instead created a modern play-landscape using a series of solid, board-marked concrete blocks and light modelling of the ground. Even at the time of writing it looks more like an abstract sculpture garden than a playground. Two concrete areas that Cramer built of one by one metre concrete slabs are placed like rugs on the homogeneous lawn. On these slabs he arranged concrete elements up to half a metre thick – walls, blocks to sit on, steps and a kind of saddle roof with steps to climb up – like oversize building blocks. Parts of

There is no sign of the climbing frame around the ventilation shafts today

Small changes have done nothing to detract from the effect of the ensemble

Shear walls and earth mounds form a striking contrast

Ernst Cramer to design the outside areas. Frau Schoch-Bockhorn was particularly concerned to create interesting play areas for children among the four- to ten-storey apartment blocks. Cramer wrote about this project at a later date:
"Young people are looking for adventure. A brave client allowed the garden architect to accommodate this urge in an unusual way by providing a climbing-wall. A sound-absorbing wall with some facing steps to sit on makes it possible to organize small-scale events as well as just ball games. The miniature theatre, the climbing-wall and the playhouse are intended to lend weight to this play area between the large apartment blocks from the outset, which cannot be achieved by planting alone, despite the use of relatively large trees."[355]

this artificial landscape were accentuated and shaded with plane trees. The building plans dating from 1962 show, along with the other walls up to five metres high, a slender concrete stela eleven metres in height.[356] The stela does not appear in the photographs taken in 1965,[357] so it is to be assumed that Cramer was making excessive demands on the client's above-mentioned boldness with this particular item. Nevertheless, in the end a "miniature theatre", as Cramer called it, was built between the apartment blocks. It uses a modern formal language and views of space that are even more marked than in the Schmidlin garden. The playground theme gave Cramer greater freedom from functional constraints and the client's

Concrete slabs for play and to shape the space in the Badener Strasse housing estate in Zurich

wishes, and thus left him more scope for the formal design, even though he was not permitted any grandiose gestures.

To what extent was an abstract complex like this appropriate for children's play at the time, and could it possibly still be used as a model today?

Unlike monofunctional play apparatus, of the kind that Cramer was still using in Olten, the nature of the play was not dictated by the architectural concrete elements. Children still play in the largely unchanged playground today, as it offers a viable spatial framework and archetypal

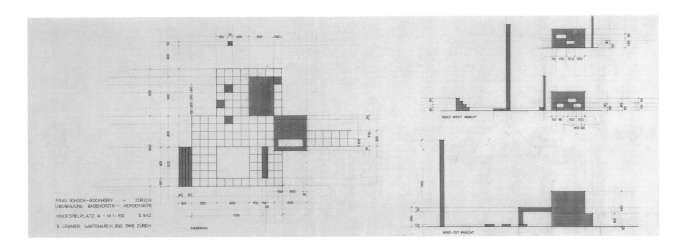

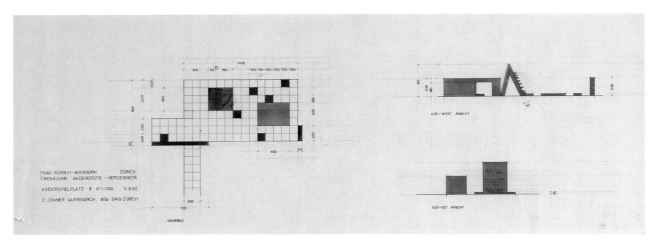

Plans for constructing the play elements in the Badener Strasse housing estate in Zurich

Not all the planned concrete elements could be realized in 1963

Climbing wall in the playground

open space elements like the spectators' steps, the "stage wall" with windows or the roof. These are timeless and serve as a setting for a wide range of activities. Only the "saddle roof" with climbing steps, an artificial mountain and a tent at the same time, has since been demolished, as children had hurt themselves while playing on it. The architectural and artistic models for this kind of open space design will be examined in the next chapter, taking the Theatre Garden in Hamburg as an example. There are clear parallels, not just in the names that Cramer chose for the two projects. The models for the Zurich and Hamburg projects were evidently identical. In Hamburg, Cramer was ultimately able to realize even the eleven metre high stela, considerably enhancing the garden's theatrical character.

International Horticultural Show IGA 1963 in Hamburg

We have already seen from the remarkable series of exhibition gardens that he produced between 1933 and 1959 that Ernst Cramer's strengths in developing and implementing new ideas were revealed particularly vividly at exhibitions. His spectacular contribution to the International Horticultural Show in Hamburg in 1963 was the high point and final flourish in this series, and it considerably enhanced the garden architect's international reputation.[358]
IGA 1963 offered Cramer a good opportunity to implement his ideas about garden design largely without restrictions. These had already clearly emerged in the Schmidlin private garden and in the housing projects Wilerfeld in Olten and Badener Strasse in Zurich. The resulting "Theatre Garden" was a sculptural work in its own right, of a kind that Cramer had not yet realized, and surpassed even the 1959 Poet's Garden in its radical abstraction. Cramer's vision of architectonic garden design reached its peak in this project.
Like many other European cities, Hamburg had removed the ring of fortifications dating from the Thirty Years' War, and thus has a green belt. Some of this was developed at a later stage, but a large part has survived as open space, and the city has used it for horticultural shows among other things. After the Second World War, IGA 1953 was held here under the direction of the established Hamburg garden architect Karl Plomin, who had already organized the German horticultural show "Planten un Blomen" (plants and flowers) on part of the same site in 1935. When the Senate IGA-commission was founded in 1957, it was already clear that Plomin was to again be involved in the overall planning of IGA 1963, in particular for the site of "Planten un Blomen". In addition, the "Kleine und Grosse Wallanlagen" (small and large ramparts) were to be made available as exhibition areas. The total area of the different sites was 76 hectares, and design suggestions were invited in an international competition, to be submitted by November 1958. 93 participants, about half from abroad, applied for the competition entry forms. Ernst Cramer was also among them, but apparently decided not to participate at an early stage, for unknown reasons. On 12 December 1958 the jury awarded the first and second prize to the garden architects Günther Schulze of Hamburg and Heinrich Raderschall of Bad Godesberg respectively. The working group that resulted, consisting of Plomin, Raderschall and Schulze, was subsequently commissioned to plan IGA 1963 in its entirety. It was divided into six sections separated by roads: section A "Planten un Blomen", a show of flowers and herbaceous plants under the direction of Karl Plomin; section B "Hall Site" for the special horticultural shows; section C "Botanical Garden"; section D "Kleine Wallanlagen" (small ramparts) with various water features; section E "Grosse Wallanlagen" (large ramparts) with German and international "Domestic Gardens from across the World"; and section F "Heiligengeistfeld" for annuals and dahlias.
After the decision had been made to display about 25 international gardens on the Grosse Wallanlagen site between Glacischaussee and Holstenwall, Karl Plomin, Günther Schulze and Heinrich Raderschall, in consultation with colleagues from abroad, personally selected the guests who were to be invited. In June 1960, after many personal exchanges and negotiations the final selection of 28 garden architects was fixed. Roberto Burle Marx, who was now a figure acknowledged and acclaimed world-wide in the field of garden architecture, had to be invited for reasons of prestige alone. The same applied to the American James Rose, who was suggested by Thomas Church, who had been approached first. Other guests alongside Ernst Cramer were Sylvia Crowe from England, Jange Blomkvist, Edvard Jacobsen and Gunnar Martinsson from Sweden, Eywin Langkilde and Georg Boye from Denmark, Morten Grindaker and Egil Gabrielsen from Norway, Onni Savonlahti from Finland, Zvi Miller from Israel, Viktor Mödlhammer from Austria, Meto J. Vroom from Holland, René Latinne from Belgium, Augustin Bonnet, Michel and Ingrid Bourne from France, Luis Iglesias Martí from Spain, Francisco Caldeira Cabral from Portugal, Jean Challet, Pierre Mas and Claude Verdugo from Morocco, Akira Sato and Kuro Kaneko from Japan, Pietro Porcinai from Italy and Franz Vogel from Bern, Switzerland who came to Hamburg in place of Walter Leder, who had originally been invited. This selection meant that the organizers had succeeded in presenting a spectrum of distinguished modern garden architecture that was unsurpassed in the history of horticultural shows. Some of the participants, above all the Europeans, were already known to Ernst Cramer from Interbau Berlin or the IFLA congresses. Cramer must have met most of the overseas garden architects, above all Roberto Burle Marx, James Rose and the Japanese Akira

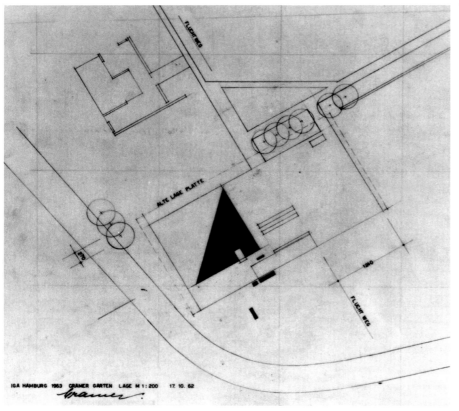

IGA HAMBURG 1963 CRAMER GARTEN LAGE M 1:200 17.10.62

Design plan for Theatre Garden
in Hamburg dating from 17 October 1962,
version with large concrete slab

Theatre Garden

Ernst Cramer worked intensively on the "Theatre Garden" for IGA 1963 from autumn 1960
onwards, and from the outset was in close contact with Günther Schulze. Schulze admired the
Zurich garden architect, which was why he had
suggested he should take part in IGA, and he remained Cramer's most important contact until
the project was finally realized. A personal letter
to Schulze dated 18 August 1961 shows that the
two garden architects met in the summer of
that year and discussed progress on the Theatre
Garden design. Cramer summed up:
*"I sense from your conversations that you are also
going through a phase of professional development and I think that this is also the case for me,
to a large and increased extent."[360]*
Hints of the direction of Schulze's further development could be found in his "Individualist's Garden",
which he designed as one of the three domestic
German Gardens. The whole surface of the walled
garden was like an arid landscape, created exclusively with sand, gravel, stone and concrete, and
reminiscent of parts of Cramer's Schmidlin garden.[361]The only plants he used were conifers,

Sato and Kuro Kaneko, for the first time in Hamburg, and it would have been most unlike him not
to have drawn new inspiration from these encounters.
Nothing was said about national gardens in the
more restricted sense in the brief,[359] and so
most of the garden architects took the opportunity to develop their designs largely independently of supposedly national characteristics.
The Grosse Wallanlagen site addressed the
theme of close links between house and garden,
and this showed particularly clearly in the three
German domestic gardens by Heinrich Raderschall, Günther Schulze and Karl Plomin, as
small houses were especially built for these gardens only. In most of the other gardens, plain,
pavilion-like structures using dark timber beams
and whitewashed walls by the German architect
Egon Jux provided the architectural accent.
Work had already started on ground modelling,
building a water-course and planting of accentu-
ating trees and shrubs when the planning documents were sent to the garden architects in October 1960. The plans that they submitted were
translated into standardized working plans in
the IGA office under the direction of Karl Plomin,
which regularly required some additional material and changes. The authors, particularly those
from different climates, had to make certain
concessions, particularly in respect of the materials and plants chosen, because of supply bottlenecks. After the tidal wave catastrophe of
February 1962, which caused considerable damage to the site, there were also major financial
difficulties. The Hamburg organizers had to im-
pose severe budget cuts, which affected the garden architects as well.

Site plan of the Grosse Wallanlagen
with the Theatre Garden (middle) at the
International Horticultural Show 1963
in Hamburg

1 Water ramp
2 Domestic gardens of nations
  (with Theatre Garden)
3 Tea pavilion
4 Museum garden
5 Baroque garden
6 Hamburg Historic Museum
7 Berlin pavilion
8 «Wallterrassen» restaurant

The dotted line indicates
the cableway track

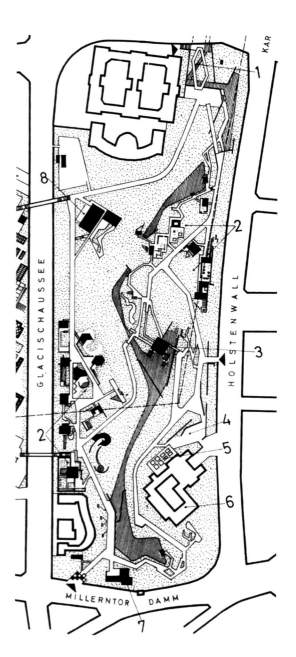

houseleeks and grasses. Given the harshness of this design, the Berlin Professor of Garden Design Gustav Allinger, who published his new book *Das Hohelied von Gartenkunst und Gartenbau[362]* to coincide with the opening of IGA, expressed his views in no uncertain terms:

"Curious lady visitors are asking how long an individualist can bear to be in this garden? [...] But one day a 'Finta Giardiniera' will perhaps tell him that he has a spleen in his head and too little green in his garden."[363]

In fact, the majority of garden architects were definitely in favour of formal clarity in garden design by this time,[364] but most were still afraid of radical simplification. It is therefore not surprising that Allinger was not particularly enthusiastic about Cramer's "Theatre Garden" either, as this was even more uncompromising in its reduction of form and content.

Unlike Günther Schulze's project and most of the other gardens, there were no plans for a pavilion near the "Theatre Garden", so that Cramer was able to develop his project entirely independently. Cramer's estate contains model photographs and plans of five different design stages for the Theatre Garden,[365] which was to be realized on a site that sloped slightly to the south-east. Knowing how Cramer worked, it is to be assumed that additional intermediate steps were also devised. In each of these design phases, Cramer not only adapted his project to the changing general conditions, which he of course had to do, but found ways of intensifying the garden's expressive qualities by means of deliberate reduction. His aim was to use the simplest resources to achieve the maximum creative effect. The design was based from the outset on the contrast between a rectangular platform to walk on, made of concrete slabs, and the existing, gently modelled grassy embankment. Concrete slabs several metres high, a triangular pool, steps and simple seating were the core elements that he was to retain until the end.

A first, partially interpretive description of the design was published a year before the exhibition:

"The Swiss garden architect Cramer of Zurich has bold plans. He has paved his 1800 sq m plot entirely in concrete, placed on it walls and columns up to eleven metres high and several metres wide, and has added to them a triangular swimming pool. He intends people to have a sense of safe seclusion when among these high walls. In his view this is a garden for men and women with a modern approach, they can meet here for parties and musical evenings. Cramer has distributed sheets of glass lit from below in the concrete floor. The only plants are a few trees that are there already and two raised triangular beds of stones. That is all. Cramer does not create any relationship between man and plant, he prefers abstraction."[366]

Even this short description shows how much Cramer was following the model of classical Modernism. At this early design stage a large

cube was attached to the square, and two wide concrete walkways thrust out from the spacious surface into the surroundings. Two free-standing slabs and a column attracted attention from a distance, and their effect was to be enhanced on the site by the shallow, half-square reflecting pool. As in the Poet's Garden, a pool without a rim was planned, sitting in the concrete as though it had been stamped out. In contrast with his Zurich masterpiece, Cramer wanted to work without an artistically created sculpture

Model of the Theatre Garden with ground-level lights and wall elements

Variant with ground-level lights and large cube

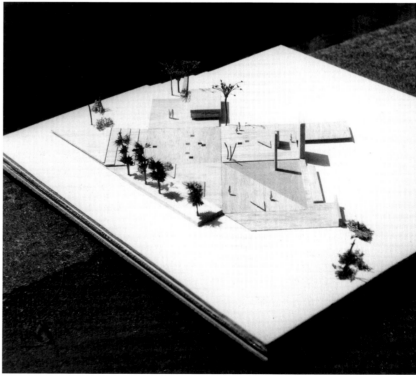

Reminiscence of Modern architecture
with Hamburg as an urban backdrop

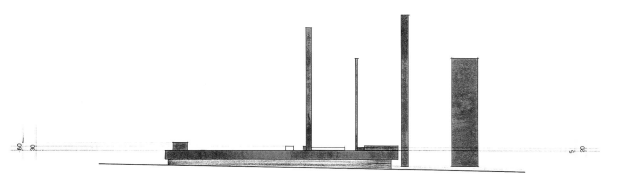

Theatre Garden as realized,
view towards the northwest

Section drawing of the
Theatre Garden (variant) with concrete
slabs up to eleven metres high

Garden space as architectonic space

from the outset in his Hamburg Theatre Garden, and instead to mark a point on the surface of the water with a simple concrete stela. This shows clearly that he self-confidently saw his garden as a sculptural place in its own right, which needed no additional artistic ingredient. The garden itself was the work of an artist.

A second design stage saw the planned paved area reduced by about half, which reduced the amount of concrete needed from 250 cubic metres to 100 cubic metres. This reduction was partly due to the IGA management's debate about excessive cost, which threatened the realization of the project for a time. [367] Cramer placed the platform as a simple rectangle parallel with the slope, and left just one long concrete walkway thrusting out over its edge. The somewhat petty-looking triangular beds had disappeared and the layout of the floodlights in the ground was altered. Two large sections of wall were added, and detached from the central platform, were set into the adjacent grassy bank at right angles to the original wall sections. Three new elements could be made out in the model: several long beams to sit on, a small island in the water and a composition made up of wall sections of about man-height that created an intricate, quasi-architectural spatial sequence at the point where the cube had originally been placed. The size and shape of the pool, produced by diagonally dividing one of the two large square sections in two, remained unchanged. The design as a whole now seemed tighter and more controlled.

In the subsequent design stages the floor lighting disappeared from the platform, along with the projecting concrete walkway and the final remnants of the intricate wall ensemble. In the end, Cramer reduced the paved area by over half again, replacing it with a lawn on the same level, so that ultimately all that was left was a long plateau 34 by 5.5 metres in size, which he fitted in as an abrupt conclusion to the edge of the slope, which had been carefully modelled geometrically. Visitors coming from the west walked down three steps, crossed the flat rectangle of lawn on a paved path 2.5 metres wide, and reached the large paved area, which raised the edge of the slope architecturally like a viewing platform. To prevent visitors from reaching the front edge of the terrace unchecked, Cramer blocked the straight, linear movement with a rostrum raised by about 25 centimetres and two by eleven metres in area. Like all the paved areas it was built of 50 by 50 centimetres concrete slabs and prefabricated concrete channel tiles. A long, plain bench opposite the rostrum was made up of eleven of these prefabricated U-shaped concrete elements. Two more provided a kind of seat on the edge of the triangular pool. One side of the pool was flush with the large paved area, and its sharply cut form thrust into the lawn.

In contrast with the strictly horizontal quality of the elements described in the previous paragraph, three large, board-marked concrete elements, up to eleven metres high, towered up into the sky like symbols. As before, a single column stood in the water of the reflecting pool. A second, smaller wall was set at right angles to the platform in the slope below the ensemble, pointing precisely at the single item in the pool. A second pair of concrete slabs, about eleven metres high, consisting of a wall 2.5 metres wide and a wall 60 centimetres wide, with 50 centimetres between them, was positioned directly on the front edge of the large platform and seemed to anchor it into the topography. Seen from the foot of the slope, a kind of reveal created the impression that the platform had a knife-sharp edge. The U-shaped channel tiles framing the paved area were set so that the inside of the U faced outwards and created a striking effect of shadow, which made the platform look almost as though it was floating. The entire layout of the complex was derived strictly from an orthogonal principle. All the edges and positions of the individual elements were thus tied into a rigid system of geometrical relations. Even the height and width dimensions of the complex were carefully proportioned: for example, the overall height of the largest slabs was double the width of the platform.

The Theatre Garden was at its most impressive at night, skilfully lit by a number of floodlights set in the ground around the ensemble. Only at night, when at least some of the surrounding area was cloaked in darkness, thus creating an illusion of distance, was it possible to sense what image Ernst Cramer had in his mind's eye when conceiving his work: the concrete walls resembled monolithic structures in the landscape, stage walls with the silhouettes of people coming into view against them. Thus the title of the garden was almost self-explanatory, without there being any temptation to seriously test the work's viability as a location for a real theatrical performance. It was incidentally never used as such, although many contemporaries would like to have seen it tried. [368] The fact that despite all this many visitors worried about the garden's ability to function is not only due to the title or to a compulsive urge to explain a mysterious garden, [369] but to Cramer's own project explanation:

"This Theatre Garden shows new ways of designing a garden space, it looks at garden life in a new way. It is intended as a component in a large landscape garden and is suitable for large-scale celebrations and theatrical performances. The range of materials used was kept to a minimum: along with the concrete columns, concrete paving and areas of water, plants appear only in the form of lawns. As in lucid modern architecture, people feel here that they are absolutely central in this garden space. To grasp this effect, visitors should sit down on one of the concrete elements; by doing this they will gain the impression that a work of this kind is a fixed and striking component of a landscape."[370]

Essentially the title "Theatre Garden" was to be read in the same figurative sense as the title "Poet's Garden". But the explanation cited above once again shows that Ernst Cramer still had difficulty with garden design that was justified purely on aesthetics, and was using the theatre motif as a functional legitimation for his design.

Of particular interest for the question as to the origins of Cramer's garden concept is the model role discharged by "lucid modern architecture", which the garden architect stresses quite

unambiguously in his short explanation. He was definitely not intending to make an analogy with the functionalistic aspects of modern architecture. Cramer may have been a pragmatist who had never subjected the theoretical basis of Modernism to academic analysis, but as a connoisseur of architecture he was undoubtedly aware of the fact that a comparison of architecture and garden based on function would have been completely out of place. He was referring rather to the specific view of space and the purely formal expression that made him partic-

Visitors silhouetted against the Theatre Garden at night

ularly keen on modern architecture, most recently in Brazil. Contrary to suppositions in other studies,[371] Japanese meditation gardens were not a serious source of inspiration to Cramer, and with the exception of the 1948 Hegner garden in Feldmeilen there is no clear reference to Japanese garden design in Cramer's work. Cramer did visit Japan to attend the 9th Congress of the International Federation of Landscape Architects in Tokyo and Kyoto, but this event did not take place until May 1964. Also, the experts assembled at the congress were unanimous that traditional Japanese gardens were extraordinarily beautiful, but could not be adapted to Western culture.[372] Richard Arioli, a Swiss participant in the congress and the first editor of the Swiss specialist magazine *Anthos*, first published in 1962,[373] added a further critical aspect. He observed "that the beautiful old gardens are cultural monuments of times past that to the approximately 30 million people living in the Tokyo-Osaka-Kyoto area are little more than museum pieces."[374]

Ernst Cramer was not interested in museum pieces; he was looking for up-to-date responses to contemporary developments. The problems that these raised in the form of unchecked urban growth could not be overlooked in Japan either. There was no doubt that he had the Congresso National building complex in Brasilia[375] in mind when conceiving his abstract masterpiece in Hamburg. Of course he could not simply copy it in miniaturized form, as this would inevitably have ended in embarrassing banality. He was interested in handling simple architectural entities, horizontal and vertical slabs, in a modern, non-hierarchical view of space and a sense of balanced geometrical proportions and relating to the landscape. All the essential morphological elements that Niemeyer had used to create his stage set-like architecture in Brazil were present in the "Theatre Garden" – with the exception of the striking hemispheres. Even the topographical situation at the sharply identified edge of a slope, which Niemeyer had deliberately used and exploited architecturally in his Brasilia complex, and the way he handled the large reflecting pool may be seen as parallels.

Perhaps Ernst Cramer was also encouraged in his conception of this extraordinary garden by an earlier American project. In 1955, the Austrian painter and graphic artist Herbert Bayer created his "Marble Garden" in Aspen, Colorado. This consisted of pieces of marble several metres high left-over from a marble quarry, which he grouped around a shallow pool. Bayer used five tall, slender stelae of white marble, and about ten more left-over pieces in the form of cuboids, pyramids and circular slabs, to stage his Marble Garden against the background of the Rocky Mountains. It was no coincidence that the formal language of this garden corresponded with the ideals of classical Modernism. Bayer had arrived the Bauhaus in Weimar as early

as 1921, and had attended Johannes Itten's introductory course, but courses with other Bauhaus artists had also left clear traces in the work of the young graphic artist.[376] From 1925, at the instigation of Walter Gropius, he was head of the new "Printing and Advertising Workshop" at the Dessau Bauhaus, and was responsible for graphics at the Bauhaus until 1928. After a few years of free-lance work for prestigious advertising agencies in Berlin and London, the young artist finally emigrated to the USA in 1938, and built a successful career as a graphic artist and exhibition curator in New York. In 1944 he met Walter Paepcke, the owner of the largest American packaging company, the Container Corporation of America, who intended to turn the former silver-mining city of Aspen into an international culture centre:

"Here an attempt was made to fit art into a living frame and to create a place of pilgrimage for an intellectual and social élite that was in need of leisure. In this sense Aspen is close to modern efforts to enliven museums and bring art and life together in a carefully planned location," wrote François Stahly in *Werk* in 1961.[377]

Herbert Bayer was entrusted with the urban design for Aspen, and he lived there to that end from 1946 to 1974. The 1955 "Marble Garden", like Bayer's artistic earth formation "Grass Mound", constructed in the same year, was one of Bayer's early sculptural works in Aspen. It is far more justifiable to identify "Grass Mound", rather than the "Poet's Garden", which was created four years later, as a forerunner of "Earthworks", the art movement known as "Land Art" in Europe, even though neither Cramer's nor Bayer's work was characterized by the pessimism about civilization and the criticicism of society that drove later pioneers of Land Art.

Was Cramer aware of this brilliant piece of work in Aspen? It is no coincidence that his and Bayer's works are illustrated and described on facing pages in Elizabeth Kassler's *Modern Gardens and the Landscape*.[378] But Kassler's book did not appear until after IGA 63, and thus could not have been the source. It is considerably more likely that Cramer's attention was drawn to the article by the French artist François Stahly in *Werk* that is quoted above. The illustration of the large lawn sculpture was so similar to Cramer's 1959 work that he would certainly have wanted

to find out more about the project. The picture printed above it showed the Marble Garden against a landscape backdrop with a view into the depths of a valley in the Rocky Mountains.[379] On the other hand Cramer's explicit reference to modern architecture and the above-

That is, unless actors try 'theatre art' and other performances to relieve the coldness and hardness of this place 'humanely'", wrote Gustav Allinger in his review.[380]

He rejected the garden as a "monument of its times", which chimed with the heartfelt view of

mentioned parallels with buildings in Brasilia suggest that the Marble Garden in Aspen was at best of minor significance for the conception of the Theatre Garden.

For Cramer the Theatre Garden was a unique opportunity to give visual expression to his enthusiasm for Brasilia's modern architecture. In one respect, however, Cramer was subject to certain illusions. Like its architectural model, the Theatre Garden was essentially conceived for the wide-open spaces of a landscape of the kind that Cramer had experienced and been so impressed by on his trip to Brazil. The Wallanlagen in Hamburg did not offer such enormous and peaceful space, which detracted from the effect of the sculptural project, in the daytime in particular. This deficiency was noted even while the garden was being realized, but there was obviously nothing that could be done about it, and after its completion most attentive observers noticed it. Of much more serious consequences was the proximity of the IGA cableway: its concrete pylon was unfortunately built only a stone's throw away. This functional element was all too similar to the concrete stela in Cramer's garden in its height and the nature of its material, and led to a certain amount of misinterpretation.

But actually it was the avant-garde aesthetic that was entirely misunderstood in the context of garden design – unlike in its manifestations in art and architecture.

"The Theatre Garden by garden architect Ernst Cramer of Zurich shows no more sign at all of the much-loved intimacy and beauty of a 'garden'.

many other critics who thought that this work took the basic idea of a garden to the point of absurdity and feared that gardeners would be downgraded to the role of concrete mixers.[381] But Allinger was probably closer to the truth with his eloquent title "monument of its times" than he was probably himself aware, as the art historian Ulrich Gertz had stated as early as 1953:

"The architectural, one might almost say: framework-like use of horizontals and verticals and their transformation into various diagonals is part of the three-dimensional consciousness of people of our day."[382]

Cramer was openly declaring his belief in the age in which he lived, and therefore chose appropriate materials and a fitting mode of formal expression.

In contrast, Allinger acknowledged the second Swiss contribution to IGA as sounding "genuinely Swiss notes". Franz Vogel's contribution, located immediately adjacent to the Theatre Garden, was certainly committed to the moderately traditional domestic garden style. But Vogel did incorporate an eye-catching artistic feature with Max Bill's abstract, two-metre-high granite sculpture "Konstruktion", which he placed on a low concrete wall like on a plinth. This is inevitably a reminder of Bill's "Kontinuität" at ZÜKA 1947[383]. The artist had also shown this latter work against a landscape backdrop, but in such a spare way, with such self-confident independence, that it could not possibly seem like Art in Building or an artistic garden accessory. However, Gustav Allinger did not waste a single

Marble Garden by Herbert Bayer in Aspen/Colorado, 1955

Grass Mound by Herbert Bayer in Aspen, 1955

word on the abstract art-work "Konstruktion",
as its placement fitted in with the practice of
many years, and on top of that, Max Bill's art
had long become acceptable: Bill had developed
"Konstruktion" as early as 1937, and later made
several versions in granite that were installed in
the early 60s at the Schachen school complex in
Winterthur and outside the Parktheater in
Grenchen.

Roberto Burle Marx too created a highly acclaimed garden design at IGA within sight of the
Theatre Garden, a large concrete sculpture that
was also very different from Cramer's contribution. Burle Marx did not abandon either his
characteristic biomorphic ground plan nor the
magnificently coloured carpets of flowers that
were so typical of the plant-lover. Of course he
couldn't use the highly expressive tropical
species and had to make do with indigenous
flowering herbaceous plants. The Brazilian designed a garden that was highly reminiscent of
his 1955 garden for the Sul-America hospital in
Rio, with its striking circular forms, concrete
walls and seats. [384] Both gardens were cen-
tred around a circular pool set off-centre in a circular paved area and were contained spatially
by a curved wall. While the pool in Rio was planted with tropical marsh plants, in Hamburg a
concrete sculpture made up of five concrete
columns six metres high was its central feature,
looking like a starkly abstract representation of
a tropical plant. Unlike Cramer's garden, a
pavilion was to be provided for the "Brazil Garden"; however, Burle Marx was not satisfied with
Egon Jux's original design, and so the architect

made a special journey to Brazil during the
preparatory period to work with the architect on
a spiral pavilion that was appropriate to the layout of the garden. Gustav Allinger wrote about
this:

*"The 'Brazil Garden' [...] is a very 'prestigious' gar-
den by a house. Here garden architect and house
architect have again created a unity by interweav-
ing their ideas. This produced a vigorous, 'exotic'
complex that is all of a piece. [...] Anyone who is*

able to imagine this garden planted with different, i.e. Brazilian trees, shrubs and flowers will recognize that this overall solution is excellent 'in its kind'."[385]

Ultimately the "Brazil Garden", despite its ground plan, which was unusual in European eyes, represented a traditional garden concept that – similar to Franz Vogel's garden – had been developed in close association with the architecture, and framed the garden with walls, at least in the central area. While the plants provided a colourful carpet like a painting on the floor, which was best viewed from an eminence, the work of art, framed by the garden design, accentuated the central focus. People in this garden were definitely cast in the role of spectators, while in the Theatre Garden they could become the actual protagonists of the scene, and had to find a view point and a focal point for themselves, in the open three-dimensional structure. For this reason Cramer's garden can by all means be seen as an "open work of art" in Umberto Eco's sense:[386] a work of art that does not dictate a particular perception, but opens up a field of interpretative possibilities.

With the "Theatre Garden", Ernst Cramer reinforced his role as a pioneer in terms of the way in which European landscape architecture and landscape art were to develop. In addition, with his controversial project he succeeded in significantly broadening the traditional understanding of garden, architecture and sculpture. The "Theatre Garden" not only combined sculptural and architectural features and made them into a remarkable architectural sculpture, and one that is undoubtedly comparable with the prominent "Satellite Towers" in Mexico City by Mathias Goeritz and Luis Barragán.[387] Cramer also consciously built landscape components into his design, so that it is legitimate to call it an architectural landscape sculpture, which did not find its counterpart until ten years later in Michael Heizer's "Complex One" project in Nevada. Very few of Cramer's contemporaries were aware of the import of his "Theatre Garden". Even so, the International Prize Jury did award him the Bronze Medal (State Prize) of the City of Hamburg at the end of the exhibition on 13 October 1963, "for outstanding achievement at IGA 63".[388] After the horticultural show was over, the Hamburg Senate discussed the future new design for the Kleine und Grosse Wallanlagen. The chairman responsible for the overall management of IGA, retired permanent under-secretary Karl Passarge, summarized every palpable argument for keeping the Theatre Garden and wrote to the Senator responsible in November 1963:

"It must once again be pointed out that it would be extraordinarily expensive to remove the so-called Theatre Garden (Cramer, Zurich). Against this fact can be placed the possibility of using it as an open-air theatre, which is something that is not otherwise available in this strip of green, but that is highly desirable. But retaining the garden would

also get rid of the impression that Hamburg is afraid to acknowledge modern solutions in the field of garden design."[389]

But they actually got rid of the Theatre Garden.

Cableway gondolas gliding
past the concrete slabs

Swiss gardens for Richard Neutra

In the year of the "Theatre Garden", Ernst Cramer met one of the greatest modern architects for the first time, the Vienna-born American Richard Neutra.

Rentsch garden in Wengen

Fritz Rentsch was a qualified printer,[390] a pupil of the typographer Jan Tschichold. He had already identified the close link between architecture and typography while training at the Meisterschule für Druckerei in Munich. Rentsch had been interested in modern architecture even before he visited the Weissenhofsiedlung in Stuttgart in 1928/29. He took over his father's printing business in 1943 – it had originally printed chocolate paper – and transformed it into one of the most successful packaging businesses in Europe during the post-war economic boom. He had long dreamed of a holiday home for his family, and in the early 60s bought a south-facing plot with a wonderful view of the Bernese Oberland Alps in Wengen, in the famous Eiger-Mönch-Jungfrau holiday region. A little later he came across Richard Neutra's book???Life and shape???.[391] He enquired eagerly at the Verlag für Architektur publishing house in Zurich whether Richard Neutra also built in Europe, and found that Neutra was due in that city only two days later. The two men arranged to meet, and agreed to build the house. Neutra asked the family to write an essay describing a day in their holiday home, and came to Switzerland with his wife Dione. Fritz Rentsch was impressed by the lively interest his American guest took in everything connected with the culture and history of the place, and undertook lengthy expeditions with Neutra.

Neutra and Cramer were obviously very similar in terms of their sensitivity to their clients' wishes, and they also had in common the fact that they had both studied under Gustav Ammann.[392] Ernst Cramer had known the Rentsch family, and Frau Rentsch in particular, for a long time, and was always consulted if something needed to be designed or looked after in their properties in Schönenwerd and Muri. So of course Cramer became involved in the new project in Wengen. Discussions with Neutra about modern architecture were very important for Cramer, even though the two were presumably not entirely in agreement about garden architecture.

The Rentsch house was not a simple project either for Richard Neutra or his on-site architects in Switzerland, the Zurich practice of Bruno Honegger, who were responsible for realizing the building. Neutra'a modern design ran counter to the local ideas of traditional houses that fitted in with the image of the place, and so the responsible authorities in the form of the local building commission and the Swiss countryside protection organization in the Bernese

Design plan for the
Rentsch garden in Wengen

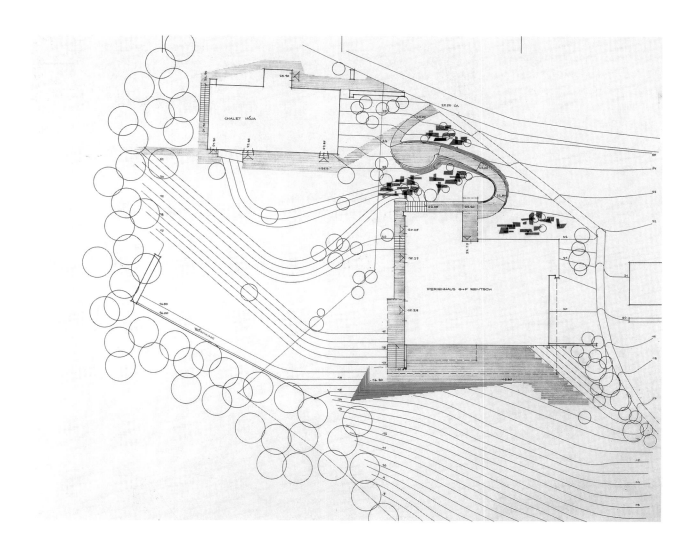

duce the danger of cracking caused by frost or water, but the architect from the responsible authority insisted that the joints should follow the traditional pattern. Neutra was ultimately able to resolve this dispute in his favour. What he finally built was a two-storey, spaciously conceived building with façades in timber, glass and natural stone, and about 420 square metres of floor space. This was divided into two separate dwellings with high, south-facing windows and sliding glass doors on to the terraces. Both floors had so-called "reflecting pools" in front of them, providing flat surfaces of water that replaced the missing balcony parapets and reflected the magnificent mountain landscape. Along with the far protruding timber beams, the pools enhanced the impression that the landscape was thrusting into the interior completely, and contributed to the contrast-filled dialogue between the warmth of the living area and the frosty chill of the snowy mountain region.

The grandiose landscape put the question of how to design the garden for the 2300 square

The shell of the Rentsch house in Wengen ...

... with a view of the Jungfrau massif

Deliberate closeness to the landscape
in the Rentsch house

Reflecting pools enhance the gandiose
scenery in Wengen

Oberland objected violently to the proposed flat roof for the holiday home, complaining that it did not fit in with the landscape and that it was setting a precedent. Neutra argued that a flat roof was the appropriate response to a landscape that was impressively framed by jagged mountain peaks.

"Nothing makes the wonderful silhouettes of the Swiss mountains look higher and fixes them so permanently in visitor's minds as the horizontal reflecting surfaces of the Swiss lakes. The horizontal line accentuates the soaring quality and does not compete with it," explained the architect in a personal letter to Fritz Rentsch.[393]

But permission to build was not granted until almost a year later, when he submitted a design with a slightly sloping gable roof with an angle in the ridge. Another point of conflict was that the architect wanted to clad part of the outer walls with a blind facing of natural stone, placing the long, narrow natural quarry-stones vertically, to emphasize that the facing was not load-bearing, and also, as the client explained, to create a relationship with the wooded surroundings. The vertical joints were also intended to re-

metre site in an unusual light. It also fitted in with Neutra's view of the garden as a frame for architecture that is left largely in its natural state, or conceived in a way that is very close to nature, and his opinion that the surrounding area should be designed formally if at all. For this reason Ernst Cramer restricted himself largely to a loose frame for the central clearing made up of trees and shrubs planted individually. As with all other examples of modern building that Cramer had encountered so far, here too we find the classical idea of the crystalline building in a free landscape designed without constraint, and the design of the informally handled access paths had to conform. In projects like this the range of opportunities available to the garden architect was certainly very limited on the surface, but his understanding of the situation and the lack of heavy-handed design is eloquent testimony of his marked sensitivity to the interplay between modern architecture and landscape. It is typical that Cramer did not publish a photograph of the garden in *Anthos*, but showed the water terrace in front of the living-rooms, with the landscape reflected in it. [394] The Zurich garden architect had already used the principle of the reflecting pool effectively in other major projects, and realized that garden design was not a matter of responding to architecture and landscape using traditional horticultural resources at any price. As if he had wanted to once again underline these correlations, the same edition of *Anthos* carried a picture of the pool in the Theatre Garden in Hamburg and a photograph of the Schmidlin garden.

Bucerius garden in Brione

A single image in the same issue also captured with unerring accuracy the second project by Richard Neutra that Cramer worked on a short time later: the house built for Ebelin Bucerius in Ticino. [395] It is dominated by a curved retaining wall accompanying an asphalted path and built of the typical, vertically placed natural quarry stone. The counterpart to this wall, which is effectfully lit at night, is a traditional Ticino rustico, an archaic-looking structure, also completely in natural stone and as homogeneous as the modern wall. A powerful natural accent is set by a large chestnut-tree, which fills that upper right-hand corner of the image. This photograph shows nothing of Neutra's actual building, nor of the garden, and yet the elegant pictorial composition with the three simple elements dating from different periods, the wall, the house and the tree, express the kind of sensitive dialogue between nature and culture that had become particularly important to Ernst Cramer. The clear lines of the built elements creating a tension-filled contrast with natural form was just as central an interest for Cramer as the art of placing tradition and Modernism in a new relationship. In particular in the Ticino gardens, Cramer had previously succeeded only with difficulty in finding a modern expressive form that emancipated itself clearly from the traditional vocabulary of design. It seems as though Neutra gave him important advice in this context, which Cramer was able to put into practice in a remarkable way years later, in his last large Ticino garden in Sonvico near Lugano. [396]

The Bucerius House, set in a picturesque landscape about 700 metres above Lago Maggiore, was built in 1966 for the Hamburg politician, publisher and journalist Gerd Bucerius and his

wife Ebelin. Ticino had started to become a popular holiday domicile for a large number of eminent Germans immediately after the war, and so the publisher and his wife found themselves in the best possible company, not far from Locarno. The German client and the American star architect were introduced to each other by an editor of *Die ZEIT*, Eka von Merveldt. [397] Bucerius, the founder of the influential liberal weekly paper *Die ZEIT* and co-proprietor of the magazine *Stern*, bought a secluded plot of land about 10,000 square metres in area above Brione and commissioned Richard Neutra to build a house with 550 square metres of floor space on a south-facing ridge, at a price of four million Swiss francs. At the time of writing, visitors still cross the valley of a little brook and continue along a long, private drive partially lined with walls of natural stone to reach the three-

would have the best views the house had to offer. The panelled ceiling of the living room reached from the staircase to the roof of the terrace, the floor of polished granite to the veranda. Ebelin Bucerius, who in the beginning had been very sceptical and was not sympathetic towards the architect, admitted later: 'This house has tremendous refinements.' [...] 'He built the house, as it were, into the mountain.'"[398]

One of the refinements was a garden floor with guest rooms and a swimming-pool about ten by five metres in size. This runs seamlessly from the interior with adjacent conservatory to the outdoor area. In the cold seasons, a sophisticated mechanism makes it possible to separate the heated indoor pool from the open-air section at the touch of a button. A large sliding glass screen shuts off the room, while part of the floor of the pool folds up under water and divides it appropriately.

But reticent design was called for in this project as well, so that the basic idea of modern architecture would not be contradicted in the midst

Tradition and Modernity
in granite at the Bucerius house

The Rustico work in the
former Bucerius garden

Richard Neutra inspecting
the building site in Brione

storey house with a flat roof, which at first blocks the extensive view. Ascending a short flight of exterior steps to the main floor and passing through the entrance hall into the spacious living-room with fireplace, it becomes clear that here too, Neutra was principally concerned with the clients' needs and with establishing close contact with nature. Neutra told his client Ebelin Bucerius:

"He would bring the mountains into the bedroom. Consequently the bedroom had two connecting glass walls which offered panoramic views across the whole of Lake Maggiore and the mountain ranges in the background. Where building regulations demanded a railing he created a moat which reflects moonlight. The kitchen would be compact in design as well as in furnishing to ease the work for the cook, the dressing room would also be the lady's study and the laundry room for the housekeeper

of the grandiose world of the Ticino mountains. But in contrast with the Rentsch house, some plans show that Cramer was rather more intensively involved in this case. [399] He was not only responsible for building the unusual natural

Cramer's informal design principle
shows clearly in this variant on the garden
plan for Gerd Bucerius

General plan with elevations of
the Bucerius house in Brione with precise
terrain modelling

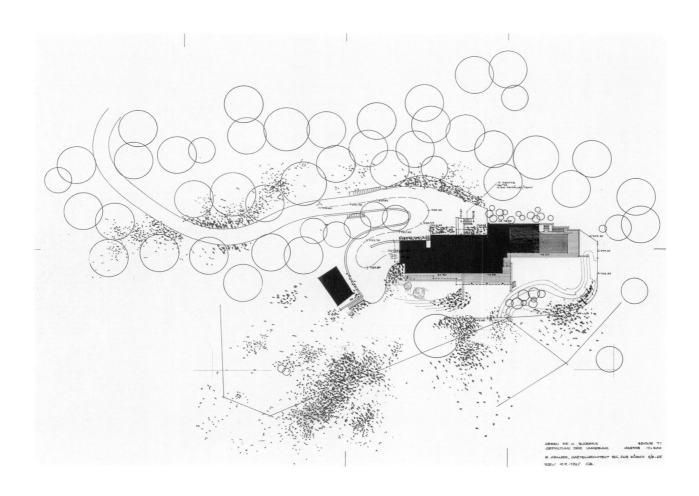

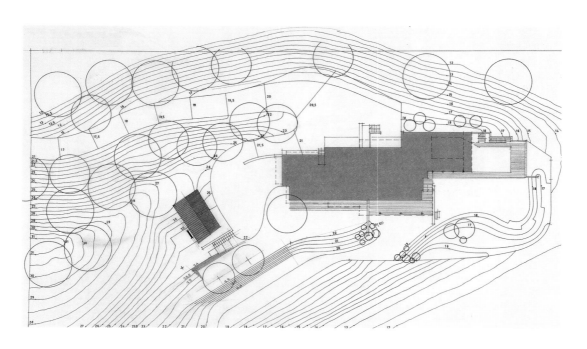

Still easily recognizable: Cramers
sensitive terrain modelling

Special finesse, yesterday as today:
the pool in the former Bucerius garden

was fond of bourgeois comforts, and fought the austerity of the modern architecture with chintz curtains at the windows and ruched cushions in the interior. [401] Cramer went for a touch of seasonal colour only at the prestigious entrance to the house, with a rhododendron planting. Otherwise he had the sloping site terraced without retaining walls, to make it easier to walk around and also as a response to the staggered nature of the architecture. The terraced site ran gradually into the topography of the surrounding area. The landscape principle was the key to the planting. Cramer created an informal transition from the garden to the surrounding wooded countryside with a fringe of shrubs. Decorative shrubs planted like a backdrop provided a loose frame for the lower edge of the slope. Existing trees that did not block the view were retained and built into the garden design.

The logic of the modern urban square

Sulzer Tower square in Winterthur

The wide range of projects on which Cramer was consulted shows how sensitively he responded to architecture and the specific brief in each case. Whether it was a luxurious villa in the Alps or a prestigious high-rise building in the foothills, Cramer's approach was always to apply a similar design strategy, which was intuitive and analytical in its way, and this also applied to what was then the tallest building in Switzerland, located in Winterthur.

Sulzer, the international technology group, did not build high-rise office building 222, completed in 1966, as a mere sign of commercial prosperity. The distinguished Basel architects Suter and Suter were also stamping their mark on the urban profile of this venerable Swiss industrial city with their elegant building, almost 93 metres high, and with a slender aluminium and steel façade. Planning began as early as 1962, when Gebrüder Sulzer, Inc. wanted to create about 2000 new office spaces for future employees and those working in temporary facili-

Tropical interior planting in the Bucerius house

View to the south-east

Slope terracing for the Bucerius house

stone walls on the drive. Correct modelling of the site and planting in the garden were particularly important as well. Neutra had set up meteorological instruments long before building started to find out precisely what the local climatic conditions were. He occasionally came to the site during the building period and erected temporary scaffolding, [400] so that he could see what the view was like from any particular point and adjust the building height where necessary. Ebelin Bucerius, the actual mistress of the house in Brione for years, was a plant-lover and wanted some colour highlights in the garden. This cannot have been greeted with much enthusiasm from either the architect or the garden architect. In general, the lady of the house

Nightscape of the Sulzer office high-rise building in Winterthur

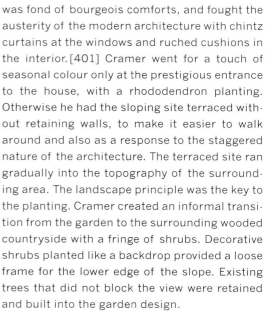

ties. With their clean architecture, meticulously adapted to functional needs, the architects' practice of Hans Rudolf Suter and Peter Suter had acquired a good reputation in booming Swiss commercial and industrial building from the 50s onwards. This project too was preceded by a comprehensive analysis. When it showed that it would not be possible to find a satisfactory solution within the cantonal building regulations with four- to five-storey buildings, a decision was taken to construct a 24-storey high-rise building with an internal access core on a square ground plan of approximately 32 by 32 metres. A second tower was originally planned, and then abandoned. The façade, articulated vertically and built in light-grey aluminium that reflected only slightly, the uniform window glazing, and the extremely slender roof cornice, without any structures on top of the building, were intended to form a crystalline structure that would accentuate Winterthur's valley site. External concrete piers about 60 centimetres wide create a three-dimensional effect that breaks all four façades down into six bays. The architects did not use these supports at the corners, and here came up with bays that were two rather than three windows wide.

Ernst Cramer was commissioned to design the prestigious outdoor areas and was required to take the adjacent line of green along the little river Eulach into account as well. It is no longer known in detail how the work was allocated. Cramer had known the Vogel-Sulzers, a family of industrialists, for years, [402] and two reasons for the commission may have been his work for Fritz Rentsch, for whom Suter and Suter had already built factories, and his excellent reputation. The first surviving plans in the estate date from December 1964; [403] all the later, detailed working plans were produced in the Basel architects' office. [404]

Cramer's design process was generally based on an analysis of the basic architectural principle and the geometrical structures of the building. As shown by the Neutra buildings, he worked – according to the task at hand – either by creating contrasts with a given structure, or else by adapting his design to the basic principles of the architecture involved. In Winterhur he pursued the second strategy and took his line directly from the striking concrete piers and the square ground plan of the high-rise building. Early preliminary designs show clearly that Cramer took up the motif of the square first, and divided the whole of the open space into a squared grid with an eleven-metre mesh, derived from the grid on which the tower's piers were placed. [405] With a few exceptions, all the planned elements were to have been subjected to this system, while the distance between the planned trees would have structured to the area regularly, but independently of the grid, and would have created a link with the strip of green by the Eulach. But the grid did not fit uniformly on all four sides of the tower, which meant that

The sign of economic prosperity in Winterthur

The entrance to the Sulzer office tower

Subtle linking of interior and exterior
in a photograph by Peter Heman

Reflecting pool with "floating" stone slabs

Island-hopping in Winterthur 1968

A skilful combination of
architecture and square design

areas of gravel would have had to compensate for this. Cramer was not content with this compromise solution.

Cramer revised the design again by simplifying the grid and attaching five bands of paving stones to each of the four façades, precisely adapted in their dimensions to the outer supports of the building, which were about 60 centimetres wide. The light bands of paving stones were set in a homogeneous asphalt and ran in a straight line to the extreme edge of the urban square, with no separate design for the pavement along the adjacent Neuwiesenstrasse and Schützenstrasse. None of the available open spaces were to have delineated edges, thus anchoring the office building in its surroundings. Cramer even continued the linear pattern on the south, opposite side of Neuwiesenstrasse, thus establishing a link with the old office building. As there were no piers on the corners of the tower, Cramer did not attach bands there, but continued the line pattern consistently, so that no part of the urban square was left blank. The original car-park markings, which were indicated on the square in a very restrained manner, identified generous parking spaces that gave the trees a lot of room and did not spoil the elegance of the design in any way. The glazed lobby with its bold roof constructed from large-format prefabricated elements on slender supports, surrounded by magnificent solitaire trees, still offers visitors a prestigious welcome. The strict limitation to a maximum of 30 centimetres of build up on the underground car-park and the air-raid shelter was not noticable in the design. The tower and its surroundings form an impressive ensemble, one of the most elegant creations in 1960s Winterthur.

The core of this ensemble in terms of landscape architecture was the large "reflecting pool" in front of the east façade of the tower. The pool measured about 16 by 32 metres, and was placed in front of the impressive façade like a mirror; it was the counterpart to the lobby in the ground

Design for the square by the Sulzer high-rise building in Winterthur (not realized)

Detailed plan, as executed, for the square by the Sulzer high-rise building

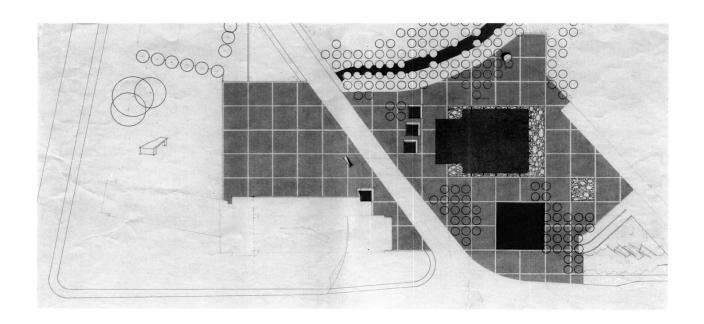

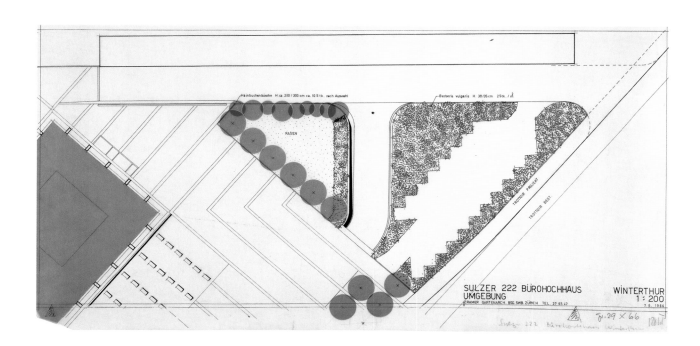

plan. In order to continue the structural lines of the square in the lobby, Cramer ordered U-shaped prefabricated concrete elements with specially finished facings, and placed them in the water similarly to the arrangement for the Poet's Garden, so that they crossed the surface like a line made up of dashes. The elements looked like stone slabs floating on the surface of the water, and tempted the children of the area into "island-hopping" in the summer. Simple concrete benches and also "floating" plant troughs in the same format and lighting arranged in a grid pattern were among the sparse furnishings in the square. Unfortunately this formerly elegant square is in a neglected state at the time of writing.[406] The pool was drained because it was leaking and the concrete elements were removed. It takes a closer look to discern that the overall design of the square was derived consistently from the structure of the building.

A logical approach to the design process and the comprehensibility of the design decisions

were crucially important both for Suter and Suter and for Cramer. The architects and the garden architect also had in common their striving for puritanical sobriety. Their mutual understanding led in later years to intensive co-operation between Ernst Cramer and Suter and Suter, who realized a whole series of industrial buildings, in particular for the Basel chemical group Ciba-Geigy.

Architecture and landscape architecture in dialogue as seen by photographer Peter Heman

By the Sulzer office tower in Winterthur today

LANDSCAPE AND GARDEN AS SCULPTURAL SPACES

While the early 50s saw a clear break in Cramer's work, the change in stylistic direction in the mid 60s was more like a correction of course. At that time, Cramer was searching for an up-to-date form of architectonic garden design, but now a new theme was emerging. This was summed up in 1987 by Emil Steiner, who had been a devoted friend of Cramer's and a journalist committed to his work for a long time: *"In the gardens he created after his 60th birthday, which can be counted as the late work, his sculptural approach increasingly gained the upper hand. Examples like the: reflecting pool outside the Sulzer tower in Winterthur, [407] the open spaces for the technical college in Winterthur, [408] a fountain in Tösstal [409] and the main square in Vaduz [410] are well-known instances of this. All his sketching and modelling developed into a kind of consistent form-giving that was not completed until, in his eyes, the greatest possible purity had been achieved."[411]* But the formal precision that Cramer had developed in his architecturally driven gardens and the sensitivity with which he responded to architecture and art continued to be characteristic features of his work. And equally, he did not abandon his inclination towards abstraction and reduction in his late work, but continued to look for formal purity and clarity of design.

"Zeitgeist", criticism of the age and Scandinavian influences in the 60s

The new sources that Ernst Cramer opened up to in the mid 60s were indicated in 1964, when a foreign colleague joined Cramer's practice. The Zurich office in Manessestrasse was coping with a large volume of commissions, which had increased enormously again since the early 60s. There were only four people working in the office and about ten to twelve employees on site, whereas Cramer was compelled to identify essential and inessential projects. He rarely considered turning down commissions. Ernst Racheter continued to direct the tree nursery in Suhr and regularly supervised projects, but he was essentially independent of the Zurich office. Heinz Rimensberger, who had looked after project management, plan drawing and model building for eight years, left the practice in 1963 and, like other former employees became a garden designer in his own right, without maintaining Cramer's garden design style. In 1964 a young colleague joined the office staff,

which consisted of Cramer's wife Gertrud Cramer, Fritz Dové and Karl Pappa. The new recruit was Christofer Bengt Eriksson, and — rather like Willi Neukom before him — he brought new ideas with him. The 25-year-old Swede was the only employee in Cramer's practice who had a university degree in garden architecture. In 1961 he had already undergone a period of practical training as a gardener in Switzerland with Walter and Klaus Leder, on the recommendation of a Stockholm garden architect. The following year he started to study garden architecture at the Royal Academy of Art in Copenhagen, which was strongly influenced by the teaching of Professor Carl Theodor Sørensen in particular. After Eriksson had been awarded his diploma in 1964, Sørensen's former assistant, the garden architect Sven-Ingvar Andersson, offered him a position in Copenhagen. But Eriksson decided to work in Switzerland again, and applied to Willi Neukom, Fred Eicher and Ernst Cramer for jobs.

Cramer accepted Christofer Eriksson's application, and first subjected the young academic, like all other new employees, to the usual test by regularly confronting him with hastily-made sketches and demanding a detailed development in ultra-quick time. [412] If the result was not satisfactory, Cramer's criticism was usually short, harsh and uncompromising. Sometimes the young garden architect was provoked and answered back. If a design had been developed satisfactorily, it was usually accepted without comment. Cramer — nothing had changed in this respect over the decades — was not a friend of office work. He did not feel in his element until out of the office and visiting sites. His employees report that Cramer liked to combine appointments of this kind with regular visits to selected restaurants. Here he would usually produce sketches for the next project on napkins, envelopes, bills or something similar, and these would then have to be interpreted and developed in the office. Cramer rarely drew plans himself, but was out and about a lot and left his employees to work out the plans, which he then often disregarded once he was back on site. Cramer's personal appearance and the extraordinary nature of his projects got the practice the reputation of being something of an outsider outfit in the mid 60s; it was always viewed somewhat sceptically by other garden architects.

Eriksson had been profoundly impressed by the elementary simplicity that C. Th. Sørensen had taught him in Copenhagen. Formal austerity, clarity of line, restrained use of carefully chosen plants and building materials, and not least a marked sense of effective spatial structuring were the characteristic qualities of Danish garden architecture even at that time. Eriksson admired this approach in Ernst Cramer's work as well, which ultimately made it easier for the two men to understand each other. After a time they were working together so well that Christofer Eriksson gradually succeeded in incorporating the design ideas that he had brought with him from Denmark into his day-to-day work, and it showed. New expressive forms started to make their presence felt in Cramer's open space design; and this was not confined to the three major projects that Eriksson was particularily involved and interested in while working for Cramer: the Looren school in Witikon, Zurich, the urban square in Aarau for the new Aargau Electricity (AEW) headquarters and the Bruderholzspital near Basel.

The Scandinavian influence on Cramer's projects showed above all in the reduced range of plants he used. Even at the time, Danish garden architecture handled woody plants in a consistent and uniform way, especially with regard to trimmed hedges. Even today the tension-filled, flexible open space concepts by Gudmund Nyeland Brandt, Carl Theodor Sørensen, Sven-Ingvar Andersson and Gunnar Martinsson, whose work Cramer had got to know at IGA 63 in Hamburg, are characterized by sensitive ground modelling and virtuoso use of hedges as space-defining elements.

We know that Cramer was interested in Scandinavian culture and especially in Danish design, which even then was considered to be timeless, not least because of his extensive travels in Denmark, Norway and Finland from 1965 onwards. He was impressed not only by the spare beauty of the Scandinavian countryside, but also admired the elegant austerity of the landscape architecture. Sven-Ingvar Andersson was always available as a host and connoisseur of Danish landscape architecture on his visits to Denmark. Carl Theodor Sørensen's pioneering work in particular, for example the well-known complex of allotments in Naerum, dating from 1948, was always top of the list of places to visit when Cramer was in Copenhagen. According to Andersson, Sørensen was very much inclined towards Futurism, and preferred to work with pragmatic, precisely articulated forms. He did not base them on simple, orthogonal systems, however, but achieved greater tension through the use of the oval, which was deployed with particular mastery in the Naerum allotments mentioned above. This composition used a large number of oval hedges of the same size – precisely trimmed hedges to enclose the allotments – to create a spatial structure of breath-taking elegance. One still moves between these man-high hedges in a dynamic space that was perfectly choreographed by the garden architect.

Cramer was impressed by the spatial and formal effect made by this design.[413] But the oval in Sørensen's work did not only appear in the form of precisely trimmed hedges, it was also important for soil modelling and as the basic shape for sunken garden spaces.

The simplicity and power of the traditional Modern formal language in Danish garden architecture is clearly present as a new and important element in Cramer's late work. He skilfully combined this new influence with his eye for creating architectural space, and continued to develop his unmistakably expressive designs in the course of the next few years. The days of strictly architectonic garden design were rapidly coming to an end for the 66-year-old Cramer, yielding to a new inclination towards more expressive, freer forms.

The biographical and creative background that influenced the change in Cramer's late work are important, but we must not overlook the accompanying social circumstances in the late 60s, a time characterized in particular by extraordinarily rapid economic and social change, reflected in all spheres of life. In Switzerland in particular a marked Neo-Liberalism led to a climate of exceptional economic growth. A remarkable building boom, the rapid expansion of the motorway network, the building of the first atomic reactor in 1965 and the swift spread of television were only a few of the external indications of this development. It was not until the end of the decade that the limits of growth were showing all over the world. Military conflicts were dominating the daily headlines and there were signs of saturation in the consumer society. A process of decay set in – accelerated by vehement youth protests – that also shook the foundations of

all the disciplines relating to the design of the environment. In fine art, against the background of a society of super-abundance that was changing in a succession of various crises, a young avant-garde started critically examining traditional views of art and the predominant system of cultural values at a very early stage. Thus Op Art, Minimal Art and Happening were increasingly successful in the United States from the mid 60s. Land Art and Arte Povera also emerged at this time of unleashed stylistic pluralism. Key Swiss names here were Bernhard Luginbühl and Daniel Spoerri, but there was scarcely any other Swiss artist in those years who so accurately captured the euphoric delusion of the belief in boundless growth as Jean Tinguely. His gigantic steel sculpture "Heureka" (Eureka) created a sensation at EXPO 64 in Lausanne.

Ultimately Cramer was not able to avoid being drawn into the 60s whirlpool of technical progress, a booming economy, falling barriers in the perception of art, social tensions, the limits of growth, and criticism of the establishment. It was only because he was so experienced that he did not lose his equilibrium in face of the wide-spread disorientation in society and culture.

when seen against the background of the way in which Cramer's formal language had developed so far. But here the key impetus for the design did not come from Cramer himself.

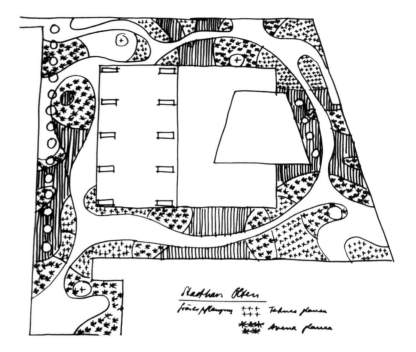

Biomorphic monochromaticism

Roof garden for the Olten town hall

The 1965 roof garden for the Olten town hall shows above all Cramer's tendency to further reduce the range of plants used, even in public gardens. The design of the paths and the handling of the lines seem like a vigorous countermovement to the architectonic garden style

The large town hall, designed by architects Frey & Egger with Werner Peterhans of Bern and Solothurn was intended to make a modern urban impact in the middle of the town and in close vicinity to the town church. Alois Egger, a former student of Hans Hofmann's at the ETH, was the architect in charge of the project. His design followed ground-breaking works by Le Corbusier. He developed a complex of buildings consisting of a single-storey base building containing the council chamber, and a ten-storey high-rise building supported by pilotis. The base building was shaped to form an atrium, into which the architects introduced a closed, windowless cube based on a trapezium-shaped ground plan, which still contains the council chamber today. Inserting this building produced two intimate internal courtyards, glazed on three sides, which provided light for the entrance hall and the corridors. To emphasize the link between the exterior and the interior, the black slate floor of the entrance hall was continued in the interior courtyards. The high-rise office volume set on top was designed to be relatively narrow, which kept it a generous distance from the neighbouring buildings and gave a view of the roof garden on the base building. "Brise-soleils" on the side façades, an integral component of the façade structure, define the outward appearance of the building. The rough-shuttered, unrendered concrete façades add to the impression that this is a Modern structure in the language of Le Corbusier.

Planting plan for the roof garden of the town hall in Olten with pfitzer juniper, fescue and ornamental blue oats

The roof garden as planted, reduced to a monochrome scheme with juniper "Pfitzeriana" and fescue (Festuca glauca "Superba")

Anyone coming up one of the two flights of stairs from the adjacent streets and into the public roof gardens of the town hall would be reminded of Rio de Janeiro and the Ministry of Education and Health. [414] There are definite parallels, not just in the relationship between the modern office high-rise and the designed roof terrace. The layout of the roof garden with its elegantly curving exposed aggregate concrete paths is entirely in the style of Roberto Burle Marx. But Cramer himself was more interested in relating to Niemeyer's architecture than to Burle Marx's garden architecture. In fact the architect Alois Egger took credit for the Brazilian look of the garden architecture. [415] Though Egger had never visited Brazil, he was so impressed by Roberto Burle Marx's work that he showed Ernst Cramer his design for the biomorphic lines for the paths almost a year before the new building was ready to be handed over to the clients. He did not have any difficulty in convincing the garden architect, whose work he greatly admired, as Cramer was enthusiastic about the work of architects and garden architects in Brazil. This explains why the basic lines for the paths and planted areas are consistent in the various designs dating from spring 1965. [416] Alois Egger had already largely defined them.

As far as the choice of plants was concerned, Cramer developed several variants ranging from colourful diversity to monochrome simplicity, then decided on reduction, and submitted a radically simplified planting plan confining the selection for the surfaces to fescue (Festuca glauca "Superba") and juniper (Juniperus chinensis "Pfitzeriana"). Cramer finally even decided to abandon the oat (Avena glauca) that had been included in an intermediate stage of the design as a third, bluish-green, plant variety, in favour of a

strictly monochromatic approach. He did not simply cover sections of the garden with one and the same plant, but superimposed another system of biomorphic areas on the defined areas, thus creating small, interrelated partial areas.

The result not only convinced Ernst Cramer, who always enjoyed criticizing the hotch-potches produced by some gardeners. The architect too, who wanted a grey-green garden composition to go with the rough-shuttered, unrendered concrete, was also satisfied when the garden and the building were completed in December 1965. But the gardening trade met the design with pronounced scepticism, not just because of alleged problems in maintaining the gardens.

"There are no dominant colours of the kind that make it possible for us to experience Burle-Marx' ornamental gardens as abstract paintings," wrote the garden journalist Heini Mathys in 1969. *"Thus the quality of the experience offered by this roof garden is reduced to a minimum, to mere formality, and to the two shades of green offered by Juniperus and Festuca. Some architects may feel that a mini-garden effect of this kind is ideal, as the primitive nature of its planting lies in the same realm as their own planting ideas. But it is easy to overlook that this primitive approach to planting courts the double danger of making mistakes in the choice of plants. The more ruthlessly the range is reduced, the more important it becomes to make the right choice, and in this respect the requisite knowledge of and experience with plants are often lacking, and this does not apply only to architects."* [417]

Other gardeners also accused Cramer of a lack of knowledge of plants, and described the roof garden planting as a complete swindle. They pointed out that the grasses chosen would never form a complete ground cover. But in fact, as

Photograph of the roof garden by Emil Steiner, summer 1968

Roof garden by Roberto Burle Marx of the Ministry of Education and Health in Rio de Janeiro as of 1999

Typical Brazilian planting in a characteristic design by Burle Marx

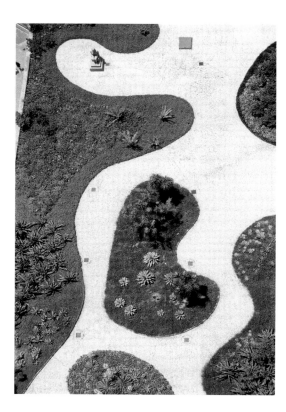

Emil Steiner described it, the planting developed quite well at first, until the caretaker started to plant brightly coloured tulips. He did so to stop visitors complaining how boring the planting scheme was. The condition of the garden deteriorated visibly from then on. [418]

Very few people realized at the time that Cramer's reduction of the range of plants was not caused by either professional ineptitude or lack of ideas, but was an attempt to set beneficial simplicity against the current design babble. Cramer responded in a similar way in the two inner courtyards of the town hall, and planted rhododendrons within the dark slate slab surface. Here too he paid particular attention to homogeneous colours and the different textures in the space. The dark, coarse leaves of the rhododendrons still make a charming contrast with the smooth slate grey of the ground. When the rhododendrons are in flower, the effect made by the colour is so much the greater, and sculptor Heinz Schwarz's bronze sculpture is shifted into a different light. In these inner courtyards the refined and reticent atmosphere has survived, but the impressive effect of the once classically Modern roof garden has been lost since it was changed into a biotope area. [419]

Spatial sequencing by topography

Open spaces for the Grüzefeld housing estate in Winterthur

The design for the open spaces on the Grüzefeld housing estate in Winterthur is one of the major projects in which new tendencies in Cramer's design showed uncompromisingly. Building started on the estate in March 1965. It was not only seen as an important contribution to the discussion on social housing, but it was significant in terms of the development of building with prefabricated concrete elements. The town of Winterthur had announced the ideas competition for this large scale project as long ago as 1960, and the winners were the CJP studio of architects Fred Cramer, Werner Jaray, Claude Paillard and Peter Leemann of Zurich and Winterthur. Building was held up for years because the town did not yet own the land, and it was not possible to make a start on the project until four cooperative housing associations had joined together. Paillard and Leemann in particular were involved in this project in realizing reasonably priced housing, with 370 dwellings and 35 different types of accommodation. The design is determined by two basic ideas: on the one hand, the entire estate was to be assembled of consistently arranged spatial groups, to be achieved by building with prefabricated elements. On the other hand, the level site was to be designed as a differentiated residential landscape with extensive open spaces, which gave Cramer significant scope in his design. Cramer was not part of the competition team, but was commissioned to design and construct the open spaces at an early stage. He was by no means an unknown partner for the young, successful CJP studio: Cramer had been responsible for the open space design for one of the studio's earliest projects, the Rainacker housing estate in Rekingen, in 1948. He had also worked for Charles Cramer, Fred Cramer's father, in Vaduz, when designing his garden.

In Grüzefeld, Cramer was confronted with a housing estate that the journalist Emil Steiner was later to call a "gigantic concrete sculpture": *"And so when looking [...] at the 'Grüzefeld' estate illustrated here we should try to understand a shape that is unfamiliar to the eye as the expression of a certain sculptural notion. Seen from a distance, it is rather like a Cubist-Constructivist sculpture (e.g. Malevich's 'Architectonics',*

Play area seen from above

Grüzefeld estate in Winterthur, a gigantic concrete sculpture

Cramer reduced the range of available structural and planting materials to very few elements, which he used consistently to build up the structure of the open spaces. Even in plan it is noticeable that Cramer consistently adapted all the estate's paths to the buildings' oblique façades, which produced a stringent system of diagonals. All the paths were paved with a type of large-format, long concrete slab, and these were skilfully laid in different variations according to use and changes of direction. The only exceptions were timber paving for certain play areas, and the use of natural stone at key points. This way of predominantly using standardized building materials was based on the theory of prefabricated building. Significant height differences were mastered with ramps or steps, and in some cases with grassed steps. These grassed steps, built with concrete slabs as risers, were a new and striking element in Cramer's repertoire, and they were used particularly effectively in one central area of the estate. Here he combined the steps with a slide and the adjacent children's playground. The children on the estate were especially fond of the simply furnished playgrounds and above all of the shallow paddling-pool by the maisonettes. Its striking shape and

1924–1928), as a 'residential castle', protecting the residents from disturbing influences from the outside world, without isolating them from their surroundings. A kind of cellular structure with living, spatially and functionally structured plasma inside, as well as a breathing outer skin that enables and partially regulates metabolism."[420]
This impression of a cellular structure referred to the prefabricated method used to build the four large residential blocks with their differentiated designs, varying between two and twelve storeys and arranged on staggered ground plans. A small section containing maisonettes and supply facilities formed the core of the estate. Despite the great variety of building heights and dwelling sizes, the estate looked homogenous because of the exposed concrete façades, all of which were grey and untreated, but also because of the open space design. This consistently matched the architecture, and had not only to be resistant to wear, but easy to maintain.

For Ernst Cramer the challenge lay in making the estate's open spaces unmistakable and homogeneous in character, while at the same time addressing a wide variety of demands imposed by use, access and maintenance. Here Cramer did without artistic and sculptural interventions of the kind he had used in the Wilerfeld estate in Olten and Badenerstrasse in Zurich. Perhaps he thought that the architecture was already sculptural enough, or possibly the budget was too tight for experiments of that kind. Instead,

attractive quality for children have been retained to the present day, despite a few changes. Residents still enjoy relaxing on the adjacent lawns and in the shade of the plane trees, which are now fully grown.
Cramer was mainly interested in the tree planting here, as that was the only thing that would still work as a framework for the space, even in another 50 years, Christofer Eriksson explained

The terrace with play apparatus
(now destroyed)

Plane-tree branches in front
of a modular concrete façade,
impression by Emil Steiner

Children's play area by
the central grassy steps

Central square in the
Grüzefeld estate with pool

Concrete boards as uniform
paving on the estate

later. And indeed even today hundreds of plane trees, placed in grids, planted as trees in avenues or to provide a tree-roof, still give the open spaces their impressive character. Cramer used the plane trees to formulate the higher, overall spatial structure of the housing estate. He used hornbeams (Carpinus betulus) only rarely as hedges to provide borders for play areas and as protective planting along the access roads. A third type of woody plant, the evergreen decorative juniper (Juniperus chinensis

Even today the large-format concrete slabs form the pavements on the Grüzefeld estate

The swimming pool in the middle of the Grüzefeld estate

An attraction for children even decades after it was constructed

"Pfitzeriana"), which Cramer also liked using in housing estates built on terraces, was used for roof planting. But the most striking feature was the mass planting with yellow dogwood (Cornus stolonifera "Flaviramea"), which he planted on all the spaces in front of the ground floor dwellings, the underground garage entrances and other areas that served very little useful purpose. The dogwood added touches of particularly fresh green in the spring and summer, and its light green, yellowish wood caught the eye in winter. This vigorous woody plant was also extremely robust and easy to trim, which was to reduce care and maintenance costs.

Once again both the residents and professionals had difficulty with this kind of mass planting. They failed to see that Cramer was concerned

first and foremost to create exciting, viable spatial sequences that responded to contemporary architecture and urbanism and could be filled with life. From this point onwards he increasingly worked with mass planting in other projects as well, in order to create clear, uniform open spaces, even though this strategy later attracted violent criticism on ecological grounds, and was sometimes even attacked as showing a lack of ability in garden design. At a time when the naturalistic garden style was still enjoying a great deal of popularity, experiments of the kind that Cramer risked had considerable rarity value. Emil Steiner also recognized this when he wrote: "The planted areas on the 'Grüzefeld' housing estate may seem like an experiment, but they are an experiment that deserves to be observed in terms of how it develops and what effect it will have in future."[421]

School yard for the Looren school in Witikon, Zurich

Some of the new design elements that Ernst Cramer had first tried out on a grand scale for the Grüzefeld housing estate reappeared in more highly developed forms in the design for the Looren school complex in Witikon, Zurich, and still give the school its characteristic appearance today. The complex, its first section completed in 1967, goes back to a competition held in 1960, which was won by the Zurich architects Eduard Del Fabro and Bruno Gerosa. In the 50s, the architects, who worked together from 1955 to 1966, had built some of the low pavilion schools typical at the time in the Canton of Zurich, and Cramer had occasionally worked on the design as well. Cramer had first worked with Eduard Del Fabro, a student of Otto Salvisberg, on building the "Im Untermoos" primary school in Altstetten, Zurich, in 1955.[422] He was also already involved as garden architect for the later "Im Feld" school project in Wetzikon, which Del Fabro and Gerosa developed between 1957 and 1967 as a complex to be extended in stages, interestingly called the "growing school building". The team was able to continue this successful collaboration for the new Looren school building.

This primary and secondary school building with two gymnasiums, swimming facilities and a double kindergarten was intended to be built in two phases, from 1964 to 1967 and from

1969 to 1971. But when it became clear, at the point when the primary school building was ready for use, that the secondary school accommodation would be needed sooner than anticipated, because of the continuing housing construction in the Witikon district, work started on the second phase in 1967. The overall design was based on the idea of two related L-shaped buildings both for the primary school and for the secondary school, each consisting of a classroom wing and a wing for the gymnasium and specialist rooms, and bordering the accompanying sports and playground areas. The main entrance to the school grounds is flanked by the two low buildings with indoor swimming pool, music room and double kindergarten. The jury report in 1960 had praised the "simplicity of the well-proportioned complex and the consistency of the entire approach."[423] The multi-storey buildings screen the open areas both from the surrounding roads and also include the existing fringe of trees along the adjacent Stöckertobel brook in the overall concept to frame the space. A characteristic feature of the open space is a difference in height of about twelve metres between the upper part of the complex on the through road and the brook. This drop is managed by the low-level main entrance to the school and above all in the central play and assembly courtyard.

"The example shows," Cramer explained, *"how important an appropriate response from the garden architect is for the architect's work. It should be a continuation of the architecture by other means. If it does not do this, it deteriorates into meaningless and in the worst case even disturbing 'decoration' or handicraft work performed on the surroundings."[424]*

The terraced courtyard, about 1,260 square metres in area, still forms the landscaped core of the school complex. It resembles the terraced landscape design for Alvar Aalto's 1961 Maison Carré in Bazoches near Paris, which Cramer was familiar with from Elizabeth Kassler's book.[425]Cramer had tried architectonic site terracing in Grüzefeld, and he now developed it into a usable, expressive "set of stands", a combination of steps and stands with grass steps.[426]This accommodates a height difference of about 2.5 metres, distributed on two sides of the school yard with slopes

of varying inclines. Cramer did not simply create a straight flight of concrete steps, but fanned the steps out at an angle, as Aalto had already done for his project near Paris. This means that the width of the steps not only increases from one side to the other, but also produces a kind of abstract amphitheatre that is regularly used for various school purposes. An artistic touch was highly valued in later years, and so the coloured, zinc-sprayed metal sculpture "II-70", by sculptor Arnold Zürcher, was placed on one side of the lowest step in front of the exposed concrete wall of the classroom wing.

While the terracing in the school yard is clearly a further development of the Grüzefeld housing estate terracing, the use of plants was even more strikingly reduced. In the school complex too, Cramer consistently packed all the areas adjacent to the road and around the kindergarten with a uniform mass planting of yellow dogwood. This not only guaranteed that all the areas that could not be used otherwise were green and easy to maintain, but also underlined the striking nature of the topography and created clearly delineated spatial units. He used isolated flowering shrubs to create a few carefully-placed highlights in the sea of dogwood. Easy to maintain does not of course mean that regular trimming can be omitted. Many landscaped areas that had been planted in this way consequently suffered from years of neglect, and today convey nothing of the precision that Cramer was looking for, with his eye on well-known Scandinavian models.

Most of the trees planted by Cramer have been neglected as well. He framed the space between the buildings with a few carefully-placed plane trees creating almost intimate spatial proportions. In both Witikon in Zurich and the Looren

Looren school complex in Witikon, Zurich, aerial photograph 1974

View of the Looren school complex from the outside

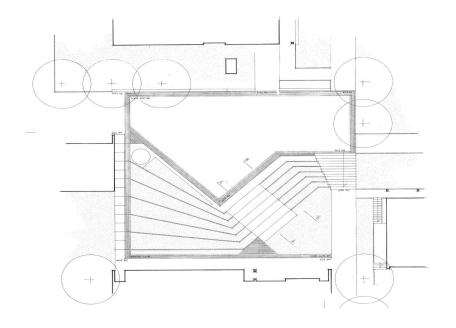

General plan of the terraced schoolyard
at the Looren school in Witikon, Zurich

The grassy steps seen from above

The planes and dogwood still give
the complex a uniform look today

Ernst Cramer at the age of 70 inspecting the
Looren school complex in summer 1968

Grassy steps and concrete steps, detail

Indoor and outdoor pools
in Frauenfeld by Bruno Gerosa and Ernst
Cramer dating from 1969–1972:

Indoor swimming pool (left) and
changing cubicles as planted shelters

View of the whole complex from
the roof of the indoor swimming pool
with young planting

Aerial view

The fully grown pfitzer junipers
establish the atmosphere today

Planes and juniper frame
the swimming baths

In the shade of the planes at the edge
of the swimming baths today

school in Maur, which was realized in the same period, he worked with his new "leading tree species", which had already been trained into an appropriate shape in the tree nurseries. Cramer always insisted that trees should be precisely positioned, and also made sure that they would be developed into green architectonic tree-roofs and cubes in the course of time. This would have required regular, expert shaping, but this maintenance measure was taken only in the rarest of cases after the gardens were completed. In the ecology movement in the 70s and 80s, when "letting things grow" became part of the new ideology of garden architecture, no one appreciated precise trimming any longer. This meant that many of Ernst Cramer's plane-tree plantatings lost their expressive power, and the uncontrolled growth of the groups of trees distorted the intended spatial proportions.

Urban square in the Obere Vorstadt, Aarau

The examples of the terracing in Grüzefeld and in the Looren school building show how Cramer gradually began to work on varying a theme that was to develop into a new design expression in the 70s. The design for the square in Aarau thrives on the consistent development of this terrace motif, the new way of handling topography and the gradual liberation from the strict use of right angles that Cramer had pursued in previous years.

The prestigious square in the Obere Vorstadt goes back to a project competition in 1961 and 1962, won by the Basel architect Guido F. Keller. The project was prompted by the increasing number of people employed by Aargau Electricity AEW and the company's search for new accommodation. While the brief was being worked out, a decision was taken to include a new cantonal court and a restaurant as part of the new development as well. The area available was

Design plan as executed of the city square in the Obere Vorstadt in Aarau between the 16-storey AEW-Tower (left), cantonal court (top) and restaurant (right)

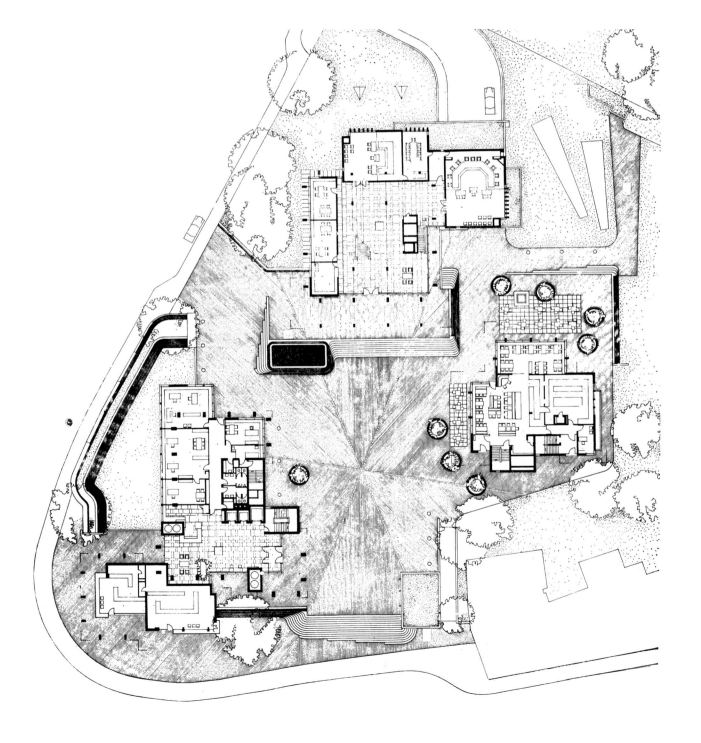

about 8,300 square metres. The intention was to produce an urban ensemble consisting of a 16-storey high-rise and two lower buildings grouped around a public square above an underground car park. Building work started on the reinforced concrete structures and the square in summer 1966, and they were completed three years later.

The landscape architecture for the public square and the buildings' surroundings was developed on the basis of one of Ernst Cramer's typical "napkin sketches".[427] Christofer Eriksson was the person in Cramer's office responsible for the detailing and implementation of the project, and he had a great deal of influence on its character. Cramer's design concept was based on the captivatingly simple idea of interpreting the square as a pedestrian-friendly "piazza" and letting all the paving run up to a central point in a star shape, "to emphasize the visual and transport-related links between the buildings and the surrounding area. The material is reddish porphyry from the Dolomites. It is placed in deliberate contrast with the grey vertical concrete walls, which form the principal boundaries of the square," Ernst Cramer explained at a later date.[428] But the reddish natural stone paving also contrasted with the light, smooth exposed concrete, which played an important part in the design of the square.

There were a large number of height differences and atriums between the buildings that had to be taken into account. To deal with this, Eriksson and Cramer developed the idea of accommodating all the height differences, which would usually have been managed with retaining walls, by building steps 14 centimetres high. This produced a kind of geological formation that is reminiscent of tufa terraces, and even included the parapets as step units. As the height differences varied considerably over the site as a whole, the realization of this unusual concept turned out to be exceptionally complex. The

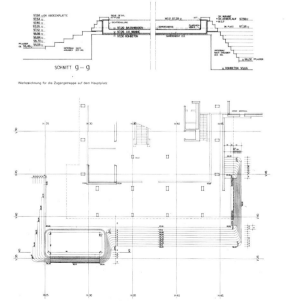

SCHNITT g – g

Werkzeichnung für die Zugangstreppe auf dem Hauptplatz

steepness of the prefabricated step units had to be precisely calculated by an engineer's office, so that the different inclines could run into each other without any disturbing breaks. Given this principle, Cramer abandoned strictly orthogonal corner solutions for the first time, and instead worked with rounded forms, contrasting with the architecture. The sculptural qualities of the complex were expressed particularly clearly in the consistent use of terracing and still underline the unusual character of the square. For the first time, this project shows a tendency, as

The parapet was fitted into the design as well

The prefabricated concrete steps look like tufa terraces

Stepped retaining walls planted with ivy

Working plan for the fountain in the town square in Aarau

2

5192

The fountain at the cantonal court building

Terraced access to the square

Concrete plant troughs, reminiscent of the geranium pot in the Poet's Garden

in the earth formations that had been developed previously, to artificially reshape the topography in an urban space with hard surfaces as well, in an almost expressive way. This sensitive sculptural approach using hard concrete was further emphasized by reduced planting and by including the nearby park in the visual scheme. The key eye-catching feature of the square is still the three by eight metre fountain, which is placed about 1.5 metres above the level of the central square on the terrace outside the cantonal court. The landscape architects wanted the fountain to present the theme of power generation, and they installed a whole battery of water jets in the pool, which shoot to different heights, following a certain programme. The water flows out of the pool down the waterfall steps to the level of the main square, and was originally intended to disappear into a simple gutter there. But subsequently a small containing wall proved to be necessary, to prevent the square from getting wet.

"Even water features in fountains," Cramer explained later in a lecture, *"can be designed following artistic ideas. Here I would like to refer to a pool in Aarau, where the shape and the play of the water are entirely in tune with the overall concept for the design of the square. The sides of the pool seem to grow out of the square like the walls and the steps. This movement of growing out of the paving is reinforced in the first phase of the water feature by the falling water, which runs in the opposite direction. In the second phase of the water feature the jets of water extend the shape of the fountain and they enclose the space that continues above the pool. The jets of water and the shape of the fountain thus create an artistically valid and uniform shape.[429]*

This "artistically valid and uniform shape" that Cramer picked out so emphatically in the case of his design for the fountain in Aarau increasingly became a leitmotif for his work. In 1967 he expressed it in a remarkable competition design that can be seen both as a clear breakthrough towards a new formal language and as an homage to Scandinavian garden design.

Volketswil cemetery competition

Ernst Cramer entered the competition for a new cemetery in Volketswil in December 1967, working with the Zurich architect Bruno Gerosa. 6600 spaces for graves and all the necessary cemetery buildings were to be planned on a slightly sloping overall area of 48,150 square metres on the edge of the town. 31 designs were originally submitted, of which ten reached the short list, including the project by Cramer and Gerosa. It surprised at first glance, based as it was on a highly succinct oval, into which all the necessary grave plots and cemetery buildings had been integrated with great ease. Cramer's commentary on this:

"This design attempts to translate the pure, closed shape of the old village cemetery for our times, and to develop a consistent form from the given site. The wood-like, ellipsoid planting makes the cemetery into a space that is closed off from its surroundings."[430]

The design sketches and the construction drawing[431] reveal the level of geometrical precision in the placement of the three ellipses of different sizes, shifted slightly in relation to each other. The largest ellipse defines the edge of the clearing that is cut precisely out of the uniform, wood-like planting. The archetypal motif of the

clearing recurs constantly from here on in many of Cramer's major projects.[432] The smallest of the three ellipses defines the form of the open central lawn that is intended to surprise the visitor with its size in the centre of the complex. The family tombs and urn graves are arranged along the edge of the lawn, while rows of graves are to be found in the area between the oval lawn and the edge of the wood, arranged in an orthogonal system with the necessary footpaths. Linear hedges were intended to provide internal articulation for this area, and at the same time to underline the depth of the space. The middle-sized ellipse, which cuts skilfully through the lawn, the field of graves and the wood, establishes the principal line for the access route. It begins at

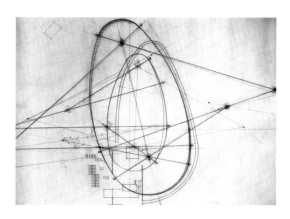

the point where Bruno Gerosa composed the simple cemetery buildings into a loose, orthogonally structured ensemble. This paved area, articulated by several pools, leads to the central lawn, accompanied by open planting. Finally, the children's graves are grouped around the cemetery chapel, the heart of the complex, which was positioned precisely at the apex of the small el-

lipse. The whole design is convincing because of the skilful overlapping of the different functions in the orthogonal system with the magnificent large-scale form of the oval.

This cemetery is clearly reminiscent of the memorable designs that Cramer had got to know in Denmark only a short time before, not just because of its striking form, but also in its generous use of space. It is not possible to establish with any certainty whether he had a particular work by Carl Theodor Sørensen in mind when drawing up his plans, or whether he was familiar with Sven-Ingvar Andersson's ellipse project for the 1967 World Fair in Montreal. But it is certain that Ernst Cramer admired the modern elegance of Scandinavian garden design, and allowed this enthusiasm to show in his design. This is also clear from a lecture manuscript called "Thoughts on the cemetery" from February 1967, containing not only a plea for simplicity and clarity in cemetery design, but also justifying a preference for spacious design with a view to Scandinavian models:

Model for the Volketswil cemetery competition

Construction drawing for the ovals

Competition plan for the new cemetery in Volketswil dating from 1967

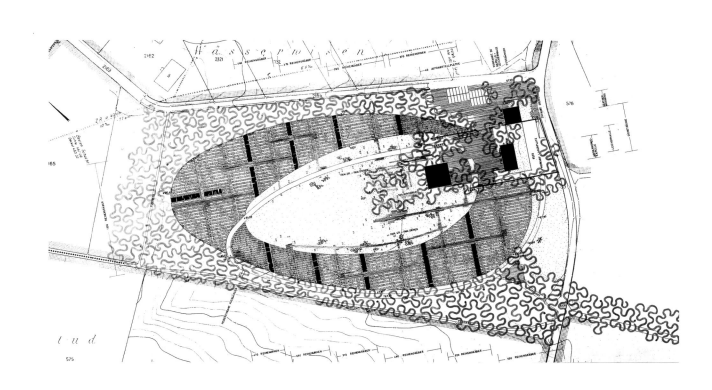

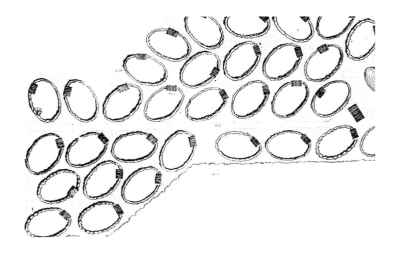

ing remark in a report on the competition in 1969:

"The jury's decision shows that solutions departing strongly from a conventional approach are not in demand. It is in any case astonishing that designs like the one submitted under the codeword Stud (author: E. Cramer, garden architect BSG/SWB, Zurich), which showed extraordinary formal qualities, and which without any doubt had the most powerful idea behind it, was not even thought worthy of a mention."[435]

Cramer's design went against the accepted conventions of cemetery design and thus gave rise to a great deal of argument. Advocates of traditional cemetery design were not at all convinced by Cramer's new interpretation of the village cemetery as a lucidly structured, clearly enclosed space. But Cramer stuck to his guns:

"Death is not a romantic idyll. It is a hard, everyday reality. And so: no park, no forest, no drama. A field of the dead."[436]

Even though Cramer was not able to realize this project, it still confirmed his authority in terms of up-to-date cemetery design. The Volketswil competition plan graced the title page of the November 1969 issue of the magazine *Garten und Landschaft*, which also ran an article by Cramer called "Tendencies in contemporary cemetery design",[437] in which he presented two of his show projects in detail: the strictly architectonically designed Pratteln cemetery and

Plan of Carl Theodor Sørensen's Nærum allotments dating from 1948

Trimmed oval hedges as garden boundaries in Sørensen's Nærum allotments

Sven-Ingvar Andersson's project for the Montreal World Fair 1967

"Can people more easily overcome their sense of mourning in a cramped space? The answer to this question must be no. Those left behind should be aware that their fate is not the fate of an individual. In a spacious cemetery they become clearly aware that transience is inextricably bound into the lives of all humans. For this reason, design on a large scale has a liberating effect, especially when the designer manages to include the horizon in the plans as well, thus conveying a new impression, that of the aerial perspective (a piece of current terminology). The cemetery in Stockholm, by Asplund, can stand as a particularly good example of a cemetery of this kind."[433]

This cemetery called "Skogskyrkogården" (Woodland Cemetery) in Enskede near Stockholm, a project by the Modern Swedish architects Sigurd Lewerentz and Erik Gunnar Asplund, was realized between 1917 and 1940. It was considered to be a timeless Modern work even shortly after it was completed, because of its generous open quality within a gently rolling forest landscape, a former gravel pit.[434] Cramer's elegant cemetery, however, was never realized. The jury decided instead on a more conventionally pleasing design by the Zurich architect Werner Gantenbein, working with the garden architect Peter Schmid. Even the journalist Heini Mathys, who was otherwise somewhat sceptical about Ernst Cramer's abstract designs, was fascinated and made the conclud-

the sculptural military cemetery on the Futa
Pass in Italy.[438] The latter project was described by Fritz Dové in a separate article.[439]
In winter 1969, Ernst Cramer and Hans-Kurt
Boehlke of Kassel were commissioned to produce a report on cemeteries in the city of Vienna. Boehlke had been director of the "Arbeitsgemeinschaft für Friedhof und Denkmal (AFD)",
the cemetery and monument study group in
Kassel[440] since 1954, of which Cramer was
also a member since 1963. Boehlke respected
Cramer as a garden architect who was forward-
looking in matters of cemetery design as
well.[441] Cramer was mainly responsible for
the explanatory sketches and drawings in their
joint report, which was to look at possibilities
for extending the cemeteries, among other
things.[442]

With the Volketswil project Cramer did not just
develop a new formal language, one now emancipated from architectonic design principles,
but he also used it to concretize a number of design tenets. Even more important than the principles of uniform use of plants and materials,
the emphasis of space, the unassertive integration of art and architecture, and the formal clarity of cemetery design are the four general design principles formulated by Ernst Cramer, for
the first time as lucidly as this, in the above-
mentioned 1967 lecture manuscript:

"Planning on a human scale.

Order in diversity.

Return to simplicity.

Keeping up with modern architecture and
art."[443]

Cramer did not want to see these four principles
applied only to the planning of cemeteries. They
were in fact the quintessence of his previous
garden design experience, and represented the
salient points from which his future projects
would emerge.

Paradigm shift – ecology versus design

Landscape design for the Bruderholz
cantonal hospital near Basel

The planning for the Bruderholz hospital near
Basel, a major project by the Suter and Suter architectural practice, was almost fully developed
when Ernst Cramer was brought in in spring
1968 to advise on designing the surroundings.
This meticulously planned large scale project
presented the experienced garden architect,
who enjoyed improvisation, with a number of
entirely new challenges that were finally too
much for him, and signalled the end of Ernst
Cramer's Zurich office.

This large hospital was built as the second cantonal hospital for the Canton of Basel-Landschaft, and along with the University Hospital in
Basel was intended to guarantee the best possible medical care. The main departments, sur-
gery, medicine, gynaecology and maternity, and
also a children's clinic and various specialist

clinics, were sited in the new complex of buildings on a wooded hill near Bottmingen. The
Bruderholz hospital was also to serve as a teaching hospital for the students of Basel University.
When complete, 1000 beds were to be provided
in the central high-rise wing. The complex included a residential area for the staff and parking facilities for about 800 vehicles in the immediate vicinity. The size of the project demanded
a correspondingly high level of planning involve-
ment by the architects and engineers. Suter and
Suter, a practice for architecture, general planning and project management, had about 300
employees at the time, and enjoyed a good reputation for hospital building. The design concept
proposed to place the central hospital complex,
the staff accommodation and the parking facilities in separate clearings in the wood, thus expressing three compact units, clearly articulated in terms of function and space, even in the
general plan. Forestry regulations required that
cleared woodland had to be replaced in the immediate vicinity.

The hospital complex occupied the largest
clearing. This was conceived as it would have
been in an overall plan for an industrial project,
with all the treatment and care departments

Aerial view of Bruder-
holzspital as of today

grouped around the core of the hospital, the ten-storey building that housed the wards. Ultimately this led to a finger-like layout for the ground plan, which at the same time enabled the subsequent extension of the building sections. A ring road still provides access to the hospital site and makes it possible for goods to be delivered from the north, separated from visitor access by car, bus or on foot from the southeast. As the site sloped to the north-west, it was possible to use natural lighting for the lower

forestry expert. [445] In the planning for the two smaller clearings he introduced a polygonal shape for the edges of the wood in each case, which fitted in with the pattern of the buildings and the access road, while for the main building he designed a spacious setting: a clearing as a large, geometrically constructed oval. His unrealized idea for the Volketswil competition was magnificently realized for the Bruderholz hospital. An avenue with three rows of trees, almost 600 in all, still provides an oval frame for a large,

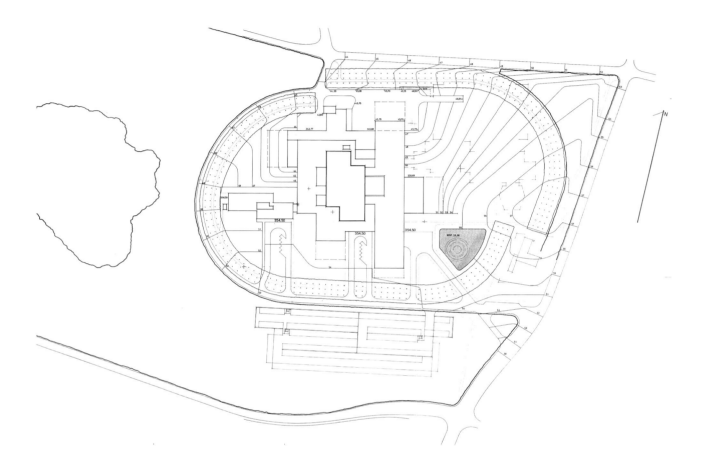

General plan of the Bruderholz cantonal hospital in Basel with the hospital complex in the centre, surrounded by the large, oval avenue of trees

floors of the hospital on the north and west sides, which meant that the site levels had to be very precisely formulated in terms of open space planning. The preliminary project was completed as early as October 1965. As the architects had worked well with Ernst Cramer not only in Winterthur, but also on other projects since, for example for the Ciba-Geigy chemicals group, [444] the Zurich landscape architect was brought in when building started in 1968.

Cramer and his staff, Christofer Eriksson in particular, were faced with a demanding task: they had to design the surrounding landscape of the large building complex in such a way that the open spaces were of high quality, supporting the identity of the hospital, but without interfering with the smooth functioning of its various departments. Re-afforestation to replace the cleared woodland around the car parks and the residential area was the least of Cramer's problems – he even explained his vision of the natural, layered structure of the new woods to the

open clearing, with the hospital building complex rising out of the centre.

As in Volketswil, here too the main intention was to create a clear open space, which would provide air to breathe. For this reason the clearing around the Bruderholzspital was developed in a balanced proportional relationship with the masses of the buildings. The unambiguous reaction to the character of the place and the expressive quality of the architecture particularly appealed to the architects, who were most enthusiastic about Cramer's proposal. It is clear at a second glance that the large oval of trees does not form a closed ring, but was interrupted at two points, resulting in a division into one third and two thirds. Cramer offset the shorter section of the ring of trees slightly outwards, to make the best possible use of the grounds' expanse despite restrictions by existing buildings on the east side and the main drive on the north side. The eastern break in the ring remains invisible, because Cramer allowed the avenues'

ends to overlap at this point. A footpath leads through the avenue made up of three rows of trees, so that it is possible to walk round the whole clearing behind the inside row of trees. Cramer knew how attractive it is to walk on the edge of a wood. Visitors can take a sheltered walk by the wood, enjoying the shade afforded by the trees in summer, and are always able to experience a framed view inwards. Cramer placed the trees with the utmost precision, and tolerated deviations from the gird only at points where important access routes cut through the ring. The underlying force of the large form was not to be weakened at any price.

But Cramer did have to make considerable concessions in the choice of trees. He originally intended to use his "leading tree species", the plane, for the ring. But a tree nursery that had been invited to tender for supplying the trees objected to the use of planes on medical grounds to the responsible cantonal authorities. [446] Fine hairs from the underside of the leaves would detach themselves in summer, often irritating the mucous membrane, which would rule out the use of planes in the vicinity of a hospital. Cramer had to abandon the idea, and

had hundreds of horse-chestnuts grown in a nearby tree nursery. When these were destroyed by a freak hailstorm, the principal architect, Heini Seiberth, and Cramer drove to a forestry nursery in the Allgäu to pick out some sycamores. This is why one of Cramer's late designs does not use planes as the main element. The story of the planes for the Bruderholzspital was circulated among Cramer's colleagues, not without some malicious glee, as a way of denouncing Cramer's lack of plant know-how. Cramer's use of plants had already been criticized on the occasion of G|59, and even decades later people were still looking for superficial – soon they were to be ecological – criticisms in an attempt to erode the progressive garden architect's reputation. In fact the generous sense of space at the Bruderholz hospital is of such crucial importance even today that the question of the kind of tree used seems to be a minor problem.

Cramer's magnificent oval formed a framework for the new complex and also provided it with a suitable image. It was to be the element that fixed the architecture and all the other landscape design measures. He planted no other trees or hedges, in order not to detract from the sense of space within the clearing. He was concerned to come up with a clear, open design for the main entrance to the hospital as well. He distanced himself from an earlier plan to narrow down the space near the entrance with another row of trees set on the arc of a circle, because he felt that the space should be left open. It is clear even in the choice of material that the garden architect was his work and its expression should relate adequately to the architecture. Working from the basic shape of a circle, Cramer devised a paved area for which he sought a special kind of concrete paving. He fi-

At the edge of the large clearing
by the Bruderholzspital

The idea of the three clearings
in the wood, with the premises for the
different facilities embedded in them

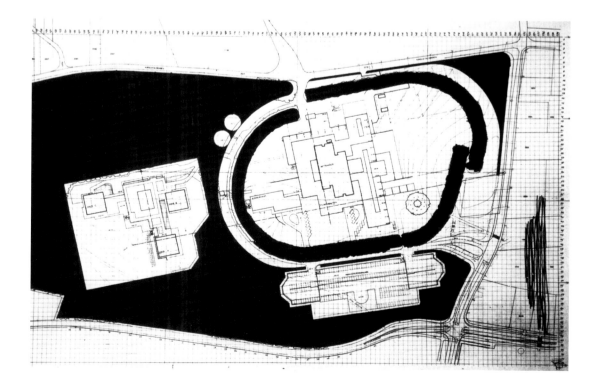

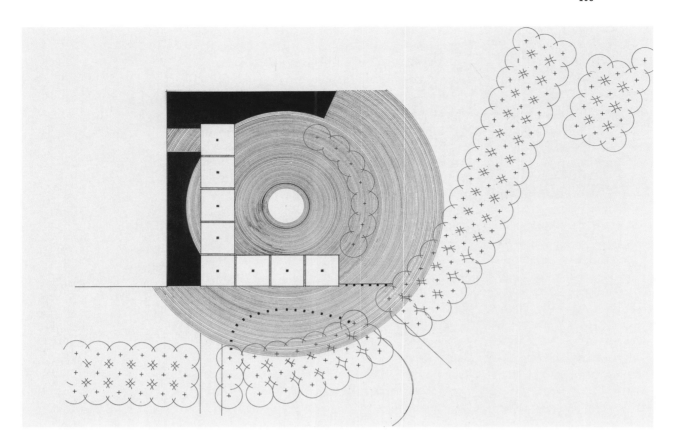

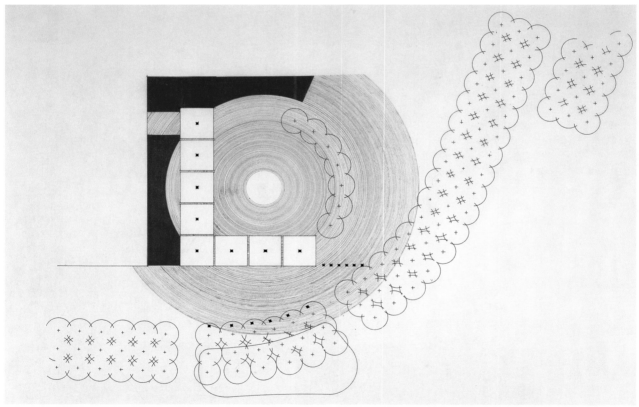

An alternative design for organizing the drive for the Bruderholzspital

In this further version the barrier elements are partly adapted to the curve of the row of trees

nally found them in a firm near Karlsruhe, and had square concrete paving-stones imported in a small, ten-by-ten centimetre paving format via a building materials business in Basel. The Bruderholz hospital was the first major building site for which this new paving system was used in Switzerland. The crucial feature here was not just the more reasonable price in comparison with the traditional granite paving-stone system. Cramer was now above all able to work with a flexible paving system that made an up-to-

date impression and could be precisely laid. Very shortly after this first use the concrete paving stones became part of the Swiss building material firm's regular range, "because of years of good experience abroad", and was extolled as reasonably priced paving material, easy to lay and maintain. [447] The three-row avenue of sycamores crossed the paved area, thus linking the square with the great ring path. Cramer had designed a special element for the centre point of the circular paved entrance area that still highlights it today: a circular fountain in smooth-cast concrete. It is made up of two concentric rings. The actual fountain basin forms the inner ring, with a central water-jet and a series of jets that shoot into the middle from the edge in a high arc. Rather like the fountain in the town square in Aarau, the jets continue the shape of the central ring, which tapers upwards conically. The outer ring is also made of smooth-cast, untreated concrete and its shape, which is also conical, is reminiscent of the crater of a volcano or a jet engine. The inner surfaces of the ring are inclined outwards at such a shallow angle that they seem like surfaces for lying down on. Individual, cubic concrete blocks are set in the inner ring and can be used as seats. Access to the space between the central fountain basin and the other ring is through three incisions in the outer ring. Cramer had used a wooden model for devising the fountain design and asked the architects' office to draw up the necessary working plans on this basis. The archetypal basic form of the fountain is reminiscent of the abstract design for an earth mound of the kind created by Herbert Bayer, for example, in Aspen, Colorado in 1955, entitled "Grass Mound".[448] But the Horace E. Dodge fountain, realized by Isamu Noguchi from 1972 to 1979 in the Philip A. Hart Plaza in the centre of Detroit, also has formal similarities with Cramer's fountain. More important than the question of whether Cramer was aware of Noguchi's work, which was produced at about the same time, is the expressive quality so typical of the period, that the two projects share. Both fountains have a formal dynamic and a

technical precision that is reminiscent of a volcano or a jet, and not by chance. The first moon landing in July 1969 had seen the start of an age that promised unlimited technical possibilities and boundless growth. This optimistic faith in technical progress was as much a feature of the late 60s as youth protests against unconditional growth. If Cramer's fountain in Aarau was dedicated to the idea of bubbling energy, the fountain at the Bruderholzspital stood for the start of the modern technological age.

"Enormous sensitivity to form and material" was the comment on Cramer made by Heini Seiberth,[449] the responsible architect at Suter and Suter, especially referring to the remarkable modelling of the terrain in the northwestern section, in the rear of the site. The aim here was to provide natural lighting for the lower level floors on the northern and western sides of the hospital. This meant that a difference in height of between four and six metres had to be compensated for within a relatively short dis-

A circular paved carpet at the entrance to the hospital

Versions with trees in the centre of the square were rejected

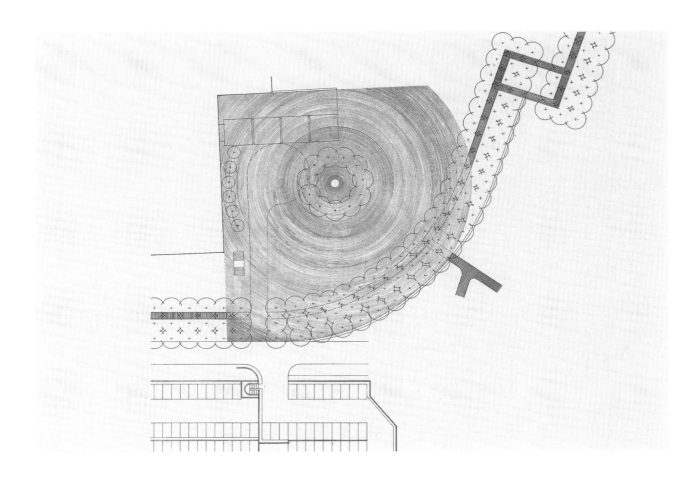

tance on this part of the site, which was bordered by the corner of the building on one side and the continuously rising ring road on the other. Cramer used this task as a reason for creating a sculptural form for the terrain that the architects christened the "giant ammonite". This is in fact an accurate description of the outer shape of the modelled earth. In principle Cramer's strategy was to terrace the land without retaining walls, fanning them out around a central pivot in the corner of the building volumes. The striking feature of this modelling is not just the steepness of the slope at the pivot. The most remarkable point is that Cramer did not adapt the lawn terraces seamlessly to the slope of the circular path on the outside, but actually retained the folding of the earth masses to the outermost edge, even increasing it a little. From the path the image is of an abstract wave of lawn, which sets the slope oscillating rhythmically. Following the model of the clearing, here too the earth sculpture is not disturbed by any other planting. Cramer had ivy planted as ground cover only on the building side, because it would have been impossible or far too complicated and expensive to mow grass in this area – so functional aspects did have a part to play.

The Bruderholz cantonal hospital in September 1973 with young maple trees in the foreground and the fountain at the entrance

The first stages of the construction of the Ammonite can be seen behind the main building. The young trees do not yet form a frame for the space

as contemporary witnesses report. He even made his own tools, so that he could shape the modelling clay better, and gave the project a sense of personal handwriting in the best sense of the word. Heini Seiberth stressed: "In principle the architects had been waiting for this kind of garden design. This was pioneering work in terms of addressing the spatial conditions."[450] Cramer's working method on site was not fundamentally different from his work on the model, with one exception: his "tool" on the site was the excavator driver and his machine. The "ammonite" was modelled on the

spot, under Ernst Cramer's supervision and following his precise instructions.

Cramer's increasingly artistic approach to his work, his frequent spontaneous changes on site and the lack of precise plans by which the work could be implemented increasingly characterized his individual handwriting as he got older, but the building foreman at the Bruderholz hospital was not the only person to be rattled by this. Cramer's intuitive approach was a constant source of argument in his own office as well.[451] Christofer Eriksson, unlike Cramer, took the view that for projects on the scale of the Bruderholz hospital there was a need for precise site surveys and very precise working plans. Otherwise the work could not be carried out cost-efficiently. But the tradition was that Cramer largely ignored financial implications, greatly to the regret of his own accounts department, and instead instructed the excavator driver on the spot about how the modelling was to be carried out. But discipline was needed for the large Suter and Suter project, and for this reason the architects, even though they were full of admiration for Cramer's creativity, were sceptical about the efficiency of his intuitive approach. Cramer lacked the patience to work his ideas out precisely on paper, Eriksson explained. This costly way of working could function with expensive private gardens and affluent clients, but the traditional strategy did not add up for large projects of this kind. As time made it clear that the Zurich office was no longer able to provide viable working plans because of Cramer's instability and because of technical

Planning such sensitive earth modelling on paper would have been very difficult, and would have made the final plans very difficult to understand. Cramer did not want to run the risk of misinterpretation. For him a plan was just an aid to implementation, and far too lacking in expressive force. He felt that a sketch on a napkin had much more of this expressive force, but he developed site modelling at this level of precision in models. Ernst Cramer made his models in white plasticine, working with great passion,

difficulties, the architects broke off the working relationship.

In this project, Cramer suddenly came up against new boundaries, mainly of an economic nature, or relating to the technical side of design implementation, that he could scarcely surmount any longer as a representative of the old generation of craftsmen. But the 70-year-old garden architect not only had to contend with economical and technical constraints. The spirit of the age had changed, and developments in the cultural and social sphere were happening so rapidly in the late 60s that Cramer and his specific view of garden architecture were not the only things that were running into trouble. It was symptomatic of the broader picture that even an institution like the Swiss Werkbund, which was committed to the moral and aesthetic renewal of post-war society, was forced on to the defensive. "The Werkbund has been accused of no longer being able to do justice to the problems of the day. What should the Werkbund do about these accusations, what can it do?" were Peter Steiger's opening remarks as first chairman of the Werkbund conference in November 1969, entitled "Give the Werkbund a chance!".[452] In the eyes of the 68 generation, in revolt and questioning everything, the establishment had made things too comfortable for itself in the years of economic growth, and was no longer sufficiently engaged in current discussions about the social questions of the future."Grandpa's Werkbund is dead!" ran the provocative slogan. A certain aspect of the discussion also touched upon a key point in Cramer's work: the old concept of the work was being called into question:

"There was disagreement about this concept of the work. It almost seemed as though the representatives of the older generation were still hankering after the Platonic idea of well designed things ('education through form'), while the younger generation are asking about the rules that govern how the work comes into being. To quote Lucius Burckhardt: 'We have lingered over appearance for too long. The product is like an iceberg'."[453]

Cramer, who had throughout his life sought after good, pure form, was undoubtedly one of the older generation that was being addressed, who felt themselves under an obligation to the con-

cept of the work and to "Die gute Form". Integrating social questions into the way he created his work was not at the top of his list of priorities. He certainly persisted in stressing that he wanted to shift people to the centre of his work, but that had nothing in common with the participatory, sociologically oriented planning propagated by Lucius Burckhardt and his fellow-thinkers. From their point of view Ernst Cramer, with his purely aesthetic and strictly formally based works, was gradually moving on to the fringes.

Cramer's work began to seem completely anachronistic when in the early 70s, in the face of world-wide environmental catastrophes, ecologically oriented landscape and environmental design became accepted, asserting itself vigorously with the slogan "Let nature grow – nature imposes its own order".[454] The Solothurn-based biologist Urs Schwarz was putting forward the idea of the natural garden as early as 1971, and put himself at the forefront of the ecological garden movement in Switzerland with his book *Der Naturgarten* (The Natural Garden).[455] Schwarz demanded categorically

Entrance to the Bruderholzspital under construction, summer 1973

Still at the centre of the entrance area today: Ernst Cramer's fountain

Prefabricated concrete screens in the entrance area

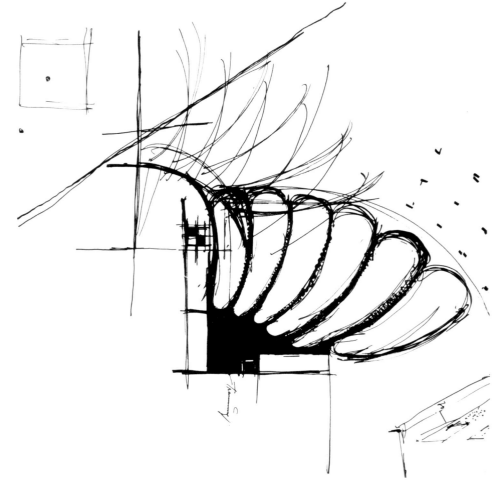

The "Ammonite" at the Bruderholzspital

Cramer's draft sketch for the "Ammonite"

The earth modelling still fascinates
visitors today

The three-row avenue of maples
frames the planted earth sculpture

New design for the historic Rechberg
Garden in Zurich, not realized, of 1968:

General plan

Large perspective drawing with view of
the newly designed Rechberg Garden

Perspective view of the new design

that there should be a general shift to "natural" garden and landscape design, and insisted:

"We must start judging private individuals by the appearance of their plot of land as far as their attitude to nature is concerned. Planting of public green spaces should reflect the community's sense of nature. As long as everyone plants their banks with foreign ground-cover and shrubs the public authorities are not going to change either."[456]

This demand suddenly questioned the whole range of plants that Ernst Cramer had used in his projects so far. Neither the plane tree nor the yellow dogwood nor the dog-rose were indigenous plants, but "weeds", according to Urs Schwarz, and they had to be eradicated:

"We consider that foreign, non-indigenous plants are weeds, and that local, indigenous ones are acceptable. And then we make a careful start on making room for the acceptable plants by getting rid of the weeds."[457]

Many of Ernst Cramer's gardens were sacrificed to the eradication of "weeds", were destroyed by allowing spontaneous, supposedly indigenous vegetation to grow, or were neglected to the point of being unrecognizable because the new dogma saw even the regular mowing of lawns, the trimming of hedges or plants into geometrical shapes as a rape of nature. "Naturalness", and no longer "Die gute Form" was now the highest distinction in garden and landscape architecture.

The Bruderholz cantonal hospital finally opened in October 1973, and is still considered one of Cramer's most impressive projects. Here the new and old values collided clearly for the first time. Cramer did not promptly withdraw in a spirit of resignation, that would have been absolutely counter to his progressive nature. But in summer 1972, two years after Christofer Eriksson and Fritz Dové had stopped working for him, Cramer closed his Zurich office and from then on ran only a small planning office in Rüschlikon, supported by his wife and Karl Pappa, his collaborator of many years' standing. Pappa also ceased working for Ernst Cramer in 1973, after 23 years. Cramer realized his last major projects on his own in the seven remaining years of his life.[458]

Cramer as a design teacher in Lausanne

Ernst Cramer started to work intensively as a design teacher at a time when he was coming up against apparently insurmountable constraints in his work and had reached a state of crisis. It certainly did not come easily to Cramer to close his Zurich office in 1972. This considerably restricted his room for manoeuvre in terms of the nature and scale of the projects he could take on, but that was not all. Cramer had always been stimulated and driven forward by working with his younger employees and engaging in critical arguments with them, and so he had lost some of his most important sparring partners. He retained his interest in exchanging ideas and his ability to work with the younger generation throughout his lifetime, and so it is not surprising that he accepted an offer to teach at the Athenaeum in 1972. But why did this Zurich man, who still had important projects to deal with in German-speaking Switzerland, decide to take up an offer to teach at a private school in Lausanne? The 74-year-old had to cope with a 200 kilometre journey in each direction each week, was compelled to find accomodations there, and spoke scarcely any French. The architect Liliane Narbel, then the head of the Athenaeum, had the impression that Ernst Cramer deliberately sought to distance himself from German-speaking Switzerland because his work was no longer afforded the proper respect by his professional colleagues there.[459] Another factor was that his unconventional approach was not in demand in educational institutions, and was almost unknown to landscape architecture students in German-speaking Switzerland. Frau Narbel came across the Zurich landscape architect's extraordinary work, which was largely unknown in French-speaking Switzerland, when looking for new, competent lecturers for her school. Cramer gratefully accepted the offer to teach in Lausanne, rented a dwelling in the town of Chexbres on Lake Geneva, 14 kilometres away, and travelled to the canton of Vaud for one day a week. The Athenaeum, Ecole d'architecture, d'architecture intérieur, d'architecture civile et d'architecture des jardins, was founded in 1945 as a private school, reformed several times after that, and moved into a new accommodation in the Avenue Fraisse in Lausanne in 1970. Liliane Narbel, who was head of the school at the time, had the task of reforming the curriculum. About 13 lecturers, most of them architects, some artists and designers and one landscape architect made up the staff there in the early 70s. The garden architecture course lasted for four years, divided into 12 terms. The minimum age for new students had been fixed at 17, and the only entrance requirement was "the ability to follow the teaching", in other words a good general school education. The first year was a kind of foundation course, then students turned to their specialist subjects and finally sat for their diploma.

Little is known about the first two years in which Cramer taught in Lausanne. A clear picture does not emerge until 1974, provided to a considerable extent by the archived sketches, plans and photographs in the garden architect's estate. Emil Steiner's journalism is also very revealing: he documented and commented on Ernst Cramer's teaching at the Athenaeum from 1975 to 1980, in photographs and some articles in *Der Gartenbau*. Steiner published his first interesting item on Cramer's teaching in Lausanne in March 1975, using the programmatic title "From inner structure to the appearance of form".[460] Cramer was working with about 15 students in 1974. Most of them came from France to study garden architecture as a specialist subject. The teaching programme and the course aims are described in the documentation as follows:

"'The teaching concentrates mainly on studio work. There students, under the direction of quali-

Ernst Cramer with his students in Lausanne

fied teachers, are taught to develop their talents harmoniously, building on architectonic composition principles and applying their technical knowledge. The practical teaching is complemented by theoretical courses. These provide an introduction to art history, stylistics, the analysis of architecture, linked with practical exercises in drawing from nature, perspective representation and decorative drawing. Students also learn how to record and present the organizational aspects of their exercises, which are largely self-chosen. The school sets great store by complete and neatly drawn plans: ground plans, sections, views and perspectives. It also requires construction details and models for the projects. Teaching in the technical field is matched to the individual subjects, with subjects like construction, mathematics, statics, material properties and drawing technique. Teaching is at the advanced level appropriate to a university, but maintains a certain necessary disci-

pline. With the exception of certain staturory requirements it represents a preparation for professional work.' [...] In the garden architecture course, specialist horticultural subjects like pedology, topography and botany are important, and so are courses that are attended with the architecture students, like urban planning, for example."[461] Cramer was not very interested in passing on theoretical knowledge. The fact that he spoke hardly any French worked in favour of teaching

The "trame"

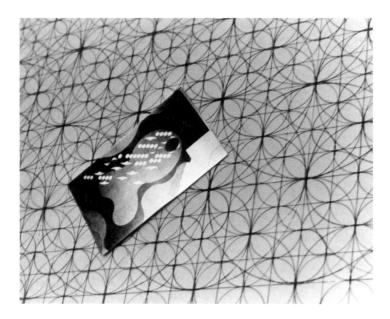

by visual means, and so his preferred means of communication was sketches, photographs and models. He did not want to hammer a particular dogma into his students, but constantly stressed the idea: "I do not have a preconceived opinion!!!" and insisted that "young people should not be educated in straitjackets".[462] He not only adopted this position in personal conversations, but also expressed himself critically in formal lectures and guest reviews, for example at the Intercantonal Technical College in Rapperswil, about the current essentially dogmatic and in his opinion uncreative approach to teaching.[463] Obviously this did not make him any friends, but he stuck to his opinion that students could only have their original delight in playing with form restored through experimental, free work. "In Ernst Cramer's opinion students' talents could best be developed by first directing their imagination to the phenomena of pure form as the source of design," Emil Steiner stated later.[464] It is clear from the statements that Cramer himself made about teaching that he had a markedly modern attitude to the exploration of form and demanded discipline from his students:

"I am thinking here above all of Mondrian's design approach. This requires and brings about strict discipline, which is not immediately understood by all students, especially not when their ideas are already fixed in a certain direction because of their

Salt model by one of Ernst Cramer's students at the Athenaeum in Lausanne

Archetypal forms in salt

previous training, But in time even these students are able to shed these preconceived ways of thinking, these clichés."[465]

An example of what Ernst Cramer meant by liberation from clichés through discipline is working with the circle-grid, the so-called "trame".[466] This drawing aid is a geometrically constructed basic grid made up of three circles of different sizes, based on an orthogonal grid with a square mesh. The centre of a medium-sized square made up of four small squares forms the centre of the smallest category of circles, which are inscribed exactly in the quadripartite square fields. The centre of the next-largest circle lies in its turn at the intersection points of the four small circle lines; this circle's radius is the same as the diameter of a small circle. The radius of the third and largest category of circle corresponds with the diameter of a medium-sized circle and is derived by the previous construction principle. A plan is produced on the basis of this geometrical construction that is completely covered with arcs of circles. The "trame" was used as the basis for designs on tracing paper. All the arcs and parts of them that appear on any general plan are thus based on this invisible circle-grid. Cramer's intentions were clear: he wanted to achieve freedom of formal language via a geometrically precise basis structure.

"A structure of this kind does not have to be directly visible in the completed work – on the contrary: its presence should be sensed only as an ordering principle running through everything in the background. For this reason we have for instance developed a circle-grid, our 'trame'. This teaches students that every curve, every apparently free line and area is derived from a pure geometrical form, in this case the circle, in other words is intended to represent a line that is part of a circle, or a combination of various parts of circles and entire circles. This circle-grid makes it easier for students to base an exercise they have been set on a clear structure. [...] By learning to design on the basis of clear principles, we escape from the danger of sterile formalism, opening up the route to humane solutions, and making our creations human again."[467]

The section of this explanation by Ernst Cramer that seeks to justify his approach is scarcely comprehensible from today's point of view, and probably has to be interpreted against the background of the discussion that was going on at the time about humane architecture and urban planning. Certainly the "trame" was a useful aid for achieving formal precision in a design, but it remains impossible to argue that this avoids formalism to any extent, and produces a more humane solution. "The product is like an iceberg" was Lucius Burckhard's fundamental criticism of the traditional concept of the work[468] and it seems that Cramer was looking for a way out of this cold formalism without wanting to abandon his principles of pure form. It is therefore to be assumed that his "humane" relates to the

popular, free formal language of the 70s, which was attractive to all design disciplines as a non-conformist alternative to an orthogonal approach, which was presumed to be cold and "inhumane". So there is no point in looking for the strictly orthogonal basic principles of earlier year in any of the projects by Ernst Cramer's students published in 1975. The students learned that there can definitely be an ordering principle behind a landscape architecture design, without the ordering grid being visible in the final outcome. Various examples examined in detail above show that Cramer regularly used this principle in his own projects, to give his de-

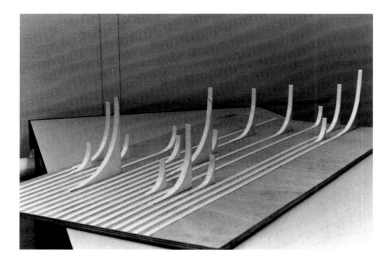

Students' model for the design of a park

Model study for Cité de Lignon housing project in Geneva

signs a high level of formal consistency. Cramer's Heuried housing estate project was also based on the *"trame"* principle. [469]

Cramer sometimes quoted the architect Louis Isadore Kahn, who died in 1974, in this context: "Design is form-making in order. Form emerges out of a system of construction. Growth is construction. In order is a creative force [...]."[470] To prevent the emergence of mere formal studies, all the student projects were based on real problems that required functional as well as formal solutions. The teacher clearly knew how to look after his students caringly, with a great deal of patience, empathy and attentiveness in terms of draughtsmanship.

"One must help everyone," he noted on a report form on which he certified that all his students were hard-working and had good to very good design abilities. [471]

People liked to accuse Cramer of formalism, but he always believed firmly: "Something formal can fulfil the purpose."[472] For this reason he tried to set up "forms for functions", to use Theodor W. Adorno's words, [473] in his own projects and in his work with students. Students usually suggested the projects they worked on with Cramer themselves. There were always a lot of different projects on the go in the studio, from large-scale urban planning projects to the design of harbour facilities. Cramer regularly lectured with slides, taking his students with him on his trips to Brazil, Japan or Scandinavia, and giving them a sense of the formal power that resided in many good gardens and urban planning concepts, without insisting that what he showed was to be seen as a model. Whenever Cramer brought something to his lectures in his little case, it wasn't usually a set of fat textbooks but fashion or design magazines in which he always found appealing formal principles that were intended to stimulate further development. One thing became clear here: Cramer's preference for dynamically flowing, space-creating forms that were always placed in dialogue with architectural spaces and bodies. If no architectural bodies were available, he developed "green pieces of architecture", austerely trimmed bodies of trees, which he used to formulate striking spaces in reality as well, for example for Roche AG in Sisseln. [474]

Creative approaches to solving design problems were also developed by the use of models as a key technique. The material used for the model did not seem to be important, it could be cardboard, clay or plasticine, and home-made tools were sometimes used for working on them. Cramer discovered an entirely new modelling material through one of his students, who was experimenting with common salt, it emerged, was particularly suitable for modelling earth reliefs, which Cramer liked his students to work on, because the material made it possible to create certain embankment angles that were very close to reality because of its specific grain qualities. Like Ernst Cramer, Emil Steiner was so enthusiastic about the potential uses of salt that he used a photograph of a sculpturally modelled salt landscape for the title page of the June 1975 issue of *Der Gartenbau*. An article called "Designed hills" illustrated some more effectively lit salt hills and also described the fascination of working with salt models.[475] Cramer used this technique in his own work for the Roche project in Sisseln, building the finely modelled earth mounds of common salt in his working model.[476] The results that Cramer had worked on experimentally with his Athenaeum students sometimes had a considerable effect on his late work, as the following project descriptions will show.

Cramer taught at the Athenaeum until his death in 1980. But the results of his teaching passed largely without mention in Switzerland, if one disregards his own projects. This is partly because of the above-mentioned shift in the paradigm of landscape architecture. In addition, the majority of Cramer's students practised as landscape architects in France, where they were in competition with peers who had studied at notable schools like Versailles. There great emphasis was laid on links with the history of French garden history, but Cramer's teaching turned out to be Modern in the classical sense in this respect as well: he rejected the lure of historical garden design and looked for his own,

new strategies for handling nature and landscape. And so one looks in vain for Ernst Cramer's legacy in the work of his former students. But this phase was all the more important for his own late work.

Heiniger private garden in Unterentfelden:

Mound composition dating from 1967

Working plan

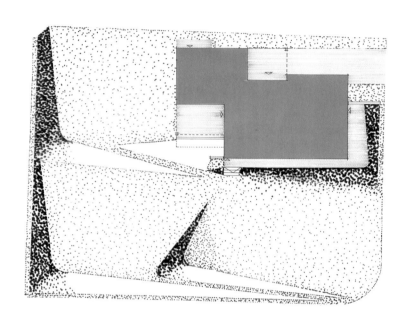

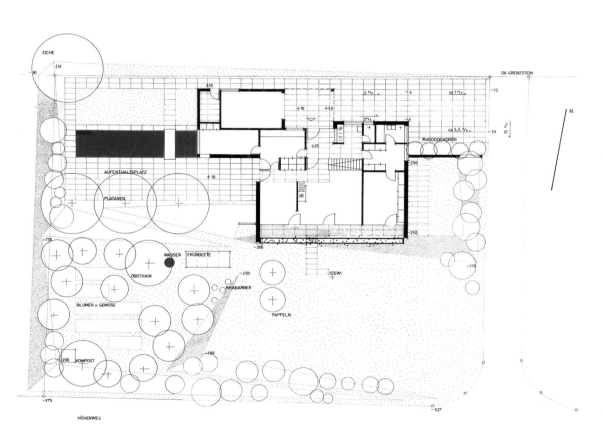

Sculptural garden zones

In the transitional period from the flourishing garden architecture practice in Zurich to the one-man-office in Rüschlikon, Cramer was responsible for a large number of private gardens, but also for a series of open spaces on housing estates, which showed his new enthusiasm for playing with earth modelling and his weakness for the use of uniform plant and construction material. The three following projects have in common that they are among the large, sprawling urban expansion projects that were planned back in the boom period of the 60s. The catchword "eco-city" did not yet exist, a fact which gave the garden architect more creative scope. But social matters definitely were important, and Cramer paid appropriate attention to them. It was in the spatial structure of the new large estates, and with the support of architects who had grown to appreciate Cramer's unconventional garden architecture from work on earlier projects, that Cramer found sufficient scope for continuing his formally simple but creatively demanding experiments.

Open space design for the Im Surinam housing estate in Basel

Access to the internal areas of the residential area is between mounds of earth planted with roses and plane trees

Grassy mounds by Ernst Cramer and apartment towers by Suter and Suter shape the image of the Im Surinam housing estate in Basel

The "Im Surinam" housing estate in Basel was planned in 1967, on a site of about 48,600 square metres that had originally been used for agricultural purposes. The estate on the main road from Basel to Riehen still exists, but none of the houses is directly on the road. The Ciba-Geigy company pension fund owned the building site and commissioned architects Suter and Suter to build the largest possible number of dwellings at reasonable rents, because the price of land was so high.[477] The architects planned three- and five-storey blocks adjacent to an existing older housing estate in the middle of the site, the edges of the new estate marked with nine- and ten-storey residential towers. The residential buildings were complemented with a hostel for Ciba apprentices, a group of shops for daily necessities and a kindergarten. There were

422 dwellings of various sizes, along with underground parking for 280 vehicles. The architects provided underground parking to keep the
open spaces on the estate free of cars and to
create room for "large green areas with varied
design".

Ernst Cramer lent the estate its unmistakable
character by using the soil excavated when the
houses were being built to pile up mounds of
earth several metres high to serve different purposes. Cramer's first aim was to support the architects' basic conception by using the expressive bodies of earth to emphasize the periphery
of the residential area. The mounds provided a
certain amount of noise insulation, in particular
along the roads, but they also created an unusual feeling of intimacy inside the estate. The impression was reinforced by the planting of plane
trees, which surrounded the spaces inside the
estate in precisely fixed rows, thus making it easier for people to find their way around. Cramer
had the planes planted not at the bottom of the
soil hills, but instead along the top, which made
the trees look even taller and accentuated the topography of the chains of little hills. All the ar-

eas where grass would not grow or would have
been too difficult to maintain were completely
planted with dog rose (Rosa rugosa). Christofer
Eriksson explained:

"*We had a great deal of success with Rosa rugosa
in our projects. You might say that I brought this
plant with me from Denmark. No one talked about
ecology in those days, and the Zurich parks and
gardens department was particularly fond of the
plant because it was very easy to trim. Actually the
rose has to be cut back to ten centimetres each
year. If you prune it every two years, the old shoots
are black and the young ones light-coloured. When
the time comes to prune them all you need to do is
send someone in among the plants with a raincoat
and boots, and explain to him that he has to cut off
all the black shoots ten centimetres above the
ground. The rose proliferates then, and flowers
very beautifully.*" [478]

Inside the estate, Cramer attached a great deal
of importance to open, free spaces with only a
few paved concrete paths, mainly curved, running through them. Extensive lawns without
trees were intended to be freely available for children to play on. He identified focal points, em-

Contours, rose plantations
and rows of plane trees are the chief
features of the plan for the
Im Surinam housing estate in Basel

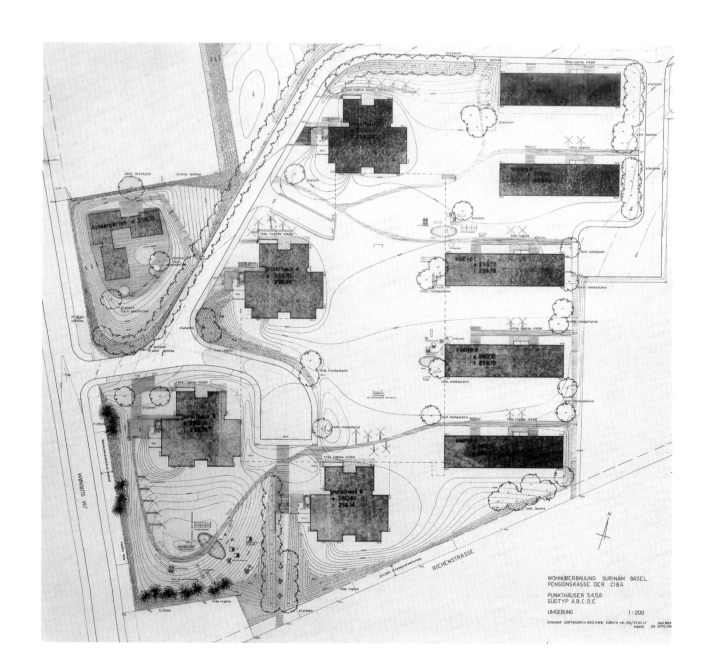

phasized the spaces between the individual buildings or created rhythmical accent in the few private gardens attached to the terraced houses with only a few individual trees or groups of trees. The typical play apparatus like slides or climbing frames were built into the artificial topography wherever possible. The low kindergarten building, set into a little artificial valley, remains a particularly impressive feature. The project's basic concept is reminiscent of the kindergarten design by Hermann Mattern and René Pechère for Interbau 1957.[479] There too, soil was modelled sculpturally to provide an intimate, protected space around the kindergarten building for the children. In Basel, to reach this area, which is ringed by trees, you still have to climb over a gentle hill from the inside of

Open space design for the Heuried estate in Wiedikon, Zurich

The specific, typical 70s character of the open space design for the Heuried housing estate in Wiedikon, Zurich also derives from an unusual combination of copious use of trees and earth modelling. But for this project Cramer went a crucial stage further than in Basel. The City of Zurich held a restricted competition for a residential development on the Heuried site, an area of about 18,000 square metres, in 1969. The programme called for the creation of 181 dwellings in fourteen ten-storey blocks, and also a kindergarten, various civil defence facilities and 296 underground parking spaces. Similarly to Suter and Suter's Basel estate, social needs were central to this public development. Here the open space design was considered to be as important as the architectural and urban planning concepts. The Zurich architects Claude Paillard and Peter Leemann won the competition between twelve invited entrants. Cramer had already worked with them on a number of housing estate projects, and most recently in 1968 on the building of the Töss church community centre in Winterthur. The architects and Cramer had shown how successfully they worked together when building the new Grüzefeld housing estate.[480] The "Im Heuried" housing estate project was the team's last major project, and was completed in 1974.

Paillard and Leemann convinced the jury with an urban planning solution proposing two long, staggered buildings. The main building was 150 metres long and up to ten storeys high, and set at a little distance from the northern boundary of the site. Even today it forms a kind of noise protection screen against the busy main road. At the same time, space was created on the north side for a wide fire brigade entrance, in the form of a simple lawn. A second, lower building and the kindergarten screen off the estate's internal open space on the south-western side. The staggered layout, terraced height sequences and a certain degree of modularity in the façade elements are reminiscent of the large estate in Winterthur, with which the team of architects had already created a stir. In Zurich they were equally concerned to create

Mound of earth Im Surinam

Earth modelling accentuated by rows of trees

Heuried housing estate, earth modelling with artistic interventions under a roof of plane trees

the estate and take a curving path down to the building with its adjacent play areas in the shade of a large solitaire tree. Cramer had the edges of the "crater" piled up so high that the building disappeared behind the hill from the estate side. Of course a row of plane trees emphasizes the edge of the little hollow here as well, forming the space and giving a feeling of security. Copious use of trees and ground modelling were the most important elements for the garden architect at "Im Surinam", and he brought them together apparently effortlessly, to form a coherent whole.

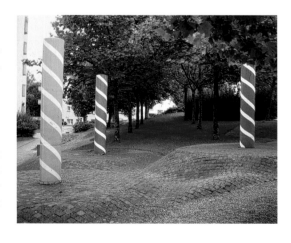

usable open spaces inside the estate that were as intimate as possible, suitable for children to play on. So-called "children's play halls" were built into the base storeys of the buildings, which confirmed this claim, and were expressly welcomed by the jury as a successful architectural feature.

It is still obvious today that the intention was to create a child-friendly environment despite the size of the buildings, and this helped to shape the image of the estate from the outset. Ernst Cramer was involved in the project in an advisory capacity, and the artists Edy Brunner and

Karl Schneider were charged with implementing the wish for attractive open spaces. The published material does not show to what extent Cramer was involved in designing the open spaces in Heuried. He was mentioned only in passing in the City of Zurich's official project brochure, while Brunner and Schneider were identified as responsible for the open space design. [481] There are two design plans dating to winter 1970 in Cramer's estate, but these are at best preliminary studies, as the estate as built differs from them considerably. [482] Only conversations with the architects responsible and analysis of the realized project have shown what a crucial part Cramer actually played in the design concept for the open spaces.

A first unmistakable sign of his handwriting is the extensive roof of trimmed planes, planted on a five metre triangular grid. Today, now that the roof of leaves has closed over, it is clear what effect the garden architect had in mind thirty years ago. He wanted to create a space with strange, squat proportions, a kind of natural counterpart to the "children's play halls". The low roof of crowns was intended to make the children feel safe and protect them from the watchful eyes of the adults in the flats above, so that they could play as they wished. Another

Heuried housing estate in Zurich with murals, play area and plane tree planting

Lawn and pavement modelling, its basic form determined by the "trame"

Earth formations similar
to Land Art in the shade of plane
trees on the Heuried estate

Paved landscapes at the sports and
recreation centre Trägerhard in Wettingen,
built in the early 70s

structed grid. This grid is not based on right angles however, but on a network of linked circles
with different radiuses: the *"trame"* that Cramer
had developed with his students in Lausanne. [483]

While we can be certain that Cramer was responsible for the basic structure of the design,
the striking earth modelling, the plane trees,
about 100 of them, and the paving, the ideas for
all the other design and play elements probably
came from the studios of the artists and architects involved. For example, Peter Leemann admitted his fondness for the Spanish architect
Antonio Gaudí. A terraced "pool mound hill"
clad with coloured ceramic tiles including a pool
of water was inspired by Gaudí. A colourfully designed play hill for sliding down, a sandpit with
a coloured ocean liner and an octopus-like creature, a "hill with ruins" with a fireplace, three
columns and seats were additional play elements for children, but they look like absurd *ob-
jets trouvés* in the middle of the grove of plane
trees. There is also a small group of five mounds
in the paved area that catches the eye; its significance and origins are unknown. This detail is almost reminiscent of an abstract depiction of a
spider. Formations like these were familiar in
the USA as cultic mounds made by the Indians
in the mid-West, and were later used by the
American Land Artist Michael Heizer as a model for his "Effigy Tumuli" in Illinois. But Heizer's
project dates only from the early 80s. Possibly
this element, which appeared almost casually,
also arose from Cramer's experimental work
with his students in Lausanne, as he always
liked setting them the task of modelling abstract hill formations in plasticine, clay or cook-
ing salt.

The earth figure was one of the least striking,
even too inconspicuous design elements in
Heuried. Other artistic features were considerably more dominant in contrast. For example,
the façades were painted with giant green and
blue silhouettes of the faces of people involved
in building the estate, to help "the residents to
relate more strongly to their home", as the city's
official project brochure put it. The same aim
was pursued with "an appeal to tenants to involve themselves in the creative process by
painting their own letter-boxes," a campaign
that was obviously very successful. [484] Thus
the open space design for the Heuried housing
estate remains a typical example of efforts to
make life more pleasant for the residents of
large housing estates by an artistic and participatory approach.

Model examples of creative design of open
spaces to counter the monotony and anonymity
of the new large housing estates were often discussed at this time. In autumn 1973, for example, the Federation of Swiss Garden and Landscape Architects paid a study visit to Paris to the
new "La Grande Borne" housing estate near
Grigny, which had been built for 15,000 residents as part of the state social housing con-

characteristic is the virtuoso handling of the topography and the almost complete lack of
steps. The whole site appears like a kind of
earth sculpture, planted with trees, and available for playing or walking on, made up not just
of areas of lawn and gravel, but also of paved
concrete surfaces. Cramer again used the same
square concrete paving that he had sought out
specially for the Bruderholz hospital project,
but this time not just in flat areas. He stretched
the paving, and this was new in Cramer's repertoire, over the modelled paths and squares,
without bordering it. Curved edges "gear" the
paved sections into the areas of grass and gravel. On closer examination is becomes clear that
almost all the elements of this inner playground
are anchored in a precise, geometrically con-

struction programme. Ernst Cramer also went on this trip as a member of the Association, and was apparently very impressed with architect Emile Aillaud's estate, which made a lively and colourful impression. Aillaud had worked with a team of sculptors and artists to create a "town as *Gesamtkunstwerk*", as the specialist press put it. Cramer then examined the landscape design and artistic features that had been used to enrich the children's lives on the French housing estate with his students in Lausanne. [485] And in fact it does seem that not just Ernst Cramer, but those responsible in the City of Zurich too were guided by "La Grande Borne" when commissioning a team of architects, landscape architects and artists to build the Heuried estate. It was a period that was looking for new, creative, even interdisciplinary solutions. "Everywhere is a playground in 'La Grande Borne', the alleyways, the yards, and the great wide meadow, the 'Prairie'. There are squares with paved hills, squares with trees, there is the sundial that shows how time is passing," wrote an enthusiastic architect in 1975. [486] Ernst Cramer shared this enthusiasm and felt moved to create the modelled paved landscape for the Heuried estate. But while natural stone had been used for the paving in Grigny, Cramer felt that concrete paving was more appropriate for the times, and omitted the rustic touch of his model. Just as in France, the Zurich artists created their colourful play features and built them into the garden architect's earth sculpture. But he did not use garish colour effects, and instead created a simple framework of landscape architecture that is still spatially viable today, and surprises people with his earth modelling. Ernst Cramer was never interested in mere copying, but in developing things that he felt were pointing the way forward.

There is no doubt of the model part played in principle by "La Grande Borne" in the Heuried design, however. Even so, there may have been a second, earlier source of inspiration that may have provided ideas not only for Heuried, but above all for a later project, the open spaces for the Technical College in Winterthur: the "Jardin sculpté" in Paris, by the French landscape architect Jacques Sgard, created in 1969. [487]

Urban planning for Homberg

The housing estate in Homberg, on the Lower Rhine, which was planned and built between 1969 and 1974, shows clearly how flexibly Cramer reacted to different general conditions. Homberg is one of the rare urban planning projects where the garden architect had to respond to existing structures. The estate in Homberg, a suburb of Duisburg, was originally a mining settlement for the Rheinpreussen cooperative housing association. [488] After being sold, it was taken over to be developed for profit by the entrepreneur Josef Kun. He wanted to pull down the old mining settlement, which would be listed as a monument today, and replace it with high-rise flats for about 5000 residents on the site, which is about 220,000 square metres in area. [489] Kun's colleague saw the De Bary high-rise flats built in Basel in 1961 by Suter and Suter and got in touch with the practice. The architect Rainer Fleischhauer, who was the manager of Suter and Suter's German office at the time, explained it was only with difficulty that Kun was persuaded to first draw up a general plan for the site that was to be developed in Germany.

The architects started planning in 1969 and proposed that as a reminiscence of the estate's history, at least the old, magnificent avenues of trees should be preserved to as large an extent as possible and built into the new design. The residential buildings were placed on an orthogonal grid in such a way that the lower buildings were on the edge of the new estate and the 70 metre long, 60 metre high towers in the centre. But as the new urban structure was not aligned

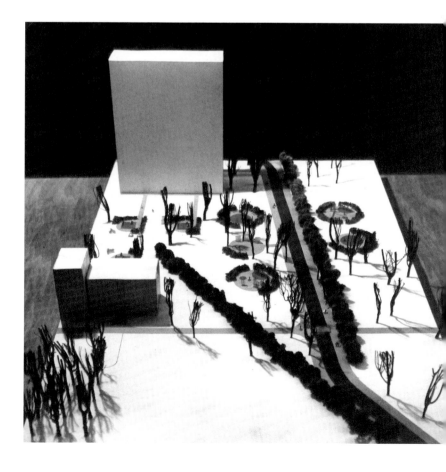

Detailed model for Homberg with
circular playgrounds and canal

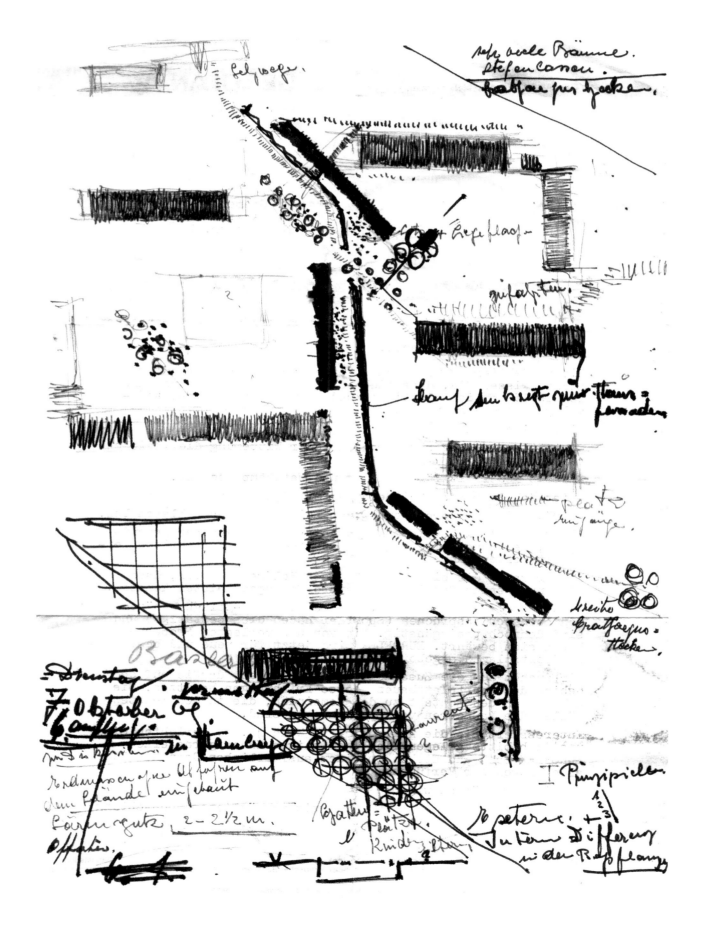

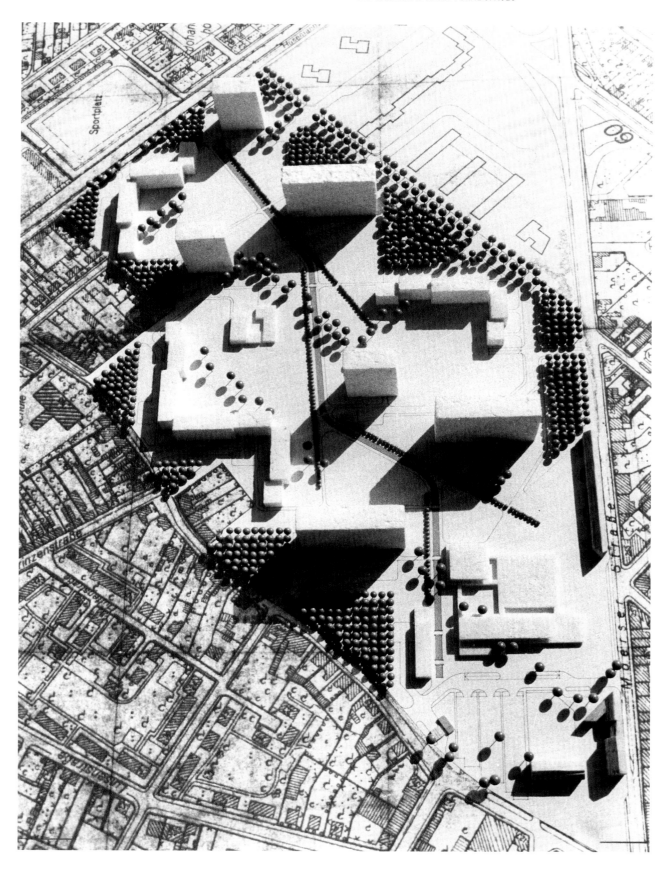

to fit in with the original development, only short sections of the original avenues remained, with the connections to the surrounding road systems positioned as their extensions. Cramer based the design for the open spaces on this motif. He proposed building a canal five metres wide and 620 metres long as the most important design element. This was to be analogous with but not parallel to the old avenues, and was to lead lengthways through the estate at a long, diagonal angle. He was apparently inspired by the endless network of canals that still run through the Ruhr region. Christofer Eriksson, who was still involved in the early stages of this project in Cramer's office, stressed that Cramer wanted to underline the horizontal nature of the landscape. The canal would have been fed with groundwater, and only 35 centimetres deep; it was to have been used as a large paddling pool in summer and for skating in winter. The ETH in Zurich produced a special report at the time to confirm that the water

Model of the Homberg housing estate with adjacent old quarters on the plan

Sketch-sheet with design ideas for the Homberg housing estate on the Lower Rhine

would flow along the canal, even though there was only a very slight difference in height between the starting point and the end of the basin.

The canal was intended to be fringed on alternate sides with hawthorn hedges, which would have led into the open spaces from the diagonal sections, and were then to have ended as abruptly as the old avenues of big trees. The design excluded any other tree planting inside the estate to allow for greater clarity of layout. A large number of small, circular playgrounds, framed with trimmed hedges, were to have been

arranged with easy access from the main paths about three metres wide that ran along both sides of the canal, via short, vertically branching side paths. This motif was again clearly reminiscent of examples of Danish garden design in the style of Carl Theodor Sørensen, but in the end hardly any of the main features of the design were realized. All that still exists are the old trees from the avenues and the modelled sound- and sight-screen on the edge of the estate. These peripheral areas are densely planted with a grid of trees, including some smoke-hardy Austrian black pines, to create a clear outer border for the space while reducing the noise within.

It is fascinating to see how Cramer did not simply completely remove or blur the old structures, but built them in, without forcing the existing elements to harmonize with the new ones. And neither did he attempt to complete the old avenues of trees, but adopted an approach that has proved itself in landscape architecture only very recently: he accepted fragmentary features, and combined them with a new, independent structure. The strategy of overlapping and linking existing and new substance in a way that was not necessarily harmonious was only developed in a forward-looking way in the late 80s. One of the most remarkable open-space projects to have made use of this strategy, among others, came into being in the 90s not far away from Homberg, in the Duisburg suburb of Meiderich: the "Duisburg Nord" landscape park, by the German landscape architecture practice of Latz + Partner. Cramer may have recognized the creative potential inherent in the old industrial landscapes of the Ruhr region. But the Duisburg Homberg project remains a remarkable exception within his œuvre.

At the new housing estate in Wädenswil as well, a paved carpet spreads with the movement of the terrain

Draft sketch for the Büelen housing estate in Wädenswil with central carpet pavement and spiral of hedges, surviving only in part

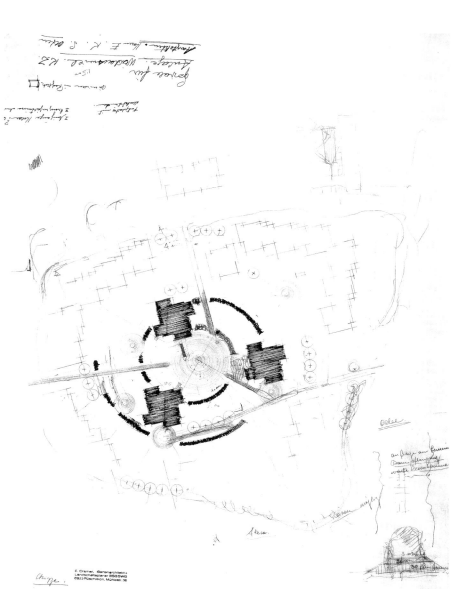

From landscape art to sculpture

"Jardin sculpté" (Jacques Sgard)

When Ernst Cramer started planning the open spaces for the laboratories at the Technical College in Winterthur in 1970, he was perceptibly influenced by Jacques Sgard's powerful sculptural design.

The French landscape architect had created a remarkable sculptural garden for the "Floralies internationales 1969" in Paris. His aim was to "enliven a space simply with the play of forms". [490] The "Jardin sculpté" was located at the south entrance to the Parc Floral de Vincennes. It was almost like a work of Land Art, consisting exclusively of elegantly shaped, curved lawn arrangements, fluently modelled concrete walls and volcano-like paved mounds. A precisely modelled, grassy rampart of earth surrounded a paved area like a sickle. Four volcanic cones up to three metres high bulged up out of the enclosed area, creating the image of a surreal landscape. In another place the mounds of earth that bordered the space were uniformly planted with hornbeam on the outside, and separated by softly modelled, metre-high concrete walls. The landscape architect made it quite clear that he had deliberately used banal materials for his abstract design. The austere precision and scale of the sculpturally imposed shapes greatly fascinated the visitors who moved through these strange spaces. Heini Mathys not only felt that this work was an exceptional phenomenon in garden architecture, but saw even then how much it had in common with the spirit of Ernst Cramer's work.

"There is undoubtedly a relationship here with the ideas inherent in E. Cramer's 'Poet's Garden' at G|59. Both garden creations embody a sculptural sense of form that – far from the usual approach to

gardening, which is often bogged down in mere decoration – expresses new formal design values."[491]

Like his Zurich colleague, who was thirty years older, Sgard worked almost exclusively with modelling paste to develop the earth formations in the models for his garden. This was the only way in which he was able to develop the sculptural, spatial structure precisely from the site. There are clear parallels with Cramer's credo in the explanation of his work:

"It is the art of a sculptor modelling abundance and emptiness, creating a rich universe of the senses by means that are always controlled, and thus rejecting the random character of vegetation that is left to its own devices, whose development changes a space that is never final."[492]

This view, which lays stress on form, of the free artistic contribution of a garden architect, whose work should always be determined by a

high degree of precision, was consistent with Cramer's ideas in just the same way as Sgard's apposite comment on topiary.

"The common habit of cutting shrubs and bushes to serve any purpose has led us to forget this sophisticated art, which requires the qualities of a sculptor and a gardener at the same time. A trimmed plant is a changing form, whose momentum one must be able to sense and maintain, without stopping it; it is a constant invention, requiring a sense of the plant, of form, of tending and of time."[493]

Unlike Cramer, Sgard was able to express his observations cogently, and argued for his way of designing urban spaces as well:

"This is the kind of response that one could make to urban space and to space in large housing estates; the latter, delivered in theoretical and specialized slices, loses its value because of its ignorance of the individual's spatial relationships to his

Ground modelling design by Jacques Sgard

Le jardin sculpté in Paris by Jacques Sgard, 1969

or her environment by creating empty surfaces devoid of emotion."[494]

Sgard's contemporaries were happy to call his sculptural work "humane" and progressive, particularly where new urban spaces were concerned, but they were critical of the rigid way in which he trimmed his plants into shape. This was increasingly coming into conflict with the ecological treatment of nature. In this respect, both Cramer and Sgard were met with the same scepticism and accused of formalism.

It has not been established whether Jacques Sgard really was familiar with the "Poet's Garden". But something over a decade later it became clear that Cramer was able to learn from Sgard in his turn. In fact, in his design for Winterthur, he went beyond Sgard's approach, and linked formal dynamics with a freer planting concept and deliberately responded to the austere architectural context.

Volcanoes at the Winterthur Technical College

The laboratory building was designed by the architects Heinrich Kunz and Oskar Götti of Zurich and Winterthur and realized from 1970 to 1974. It was conceived as a functional skeleton structure with flat reinforced concrete ceil-

ings and steel supports. The two upper floors were pulled together into a tight cube and placed on top of a transparent entrance hall. A central stairwell core, which adds a highlight to the entrance hall, provides access to the five floors and an attic storey, and also serves to reinforce the structure horizontally, along with two shear walls. The transparent entrance hall was intended to create a fluent transition between the interior and the exterior.

Cramer and his employee Karl Pappa were faced with the task of designing the square above the underground car park, the atriums by the building and the floor covering in the entrance hall. Cramer noted three variants for possible design approaches in an undated sketch, presumably dating from 1970. [495] He called the first vari-

Winterthur building site in summer 1974

ant "a carpet over the whole site". Cramer noted "radiation from the corridors" on the second variant and planned radiations "from certain centres" as a third variant. The concluding notes "everything possible from one centre" and "all further forms lié/integrated" show that Cramer was working from the outset on the idea of designing the whole area uniformly, working from a central point. He drew a grid of trees on the same sheet, set on paving patterned in concentric circles. In an advanced, expressive preliminary design, which was also published as the title page of the magazine *Anthos*, he chose the main entrance to the lecture rooms as the centre point for his design. [496] But instead of interpreting this zone as a centre for concentric circles, Cramer drew a network of radial lines on transparent paper with powerful strokes of felt-tip pen, covering the whole site like a carpet of rays. He then built eight smaller circles freely into this carpet, which in their turn formed the centre of radial rings of rays. The diameter of the "satellites" was always the same, 4.5 metres, but the diameter of their subordinate rings of rays varies between nine and twenty-two metres. In the final version the largest ring of rays is almost 40 metres in diameter. Cramer finally decided on the central stairwell as the centre for the whole carpet.

"Garden architect Ernst Cramer's ideas led to free spatial development without any sense of setting borders. He takes his cue from the immediate vicinity and aims to create a moving area that fuses with the architecture of the new building despite being the exact opposite in design terms. It is possible to meet, spend time, move about and talk, play, celebrate, feast in the human scale of the open space."[497]

This official project report reveals Cramer's motivation: he wanted to design a fluent open space that contrasted formally with the architecture, but without reclaiming the traditional landscape vision of classical Modernism. Cramer in fact had an abstract, sculpturally designed landscape in mind that was intended to emphasize the human scale. What looked like a powerful, expressive pattern of rays in the preliminary design, in reality became an ordering, but by no means over-insistent structure, because he simply used the rays to fix the pattern for laying the uniformly grey composite stone paved surface. The use of composite stone paving was still not common at the time, and certainly not in this expressive way. The elaborate pattern on which it was laid, with its countless radials, had to be pre-constructed in minute detail in order to avoid undesirable leftover areas or intersections. Karl Pappa thus made sure that the working plans were extremely precise; now that the number of projects in Cramer's studio had become manageable again, it was again possible to provide the precise working plans that were required.

Cramer and the architects wanted to make a seamless transition from interior to exterior in

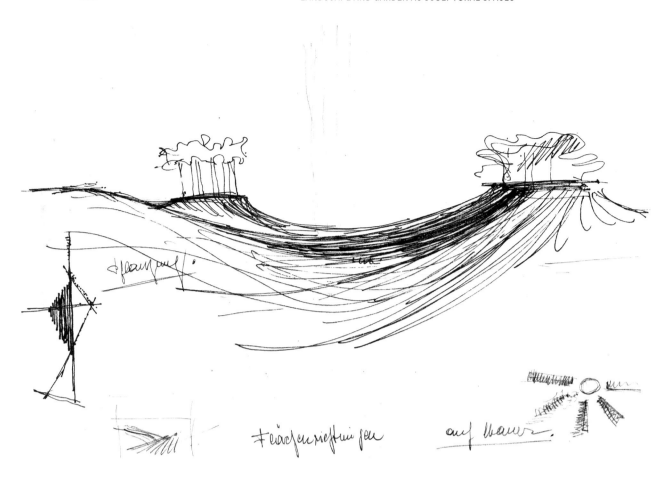

the entrance hall, and so they decided on an unusual measure. The grey composite stone paving
was used as a floor covering inside the hall as
well. Even here Cramer laid out his paved carpet
in such a way that no steps were needed, despite
some small height differences. Thus the staircase
tower makes its full impact. Only the floor-to-ceil-
ing panes of glass separate the interior from the
exterior. Today one looks from the entrance hall
into a futuristic landscape: the strange pattern of
rays in the general plan concealed not only a clev-
erly devised pattern for the paving, but also some
unusual design elements: "volcanic cones" 1.5
metres high, planted with free-growing hornbeam bushes. Heini Mathys wrote:

*"The excrescences, largely planted with horn-
beam, as far as we know the first shapes of this
kind to be executed using composite concrete
bricks, not only provide raised green volumes –
largely safe from damage – but also invite people
to lean on them or lie down, all around the site.
Thus an unusual design idea has at the same time
produced relaxation areas that are enjoyable to
use."[498]*

In functional terms, the "chlorophyll satellites",
as Mathys called them, were nothing more than
large plant containers on the roofs of the underground car park and the civil defence accommodation. But the sketches Cramer made in spring
1973 show that he did in fact want the plant

Ernst Cramer's sketch for the
planted volcanic cones for the
Winterthur Technical College

Funnels and concrete cubes
as seating elements as realized
in the mid 70s

The volcanoes today

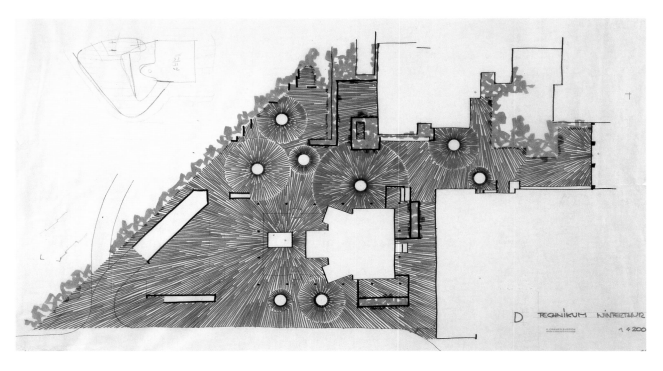

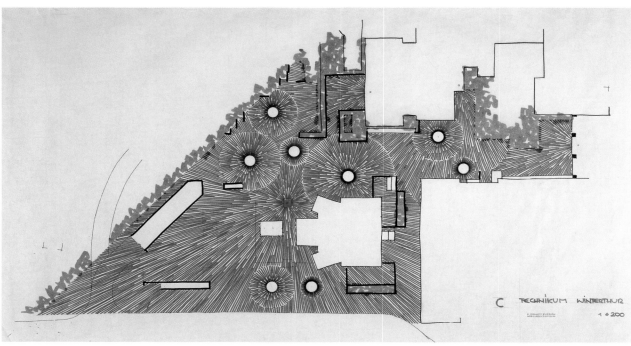

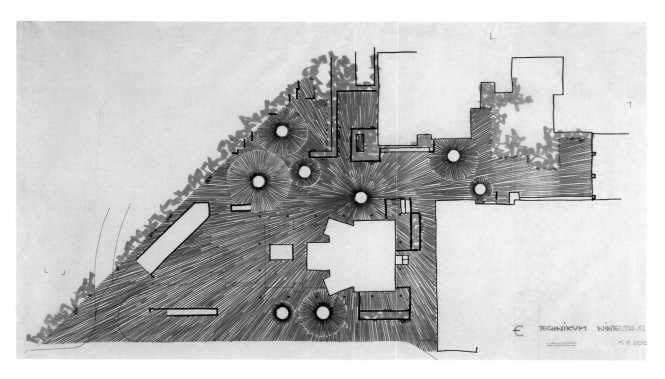

cones to be sitting and lying areas in the shade of picturesque groups of trees. But the hard paving could obviously never be used as a proper area to lie down in, and for this reason Cramer designed extra cubic concrete elements to sit on. These 50 centimetre high seat-blocks with a special profile were used for various purposes: as barrier bollards, wall elements, bases for information panels, stools in the entrance hall with appropriate cushions and as a base for the outdoor lighting units. The overall result was a very uniform look for the furniture. Later the

concept of consistently spreading a single carpet without an edge over the whole area. He was also committed to using an up-to-date material in the open space, and demanded the kind of precision in execution that had been important to him throughout his life. And of course Cramer also used his "leading tree species", the plane, in Winterthur. They were introduced mainly to provide shade in the western half of the square, which can be interpreted as a natural counterpart to or even as a continuation of the glazed entrance hall.

Draft plan for the square for Winterthur Technical College

Design variant C

Design variant E for the square at Winterthur Technical College

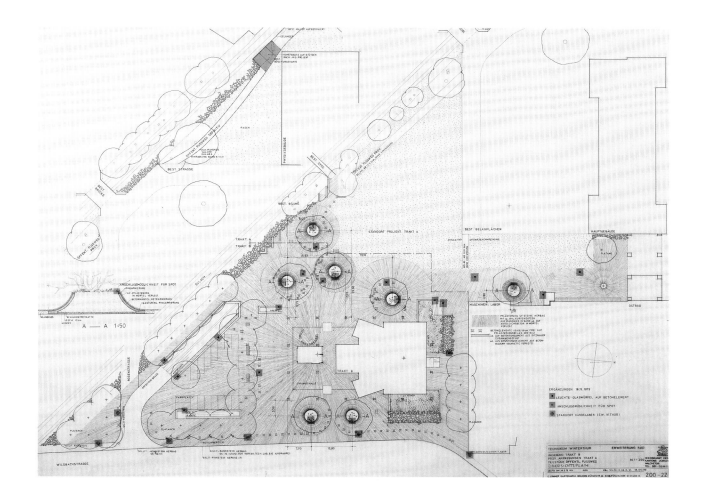

cubic lighting elements, also specially manufactured, were replaced by simple spherical lamps on tubular stands, but the impression of an artificial, swirling topography on an unusual scale is still present.

Once more it becomes clear that in principle Cramer was always concerned about the function of his design, and did not acknowledge purely artistic work, like Sgard. Possibly it was also simpler for him to persuade his clients this way that his unusual approach to open space design made sense. It was certainly easier to justify the cones as plant containers that invited people to sit down than as an artistic game with form played out in a square. Cramer's approach was also fundamentally different from Sgard's paved mounds in the way materials were chosen. He did not opt for building up the cones using composite paving simply because of the

"*Viktor Vasarely demanded 'integrated open space' in a 'struggle against the visual depravity of the modern town' that he raised almost to the status of a working programme,*" wrote Heini Mathys."*And here we have an example of 'integrated open space' of this kind."[499]*

Working plan for constructing the Technical College square

Postplatz in Vaduz

Cramer returned to the sculptural approach he had continued to develop and implement in Winterthur a short time later in Vaduz. Here he had the long-awaited opportunity to realize a large-scale design free of strictly functional constraints.

In the early 70s the City of Vaduz decided to build a new post-office and administrative building in the centre of the Principality of Liechtenstein's main town. The planning scheme for the centre allotted the project a site between two main streets immediately adjacent to the National Bank, the National Museum and the Art Gallery. The extraordinary feature of this site is still that the adjacent steep wooded escarpment thrusts into the urban space through a great gap in the buildings as a powerful natural component. The architect commissioned to build the new administrative building, Franz Marok of Schaan, addressed the constellation of the urban space by giving his building an angular ground plan facing the steep escarpment and forming the north-western edge of the new square. The National Bank frames the south-western edge of the long, trapezoid open space as a counterpart to the new building. The new administrative building mediates between two different levels of terrain: its ground floor is adjacent on the west side to Äulestrasse, which is lower, and which still leads to the underground car-parks, the delivery entrance and the bus stops. The actual town square, which has a two-floor car park underneath it, is located along Städtlestrasse, about three metres above the level of Äulestrasse. The three-storey office section with attic storey is placed transversely above the base storey of the building complex. It dominates the urban space with its façade clad in dark-brown, prefabricated concrete elements. Ernst Cramer was consulted already during the planning phase in late 1971, on the recommendation of a Zurich architect, presumably Werner Jaray. The aim was to fix the principles of the design for the surroundings as part of the planning permission process.

"The problem of ventilation for the underground car park had to be solved, in addition to integrating

Project unknown: concept for a free arrangement of stelae dating from June 1978

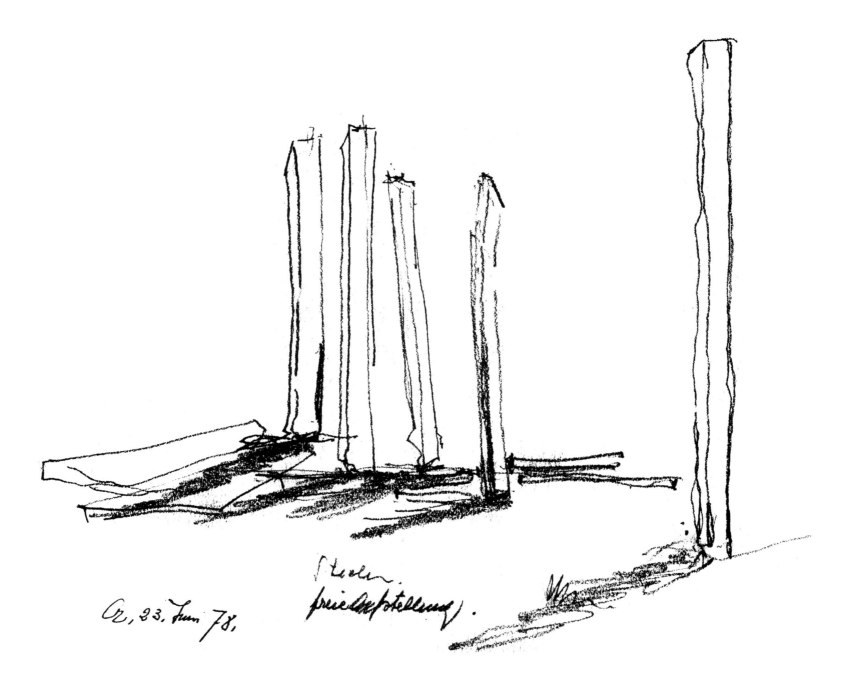

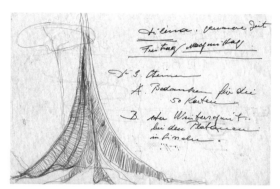

seats and barrier bollards. He was not happy with the stelae which were supposed to establish a structure of spatial relationships. They had the right proportions, but were too similar to the vertical quality of the architectural background and seemed too rigid. The solution lay in dynamizing the basic form.

Tall, tower-like structures can be identified in the first sketches made in March 1975, thus developing a new form for the stelae. [502] The towers are based on a rectangular ground plan but taper dynamically towards the top on one side. Each tower consists of a vertical wall and a second wall, curved parabolically, approaching the vertical in the upper section. Cramer noted that these forms could complement each other. If their vertical walls were placed together, two of them would have produced a tall, volcano-like form, which suggests that the concept might be a further development of the Winterthur volcanoes. But this is not an adequate explanation for this extraordinary design. The sculptural structures in prefabricated, smooth-cast concrete had an elegance that is once more reminiscent of

First experiments on a red lace cloth for the design of the Postplatz in Vaduz

Study drawing of a tropical buttressed tree

the bank site and the centre planning. We felt that that the proposal to design the 7 m high tube intended for ventilation in a concrete, spirally repeating form could create a good effect in the square. […]," wrote the representative of the Vaduz building department responsible for the project, Walter Walch, stressing the fact that: *"The proposed design for the square is an integral part of the post-office project. The proposal deviates from the otherwise customary image (shrubs, little benches, lawns etc.), and is thus particularly striking. It seems to us that this square design is being interpreted as 'Art in Architecture', which in this sense, however, is not the opinion of those responsible."[500]*

In the project report, which gives no information about precise locations and dimensions, a model photograph shows five concrete stelae about four metres high and two rows of trees spiralling out from a large pool. The circular pool was ten metres in diameter and was intended as a the key element in the design of the square from the outset. Cramer first developed the idea for the spiral arrangement of the stelae on a small, improvised working model. [501] He experimented with 23 small polystyrene cubes, which he grouped – on a red lace cloth – in various linear, circular and spiral arrangements around a circular piece of glass as a placeholder for the central pool. In fact the paving, patterned in black, grey and red, that was later realized was similar to a dressmaking pattern in some ways. At one phase in this little experiment it is possible to make out five stelae, consisting of five cubes piled one on top of the other, and positioned on an invisible spiral line. In the realized project, Cramer used concrete cubes with edges 50 centimetres long, but only, as in Winterthur, as

a source of inspiration that Cramer had been seized with since 1960. He still drew on the trip to Brazil that he had made at that time, as became clear on another excursion he made in 1979, when he and his wife took part in a group trip to Madeira, directed by the specialist journalist Emil Steiner. When the group was visiting the Royal Gardens, Cramer disappeared and explored the island on his own. In the evening, when the group met again and was talking about what they had seen in the gardens, Ernst Cramer reported proudly that he had discovered something much more interesting: Oscar Niemeyer's Casino Park Hotel in Funchal. Emil Steiner had the impression that this was a project after Cramer's own heart, because it seemed to him as though it had been sculpted by hand, and was full of formal dynamic power. [503]

Draft sketch for the Postplatz in Vaduz dating from June 1975

Working plans for the arrangement
of the prefabricated concrete sculptures
around the central pool

The Postplatz in Vaduz under construction
with the concrete sculptures in front of the
covered façade of the office building

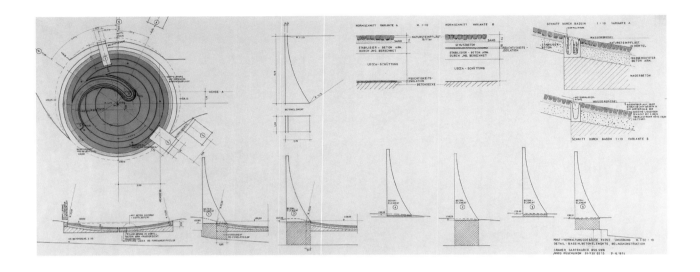

The form of the 6.4 metre high concrete towers in Vaduz obviously derives directly from Niemeyer's sail-like columns in Brasilia. Sketches Cramer made with his own hand of Niemeyer's columns and the cathedral in Brasilia are clear indications of this link.[504] Cramer's own explanation is reminiscent of Oscar Niemeyer's comments on the columns of the Palácio da Alvorada.[505] Cramer argued: "The weight of the concrete is cancelled out. The plane trees and the geometrically derived parabolas come together in a classical-modern new beginning."[506] But the heart of the matter was that Cramer liberated the sail-like structures from the last remnants of their functionality – one of the six concrete structures in Vaduz contained the ventilation shaft for the underground car park – and allowed them to show themselves to full aesthetic advantage as sculptures in this urban square. Cramer set up the prefabricated concrete columns in the spirit of Swiss Concrete and Constructivist art, which sought a new link between formal abstraction and aesthetic eloquence. The white concrete sculptures presented a puzzle picture made up of static and dynamic components that could be experienced by walking through the group of sculptures. Seen from the front, they were just static, rectangular bodies. But the formal dynamic that was already present in Niemeyer's columns was sustained in the side view, and was further enhanced by a sense of movement, which seemed to continue infinity. The individual positioning of the six sculptures of different widths made it possible to perceive the different views at the same time. The contrast between the vigorous bodies, the wooded escarpment in the background and the volume of the multi-story building masses of the post-office and administration buildings could

hardly have been more striking. About 50 plane trees, which the landscape architect planted all around the complex of buildings, linked the newly designed square with the natural backdrop. Nature in different degrees of cultural transfor-

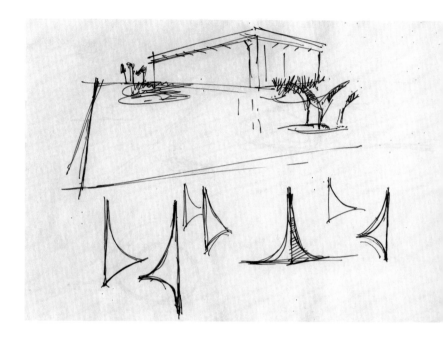

mation met at the Postplatz, and formed a unique sculptural space at the heart of Vaduz. Cramer changed the pool of water, which originally made a striking centre as an independent shape in the 4000 square metre urban space, into a paved hollow filled with water, around which the concrete sculptures were placed. Five radially arranged jets of water enlivened the surface of the pool. The plane trees in the immediate vicinity were positioned, like the concrete sculptures, on different arcs of circles around the water. To stress the continuity of the

Ernst Cramer's study drawings
of Oscar Niemeyer's columns in Brasilia

The Postplatz in Vaduz as realized
(no longer in existence)

Concrete sculptures surround the pool

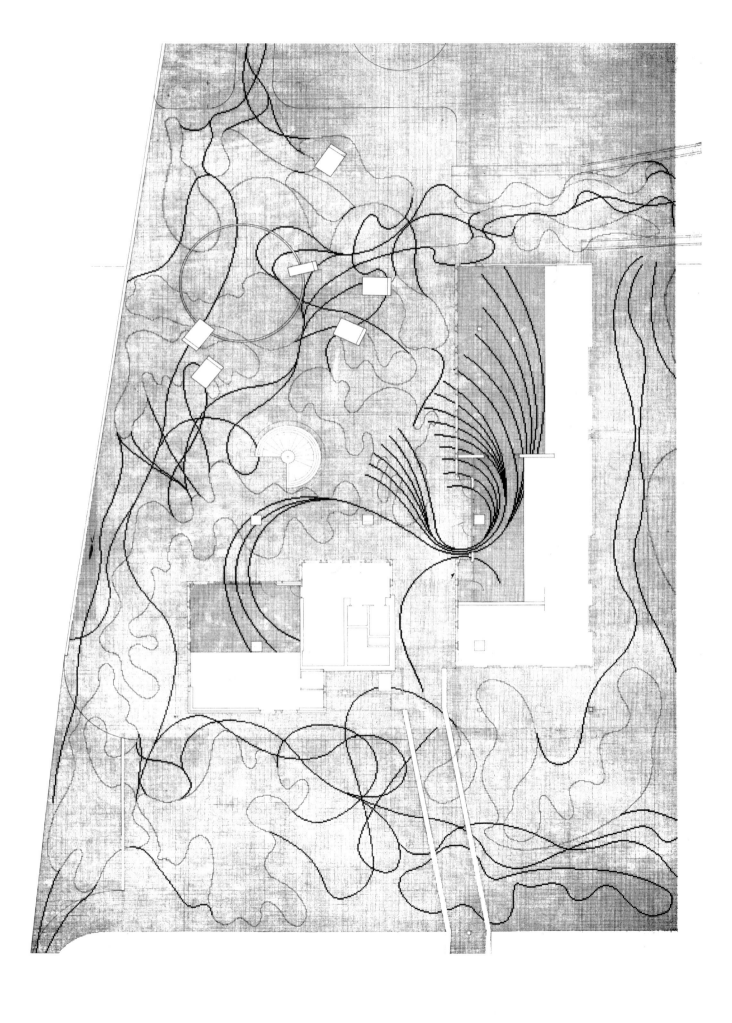

square, Cramer not only ran the paved surface over all the areas around the building complex like a carpet, but also had the pool paved with the same concrete material. He wanted to underline the complex links within the square, with its complicated, overall paved pattern of grey

work, and paled almost into unrecognizability with the passage of time.

This sculpturally designed square with all its remarkable spatial and formal force was completed in November 1976. Cramer, who was almost 80 years old, not only poured his experience of

and red areas and a confusingly large number of black lines with the title "Interconnection!!!".[507] As in Winterthur, Cramer continued the square concrete paving stones into the post office counter-hall and the foyer of the office building and emphasized the links between interior and exterior space and between the entrances to the buildings with bundles of black lines. Otherwise the logic of the lines is certainly not unambiguously comprehensible and is reminiscent of a somewhat confused dressmaking pattern.

With regard to Cramer's points of reference, a comparison with Roberto Burle Marx's artful paving work suggests itself. But despite various similarities in the free, biomorphic formal design, it soon becomes apparent that Cramer was not trying to imitate a model but to achieve his own form of creative expression. While Burle Marx's work includes individual homogeneous colour fields and patterns, and these determine the rhythm, Cramer's work tends to be characterized by arhythmia. Lines drawn apparently at random border colour fields or link individual areas of the square like guide rails. The effect of Cramer's paving pattern, however, was far from the magnificent colours found in Burle Marx's

four decades of Swiss garden architecture into it, but also demonstrated his irrepressible urge to find artistic freedom, combined with social responsibility. But what started as a protest by individual politicians and criticism from outraged taxpayers in the newspapers during the realization phase in the 70s,[508] ended about twenty years later with the demolition of the entire ensemble. The National Bank was being rebuilt, and there was a sense that this opportunity should be taken to redesign the square according to a traditional sense of beauty, and thus to expunge a supposedly ugly feature from the centre of the city. Walter Walch had mentioned the "otherwise customary image" of square design with "shrubs, little benches, lawns" and "Art in Architecture" in his official note quoted above, and this did indeed become reality in the mid 90s. This led to the irrevocable destruction of the successful, abstract late work of one of the most important protagonists of Modern Swiss garden architecture in the 20th century.

Drawing developing the paving pattern and the concrete sculptures, July 1975

Design plan for the Postplatz in Vaduz with post-office building (right) and office building (below)

The "Flame" in Sisseln

Even while the Postplatz in Vaduz was still being built, Ernst Cramer became involved in a project that gave him even more freedom in terms of artistic design than he had already enjoyed in Liechtenstein. At last he was able to realize a sculpture that had to meet absolutely no functional requirements at all, unlike all his previous sculptural projects. In the early 70s, the Preiswerk building company was planning to develop the Roche AG chemical group's 800,000 square metre factory site in Sisseln near Basel. Originally it was Otto Salvisberg, and then the architect Roland Rohn, who regularly built for the Hoffmann-La Roche group. Preiswerk was a firm of building contractors who also became involved in planning buildings for Roche after the death of Rohn. The industrial architect who managed the project in Sisseln from 1974 – Georg Steiner of Basel – was faced with the challenging task of designing not only the new buildings, but also supervising the entire industrial landscape development. A large central square serving as transport intersection and prestigious core of the factory site, was to be constructed in front of one of the new buildings, office building 324 of 1974. When Georg Steiner found he was not getting any further with the landscape architecture concept for the situation, he asked the journalist Emil Steiner for advice. [509] Steiner realized that it would not be possible to do justice to this substantial task us-

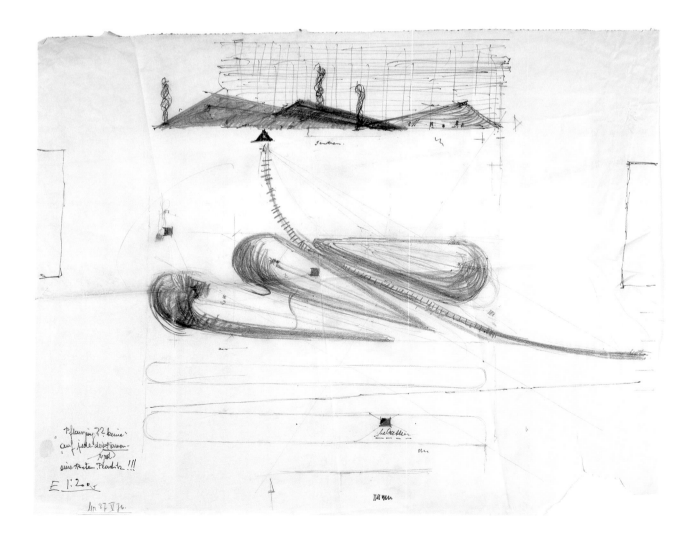

ing the usual horticultural strategies. And so as someone who was very familiar with Ernst Cramer's work, he recommended the architect to commission the Zurich landscape architect to work on the project. The brief was made all the more interesting by the fact that Preiswerk had expressed a wish to present Roche with a large sculpture at the end of the project, as Roche were celebrating an anniversary. But it was finally decided, in agreement with the factory management, that Preiswerk would instead present an anniversary gift for the entrance hall of the new workshop building. Roche would in

Model of the "Flame" with two mounds of salt in front of Office Building 324

Mound compositions for Roche AG in Sisseln

turn take over the design for the square, and Steiner was to develop appropriate proposals.[510]

Ernst Cramer did not need much persuading to take on the project. When Emil Steiner told him about the proposed sculpture, and that a sculptor was being sought, Cramer spontaneously announced that he was ready and able to take on this part of the project as well, and would work out a proposal of his own. Building 324 was not even completed when the garden architect had his first designs ready in January 1974.[511] He suggested that the soil excavated during construction should be piled up in the form of large, long mounds. Photographs of models show that Cramer wanted to create a total of four mounds about 50 metres long and about six metres high. The mounds were to be in the shape of long teardrops, and were to reach their maximum height at the wide end in each case. Two mounds would be fitted together in each case in such a way that the slopes, rising in opposite directions, would produce an artificial valley running diagonally. Cramer placed a pair of mounds, lavishly planted on the outer sides, transversely in front of the five-story office building 324. A second mound, with less dense planting, was to have screened off the car park, which was placed somewhat to the side. The earth formations and the strategy of planting on one side only are clearly reminiscent of Cramer's "Poet's Garden" and also of Jacques Sgard's earth formations in the "Jardin sculpté". In fact Ernst Cramer's notes include some sketches dating from May 1976, showing long pyramids of soil rather than teardrop-shaped mounds.[512] But Cramer did not want to repeat himself: according to Emil Steiner's reports, a shallow pool paved in glittering mosaic and a fountain was to be placed between the mounds.

The Roche authorities did not approve this design. Presumably the office building would have disappeared almost completely behind the mounds from a pedestrian's point of view, and the building costs would also have been considerable. But the factory managers were interested in a sculpture, placed somewhat to the side of the square, that was proposed even in the first sketches and model photographs: the Flame. As in many of the preceding projects, whether it was the fountain in Aarau or the Bruderholzspital, the volcanoes in Winterthur or the concrete sculptures in Vaduz, the expressive dynamics of the sculptural elements had a central part to play in Sisseln as well. Given the importance of the element of fire in chemistry, in oxydization processes and in a figurative sense in other biochemical processes, the surging dynamic of a flame was to be embodied. Cramer bought himself some multi-coloured electrical wire and started to develop his idea in models. In the early variants he placed a sculpture about 14 metres high, made up of five snaking poles, south of the main entrance to the

office building. The next recorded stage proposed not just one but six flame sculptures of this kind in the central square, marking out a broad arc running from the entrance to the office building across the square, ending up between the factory buildings. The mounds had

now been replaced by compact, architecturally shaped "bodies of trees" in front of the building. They were intended to change the spatial structure and enter into a dialogue with the buildings. Cramer was later to explore the potential of this motif thoroughly again in 1977,[513] in a set of revealing sketches called "The Tree Town" and "The Green Town", but the idea was realized only in Sisseln. Of course this new spatial element was to be made up of plane trees. As he probably felt that planting in simple rows or on a grid pattern was too boring for the orthogonally organized factory site in front of the austerely structured façade, Cramer devel-

"The tree is architecture",
sketch dating from 1979

Cramer's idea of a tree town
consisting of masses of trimmed trees
among modern high-rise buildings

Design for Roche AG in Sisseln
on an envelope, April 1977

Two centres define the character
of the square in this design

Five Flames and architectonically
trimmed bodies of trees in front of
the Roche AG office building

The whole complex of Roche AG
in Sisseln today with a view
across the Rhine into the foothills
of the Black Forest

"Living concrete " among
wintry plane trees

The "Flame" in model form

The sculpture in dialogue
with the factory chimney

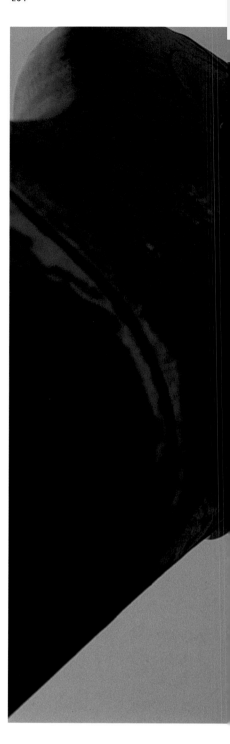

The "Flame" flickers skywards

The "Flame" in the newly planted grove of plane trees

Flickering flame and drifting smoke

still able to come up with. The final design was completed in early 1977, and included only a single circular screen of trees covering the whole square. Unlike the preceding variants, the tree planting is now imbued with much greater simplicity and power. The trimmed mass of trees is made up of six arcs of circles of different dimensions on which 79 plane trees seem to be placed randomly at first sight. It is only at a second glance that the precise principle on which they are arranged is revealed. In front of the main entrance to the office building there is – still – a kind of clearing or curved corridor in the stand of trees. The entrance no longer sets the tone in a compelling way, but benefits almost casually from the spatial concept of the tree planting. The significance of the clearing is reinforced by the large, 15-metre-high sculpture, which has shifted closer to the main drive. This change in position also helped to avoid marking the entrance to the building too insistently, and to underline the more generous approach to the handling of space. In an almost symbolic way, to this day the Flame is the focal point, but not the centre of the tree-covered square, without making a monumental effect.

After Cramer had succeeded in persuading all concerned with the help of a wire model, he built a larger model in wood, about 80 centimetres high, in order to emphasize his vision of "living concrete". All seven elements of the sculpture were shaped identically and each made up of two-and-a-half S-shaped curves. In cross-section the poles were circular and minimal in their dimensions, and at the curves they had to have a thicker, oval cross-section, for static reasons. The feet of the seven elements were placed on a strictly square grid with sixteen possible positions. After that the poles were arranged so that their curves pointed in five different directions; this means that only two pairs follow the same direction and curving movement, but these too are positioned on the grid in such a way that observers have difficulty in making out that they are in fact facing the same way. Only one pole is not arranged on one of the four points of the compass, but points south-east with its first curve. The strategy is clear: Cramer wanted to work with standard elements and to follow the strictest rules, but to create a lively image despite this. The simplest thing would have been to shape and weld seven slender steel tubes appropriately. But Cramer's concept of living concrete would have been contradicted fundamentally, especially as it would have been possible to perceive an unintended analogy with the pipework of the chemical plant. This was why Georg Steiner supported Cramer in his search for ways of shaping concrete appropriately. The slender elements could not be manufactured in a single mould, and so they had to be assembled from precisely prefabricated elements. Astonishingly enough, calculations made by Preiswerk's structural civil engineer showed that Cramer had intuitively

oped a planting pattern for two large, round groves of trees, each of them made up of several eccentrically arranged circles of trees. The two geometrically trimmed masses of trees were arranged so that a dynamically compressed space was produced between them, intended to lead to the main entrance of the office building like a suction head. Additional articulating corridors of light were created at the points where the factory roads cut through the groves. The Roche management approved most of the components of this design. [514] However, the idea of drawing the arcs of the circles visibly on the ground was to be abandoned, along with five of the six sculptures. But the one outside the entrance, with seven elements, was definitely to be realized.

It is not possible to establish how many revisions of his project Cramer delivered in the course of the years. In any case, Georg Steiner was impressed by the spontaneity and apparently inexhaustible quantity of new ideas that the almost 80-year-old garden architect was

chosen the right dimensions for the round and oval cross-sections with his model. Switzerland was searched in vain for a concrete moulding equipment factory that could manufacture the shuttering, but finally an Italian firm was able to oblige. The 42 elements were poured in red pig-mented concrete, each even more slender in dimension. The oval interfaces were provided with a connecting pin to assist the assembly process statically. Six sections were fitted together in each case with the newly developed adhesive "Araldite" to form a single pole. The buckling

Ernst Cramer and his "Flame" in June 1977

load of the components made the installation of the poles another difficult procedure, but the work was finally done with two heavy mobile cranes. The completed sculpture was ready for unveiling on 19 June 1977.

Ernst Cramer's visions of "living concrete" and the "Tree Town" had become reality. The ensemble of precisely formulated green space and the sculpture anchored in it is still impressive today. The sculpture enters into a stimulating dialogue with the surrounding industrial landscape and also with the trees at any time of the day or year, according to the changing weather and light. In Sisseln, similarly to Vaduz, architecture, sculpture and landscape architecture have joined to form a kind of *Gesamtkunstwerk* that is considerably more than the sum of its parts. Neither work reveals the precision of its composition at a first glance, but they both reveal it only as the visitor moves through the space. This principle is still perfectly preserved in Sisseln at the time of writing. Here Cramer was not just promoting the dynamic of a static, functional spatial structure, but also set the viewers in motion. And he still allows them to experience a piece of industrial landscape from new and exciting perspectives.

A Persian garden

Holiday resort in Zibashar

A positive experience of working with Ernst Cramer motivated Georg Steiner to involve him in another extraordinary project: planning the holiday resort of Zibashar on the shores of the Caspian Sea. [515] The Basel firm Pro-Plan-Ing AG, Preiswerk's planning company, in collaboration with the Reveca Catering Company Ltd. Zurich Airport, had been commissioned by a court official of the Shah of Persia on behalf of the Teheran Redevelopment Company (TRC) to build a holiday resort with about 15,000 beds on a site with an area of 1.3 square kilometres. In addition, there were to be about 400 apartments and holiday homes that would be sold to

Variation on the theme of the Tree Town

an affluent clientele from at home and abroad. Anyone who was anyone in Iran at the time owned a holiday home on the Caspian Sea. Zibashar was intended to become one of the most desirable holiday destinations on the Caspian coast, with a first-class hotel with 600 beds, a casino, a spa, a bazaar, a wide range of tourist attractions and a variety of sports facilities.

When Cramer started work on this project in 1977, a team of architects had already been engaged on it for some time. They had sketched out a rough draft of an enormous town. The centre was intended to feature an urban complex on a large empty plain. The complex was to have an overwhelming mass of buildings and a gigantic tower reminiscent of Manhattan or Houston. When Cramer found out what this project was all about he reprimanded the architects and explained to them that it was entirely impermissible to concentrate a mass of buildings at the centre of a Persian town. "We are in Persia, and in Persia the centre is the eye of God."[516] Cramer knew that gardens had always occupied a central position in Persia. The word "paradise" comes from the Ancient Greek, and appeared there as a name for Persian gardens. Persian carpets, on which Cramer based his design, were nomads' mobile gardens as it were, which they unrolled in their tents at the end of a day's journey. As a rule, there was a blue area in the middle of these carpets as well: the pool, the Eye of Allah. Cramer was successful in persuading the architects to rethink their plan thoroughly – a large, square pool of water appeared in the design, in the centre of the planned settlement.

Around the pool, the team devised two large, octagonal carpet estates in the north and a cultural district, also octagonal, with housing around it in the south-west as well as a hotel complex, octagonal in its turn, the only six-star hotel in the world, with direct access to the coast and a private beach. The central articulating and linking element was to be a large canal, with canals branching off from the central pool into the four districts. But Cramer did not just put his stamp on the general plan with expanses of water. He also developed a meticulously devised structure of greenery. The mild climate on the Caspian coast made it possible to work with plants similar to the ones he had used in Ticino. Thus the planting list included a whole series of decorative varieties from the Ticino version of "Cramer's magnificent flower composition". In a large number of sketches and drawings for the extensive parks, inner-city oases and hotel gardens, Cramer once more developed the kind of romantic planting that he had been so enthusiastic about at the beginning of his professional career. [517] It almost seems that in this project, at the age of 80, he had come back to his roots and his love for plants in all their diversity. Cramer paid particular attention to the transitions between town and countryside and the way in which architecture was integrated into

The curved edge of a city by the sea.
Sketch by Ernst Cramer for the holiday resort of Zibashar dating from October 1977

Cramer's drawing of the canal flowing
into the Caspian Sea, autumn 1977

the overall concept. In this respect as well, the plan shows the characteristics of the new design strategies. Trees supported the structure of the resort in strictly geometrical formations, arcs of circles, straight lines and grids. The carpet housing in particular has conspicuous rows of trees that are shifted strikingly off the prescribed street axes, creating an unusual tension.

Ernst Cramer took particular care with his work on the three-by-three metre model of the paradise town, made up of hundreds of brass screws and components, and thus called "Schrüblistadt" (Town of Screws) by the team. The golden-gleaming model, mounted on separable boards and underlaid with mirrors representing water, was intended to convey the radiant magnificence of the new and luxurious town, with its marina, golf course and sandy beaches. Again working in laborious detail, Cramer created the landscape on the model with hundreds of pins, insisting on the utmost precision. The intention was that even the model, despite its small scale, should show the charm of the park landscape and the atmosphere on the path leading along the great canal under the magnificent bridge to the point where the canal meets the sea. Georg Steiner said admiringly of Cramer: "He was a garden and landscape ARCHITECT. He made architecture with plants!"[518] The model was broken down into many pieces and sent on its travels. An elaborate concertina album was also produced,[519] with written descriptions of the luxury of the new town, vividly supported by atmospheric model photographs and sketches by Ernst Cramer and the architects. But when Shah Mohammad Reza Pahlewi was overthrown by the Shiite opposition in 1979 and had to leave Iran, all the Western companies were also forced to leave the country and break off trade relations. Zibashar remained a magnificent vision, whose intoxicating atmosphere Cramer had also been able to drink in for a time.

General plan of the projected holiday resort of Zibashar on the Caspian Sea

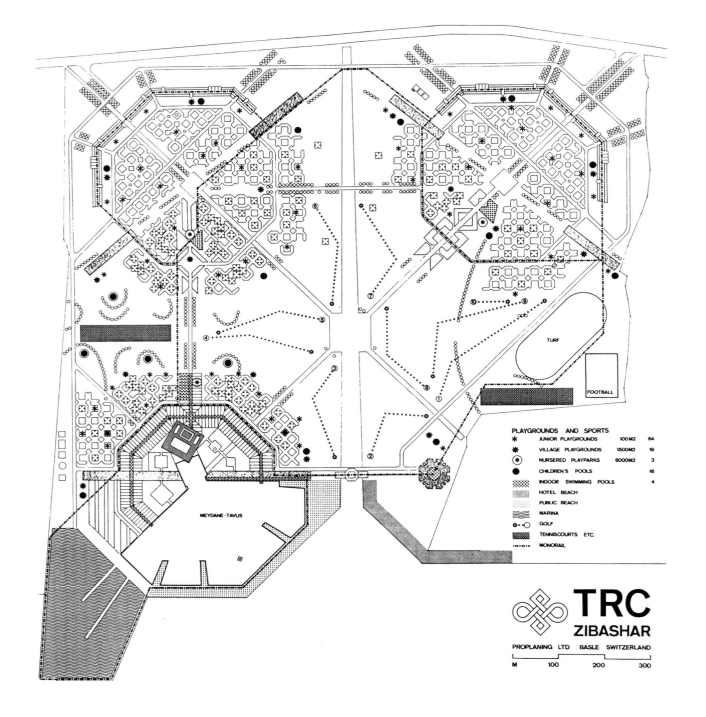

PLAYGROUNDS AND SPORTS

✳	JUNIOR PLAYGROUNDS 100M2	64
✴	VILLAGE PLAYGROUNDS 1500M2	19
⊙	NURSERED PLAYPARKS 8000M2	3
●	CHILDREN'S POOLS	16
	INDOOR SWIMMING POOLS	4
	HOTEL BEACH	
	PUBLIC BEACH	
	MARINA	
○•◦◦	GOLF	
	TENNISCOURTS ETC.	
·--·--·	MONORAIL	

TURF

FOOTBALL

MEYDANE·TAVUS

TRC
ZIBASHAR

PROPLANING LTD BASLE SWITZERLAND

M 100 200 300

Overflowing creativity

Cemetery in Gränichen

The cemetery in Gränichen offered Cramer a rare opportunity to prove himself as a garden architect, architect, sculptor and painter. In his last large cemetery project he invested much, perhaps too much creativity.

As long ago as the early 60s, when the old cemetery surrounding the Reformed church in Gränichen had to be closed as part of the separation of church and state, Cramer had been brought in to redesign the walled area around the church as a public open space. He had to create a new cemetery opposite – a task that he had discharged with relatively simple resources, and as compellingly as ever. In the mid 60s he submitted a plan including the building of a low

cemetery building, but this was not realized for financial reasons. In the early 70s the town decided to hold a small, invited project competition and asked Cramer to take part, along with three local architects. A jury selected his "Cheops" project in May 1974 and recommended that it should be realized. The garden architect was extraordinarily pleased to have succeeded, as he had always harboured a secret wish to work as an architect. There was a time when he even forbade his employees to fold plans, because he preferred to appear with a large roll of plans at meetings with clients and architects. [520]

The project convinced the jury with its unusual combination of landscape design and architecture. Cramer retained the earlier square concept for the ground plan with a side length of 18 metres, subdivided into four units of almost equal size for the various uses: two of the quarters contained staff rooms, the garage and the workshop, one quarter contained the visitors' room with three adjacent mortuaries, and the last quarter, facing the cemetery, was conceived as an open shelter. The ambitious shape of a curved, tent-like roof was proposed for the 12.5 metre high roof, clad with Eternit asbestos cement slabs; this was intended to create a dominant feature for the residential quarter and a centre for the cemetery. [521] Was Cramer aware of the demanding power of this

The large model, called Town of Screws, with the hotel in the foreground and the casino above the mouth of the canal

Cramer marked out the structure of the green areas meticulously with pins on the model

Cramers design sketch for
the cemetery in Gränichen

Model with planted mound
of earth and funeral chapel

The Gränichen earth moulding
in model form

architectural form? He was proceeding in a similar way as for the volcanic cones at Winterthur technical college and Postplatz in Vaduz, intending above all to achieve unity of architecture and landscape. The roof was to initiate a curving movement that would lead into the movement of the surroundings as smoothly as possible. The site was placed within a precisely shaped circular wall of earth, formed like a dish. This volcanic cone with an exterior diameter of about 80 metres was formally very similar to the fountain outside the Bruderholzspital, [522] and still fulfils three important functions today. It creates a closed, almost intimate space around the building; it is used as a field for urn internments and above all it forms a space that is screened visually from the extensive field of graves with its countless tombstones. Cramer wanted to create a sense of spatial peace for the mourners, before they carried their dead to the cemetery. The surrounding bank of earth is about three metres high, the same height as the lavishly glazed ground floor of the funeral chapel. It guides the eye upward and gives viewers the illusion that they are looking beyond a distant horizon.

After intense discussions, the local council decided that the elaborate shape of the roof of the building was not justifiable functionally, financially and aesthetically. [523] The flat roof version, which Cramer had already proposed in his first design in 1967, was also rejected. After the design had been revised in consultation with an architect from Gränichen, a simple pyramid roof was built that no longer had the original dynamic force. And so Cramer paid all the more attention to making the open space design more dynamic. Here the circular embankment played a crucial role. While it was planted with ivy and individual shrubs on the outside surfaces, Cramer laid lawns on the inside, and completely covered one part with cotoneaster. The start of the main access path was marked with a sharp incision in

A design idea for the Gränichen cemetery developed by Ernst Cramer by drawing and painting

the ring. At another point Cramer opened up a broader view of a part of the cemetery that was intended to be more open and without graves. Visitors were to find themselves in a spacious, open cemetery landscape. But it was precisely this spaciousness that was missing in reality.

Based on the structural principle of the *trame*, two more circular hedges were drawn closely round the building like bowls. They were intended to serve as space-defining and screening elements. The smaller space enclosed by these hedges seems like a green extension of the visitor's room in the building, while the larger hedge-wall surrounds the service courtyard. In plan the hedge formations and the earth modelling complement each other to form an almost closed full circle. Cramer paid a great deal of attention to the paving as well. He used exactly the same square concrete paving that he had chosen for the Bruderholzspital and in Vaduz. As in Vaduz, the design underlines the way in which visitors move from the entrance of the cemetery to the anteroom and finally into the mortuaries, using an elegantly curved, red and dark grey

pattern in the paving. The paving is laid both in the open space and in the public interior in Gränichen as well, to stress the close relationship between the interior and the exterior. Here Cramer even had the low plinths for the three glazed catafalques for the coffins in the mortuaries made in the same coloured concrete paving, and conceived the ceiling lighting in curved lines, in the spirit of the flowing rhythms of the space. Even the hedges were to have been trimmed so that the top moved rhythmically, but he was finally advised against this because of maintenance costs.

Cramer was not prepared to renounce the privilege of designing a sculpture for the communal grave in the ring embankment, intended to provide a further highlight for the location. A first suggestion in summer 1977 was that a Corten steel sculpture about 4.4 metres high should be erected. A double S-shaped incision was to be made in the 80 centimetre wide slab, so that the two halves of the wall could be bent out in different directions, thus creating a puzzle picture made up of static and dynamic compo-

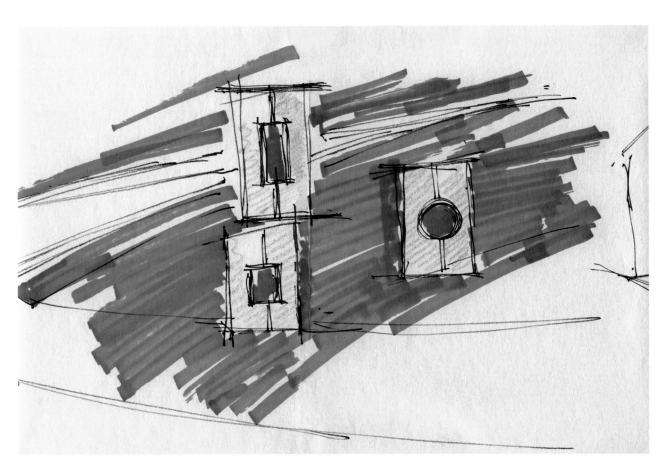

like abstract chessmen on the rising surface of the earth mound. The slight shift between the two parts of each sculpture establishes a certain tension within the objects. The three sculptures and also the two halves of each individual sculpture shift in relation to each other according to the standpoint of the viewer. The clarity of the image on first sight is even more subtly distorted with the movement of the observer. Cramer himself did not offer his clients any interpretation of his group of sculptures, but his sketches suggest that he was less concerned with a certain symbolism than with "light penetration" and perspectival spatial relationships. [525] Encouraged by the clients' openness and delight in experimentation, Cramer's urge to design knew no bounds, even beyond this point. He designed a number of variants for the entrance gates, the enamelled door handles, the lamps, fences and curtains, but one day he also presented the building expert responsible with a proposal for a coloured mural that he wanted to present to the parish as a gift. After a few consultations, Cramer's surprising offer was accepted, and he went to work single-handed. Cramer composed an abstract mural for the wall of the visitors' room in the funeral chapel, made up of dark shades of blue, red and green applied horizontally in freely painted brushstrokes that flowed into each other. Apparently, even this creative intervention was mainly about creating an atmosphere in the room, and not about representing a particular content.

It is worth pointing out that in the case of the Gränichen cemetery project, which was com-

nents. [524] But this proposal was not greeted with enthusiasm because of the neglected appearance of the rusty steel. Instead, Cramer developed a group of sculptures in the same year consisting of three concrete units about two metres high, each consisting of two identical concrete elements in a reddish colour, which were set up as mirror images of each other, like abstract brackets. Each sculpture was rectangular in plan, but had a different central window in each case: circle, square and rectangle. The elements stand staggered one behind the other

Design for three concrete sculptures
in the Gränichen cemetery

Simple design for the Gränichen colour
scheme dating from July 1977

pleted in 1978, Cramer obviously lost sight of some aspects of his own principles formulated in 1967:

"Planning on a human scale.

Order in diversity.

Return to simplicity.

Keeping up with modern architecture and art."[526]

It is certainly not possible here to speak of a return to simplicity in comparison with other of his projects. Each individual design measure may correspond to this principle. Powerful earth modelling, simple planting and skilful handling of spatial constellations point in this direction. But the multiplicity and variety of the individual ideas realized, raising claims for Cramer's status as architect and artist, as well as landscape architect, was unable to achieve the kind of creative calm that was otherwise so important for him. It seems as though in this project he yielded to the temptation to use the freedom offered to aspire to solving every aspect of the design single-handed – at the price of losing sight of the integrity of the whole in the midst of his tumultuous urge to create.

Staging the view

Gasser garden in Sonvico

Designing private gardens was important for Cramer to the end, although it was no longer anywhere near as important as it had been in the 60s, when over half of his commissions related to private projects. Now as then, in private gardens the clients laid down the guidelines for the design. Cramer accepted this rule of the game effortlessly in his reticent way, and always made his clients feel confident that their personal wishes were being taken into account at all times. The consequence was that he could only draw on his creative potential to a limited extent when designing private gardens. Two private gardens created in the 70s, one of them the last that Ernst Cramer worked on before his death, clearly shows his unbroken intensive efforts relating to the spatial and formal qualities of these private paradises.

Aldo Gasser, the proprietor of a distinguished fashion house in Lugano, commissioned a Ticino architect to build him a villa in Sonvico in the early 70s. [527] The building plot in the Ticinese mountains near Lugano had a magnificent view of the picturesque mountain and forest landscape with Lugano and the lake in the distance, and this had to be taken into account when building the house and planning the garden. The commissioned architect designed a house that was characterized by both traditional elements of Ticino architecture and a relatively austere formal language. The high walls clad in natural stone in particular had hints of the simplicity

Proposal for a coloured wall design in the Gränichen cemetery dating from October 1977

that Cramer preferred. The architect died shortly before building started, and the client asked
the owner of a Ticinese gardening business that
he regularly bought plants from for advice:
Arnoldo Manni, a former partner in the firm of
Manni – Cramer & Surbeck. [528] Manni showed
Gasser some of the gardens that he had realized with Ernst Cramer in Ticino since the 40s.
Gasser was so impressed that he decided in
1972 to commission Ernst Cramer to design his
new garden. At the first meeting, Cramer expressed his enthusiasm for Tuscany, with its avenues of cypresses and pine-woods, and suggested similar motifs for the design of the garden. It seems reasonable to assume that in Ticino he went back to the romantic garden images
that he had used over thirty years earlier. And
the projects that Gasser had seen raised expectations of a picturesque Ticino garden. But first
of all Cramer made a plaster model of the gar-

Expressive design for the concrete
paving in the Gasser garden

Preliminary design plan for the Gasser
garden in Sonvico with a striking shape for
the topography and the tree backdrops

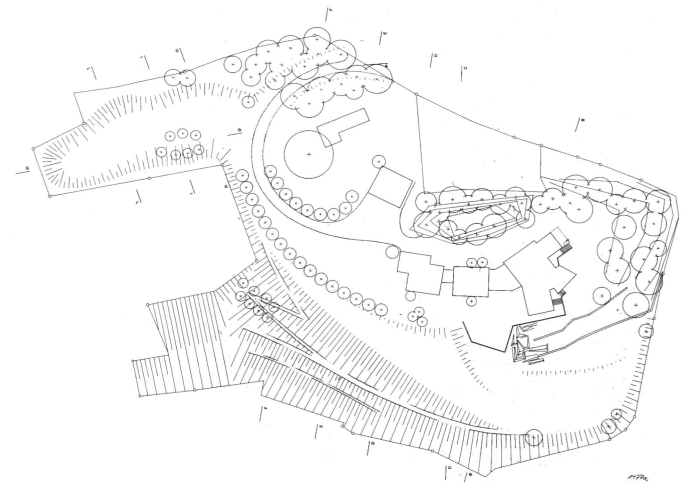

den, in which he more clearly defined its spatial structure. The days of picturesque images that could be looked at from an ideal viewpoint were long gone for Cramer, even though the plants chosen were scarcely any different from those he would have used in the 40s. Cramer wanted to create spaces, but he also wanted to frame the view of the surrounding landscape, and he devised a variety of motifs for both purposes. In summer 1973 the client and his garden architect travelled to Pistoia together, to order pines and cypresses from the famous tree nurseries there, to be delivered and planted in winter.

At the same time, a start was made in Sonvico on the earth modelling and the construction of the roads and paths. A long, tarred drive was intended to branch of from the entrance gate on the main road and lead along the edge of the slope to the garages, which were slightly set back. There the surface changed from tar to small granite paving stones, and a narrow path between the ridge and the villa led to the front door. To formulate this space precisely, Cramer had a section dug out of the bank formed by the

Drive to the Gasser house in Sonvico

Building the retaining wall

ridge so that he could build a high, slightly curved retaining wall in natural stone. This produced a simple space, uniformly clad in stone, defined by the natural stone paving, the retaining wall and the natural stone façade of the house. The precise way the materials were used and the management of the space are reminiscent of the drive leading to the Bucerius house in Brione, even though the masonry stones were placed vertically there.

But the driveway to the house did not quite become an impressively choreographed spatial experience until the main gate was built, with its accompanying planting on either side. Cramer deployed a traditional touch for the start of the drive, using a large gate that was essentially classical in design. When the gate opened, visitors looked directly into a cypress avenue, which seemed to extend to the far horizon. Cramer created this optical illusion by building a ramp along the axis of the view from the gate, planting an avenue of slender cypresses on it, then reducing the distance between the two rows as they got further away, thus reinforcing the perspective effect. But before running straight into this false avenue, the drive in fact swung left in a great curve. The garden architect underlined the drive's swoop along the edge of the slope by modelling a shallow earth embankment to accompany it. This also served to raise the horizon and render it more precise, and made visitors even more curious to look beyond the embankment into the surrounding countryside. The drive and the embankment did not run parallel.

View down the cypress avenue that seems to lead into the distance

The row of pines on the modelled embankment

Detailed plan for the portal design and the garden drive with avenue of cypresses

They came up close to each other at first, and then gradually separated again.

Cramer had about 15 umbrella pines planted at regular intervals on the boundary embankment – a powerful, unexpected gesture. It seemed absurd at first to block the magnificent, uninterrupted view with trees. The tree-trunks break the view down into individual images like in a film-

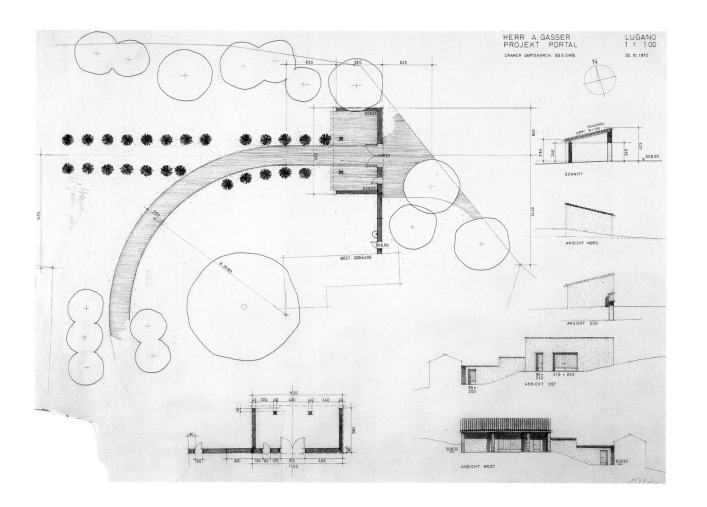

strip, which deliberately increases the observer's sense of movement. This kind of curved, fluent handling of lines is typical of the layout of the whole garden, and it also shows up in some interesting details of the paving, which are reminiscent of the fanned bundles of lines in the paving of the Postplatz in Vaduz. Cramer wanted to frame the picture, and to create a fore-

tate, to talk about the handling of space and the conscious inclusion of the landscape in the garden.[529]

ground to reinforce the effect of depth. The edges of the drive, the top of the embankment and the crown of the trees define a dynamically curved space that gives the driveway an astonishing power to this day.

The drive and the subsequent approach to the house were precisely formulated and matched to each other with the utmost accuracy. They were the most impressive places in the garden, as the rest of the site was planted essentially in an open and traditional landscape style. It is therefore not surprising that Cramer made a detailed photographic record of the drive. His instinct for creating dynamic spaces could develop to the full here, and linked the client's expectations with his own ideas in a skilful way. The last planting in Sonvico was done in summer 1978. Cramer liked to bring visitors to the es-

The magnificent view of the countryside and Lake Lugano, broken down into individual images like a film strip

Contemporary Baroque

Metzner garden

The new design for the garden at the stately 18th century home of the noble Solothurn von Sury family was the first and only recorded opportunity that Ernst Cramer had to create a new garden within a historical structure. He had never come into contact with such a well-preserved historical garden before.

In spring 1979, Emil Steiner[530] sent Cramer in Rüschlikon a copy of an article by Albert Baumann in the 1961 *Gartenbaublatt*. [531] The article dealt with Italian influence on "Solothurn gardens in the 17th, 18th and 19th centuries". Baumann described the surviving remains of the gardens at the von Sury house as a masterpiece:

"The axis of the surviving garden leads through the service courtyard. The axis starts by the entrance to the coach-house, the main house is on the right, on the left is a pretty pheasantery (faisandrie). In front of the house is a large, solid terrace, protected by a wall of green on the west-

"Contemporary baroque is allowed", entry in the sketch-book dated March 1980

Design sketch for the Metzner garden called "Nonsymmetry"

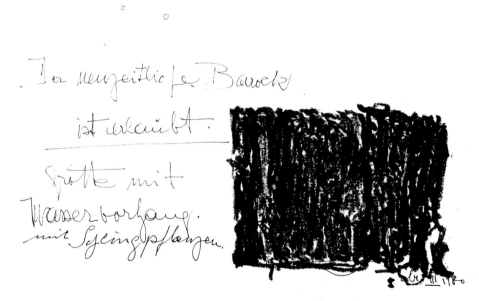

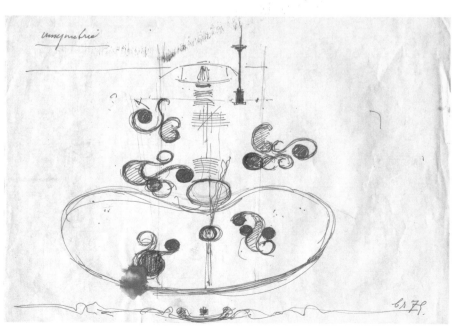

ern side, and opposite this, slightly raised, is a little promenade, shaded by an avenue of lime trees. The axis continues in a semicircular projection, marked by a mighty horse-chestnut. From this vantage point a beautiful, functionally handled group of steps leads on the axis to the lower part of the garden. Two paths thrusting out on the sides, adapted to the terrain, serve the same purpose. In the lowest part of the garden we find a large oval area like a parterre, cut by a path on the garden's axis. This area is highlighted by a pool, a bench, and flowerbeds at the sides. The larger areas of the oval are planted with vegetables, but could conceivably be adorned with lawns. The various spaces produced by the way the garden is divided are framed with trees and shrubs. A small grotto dating from the last century is built into the slope before the lime avenue."[532]

Baumann provided a plan of the garden that he had drawn up in 1958 as a further description, and Emil Steiner noted on the copy that the garden had survived in this form, with the exception of the beds. Steiner wrote a few lines to Cramer on the back of the copy, asking whether he would be interested in the project, which he saw as "monument preservation project". [533] The building contractor Metzner had acquired the plot of land and the historic family house with its large, overgrown garden in the late 70s, and was thinking of redesigning the site, but paying due attention to the historical substance. He turned to Emil Steiner, the Solothurn monument preservation consultant and editor of the *Gartenblatt* for expert advice. At first the intention was to recover the basic structure of the historical garden, but when the owner pointed out that he wanted to be able to use the garden with his family in their leisure time, and thus to make appropriate changes, Steiner decided to involve his friend Cramer. The three men met for a first walk round the garden in February 1979.[534]

Cramer made a large number of sketches, as usual on old envelopes, advertising brochures, cardboard boxes and wallpaper patterns, looking for the correct formal language for the baroque garden with a draughtsman's impatiently seeking strokes. In spring 1980 he came to the conclusion: "Contemporary baroque is allowed."[535] He thought that it was perfectly permissible to use baroque formal language in this context, to the extent that it conformed with the rules of simplicity and did not end up as symmetrical figures. Another note in large red writing reads: "This situation needs large masses of green + simple forms."[536]

Cramer moved away from all his previous design processes and seemed to have been working more intuitively than ever before for this project. The design is not based on a grid, and the *trame* was not used to develop the solution. Photographs of a plasticine model dating from March 1980 show a first concept. [537] Cramer could see only one good solution for a new swimming-pool that the client wanted in his garden:

ly daring. It was to be on the upper level of the terrace and would have effectively leapt over the swimming-pool, with a protruding shelf of water. A broad curtain of water would have become the new main attraction in the garden, against the background of the mighty old horse chestnut. For the lower level of the garden, Cramer imagined an almost surreal ensemble of six large, geometrically trimmed hedge figures, placed irregularly around the central garden area like chessmen. All the elements were constructed strictly geometrically, and Cramer noted: "Stonework – no curves, except the form of the pool and this is still to be based on right angles – is permitted. Technology must not be visible anywhere."[538] He designed the cross-section of the geometrically rounded Jurassic limestone edging stones for the pool with the utmost meticulousness.

Everyone involved felt that the intensity of the work, which had taken over a year, had been worth while. The planned garden would skilfully link the historic with the new, and so everyone was looking forward calmly to the crucial meeting with the monument preservation department in mid-September. "Model very good … free baroque my view … Certainly necessary to show monument people. I'm working." These were probably Cramer's last jottings about his ideas for the project. But the all-important meeting never took place. Cramer died unexpectedly on 7 September 1980 after a short illness, three months before his 82nd birthday, in Rüschlikon.

it had to be placed at the foot of the central retaining wall in the garden in such a way that it would only be recognizable at a second glance. Even so, a pool 2.8 metres wide and over 14 metres long was planned. The new central element of the garden was to be a cascade on the central axis, which would run down to the large oval. The plan for the start of the cascade was particular-

Ernst Cramer and his client
in Solothurn in February 1979

Design sketch for the Metzner garden
in Solothurn dating from 1979

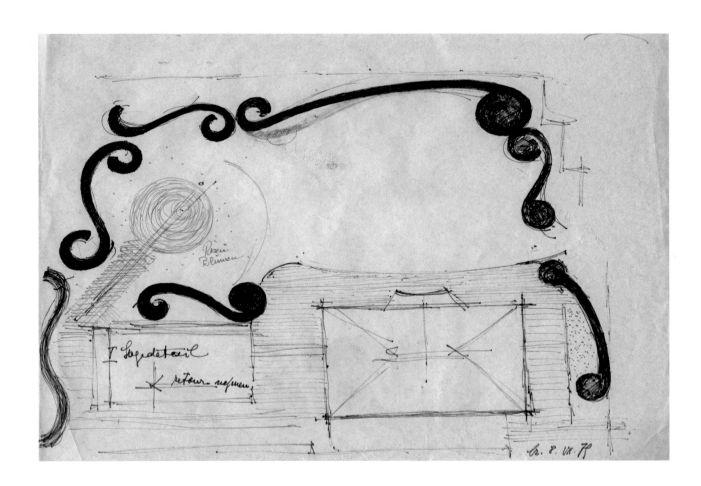

A MODEL FOR CONTEMPORARY LANDSCAPE ARCHITECTURE?

Ernst Cramer's openness to current cultural trends, his unprejudiced collaboration with progressive artists and architects, and his ambition to make an independent and relevant contribution to the culture of his day remain the defining features of his importance as a garden architect. At G|59 he not only made a courageous break with his own past, but he also unambiguously rejected the conventions of garden design and gave a valuable impetus to the renewal of garden culture by committing himself openly to the garden as a means of artistic expression. This impetus did not trigger any serious movement in garden architecture at the time, neither in Switzerland, nor in the neighbouring countries. This was due to a large extent to the profound gulf, still scarcely bridged today, that was opened up between the artistic and the everyday world, above all by modern abstract art with its autonomous system of signs. Cramer's abstract gardens were mysterious artefacts to many of his contemporaries, belonging to a world that lay beyond the everyday. Both the "Poet's Garden" and the "Theatre Garden" are still seen mainly as abstract works of art, and not as visionary landscape architecture. The change of paradigm from artistic to ecological aesthetics in the early 70s, as well as the considerable time-lapses that occur before innovations in art and culture become generally accepted in landscape architecture[539] are additional reasons why Cramer's visionary gardens were almost forgotten and are only recently being rediscovered.

Ernst Cramer could never be moved to explain his visions in detail during his lifetime. To this day not even the universities have engaged in a targeted theoretical examination of his work. His comrades-in-arms – this became clear from numerous in-depth conversations – could not really understand his change of direction or the significance of his avant-garde projects. "If you heard him talking about a garden a few years later," Hans Jakob Barth admitted, for example, "you were puzzled by such a change of mind through 90 to 180 degrees."[540] But the fact that none of them picked up on and consistently took the new design approaches any further can also be explained by the former employees' aspirations to emancipate themselves. Anyone who left the practice to become an independent garden architect wanted to break away from Cramer's creative dominance and develop a style of his own. Willi Neukom, for example, who was known for his openness towards innovations in art and architecture, founded a very

successful studio of his own and created some remarkable artistic projects. But he too did not succeed in cultivating Ernst Cramer's progressive impetus in a way that could have led to a regenerative movement in landscape architecture. "Dieter Kienast at Rapperswil was passionate when he introduced us to Ernst Cramer's work. His enthusiasm was infectious," declared the Swiss landscape architect and former student at the Intercantonal Technical College in Rapperswil, Olivier Lasserre, in an interview that was published recently.[541] Kienast realized the implications of Ernst Cramer's work even in the early 80s. He discovered him as one of the central models in current landscape architecture and nailed his colours to the mast like no one else.[542]

"The things which were relevant in the early eighties are not the same as those which are relevant in 1995, but, despite this, the works of Ernst Cramer still inspire me today [...]. [The] deductive principle, concentration on a few elements, becoming more powerful in consequence, made a lasting impression on me. Cramer's work was certainly the more forceful and followed an approach which was more innovative and programmatic."[543]

Years later Stefan Rotzler, who had started to take a first thorough look through the estate with Gertrud Cramer, joined with Emil Steiner and Heini Mathys and sketched out the idiosyncratic garden architect's career and some of the most important projects for the first time in *Anthos*.[544] The fact that Cramer's work has started to seem relevant again since the mid 80s to the younger generation of landscape architects as well, can be explained only against the background of a switch in trends that takes place almost cyclically in landscape architecture: "design versus ecology".[545] Purely ecologically oriented, scientifically legitimated landscape design has become paralysed in a dry academic approach in recent years, which led at best to mere imitation of nature but even more frequently to inarticulacy in design.[546] The motto *Design with nature*,[547] based on a physiocentric concept of nature, was used well into the 80s to demand that design be abandoned in favour of ecology, as nature was seen as the better designer and would take care of the aesthetic quality of the project herself. Dieter Kienast vehemently criticized outgrowths of this development as "eco-design", and demanded a theoretically sound renewal of garden culture with an eye to Cramer's pioneering achievements:

"Mother Nature provides us with the new ideal of beauty for the garden. If this is not enough for

Geometrically constructed paths lead through the abstract hilly landscape of the "Berggarten" in Graz by Kienast Vogt Partner

technical reasons, then people go back to rustic ways of processing 'natural' materials. Anything visibly artificial, any design, is taboo, straight lines are godless and concrete is the source of all evil. The highest esteem is paid to showing particular exquisite natural images: the jungle wilderness, the splashing stream, the lake with its beds of reeds, the blossoming Alpine meadow. And because the natural requirements are not in evidence, they have to be created artificially. And at the same time it is essential to cover up this artificiality as much as possible. 'Eco-design' is what we intend to call the kind of garden design that takes its cue from the image of nature without the resulting image relating even remotely to the essence of the situation. [...] The renewal of garden culture is not a problem of form, but a problem of content. The difference between a banal bit of green that is easy to look after, a completely overgrown area that is left to its own devices and a garden is that a garden has a viable concept behind it, a score or a vision. The garden must become a signifier again, it should sharpen our awareness and awaken our senses."[548]

The "Poet's Garden" met these requirements exactly in 1959: it did not need to draw on the past, but became a signifier of the present through the unprejudiced use of modern building materials. Above all through its up-to-date design vocabulary, however, it sharpened our awareness of the garden as an independent, topical cultural product, stimulated discussion and aroused the viewers' senses.

Ernst Cramer tried time and again to integrate artistic and abstract earth formations not just temporarily at garden shows, but also as permanent design elements within landscape architecture. His realized designs for the Wilerfeld housing estate in Olten, the Winterthur Technical College or even the "Ammonite" at the Bruderholz hospital near Basel are just some of the most familiar examples of his virtuoso handling of artistic earth modelling in everyday open space design. The grassy pyramids in the "Poet's Garden" brought Cramer a great deal of kudos, but he was never again able – although he suggested it for the Roche project in Sisseln, for example – to realize them in this succinct form. And this was not always just because peo-

ple did not understand modern artistic landscape design, but also because architects were afraid that architectonic landscape design would mean unacceptable formal competition for the building. This scepticism still prevails in many architectural circles today, and shows a view of the garden that was lastingly shaped by classical Modernism: the ideal of an architectural structure in surroundings that have been left in as natural a state, or designed as naturally, as possible. Even more recent architecture – emancipating itself formally from Modernism by using terms like "landscaping", "decontextualization" and "hybridization" and trying to achieve a new relationship with nature in its programmatic approach – prefers to present itself as embedded in idealized images of nature and landscape of the kind that had been staged with consummate mastery by garden artists in 18th century landscape gardens.

Fear of excessively high construction and maintenance costs for landscape architecture often only reinforces many garden architects' and clients' reservations above gardens that do not conform to an aracadian ideal. Of course all gardens, but especially gardens of this kind, like any piece of landscape that has been transformed by man, need a certain level of care if they are not to deteriorate rapidly. What happens when this factor is neglected can be seen in many of Ernst Cramer's projects that have not been maintained with sufficient attention. The value in principle that a society accords to its culture can thus also be deduced from the condition of its gardens, parks and squares. Cramer obviously crossed a certain threshold with many of his works in this respect, and this same threshold repeatedly sets tight boundaries for experiment in current open-space design as well.

Brühlpark in Wettingen (Dieter Kienast)

Dieter Kienast did not just adopt Cramer's ideas, he consistently developed his radical approach to design in subsequent decades, and thus ensured continuity in the history of garden architecture also in practice. Brühlpark in Wettingen, dating from 1982/83, was the first project in which Kienast clearly borrowed from Cramer's abstract formal language in terms of design.

Earth pyramids in the Brühlpark in Wettingen in dialogue with the Jura foothills in the background

Kienast did not at first feel comfortable with the fact that he was so recognizably close to the model – the topography of Brühlpark is marked by two large earth pyramids and an earth cone – as this fact forced him to face his own principles and justify such recourse to the past.

happened decades earlier, critical voices multiplied even while Brühlpark was under construction, complaining about the lack of flowers and predicting that the geometrical mounds would not stand up to everyday use. But Kienast stuck to his idea in the teeth of demands for natura-

Plan of the Brühlpark in Wettingen by Dieter Kienast dating from 1982/1983

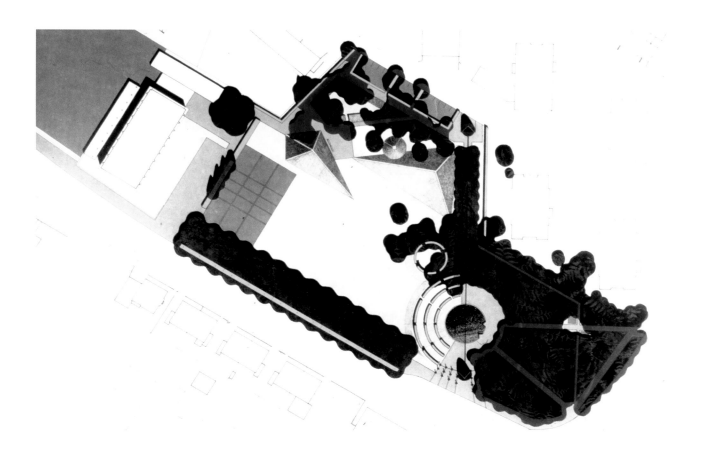

"The earth pyramids are reminiscent of Pückler and Cramer. I did not intend this relationship to be, and this could have led to a new formal design with a large number of mounds of earth, but I finally left it as it was because I felt that the park could only cope with few simple elements. The mounds were intended to form a contrast with the flat surroundings and the Lägern mountain ridge."[549]
In fact the asymmetrical, long shapes of the free-standing, three- and four-sided pyramids in Wettingen were more reminiscent of the Zurich model than of the earth structures in the park in Branitz. The fact that the pyramids were built despite Kienast's scruples is not so much a sign of a recourse to tradition than evidence of the progressive nature of Cramer's 1959 concept. He had recognized that it would be impossible for garden architecture to make a contribution to contemporary culture, which at the time meant the vaunted moral and aesthetic renewal of post-war society, until garden architects shook off the dictates of traditional imitation of nature and openly devoted themselves to innovations in art, culture and architecture. "Not clinging to what we already have or even wanting to look for a style, but liberating ourselves, that should be the lesson," Cramer's teacher Gustav Ammann had already demanded.[550] As had

listic forms and proved that the abstract earth mounds were viable in terms of day-to-day wear and tear.

Berggarten in Graz (Kienast Vogt Partner)

The earth pyramids in the "Poet's Garden" and Brühlpark were still free-standing individual structures, but just under two decades later an artificial ground sculpture to walk on was created from 29,000 cubic metres of earth in Graz. Impetus drawn from the "Poet's Garden" produced an independent work of landscape art in the year 2000 that can be called a cultural product of our day, and need in no respect fear comparisons with the historical model.
The scenery is surreal: almost as though they are sleepwalking, the public move through a landscape architecture stage setting, just under five hectares in area, consisting of long, grassy pyramids up to eight metres high. Spectators become protagonists, disappearing into geometrically formed folds in the earth, exploring stepped pyramids or enjoying the shade of small groups of trees, in order to peacefully watch the abstract scene's moving double on the surface of the wood's pond. The whole scene is carpeted with the sounds of the 21st century: the music of the spheres, the chatter of the vis-

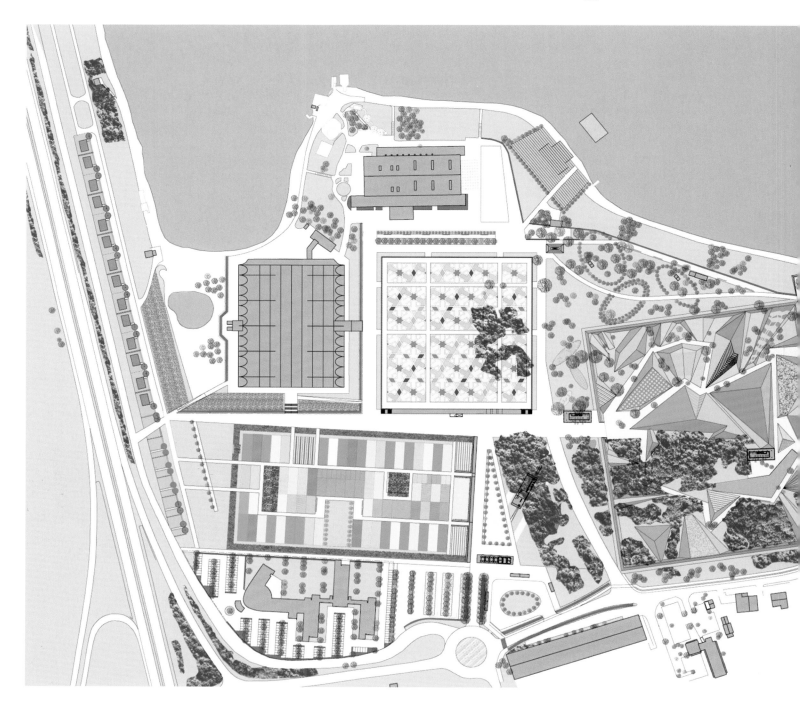

Realised plan for the Horticultural Show site in Graz by Kienast Vogt Partner

itors and from time to time the turbines of an aircraft taking off.

"You [...] bring to us a completely new landscape, you create a sense of space that I have never felt before in the open air. You prove that given an ingenious mind and precise use of the craft, it is not absolutely necessary to use this valuable material soil in a way as the forces of nature do. You do not create an imitation of a natural event, but you create a work in a way that we abstract painters and sculptors have been trying to achieve by concrete means for years." [551]

There is no doubt that Hans Fischli's enthusiastic commentary on the "Poet's Garden" dating from 1959 could also have applied to the "Berggarten" (Mountain Garden) at the International Steiermark Horticultural Show 2000 in Graz. Cramer's work is rightly seen as a forerunner to the park by Kienast Vogt Partner. But unlike its model, the "Berggarten" survived as a public park after the end of the exhibition.

Today, four decades after G|59, landscape architects can benefit from an avant-garde landscape art that caused a furore in the late 60s with spectacular "Earthworks" in remote American desert areas: Land Art. Unlike Ernst Cramer, the American avant-garde artists with their gigantic earth formations were interested neither in the abstract representation of nature nor in gardens in the strict sense. This would be reason enough – as pointed out earlier [552] – not to call Cramer a pioneer of Land Art.

Unlike many of his professional colleagues, Ernst Cramer did not look for inspiration only in masterpieces of landscape or garden design. In his search for the "unified form of artistic value", [553] he preferred to draw on sources from modern art and architecture. To him the central challenge was to decode the essential qualities of advanced art and buildings and to use them to generate a language for landscape architecture that was appropriate to its day. Nothing has

again entering into a dialogue with related disciplines. The obvious thematic, media and contextual parallels between Land Art and landscape architecture, for example, have in recent years repeatedly created a temptation to fall short of the minimum critical distance to art. Unreflecting imitation of elements of landscape art, following the motto "Land Art rather than landscape architecture", has often led to pseudo-artistic projects that did not meet the criteria of either fine art or those of meaningful environmental design.

An approach to landscape architecture that concentrates exclusively on creating individual garden art objects is bound to fall short today, regardless of whether it is landscape art or Cramer's abstract gardens that provide the model. The complexity and changeability of modern man-made landscapes, including urban and industrial landscapes, requires a di-

changed with respect to this challenge today, regardless of whether the source is artistic, architectural or natural in origin. Even Cramer at the time was in danger, when designing the gates for the Pratteln cemetery, of simply imitating Mondrian's painting formally, thus risking his credibility as a designing garden architect. But ultimately he succeeded in most of his works in enriching the genuine vocabulary of landscape architecture and considerably increasing people's understanding of gardens and landscapes. In the "Theatre Garden" in particular, in which sculptural, architectural and landscape-architectural features combine to form an architectonic land sculpture, Cramer showed his extraordinary abilities as a "go-between" for disciplines who relished experiment, but always remained aware of his own professional origins. Cramer's strategy of intelligent migration between professions is growing particularly significant today, when landscape architecture is

verse repertoire of strategies for landscape architecture in dealing with the given context. Ensembles like the "Poet's Garden" will continue to provide important, if sometimes temporary stimuli for current perceptions of nature and the environment, but only to the extent that they are not allowed to deteriorate into merely decorative studies.

Fine art too tends to risk its own credibility when it uses labels like "Plant Art"[554] and – worse yet – plays with the general sensitivity of the unprejudiced observer to the qualities of the designed and the natural environment by crossing boundaries in a way that is naïve, almost negligent. In recent years, many artists who enjoy experimenting have found the right atmosphere for trying new things in public parks and gardens, which provide open space in the truest sense of the word in the dense functional network of cities. In the best cases this does not just produce a dialogue between the impartial

View over the "Berggarten" in Graz

Graphic planting, here with lavender, highlights parts of the grassy hills

The hill formation is laid out before the visitor like an open book

viewer and the work, but also a give and take between the landscape architect's space-time works of art and the fine artist's creative intervention. Exciting conversations develop particularly when garden and park are not used merely in a traditional way, as pretty pictorial backgrounds, but are respected as equal partners and are actively involved. This requires a certain knowledge of garden history and certainly a fine sense of spatial dimensions and vital natural processes in parks and gardens.

If one keeps in mind how difficult landscape architecture has found it in the past two decades to intelligibly integrate creative approaches of landscape art into their work, then it becomes clear how far ahead of his time Ernst Cramer was in this respect as well. He was successful decades before Land Art, similarly to the garden architects Carl Theodor Sørensen and Roberto Burle Marx, or the artists Isamu Noguchi and Herbert Bayer, in using sculptural earth modelling to expand the view of sculpture and garden in such a way that the landscape was not merely a picturesque background, but the actual object of artistic production.

Cramer's precise handling of physical space, which he formulated by the use of tree volumes, hedges, walls or screens, his sensitive approach to earth modelling, and the fact that he confined

himself to few interventions into the landscape, the garden or the square that were all the more powerful for this, create an abstract austerity in many projects even today, and people like to associate this with the idea of "Minimalism". Cramer himself did not use this term, but both the "return to simplicity" and "order in diversity"[555] were fundamental interests of his. These are being discussed in detail today both in architecture and landscape architecture against the background of a seemingly threatening flood of media images.[556] Inclining towards fundamentals, towards simplicity, as a reaction to luxurious exuberance and complexity is a cyclical phenomenon that can be observed in places other than the history of art. In his book *Architecture and the Human Dimension*,[557] Peter F. Smith points out a three-phase cycle in cultural history, tracing a development from ordered classicism to anarchic romanticism. The speed at which this cultural cycle runs has increased so much in the course of history that the individual phases can no longer be told apart unequivocally. The modern movement, with its commitment to abstraction, to universality, to the elementary can probably be seen as one of the last significant manifestations of the first phase. But Piet Mondrian demanded of the truly modern artist that he should choose abstraction in the spirit of a New Creativity, and free himself from the dictates of the natural (individual). A creative discipline like garden architecture, which felt bound to nature in the most intimate way, and saw her as its teacher, had to be distrusted on principle from the point of view of Modernism. And therefore unlike architecture, garden architecture of the day did not succeed in formulating convincing responses to the demands of Modernism using its own specific expressive devices; it saw itself trapped in a hopeless dilemma, and oscillated between admiration of the ideal image of unspoiled nature and an inclination towards architectonic garden design that frequently ended in decorative formalism.

The late 20th century again saw a high point of growth-oriented development in Western society, and as a result, simplicity, naturalness, directness, genuineness have once more become irresistibly attractive. But as delight in extravagance is rooted in man's deepest instincts, according to the poet-analyst of contemporary issues and essayist Hans Magnus Enzensberger, private luxury will never completely disappear. However, it will presumably survive under quite different conditions and in a quite different form. "The luxury of the future will say goodbye to excess and strive towards the necessary, which, it is to be feared, will be available only to the very few."[558] Elementary necessities of life like freely disposable time, free definition of interest, space for free movement, calm, an intact environment, and security will be among the luxury goods of the future. None of these luxury goods will be available without renunciation and self-restraint, as the present social system is draining these resources massively while effectively pretending that this is done in the interest of unrestricted individual freedom. "Minimalism and renunciation could turn out to be as rare, expensive and sought-after as ostentatious extravagance used to be", [559] is Enzensberger's analysis.

"Planning on a human scale. Order in diversity. Return to simplicity. Keeping up with modern architecture and art."[560]

Ernst Cramer's design principles, dating from 1967, which he supported impressively with his work, seem from today's point of view like a reply to current tendencies towards design loquacity that Dieter Kienast repeatedly denounced. But the rationally developed formal language, the rigid basic structure of the garden designs and the reduced range of plants in many of Cramer's gardens repeatedly made observers suspect that he was concerned only with dogmatic austerity, and Kienast noted appositely in this context:

"His example is becoming the accepted thing for gardeners and garden architects, but they have been interested not so much in realizing the artistic concept as in saving effort, time and knowledge of plants. Even architects are taking advantage of this propitious situation, and a lack of knowledge about plants when designing the surroundings is covered up by referring to the new garden concept. And in tree nurseries horticulturally prestigious, varied and elaborate ranges are given up in favour of the robust mass appeal of a smaller number of plant varieties. Thus a formerly outstanding garden design concept has degenerated into a national plague of the uniform green of our balcony boxes, gardens and parks, aseptic and easy to look after."[561]

The misunderstanding that Cramer avoided elaborate planting because he did not know enough about plants still persists today, just as the erroneous belief that the minimalist simplicity of his work had something to do with merely rational-functional design or thoughtless formalism. Cramer was well aware that a straight line in plan would never be as hard when it crossed the landscape; vegetation in its inherent vitality, unlike architectural building materials, admits neither merciless severity nor paralysis in abstraction. The dialogue between a simple, rational basic structure and plant vitality that is to be found in numerous designs by today's young landscape architects was in many cases crucial to the emergence of the poetic element in Cramer's gardens. Cramer knew that simplification not only means eliminating unnecessary elements, but entails seeking universality, openness and significance.

Pyramids reflected in the water.
Memories of the Poet's Garden

NOTES

[1] VON MOOS, Stanislaus: "Recycling Max Bill" in: Bundesamt für Kultur (publ.): Minimal Tradition. Bern 1996; p. 9

[2] DUNINGTON-GRUBB, H.B.: "Modernism arrives in the Garden – To Stay?" in: Landscape Architecture, issue 4/1942; pp. 156–157

[3] cf. also: IMBERT, Dorotheé: The Modernist Garden in France. New Haven, London 1993

[4] ZULAUF, Rainer et al.: "Freiräume" in: Werk, Bauen + Wohnen, issue 9/2000; pp. 44–47

[5] MUTHESIUS, Hermann: Landhaus und Garten. Munich 1907; p. 25

[6] GOTHEIN, Marie Louise: Geschichte der Gartenkunst. Volume Two. Jena 1926; p. 455

[7] cf. Die Gartenkunst, issue 6/1904; pp. 15–16, 52–56, 53–54

[8] MERTENS, Oskar: "Über Gartenkunst" in: Das Werk, issue 5/1918; p. 80

[9] cf. project at Hardlaubstrasse 36, Zurich 6 (1916–1918), described in Ernst Cramer's report book; ASL Dossier 01.03.006

[10] CRAMER, Ernst: Report book of 1916–1918; Archiv für Schweizer Landschaftsarchitektur (ASL) Dossier 01.03.006

[11] NEUTRA, Richard in: AMMANN, Gustav: Blühende Gärten. Landscape Gardens. Jardins en fleurs. Erlenbach-Zürich 1955; p. 7

[12] founded in 1925

[13] founded in 1913; German Werkbund founded in 1907

[14] cf. MATHYS, Heini: "Gratulation. Ernst Cramer 80jährig" in: Gärtnermeister, issue 49/1978; pp. 1076–1077. There is no record in Ernst Cramer's estate of his work in Correvon's gardening firm

[15] Various photographs of Ernst Cramer with his fellow students were taken here

[16] cf. p. 80

[17] CRAMER, Ernst: note accompanying motto: Meine Zeit steht in Deinen Händen (My time is in your hands), Oeschberg-Koppigen 1922; ASL Dossier 01.03.022

[18] AMMANN, Gustav: "Sollen wir die Form ganz zertrümmern?" in: Die Gartenkunst, vol. 39/1926; p. 81

[19] ibid. p. 83/cf. AMMANN, Gustav: "Mensch, Bauwerk und Pflanze im Garten" in: Das Werk, issue 6/1926; p. 181 ff.

[20] GIEDION, Sigfried: Befreites Wohnen, Zurich 1929

[21] cf. RÜEGG, Arthur/MARBACH, Ueli: Werkbundsiedlung Neubühl. Zurich 1990

[22] HARBERS, Guido: Der Wohngarten. Seine Raum- und Bauelemente. Munich 1933

[23] AMMANN, Gustav: "Alte Bindungen – Neue Verbindungen" in: Gartenschönheit, issue 1/1933; no page

[24] MAASZ, Harry: Der Garten – Dein Arzt. Fort mit den Gartensorgen. Frankfurt an der Oder 1927, 6th-8th ed. 1931, 9th-10th ed. 1936

[25] ibid. p. 7

[26] ibid. pp. 41/42 and pp. 53/54

[27] cf. "The Zurich Cantonal Horticultural Show, Züga 1933"; p. 23

[28] ibid. p. 13

[29] ibid. p. 54

[30] cf. MEDICI-MALL, Katharina: Im Durcheinandertal der Stile. Architektur und Kunst im Urteil von Peter Meyer (1894–1984). Basel Boston Berlin 1998

[31] MEYER, Peter: "Zürcher Gartenbauausstellung ZÜGA 24. Juni bis 17. September 1933" in: Das Werk, issue 7/1933; p. 193

[32] ibid.

[33] SCHNEIDER, Camillo: "Die Zürcher Gartenbau-Ausstellung (Züga)" in: Gartenschönheit, issue 10/1933; p. 199

[34] cf. AMMANN, Gustav et al.: "'ZÜGA' Die Zürcher Gartenbau-Ausstellung 1933" in: Schweizerische Bauzeitung, issue 10/1933; pp. 120–125

[35] The first small-gauge corrugated asbestos cement slabs were manufactured in 1926–1929 and used only as roof coverings at first.

[36] AMMANN, Gustav: "Rückschau auf die 'ZÜGA'" in: Gartenkunst, issue 46/1933; pp. 169–171

[37] AMMANN, Gustav: "Garten und Landschaft. Organische Gartengestaltung und landschaftsfremde Gärten" in: Werk, issue 9/1943; p. 285

[38] cf. MAASZ, Harry: Gartentechnik und Gartenkunst. Nordhausen 1931, p. 489

[39] Cramer's estate contains various photographs prepared by the Zurich photographic studio of J. Meiner & Sohn. Cf. ASL Dossier 01.02.282

[40] VALENTIEN, Otto: Zeitgemässe Wohn-Gärten. Munich 1932

[41] cf. Künstler-Lexikon der Schweiz

[42] Claus Vogel worked in England for a few years as a Sulzer representative.

[43] cf. ASL Dossier 01.02.311, 01.02.144, 01.02.186

[44] no author: "Raum und Landschaft. Ausschnitte aus einem Garten der Firma Cramer & Surbeck, Gartenarchitekten, Zürich." in: Das ideale Heim 1945; pp. 399–404

[45] ibid.; p. 399. The style of the article suggests that Cramer wrote it.

[46] ibid.; p. 400

[47] ibid.; p. 404

[48] CRAMER, Ernst: "Wir betrachten Gartenbilder …" in: Schweizer Garten, issue 7/1937; p. 221 (cf. also title page of the issue)

[49] CRAMER, Ernst: "Wir betrachten Gartenbilder …" in: Schweizer Garten, issue 8/1937; pp. 227–233

[50] CRAMER, Ernst: ibidem: issue 7/1937; p. 221

[51] CRAMER, Ernst ibidem issue 8/1937; p. 230

[52] built by the Zurich architect André Bosshard for the then president of the Swiss-Italian Trade Association

[53] cf. ZELTNER, Hans M.: "Neuzeitliche Wohnbauten" in: Das ideale Heim 1937; pp. 279–290

[54] cf. Kunsthaus Zürich (pub.): 30er Jahre Schweiz. Ein Jahrzehnt im Widerspruch. Zurich 1981

[55] cf. ETTER, Philipp: "Sinn der Landesverteidigung. Ansprache zur Eröffnung der Zürcher Hochschulwochen für Landesverteidigung am 11. Mai 1936 in der Eidgenössischen Technischen Hochschule in Zürich." in: ETH Zurich (pub.): Kultur- und Staatswissenschaftliche Schriften, issue 14. Aarau 1936

[56] MEYER, Peter: "Die Architektur der Landesausstellung – kritische Besprechung" in: Das Werk, issue 11/1939; p. 340

[57] MEILI, Armin: Lecture to the Grosse Ausstellungskommission on 18 February 1937, p. 2. Staatsarchiv Zürich, document O 59

[58] MEDICI-MALL, Katharina: "Trotz alledem und alledem modern" in: Der Architekt, issue 1/1996; p. 38

[59] FRISCH, Max: Dienstbüchlein. Frankfurt 1970; p. 72

[60] MEYER, Peter: "Schweizerische Landesausstellung" in: Das Werk, issue 5/1939; p. 133

[61] MEYER, Peter: "Garten, Landschaft, Architektur Vortrag gehalten im Z.I.A. am 25. October 1939" in: Schweizerische Bauzeitung, issue 18/1939; p. 211

[62] LEDER, Walter: "Blühend grüne Landi!" in: Schweizer Garten, issue 9/1939; p. 273

[63] cf. AMMANN, Gustav: "Garten und Landschaft. Organische Gartengestaltung und landschaftsfremde Gärten" in: Werk, issue 9/1943; pp. 285–289

[64] MEYER, Peter: "Die Architektur der Landesausstellung – kritische Besprechung" in: Das Werk, issue 11/1939; p. 337

[65] cf. Das Werk, issue 7/1939; p. 200

[66] cf. ASL Dossier 01.02.253 and 01.02.304

[67] cf. Das Werk, issue 7/1939; pp. 200/201

[68] cf. MERTENS, Oskar: "Formprobleme der heutigen Gartengestaltung" in: Das Werk issue 9/1941; p. 246 and in: Schweizer Garten, issue 11/1942; p. 299

[69] HOFMANN, Hans: "Gedanken über die Architektur der Gegenwart in der Schweiz" London 1946, quoted from: LUCHSINGER, Christoph (ed.): Hans Hofmann. Zurich 1985; p. 136

[70] ZELTNER, Hans M.: "Moderne Schweizer Wohngärten" in: Das ideale Heim 1940; p. 30 ff

[71] SCHWEIZER, Johannes Erwin: "Der Bund Schweizerischer Gartengestalter (BSG) zeigt neue Arbeiten seiner Mitglieder" in: Schweizer Garten, issue 1/1942; pp. 1–30

[72] SCHWEIZER, Johannes Erwin: "Gedanken über Bilder aus neuen Gärten" in: Das ideale Heim 1942; pp. 183–192

[73] cf. Schweizer Garten, issue 11/1940

[74] MERTENS, Walter: "Einführung in das Thema der Landschaftsgestaltung" in: Schweizerische Bauzeitung, issue 15/1941; p. 161

[75] AMMANN, Gustav: "Das Landschaftsbild und die Dringlichkeit seiner Pflege und Gestaltung" in: ibid. pp. 172–174

[76] MERTENS, Walter: "Einführung in das Thema der Landschaftsgestaltung" in: Schweizerische Bauzeitung, issue 15/1941; p. 161

[77] SCHILLER, Hans: "Ist der Hausgarten auf dem richtigen Weg?" in: Gartenschönheit, issue 10/1940; p. 186

[78] cf. MERTENS, Oskar: "Formprobleme der heutigen Gartengestaltung" in: Das Werk, issue 9/1941; pp. 244–246 and in: Schweizer Garten, issue 11/1942; pp. 297–300

[79] AMMANN, Gustav: "Gestaltungsprobleme in Garten und Landschaft" in: Gartenkunst, issue 54/1942; p. 101.

[80] EGENDER, Karl: "Gärten im 'Heimatstil'" in: Schweizer Garten, issue 10/1942; p. 275

[81] cf. ASL Dossier 01.02.232

[82] VON WYSS, Roland: "Blühender Herbst" in: Schweizer Garten, issue 10/1942; p. 275

[83] cf. Bianca garden in Zollikon (1936–1937), Schoeller garden in Erlenbach (1934–1937), Kägi garden in Vitznau (1943)

[84] e.g. Vogt, R. garden in Locarno Monti (1941–1948)

[85] cf. ASL Dossier 01.02.178

[86] cf. ASL Dossiers 01.02.176 and 01.02.175

[87] cf. CRAMER, Ernst: "Gärten, Land-schaft und Bauliches. Eine kleine Bildreportage aus Arbeiten von E. Cramer, Gartenarchitekt B.S.G., Zürich" in: Schweizer Garten, issue 3/1943; pp. 57–63

[88] cf. SEIFERT, Alwin: "Gedanken über bodenständige Gartenkunst" in: Garten-kunst, issue 42/1929, p. 118 ff. and: SEIFERT, Alwin: "Bodenständige Gartenkunst" in: Gartenkunst, issue 43/1930, p. 162–169

[89] AMMANN, Gustav: "Garten und Landschaft. Organische Gartengestaltung und landschaftsfremde Gärten" in: Werk, issue 9/1943; p. 287

[90] ibid.; p. 288

[91] SURBECK, Ernst: "Den Garten einmal zeichnerisch gesehen" in: Schwei-zer Garten, issue 1/1945; p. 8

[92] BILL, Max: "Malerei, Architektur, Plastik – Kunst im halben Jahrzehnt" in: RUTISHAUSER, Max: Die 40er Jahre. Ein dramatisches Jahrzehnt in Bildern. Zofingen 1976; p. 109

[93] RÜEGG, Arthur: "Ideenflüsse" in: MESEURE, Anna et al: Architektur im 20. Jahrhundert. Schweiz. Munich 1998; p. 67

[94] cf. Werk, issue 1/1944

[95] cf. "Landscape rules?"; p. 40

[96] ROTH, Alfred: "Planen und Bauen nach dem Kriege von der Schweiz aus gesehen" in: Werk, issue 1/1944; p. 4

[97] cf. Das Wohnen, issue 2/1944; p. 41

[98] cf. Finanzamt der Stadt Zürich (ed.): 50 Jahre Wohnungspolitik der Stadt Zürich 1907–1957. Zürich 1959; p. 34

[99] ibid.

[100] cf. HÄSLER, Alfred A.: Einer muss es tun. Leben und Werk Ernst Göhners. Frauenfeld, Stuttgart 1981; p. 94 ff.

[101] cf. ASL Dossier 01.02.180

[102] cf. also Zollikerberg housing estate ASL Dossier 01.02.319

[103] AESCHLIMANN, Max: "Das Projekt Wasserwerkstraße der Baugenossenschaft des eidgenössischen Personals Zürich" in: Das Wohnen, issue 12/1944; pp. 211–212

[104] HOFFMANN, Hans: inaugural lecture on 30 May 1942 in Auditorium III of the ETH Zurich. Special print from: Schweizer Bauzeitung, 20 June 1942

[105] VOLKART, Hans: Schweizer Architektur. Ein Überblick über das schweizerische Bauschaffen der Gegenwart. Ravensburg 1951; p. 38

[106] cf. ROTZLER, Willy: "Wohnbau und Grünflächen" in: Werk, issue 3/1950; p. 65–72

[107] cf. VOLKART, Hans: ibid.; p. 37

[108] ROTZLER, Willy: "Wohnbau und Grün-flächen" in: Werk, issue 3/1950; p. 72

[109] cf. BILL, Max: Wiederaufbau. Dokumente über Zerstörungen, Planungen, Konstruktionen. Zurich, Erlenbach 1945

[110] cf. SURBECK, Ernst: "Kosten von Gar-tenanlagen" in: Werk, issue 2/1946; p. 101

[111] The company register in the Canton of Zurich Trade Registration Office has an entry for 2 July 1945, stating that a com-pany called Cramer & Surbeck, garden arch-itects' practice and horticultural busi-ness, with its headquarters at Bleicherweg 18, was founded in Zurich on 1 January 1945. cf. Firmenregister des Handel-registeramtes Kanton Zürich, Fol. 26368; Handelamtsblatt Nr. 154; p. 1587

[112] SURBECK, Ernst: "Den Garten einmal zeichnerisch gesehen" in: Schwei-zer Garten, issue 1/1945; pp. 1–8

[113] AMMANN, Gustav: "Ist das 'Natürliche' ein Form-Ersatz?" in: Schwei-zer Garten, issue 2/1945; pp. 33–38

[114] OERI, Georgine: "Über das 'Natürliche' als Formersatz" in: Werk, issue 1/1945; pp. 9–10

[115] CRAMER, Ernst: "Wo stehen wir heute im Gartenbau?" in: Werk, issue 3/1946; pp. 85–88

[116] cf. "The Vogel-Sulzer garden in Itschnach"; p. 26

[117] cf. "Early residential and housing estates"; p. 52 f

[118] SCHMIDT, Georg: "Abstrakte und surrealistische Kunst in der Schweiz" in: Werk, issue 1/1943; p. 45

[119] cf. page 21

[120] CRAMER, Ernst: "Wo stehen wir heute im Gartenbau?" in: Werk, issue 3/1946; p. 86

[121] BARTH, Hans Jakob: "Gärten wie Blumensträusse" in: Anthos, issue 2/1987; pp. 5–12

[122] ibid.; p. 8

[123] cf. V.S.: "ZÜKA. Zürcher Kantonale Gewerbe- und Landwirtschaftsausstellung" in: Werk, issue 10/1947; pp. 113–114

[124] SCHMID, Willy: "Der Gartenbau an der 'Züka'" in: Schweizer Garten, issue 9/1947; p. 305

[125] MEYER, Peter: "ZÜKA" in: Schwei-zerische Bauzeitung, issue 9/1947; p. 540

[126] VON WYSS, Roland: "Die Gärten an der 'ZÜKA' in Zürich" in: Schweizer Garten, issue 10/1947; pp. 274 and 311

[127] cf. "Autumn in Bloom, horticultural and flower show 1942"; p. 41

[128] cf. ASL Dossier 01.02.117

[129] V.S.: "ZÜKA. Zürcher Kantonale Gewerbe- und Landwirtschaftsausstellung" in: Werk, issue 10/1947; p. 113

[130] BILL, Max: "Ausstellungen. Ein Beitrag zur Abklärung von Fragen der Ausstellungs-Gestaltung" in: Werk, issue 3/1948; p. 71

[131] from a conversation with Albert Zulauf in April 1998

[132] 20 to 29 September 1947

[133] cf. VON WYSS, Roland: "Die Gärten an der 'AGA' in Aarau" in: Schweizer Garten, issue 10/1947; pp. 312–313

[134] SCHMIDT, Georg in: Werk, issue 3/1948; p. 77

[135] VON WYSS, Roland: "Die Gärten an der 'ZÜKA' in Zürich" in: Schweizer Garten, issue 10/1947; p. 308

[136] cf. Werk, issue 3/1948; p. 71

[137] cf. ASL Dossier 01.02.172

[138] Max Bill was certainly not displeased at a later stage when "Kontinuität" was sometimes seen as a forerunner of Ameri-can Land Art. cf. SPIESS, Werner: Kontinuität. Granit-Monolith von Max Bill. Zumikon 1986

[139] cf. MEDICI-MALL, Katharina: Im Durcheinandertal der Stile. Architektur und Kunst im Urteil von Peter Meyer (1894–1984). Basel Boston Berlin 1998; p. 59 ff

[140] AMMANN, Gustav: "Kleinarchitektur und Plastik im Hausgarten" in: Schweizer Garten, issue 10/1948; pp. 289–298

[141] LEDER, Klaus: "Plastik im Garten" in: Schweizer Garten, issue 10/1948; pp. 299–310

[142] The number of projects in 1947 was more than five times greater than in the previous year. Most of the projects involved private gardens.

[143] MAURER, G.: "Die neue Einheit von Haus und Garten" in: Das ideale Heim, issue 9/1948; pp. 462–467

[144] cf. ASL Dossiers 01.02.126 and 01.02.181

[145] cf. page 37

[146] cf. Schweizer Garten, issue 10/1948; p. 295; and ASL Dossiers 01.02.293 and 01.04.602. The company produced watchmakers' jewels

[147] cf. "Autumn in Bloom, horticultural and flower show 1942"; p. 41

[148] cf. ASL Dossier 01.02.234

[149] A photograph of this construction was published in the same issue in 1948.

[150] AMMANN, Gustav: "Kleinarchitektur und Plastik im Hausgarten" in: Schweizer Garten, issue 10/1948; p. 292

[151] BILL, Max: "Malerei, Architektur, Plastik – Kunst im halbierten Jahrzehnt" in: RUTISHAUSER, Max: Die 40er Jahre. Zofingen 1976; p. 108

[152] cf. SWB Geschäftsbericht 1949

[153] cf. BROGLE, Theodor: "Der Qualitäts-und Formgedanke in der schweizerischen Industrie" in: Werk, issue 8/1949; p. 259 ff.

[154] BILL, Max: "Schönheit aus Funktion und als Funktion" in: Werk, issue 8/1949; p. 274

[155] BILL, Max: Form. Eine Bilanz über die Formentwicklung um die Mitte des 20. Jahrhunderts. Basel 1952

[156] BILL, Max: "Schönheit aus Funktion und als Funktion" in: Werk, issue 8/1949; p. 274

[157] SMITH, G. E. Kidder: Switzerland Builds – Its native and modern Architec-ture. New York, Stockholm 1950; p. 153

[158] SURBECK, Ernst: "Über die gärtne-rische Gestaltung von Schulhausanlagen" in: Werk, issue 6/1949; pp. 216–217

[159] cf. VOLKART, Hans: Schweizer Architektur. Ein Überblick über das schweizerische Bauschaffen der Gegen-wart. Ravensburg 1951; pp. 105/106

[160] cf. Schweizerische Lehrerzeitung, issue 45/1950; p. 897

[161] from a conversation with Albert Zulauf in April 1998

[162] cf. "Outdoor areas for the Dorf primary school in Suhr"; p. 71

[163] cf. Firmenregister des Handelregister-amtes Kanton Zürich, Fol. 26368

[164] from a conversation with Wolf Hunziker in spring 1998

[165] cf. ASL Dossier 01.04.318

[166] ibid.

[167] cf. CRAMER, Ernst: "Gärtne-rische Planungen" in: Schweizer Garten, issue 2/1953; pp. 41–48

[168] from a conversation with Willy Guhl in March 2000

[169] cf. ROTZLER, Willy: "Neue Schweizer Pflanzenbehälter" in: Werk, issue 6/1952; pp. 192–193

[170] cf. CRAMER, Ernst: "Gärt-nerische Planungen" in: Schweizer Garten, issue 2/1953; pp. 41–48

[171] ibid.; p. 42

[172] ibid.; p. 44

[173] cf. VALENTIEN, Otto: Neue Gärten. Ravensburg 1949

[174] REICH, Alfred: "Zürich und Basel – Garten und Landschaft. Fachliche Reise-eindrücke aus der Schweiz" in: Garten und Landschaft, issue 8/1950; p. 6

[175] cf. VALENTIEN, Otto: "Eindrücke der heutigen Schweizer Gartengestaltung" in: Garten und Landschaft, issue 1/1953; p. 16

[176] no author: "Eindrücke junger Weihen-stephaner Gartengestalter in der Schweiz" in: Garten und Landschaft, issue 8/1951

[177] cf. "Who's afraid of experiments"; p. 74

[178] cf. BARTH, Hans Jakob: "Beton-platten im Garten?" in: Garten und Land-schaft, issue 1/1953; p. 8

[179] VALENTIEN, Otto: "Neues Bauen – Neue Gärten. Der Gartenarchitekt" in: Garten und Landschaft, issue 1/1953; p. 2

[180] cf. ibid.; pp. 15–16

[181] ROTH, Alfred: "Zeitgemäße Architek-turbetrachtungen. Mit besonderer Berück-sichtigung der schweizerischen Situation" in: Werk, issue 3/1951; pp. 70–71

[182] cf. ROTH, Alfred: "Rückblick auf die Jahrgänge 1943–1956" in: Werk/Oeuvre, issue 12/1973; pp. 1569–1572

[183] FRISCH, Max: "Cum grano salis. Eine kleine Glosse zur schweizerischen Architektur" in: Werk, issue 10/1953; pp. 325–329

[184] ibid.; p. 329

[185] cf. ROTH, Alfred: "Zeitgemäße Architekturbetrachtungen. Mit beson-derer Berücksichtigung der schweizerischen Situation" in: Werk, issue 3/1951; pp. 68–69

[186] GIEDION, Sigfried: "Brasilien und die heutige Architektur" in: Werk, issue 8/1953; pp. 238–240

[187] ibid.; p. 240

[188] GIEDION, Sigfried: "Roberto Burle Marx und das Problem der Gartengestal-tung" in: Werk, issue 8/1953; p. 253

[189] cf. CURJEL, Hans: "Roberto Burle Marx" in: Werk-Chronik, issue 12/1956; p. 247

[190] cf. CROWE, Sylvia: The Landscape of Power. London 1958

[191] cf. "The First Swiss Horticultural Show G|59"; p. 102

[192] cf. CURJEL, Hans: "Roberto Burle Marx. Neuere Arbeiten des Brasilianischen Gartengestalters. Kunstgewerbemuseum 14. Oktober bis 16. Dezember" in: Werk-Chronik, issue 12/1956; p. 247

[193] BAUMANN, Albert: Neues Planen und Gestalten für Haus und Garten, Friedhof und Landschaft. Münsingen 1953

[194] AMMANN, Gustav: Blühende Gärten. Landscape Gardens. Jardins en fleurs. Erlenbach, Zurich 1955

[195] BAUMANN, Ernst: Neue Gärten. New Gardens. Zurich 1955

[196] cf. BAUMANN, Albert: "Neues Planen und Gestalten für Haus und Garten, Friedhof und Landschaft." Münsingen 1953; p. 31 and p. 177

[197] ibid.; p. 9

[198] cf. NEUTRA, Richard: Life and shape. The autobiography of Richard Neutra. 1962

[199] cf. AMMANN, Gustav: Blühende Gärten. Landscape Gardens. Jardins en fleurs. Erlenbach, Zurich 1955; pp. 113–127

[200] NEUTRA, Richard: "Der Gartenarchitekt – Seniorpartner des Architekten" in: EXNER, Hermann/NEUTRA, Dione (ed.): Richard und Dion Neutra. Pflanzen Wasser Steine Licht. Berlin/Hamburg 1974

[201] WALKER, Peter: "The practice of landscape architecture in the postwar United States" in: TREIB, Marc (ed.): Modern Landscape Architecture: a critical review. Cambridge/Massachusetts, London 1993; p. 251. Peter Walker had worked in Lawrence Halprin's office himself as a young man.

[202] AMMANN, Gustav: Blühende Gärten. Landscape Gardens. Jardins en fleurs. Erlenbach, Zurich 1955; p. 113

[203] cf. ibid.; p. 16

[204] Ammann's son, Peter Ammann and his friend, Arnold Vogt, both garden architect's completed the book project.

[205] Verlag "Das ideale Heim" (publ.): Special issue Wohngarten. Winterthur 1956

[206] cf. CRAMER, Ernst/GOLLWITZER, Gerda: "Schweizer Gartengespräch" in: Garten und Landschaft, issue 12/1956; pp. 357–358

[207] Im Untermoos primary school building, built by Eduard Del Fabro in Altstetten, Zurich in 1955; cf. ASL Dossier 01.04.113

[208] CRAMER, Ernst/GOLLWITZER, Gerda: "Schweizer Gartengespräch" in: Garten und Landschaft, issue 12/1956; pp. 357–358

[209] cf. p. 67 f.

[210] EICHER, Fred in a conversation with the author in May 2000

[211] cf. "Open space design at the Bernarda Seminary for Female Teachers in Menzingen"; p. 86

[212] CRAMER, Ernst/GOLLWITZER, Gerda: "Schweizer Gartengespräch" in: Garten und Landschaft, issue 12/1956; p. 357

[213] cf. LEHR: "Hausgartenwettbewerb des Arbeitskreises junger Gartenarchitekten" in: Garten und Landschaft, issue 7/1954; p. 16

[214] cf. no author: "Stimmen zum Wettbewerb 'Garten am Wilhaditurm'" in: Garten und Landschaft, issue 6/1956; p. 183

[215] cf. IMBERT, Dorothée: The modernist garden in France. New Haven, London 1993

[216] cf. CURJEL, Hans: "Piet Mondrian" in: Werk-Chronik issue 5/1955; pp. 132–134

[217] cf. "Mondrian as a model?"; p. 120

[218] FINSLER, Hans, quoted from MARTINSSON, Gunnar in: Garten und Landschaft, issue 6/1956; pp. 183–184. cf. also: FINSLER, Hans: "Der Werkbund und die Dinge. Vortrag von Hans Finsler, gehalten an der Generalversammlung des Schweizerischen Werkbundes in St. Gallen am 5. November 1955." in: Werk issue 9/1956; pp. 269–272

[219] MARTINSSON, Gunnar in: ibid.

[220] cf. "Menzingen weiht das neue Seminar Bernarda ein" in: supplement to the Zuger Nachrichten dated 24 October 1958

[221] cf. ASL Dossier 01.02.098

[222] cf. no author: "Grünanlage am Lehrerinnenseminar in Menzingen/ Schweiz" in: Garten und Landschaft, issue 9/1959; pp. 267–269

[223] It is particularly regrettable that the strikingly striped surface of the courtyard has been obliterated by a new tarred surface

[224] CRAMER, Ernst: "Das heutige Gestalten (Richtlinien für den Bauherrn)" in: unknown; pp. 240–242

[225] cf. STUCKY, Fritz: "Haus mit 3 Wohnungen in Zug" in: Bauen + Wohnen, issue 1/1957; pp. 14–17

[226] cf. REICHOW, Hans Bernhard: Organische Stadtbaukunst. Von der Grossstadt zur Stadtlandschaft. Braunschweig-Berlin-Hamburg 1948

[227] GÖDERITZ, Johannes/RAINER, Roland/HOFFMANN, Hubert: Die gegliederte und aufgelockerte Stadt. Tübingen 1957

[228] DOLF-BONEKÄMPER, Gabi: Das Hansaviertel. Internationale Nachkriegsmoderne in Berlin. Berlin 1999; pp. 34–35

[229] BOURNOT, Helmut: "Koordinierung und Gesamtplanung der Grünflächen im Hansaviertel Berlin" in: Garten und Landschaft, issue 10/1957; p. 258

[230] cf. ibid.

[231] ROSSOW, Walter: "Städtebau und Landschaft" in: Interbau Berlin 1957. Amtlicher Katalog der Internationalen Bauausstellung Berlin 1957. Berlin 1957; pp. 331–334

[232] cf. Garten und Landschaft, issue 10/1957; p. 260

[233] cf. ibid.

[234] cf. "Poet's Garden"; p. 106

[235] Ernst Cramer photographed his encounter with Otto Senn, Ludwig Lemmer and other Interbau architects. cf. ASL Dossier 01.02.189

[236] cf. SENN, Otto: "Raum als Form" in: Werk, issue 4201955; pp. 368–393

[237] cf. ASL Dossier 01.04.125

[238] cf. PERSITZ, Alexandre: "Berlin 1957 – Bâtiments divers" in: l'architecture d'aujourd'hui, issue 75/1957; p. 8

[239] no author: "Objekt 14, 7-geschossiges Wohnhaus" in: Interbau Berlin 1957. Amtlicher Katalog der Internationalen Bauausstellung Berlin 1957. Berlin 1957; pp. 90–91

[240] cf. DOLF-BONEKÄMPER, Gabi: Das Hansaviertel. Internationale Nachkriegsmoderne in Berlin. Berlin 1999; p. 55

[241] There are photographs of the building in Cramer's collection of photographs. cf. ASL Dossier 01.02.189

[242] FILS, Alexander: Brasilia. Moderne Architektur in Brasilien. Düsseldorf 1988; p. 125

[243] LE CORBUSIER quoted from: BARDI, Pietro Maria: Lembranca de Le Corbusier: Athenas, Italia, Brasil. Sao Paulo 1984; p. 114; see also: FILS, Alexander: Brasilia. Moderne Architektur in Brasilien. Düsseldorf 1988; pp. 102–104

[244] ibid.; p. 78

[245] BILL, Max: "Report on Brasilien architecture" in: Architectural Review, issue 116/1954; pp. 235–250

[246] cf. "'Good form' as a model"; p. 67

[247] cf. p. 79

[248] STUCKY, Fritz in a conversation with the author in Mai 2000

[249] cf. p. 92

[250] STUCKY, Fritz in an unpublished information brochure about the history of the architectural practice.

[251] STUCKY, Fritz: "Terrassenhäuser in Zug" in: Werk, issue 2/1961; p. 59

[252] cf. "Landscape design for Walter Jonas's Intrapolis"; p. 142

[253] cf.: no author: "Was bringt die Gartenbau-Ausstellung?" in: Schweizer Garten, issue 3/1959; p. 80

[254] STEINER, Emil: "Die Form in der Gartengestaltung" in: Schweizerisches Gartenbau-Blatt, issue 25, 25 June 1959; p. 649

[255] cf. MATHYS, Heini: "G/59 – Eine neue Gartenwelt am Zürichsee" in: Schweizer Garten + Wohnkultur, issue 5/1959; p. 117

[256] The first general plans and individual designs were published in July 1958. cf. NEUKOM, Willi: "Erste Schweizerische Gartenbauausstellung in Zürich 1959" in: Bauen + Wohnen, issue 7/1958; p. 248

[257] GOLLWITZER, Gerda: "Gärten am See. Zur 1. Schweizerischen Gartenbauausstellung Zürich 1959" in: Garten und Landschaft, issue 8/1959; p. 228

[258] NEUKOM, Willi: "Zu den Gärten des rechten Ufers" in: ibid.; p. 235

[259] NEUKOM, Willi: "Gartenvariationen" in: Bauen + Wohnen, issue 3/1956; p. 101

[260] cf. also: ZEVI, Bruno: "Ein Gartenarchitekt in den Tropen. Aus dem Schaffen von Roberto Burle Marx" in: Garten und Landschaft, issue 10/1958; pp. 261–263

[261] NEUKOM, Willi: "Erste Schweizerische Gartenbauausstellung in Zürich 1959" in: Bauen + Wohnen, issue 7/1958; p. 248

[262] NEUKOM, Willi: "Schweizerische Gartenbauausstellung G/59 in Zürich 1959" in: Bauen + Wohnen Chronik, issue 10/1959; p. X6

[263] cf. NEUKOM, Willi: "Erste Schweizerische Gartenbauausstellung in Zürich 1959" in: Bauen + Wohnen, issue 7/1958; p. 248

[264] NEUKOM, Willi quoted from: Garten und Landschaft, issue 8/1959; p. 230

[265] cf. IMBERT, Dorothée: The modernist garden in France. New Haven, London 1993; pp. 126–129

[266] NEUKOM, Willi: "Schweizerische Gartenbauausstellung G/59 in Zürich 1959" in: Bauen + Wohnen Chronik, issue 10/1959; p. X6 ((?))

[267] cf. "The Zurich Cantonal Agriculture and Trade Exhibition, ZÜKA 1947"; p. 60

[268] FRISCHKNECHT, Walter in conversation with the author in June 2000

[269] cf. NEUKOM, Willi: "Erste Schweizerische Gartenbauausstellung in Zürich 1959" in: Bauen + Wohnen, issue 7/1958; p. 248

[270] NEUKOM, Willi: "Schweizerische Gartenbauausstellung G/59 in Zürich 1959" in: Bauen + Wohnen Chronik, issue 10/1959; p. X6

[271] cf. GROSS, Roland: "1. Schweizerische Gartenbau-Ausstellung 1959 in Zürich" in: Werk, issue 10/1959; p. 347

[272] cf. Bauen + Wohnen Chronik, issue 10/1959; p. X1

[273] cf. ASL Dossier 01.04.262

[274] A reconstruction model was prepared from this information at the ETH in Zurich. cf. ASL Dossiers 01.04.262, 01.02.033 to 01.02.037

[275] The two intersecting pyramids were not drawn in correctly until the general plan for G | 59.

[276] cf. e. g.: "Outdoor areas for the Dorf primary school in Suhr", p. 71 and "Leisure garden for Riwisa in Hägglingen", p. 83

[277] SCHEIDEGGER, Alfred: "Der Bildhauer Bernhard Luginbühl" in: Werk, issue 1/1960; pp. 65–66

[278] cf. ROTZLER, Willy: "Kunst im Grünraum" in: Werk, issue 10/1959; pp. 351–356 and in: Offizieller Katalog. 1. Schweizerische Gartenbau-Ausstellung Zürich 1959. 25.April – 11.Oktober. Zurich 1959; pp. 68–69

[279] from a conversation with Willy Rotzler's son Stefan

[280] ROTZLER, Willy: "Kunst im Grünraum" in: Werk, issue 10/1959; pp. 351–356

[281] STEINER, Emil in a conversation with the author in 1998

[282] NEUKOM, Willi: "Schweizerische Gartenbauausstellung G/59 in Zürich 1959" in: Bauen + Wohnen Chronik, issue 10/1959; p. X6

[283] cf. no author: "Fürst Pücklers Tumulus im Park zu Branitz" in: Garten und Landschaft, issue 2/1958; p. 35

[284] cf. also the discussion about the 'Garden for the Wilhadi Tower' competition p. 85

[285] MATHYS, Heini: "Der Garten des Poeten" in: Schweizer Garten + Wohnkultur, issue 7/1959; p. 154

[286] STEINER, Emil: "Die Form in der Gartengestaltung" in: Schweizerisches Gartenbau-Blatt, issue 25/1959; p. 649

[287] BENN, Gottfried, quoted from: MATHYS, Heini: "Der Garten des Poeten" in: Schweizer Garten + Wohnkultur, issue 7/1959; p. 154

[288] cf. "The Zurich Cantonal Agriculture and Trade Exhibition, ZÜKA 1947"; p. 60

[289] FISCHLI, Hans: letter to Ernst Cramer dated 26 August 1959; ASL Dossier 01.03.013

[290] cf. the remarkable book by: JOST, Karl: Hans Fischli – Architekt, Maler, Bildhauer. Zurich 1992

[291] FISCHLI, Hans, quoted from: ibid.; p. 144

[292] ibid.; p. 168

[293] cf. ROWE, Colin/SLUTZKY, Robert: Transparenz. Basel 1997

[294] BILL, Max in the catalogue for "Konkrete Zürcher Kunst" 1949, quoted from: ROTZLER, Willy: Konstruktive Konzepte. Eine Geschichte der konstruktiven Kunst vom Kubismus bis heute. Zurich 1977; p. 130

[295] MATHYS, Heini: "G/59 – Eine neue Gartenwelt am Zürichsee" in: Schweizer Garten + Wohnkultur, issue 5/1959; p. 107

[296] GIEDION-WELCKER, Carola: "Plastik des XX. Jahrhunderts. Volumen- und Raumgestaltung". Zurich 1954

[297] cf. "International Horticultural Show IGA 1963 in Hamburg"; p. 151

[298] My thanks to Ms Cornelia Hahn Oberlander, landscape architect in Vancouver, for this point.

[299] KASSLER, Elizabeth B.: Modern gardens and the landscape. New York 1964; p. 57

[300] cf. ROTZLER, Stefan: "Ernst Cramer, Landschaftsarchitekt, 1898–1980" in: Anthos, issue 2/1987; p. 1

[301] cf. ASL Dossiers: 01.02.072 to 01.02.074, 01.04.165, 01.04.141 and 01.04.754, and also: no author: "Bericht über einen Projketwettbewerb für die Erstellung eines Friedhofes in Pratteln BL" in: Kunst und Stein, issue 3/1959, special issue on the occasion of the cemetery and monument show at the G/59 in Zurich; pp. 33–39

[302] cf "Cramer as a design teacher in Lausanne"; p. 205

[303] CRAMER, Ernst, quoted from STEINER, Emil: "Von der inneren Struktur zum Erscheinen der Form" in: Der Gartenbau, issue 11/1975; S. 379

[304] cf. e.g. GERSTNER, Karl: Kalte Kunst? – zum Standort der heutigen Malerei. Teufen 1957

[305] cf.. ARIOLI, Richard in a personal letter to Emil Steiner dated 04.02.1987; ASL Dossier 01.05.048

[306] cf. "Interbau Berlin 1957"; p. 94 ff.

[307] cf. pp. 79, 98 and 105

[308] ROTZLER, Willy: "Kunst im Grünraum" in: Werk, issue 10/1959; p. 354

[309] cf. ASL Dossier 01.02.322

[310] cf. p. 98

[311] ECO, Umberto: Theory of Semiotics. Indiana 1978; p. 356

[312] cf. FILS, Alexander: Brasilia. Moderne Architektur in Brasilien. Düsseldorf 1988; pp. 120–124

[313] NIEMEYER, Oscar: "Meine Erfahrung in Brasilia". Rio de Janeiro 1961, quoted from: FILS, Alexander (ed.): Oscar Niemeyer. Selbstdarstellung, Kritiken, Oeuvre. Düsseldorf 1982; p. 53

[314] cf. p. 99

[315] cf. "Postplatz in Vaduz"; p. 224

[316] cf. "International Horticultural Show IGA 1963 in Hamburg"; p. 151

[317] cf. Interview with Roberto Burle Marx in March 1981 in: FILS, Alexander (ed.): Oscar Niemeyer. Selbstdarstellung, Kritiken, Œuvre. Düsseldorf 1982; pp. 143–144

[318] But so far no photographs of this garden have appeared in Cramer's estate. It is however not impossible that the photographs in question have disappeared in the course of the decades

[319] cf. Werk-Chronik issue 10/1959; pp. 206–207. Kunst und Stein, issue 5/1959. Garten und Landschaft, issue 11/1969; pp. 353–354; and ASL-Dossiers 01.02.072 – 01.02.074, 01.04.141, 01.04.165, 01.05.022

[320] DOVÉ, Fritz in a conversation with the author in summer 1998

[321] cf. "Interbau Berlin 1957"; p. 94

[322] CESCON, Ermes in a conversation with the author in summer 1998

[323] LANDER, Helmut in a conversation with the author in summer 2000

[324] cf. HANSJAKOB, Gottfried und Anton: "Krieg und Friedhof" in: Garten und Landschaft, issue 12/1969; pp. 375–376

[325] DOVÉ, Fritz in a conversation with the author in summer 1998

[326] OESTERLEN, Dieter: Dieter Oesterlen. Bauten und Texte 1946–1991. Tübingen-Berlin 1992; pp. 84–86

[327] cf. "Early Ticino Gardens"; p. 42

[328] cf. ASL Dossier 01.02.132

[329] cf. p. 100

[330] DOVÉ, Fritz in a conversation with the author in summer 1998

[331] GRAMENZ, Gisela: "Beton macht den Garten wohnlich" in: Schöner Wohnen, issue 2/1967; p. 197

[332] SCHMIDLIN, Josef in a conversation with the author in summer 1998

[333] cf. ASL Dossier 01.04.768

[334] SCHMIDLIN, Josef, quoted from: GRAMENZ, Gisela: "Beton macht den Garten wohnlich" in: Schöner Wohnen, issue 2/1967; p. 201

[335] cf. "International Horticultural Show IGA 1963 in Hamburg"; p. 151

[336] cf. GRAMENZ, Gisela: "Notizen von einem Streifzug durch die IGA 63" in: Schöner Wohnen, issue 7/1963; pp. 92–101

[337] CRAMER, Ernst, quoted from: SCHMIDLIN, Josef in a conversation with the author in summer 1998 [338] KLOTZ, Heinrich (ed.): Vision der Moderne. Das Prinzip Konstruktion. Munich 1986

[339] cf. GLEININGER-NEUMANN, Andrea: "Technologische Phantasien und urbanistische Utopien" in: ibid.; pp. 56–65

[340] JONAS, Walter: "Das Trichterhaus – Vorschlag zu einer Massensiedlung" in:

Bauen + Wohnen, issue 3/1962; p. 136

[341] JONAS, Walter: Das Intra-Haus. Vision einer Stadt. Zurich 1962; p. 9

[342] JONAS, Walter: "Intrapolis – ein städtebauliches Projekt" in: SCHMID, Heinrich E.: Walter Jonas. Maler Denker Urbanist. Zurich 1980; p. 124

[343] cf. KLOTZ, Heinrich (ed.): Vision der Moderne. Das Prinzip Konstruktion. Munich 1986

[344] BURCKHARDT, Lucius: "Neues aus Intropia" in: Werk-Chronik issue 7/1964; p. 145

[345] JONAS, Walter: Das INTRA-HAUS. Zurich 1962

[346] cf. "Interbau Berlin 1957"; p. 94

[347] cf. "Villas and terraced buildings"; p. 99

[348] cf. STEINBRÜCHEL, Franz: "Intrapolis oder der Mut zum Ungewohnten" in: SCHMID, Heinrich E.: Walter Jonas. Maler Denker Urbanist. Zurich 1980; pp. 141–142

[349] cf. Werk-Chronik issue 7/1964; p. 146

[350] CRAMER, Ernst: "Bauwerk und Natur" in: JONAS, Walter: Das INTRA-HAUS. Zurich 1962; pp. 59–61

[351] KOCH, Michael/MAURER, Bruno: "Zauberformeln. Episoden auf dem Weg der Schweizer Architektur in die Welt 1939–1968" in: MESEURE, Anna et al: Architektur im 20. Jahrhundert. Schweiz. Munich 1998; p. 43

[352] cf. "International Horticultural Show IGA 1963 in Hamburg"; p. 151

[353] CRAMER, Ernst: "Wohnkolonie Wilerfeld, Olten" in: Anthos, issue 4/1964; p. 29

[354] cf. ASL Dossier: 01.04.161

[355] CRAMER, Ernst: "Wohnkolonie Badenerstrasse in Zürich" in: Anthos, issue 4/1964; p. 34

[356] cf. ASL Dossier 01.04.200

[357] cf. ASL Dossier 01.02.104

[358] Dr. Marketa Haist wrote her dissertation entitled "Achtundzwanzig Männer brauchen einen neuen Anzug. Die internationalen Gärten auf der Internationalen Gartenbau-Ausstellung 1963 in Hamburg" in 1994 at the University of Karlsruhe (TH). In it she discusses the concept of the show and the contributions by all the garden architects, including Ernst Cramer, in detail. A shorter version of this comprehensive work appeared under the same title in: Die Gartenkunst, issue 2/1996; pp. 252–314

[359] cf. ALLINGER, Gustav: "Große und kleine Gärten auf der Internationalen Gartenbau-Ausstellung 1963 in Hamburg" in: offprint from the Deutsche Gärtnerbörse, issue 40,42,44/1963; p. 7

[360] CRAMER, Ernst in a personal letter to Günther Schulze dated 18 August 1961; Archiv für Schweizer Landschaftsarchitektur, Rapperswil

[361] cf. "Schmidlin garden in Aarau"; p. 136

[362] ALLINGER, Gustav: Das Hohelied von Gartenkunst und Gartenbau. Berlin-Hamburg 1963

[363] ALLINGER, Gustav: "Große und kleine Gärten auf der Internationalen Gartenbau-Ausstellung 1963 in Hamburg" in: offprint from the Deutsche Gärtnerbörse, issue 40, 42, 44/1963; p. 13

[364] cf. REICH, Alfred: "Entwicklung zu klaren Formen?" in: Garten und Landschaft, issue 1/1962; pp. 14–16

[365] cf. ASL Dossier 01.02.042

[366] Deutsche Gärtnerbörse issue 4/1962, quoted from: Schweizerisches Gartenbau-Blatt issue 7/1962

[367] cf. IGA minutes dated 7 December 1962

[368] cf. GLINZ, Martin in: Schweizerische Gärtnerzeitung, issue 38/1963; p. 317

[369] cf. GREBE, Reinhard: "Die Gärten der Nationen auf der IGA 63 in Hamburg" in: Die neue Landschaft, issue 9/1963; p. 265

[370] CRAMER, Ernst: "Theatergarten" in: Garten und Landschaft, issue 8/1963; p. 250

[371] cf. HAIST, Marketa: "Achtundzwanzig Männer brauchen einen neuen Anzug. Die internationalen Gärten auf der Internationalen Gartenbau-Ausstellung 1963 in Hamburg." in: Die Gartenkunst, issue 2/1996; p. 283

[372] cf. report on the 9th IFLA-Kongress in: Garten und Landschaft, issue 10/1964; pp. 338–346

[373] Richard Arioli was editor of the Swiss specialist magazine Anthos from 1962 to 1965; it first appeared in March 1962. According to Willi Neukom, Ernst Cramer was president of the Anthos editorial commission in 1963 und 1964

[374] ARIOLI, Richard: "9. Kongress der IFLA in Japan" in: Anthos, issue 2/1964; pp. 39–40

[375] cf. p. 125

[376] cf. Denver Art Museum (publ.): Herbert Bayer. Collection and Archive at the Denver Art Museum. Seattle-London 1988

[377] STAHLY, François: "Aspen – ein amerikanisches Kulturzentrum" in: Werk, issue 7/1961; p. 249

[378] cf. p. 118

[379] STAHLY, François: ibid.; p. 250

[380] ALLINGER, Gustav: "Große und kleine Gärten auf der Internationalen Gartenbau-Ausstellung 1963 in Hamburg" in: offprint from the Deutsche Gärtnerbörse, issue 40, 42, 44/1963; p. 9

[381] cf. e.g. HANISCH, Karl Heinz: "Gärten auf der IGA 63" in: Pflanze und Garten, issue 8/1963; pp. 196–198

[382] GERTZ, Ulrich: Plastik der Gegenwart. Kunst unserer Zeit. Vol. 8. Berlin 1953; p. 19

[383] cf. "The Zurich Cantonal Agriculture and Trade Exhibition, ZÜKA 1947"; p. 60

[384] cf. p. 106

[385] ALLINGER, Gustav: "Große und kleine Gärten auf der Internationalen Gartenbau-Ausstellung 1963 in Hamburg" in: offprint from the Deutsche Gärtnerbörse, issue 40, 42, 44/1963; p. 12

[386] cf. ECO, Umberto: The Open Work. London 1998

[387] cf. STEGMANN, Markus; Architektonische Skulptur im 20. Jahrhundert. Tübingen 1995

[388] cf. ASL Dossier 01.05.014

[389] PASSARGE, Karl in a letter to Senator Keilhack dated 15 November 1963

[390] RENTSCH, Fritz in a conversation with the author in summer 1999

[391] NEUTRA, Richard: Life and shape. The autobiography of Richard Neutra. 1962

[392] cf. p. 81

[393] NEUTRA, Richard in a letter to Fritz Rentsch dated 14 March 1962; client's personal archive

[394] no author: "Ferienhaus in Wengen/Schweiz" in: Anthos, issue 2/1966; p. 8

[395] ibid.; p. 9. Photograph by the Bern photographer Martin Hesse

[396] cf. "Staging the view"; p. 245

[397] cf. DAHRENDORF, Ralf: Liberal und unabhängig. Gerd Bucerius und seine Zeit. Munich 2000; pp. 180–186

[398] BUCERIUS, Ebelin, quoted from: SACK, Manfred: Richard Neutra. Zurich-Munich-London 1992; p. 17

[399] cf. ASL Dossier 01.04.440

[400] cf. ASL Dossier 01.02.046

[401] from a conversation with the current owners of the house in summer 1999

[402] cf. "The Vogel-Sulzer garden in Itschnach"; p. 26

[403] cf. ASL Dossiers 01.04.150 and 01.04.187

[404] cf. private archive of Suter & Suter AG in the Schweizerisches Wirtschaftsarchiv Basel (SWA), Dossier PA 510: 0084/1

[405] cf. ASL Dossier 01.04.765

[406] cf. WEILACHER, Udo: "Gartenarchitektur als lebendiger Ausdruck Schweizer Zeitgeschichte" in: DISP 139/1999; pp. 13–16

[407] cf. "Sulzer Tower square in Winterthur"; p. 168

[408] cf. "Volcanoes at the Winterthur Technical College"; p. 220

[409] Fountain near the Zehntenscheune in Rikon, converted in 1961 as the canteen for the Heinrich Kuhn Metallwarenfabrik AG; cf. ASL Dossier 01.02.060

[410] cf. "Postplatz in Vaduz"; p. 224

[411] STEINER, Emil: "Begegnung mit Ernst Cramer" in: Anthos, issue 2/1987; p. 18

[412] ERIKSSON, Christofer in conversation with the author in March 1998

[413] This shows clearly in the many colour slides of the gardens that Cramer took on another visit in September 1975; cf. ASL Dossier 01.02.324

[414] cf. p. 98

[415] EGGER, Alois in conversation with the author in October 2000

[416] cf. ASL Dossiers 01.04.278 and 01.04.136

[417] MATHYS, Heini: "Dachgarten in Olten" in: Schweizerische Gärtnerzeitung, issue 15/1969; p. 163

[418] STEINER, Emil in conversation with the author in 1998

[419] Situation in October 2000

[420] STEINER, Emil: "Das Grün der Siedlung 'Grüzefeld' in Winterthur" in: Der Gartenbau, issue 1/1970; pp. 12–13

[421] ibid.; p. 16

[422] cf. Interview p. 83

[423] Bauamt II der Stadt Zürich: Wettbewerb zur Erlangung von Plänen für ein Primar- und Sekundarschulhaus mit Lehrschwimmbecken und Doppelkindergarten an der Katzenschwanzstrasse im Quartier Witikon. Bericht des Preisgerichtes. Zurich, 9 November 1960; p. 7

[424] ibid.

[425] cf. KASSLER, Elizabeth B.: Modern gardens and the landscape. New York 1964; p. 85

[426] CRAMER, Ernst: "Pausenplatz zum Schulhaus Looren in Witikon/ZH" in: Anthos, issue 4/1971; p. 22

[427] All the following observations about this project are based on information provided by Christofer Eriksson in conversation with the author in March 1998.

[428] CRAMER, Ernst: "Stadtplatz in Aarau/Schweiz" in: Garten und Landschaft, issue 8/1970; p. 259

[429] CRAMER, Ernst quoted from: Anthos, issue 2/1987; p. 23

[430] CRAMER, Ernst: "Friedhof im Züricher Oberland" in: Garten und Landschaft, issue 11/1969; p. 346

[431] cf. ASL Dossier 01.01.007

[432] cf. "Paradigm shift– ecology versus design"; p. 195

[433] CRAMER, Ernst: "Gedanken zum Thema Friedhof", lecture manuscript dated 16 February 1967; ASL Dossier 01.03.008

[434] cf. KASSLER, Elizabeth B.: Modern gardens and the landscape. New York 1964; p. 77

[435] MATHYS, Heini: "Rückblick auf den Wettbewerb für den Friedhof 'Hinderneuwies' in Volketswil" in: Anthos, issue 4/1969

[436] CRAMER, Ernst: "Fried-Hof", an explanatory report for an unidentified cemetery competition, presumed to be near Neu-Perlach; ASL Dossier 01.03.008

[437] CRAMER, Ernst: "Tendenzen heutiger Friedhofgestaltung" in: Garten und Landschaft, issue 11/1969; pp. 343–347

[438] cf. "Military cemetery at the Passo la Futa, Italy (Dieter Oesterlen, Walter Rossow)"; p. 126

[439] DOVÉ, Fritz: "Soldatenfriedhof Futa-Paß/Italien" in: Garten und Landschaft, issue 11/1969; pp. 353–354

[440] founded in 1951

[441] BOEHLKE, Hans-Kurt in conversation with the author in autumn 2000

[442] cf. ASL Dossier 01.01.018

[443] CRAMER, Ernst: "Gedanken zum Thema Friedhof", lecture manuscript dated 16 February 1967 in ASL Dossier 01.03.008

[444] another project with Suter and Suter under the architect Albert Brunner: e.g. Ciba Photochemie AG Fribourg, Marly research centre, 1965

[445] The author gained a great deal of information on this project from a detailed conversation with Hans-Rudolf Suter, Heini Seiberth and Rainer Fleischhauer in May 1999

[446] cf. ARIOLI, Richard in a personal letter to Emil Steiner dated 4. February 1987; ASL Dossier 01.05.048

[447] cf. the building material firm's advertising brochure in ASL Dossier 01.05.002

[448] cf. page 158

[449] SEIBERTH, Heini in conversation with the author in May 1999

[450] ibid.

[451] ERIKSSON, Christofer in conversation with the author in March 1998

[452] STEIGER, Peter: "Dem Werkbund eine Chance!" in: SWB-Kommentare 14, February 1970; pp. 121–122

[453] HERNANDES, Antonio: "Randnotizen zur Tagung" in: ibid.; p. 123

[454] cf. LEROY, Louis G.: Natur ausschalten – Natur einschalten. Stuttgart 1973

[455] cf. SCHWARZ, Urs: Der Naturgarten. Frankfurt 1980

[456] SCHWARZ, Urs: ibid.; p. 88

[457] ibid.; p. 89

[458] From 1971 to 1973 the number of commissions sank to the level of the late 30s

[459] NARBEL, Liliane in conversation with the author in November 2000

[460] STEINER, Emil: "Von der inneren Struktur zum Erscheinen der Form" in: Der Gartenbau, issue 11/1975; pp. 377–384

[461] ibid.; p. 377

[462] CRAMER, Ernst, quoted from ASL Dossier 01.03.034

[463] ROTZLER, Stefan in a personal conversation with the author in spring 1998

[464] STEINER, Emil: "Begegnung mit Ernst Cramer" in: Anthos, issue 2/1987; p. 34

[465] CRAMER, Ernst quoted from STEINER, Emil; ibid.; cf. "Mondrian as a model?"; p. 120

[466] cf. p. 214

[467] CRAMER, Ernst, quoted from: ibid.; pp. 380–381

[468] cf. p. 201

[469] cf. "Open space design for the Heuried estate in Wiedikon, Zurich"; p. 212

[470] KAHN, Louis I., quoted from: STEINER, Emil: "Gestaltete Hügel" in: Der Gartenbau, issue 25/1975; p. 981; cf. KAHN, Louis I.: "Order and Form" in: Perspecta, The Yale Architectural Journal, issue 3/1955; p. 59

[471] cf. ASL Dossier 01.03.035

[472] cf. ASL Dossier 01.03.034

[473] cf. ADORNO, Theodor W.: Ohne Leitbild. Frankfurt 1969

[474] cf. 'The "Flame" in Sisseln'; p. 230

[475] STEINER, Emil: "Gestaltete Hügel" in: Der Gartenbau, issue 25/1975; pp. 981–982

[476] cf. p. 231

[477] cf. Suter und Suter AG: "Wohnüberbauung 'Im Surinam', Basel" in: Schweizer Journal, issue 10–11/1972; p. 69

[478] ERIKSSON, Christofer in conversation with the author in March 1998

[479] cf. page 97

[480] cf. "Open spaces for the Grüzefeld housing estate in Winterthur"; p. 180

[481] cf. Stadt Zürich (publ.): Wohnsiedlungen Heuried und Utohof in Zürich-Wiedikon. Zurich 1978

[482] cf. ASL Dossier 01.04.648

[483] cf. "Cramer as a design teacher in Lausanne"; p. 205

[484] Stadt Zürich (publ.): Wohnsiedlungen Heuried und Utohof in Zürich-Wiedikon. Zurich 1978; p. 22

[485] cf. STEPHANUS, Bernd: "Grigny eine Stadt?" in: Werk, issue 3/1973; pp. 280–287 and STEINER, Emil: "Von der inneren Struktur zum Erscheinen der Form" in: Der Gartenbau, issue 11/1975; p. 383

[486] WEBER, Hans-Ulrich: "Gedanken zu 'La Grande Borne' in Grigny" in: Anthos, issue 3/74; p. 4

[487] cf. SGARD, Jacques: "Le 'Jardin sculpté' der 'Floralies 1969' in Paris" in: Anthos, issue 4/1969; pp. 39–44. cf. also p. 220

[488] The author is grateful to Rainer Fleischhauer, the architect responsible at the time, for detailed information about the history of the housing estate conveyed in a conversion in May 1999.

[489] cf. no author: "Stadtsanierung in einem Ballungsgebiet" in: Anthos, issue 4/1972; pp. 8–9

[490] SGARD, Jacques: "Le 'Jardin sculpté' der 'Floralies 1969' in Paris" in: Anthos, issue 4/1969; p. 39

[491] MATHYS, Heini in: ibid.

[492] SGARD, Jacques in: ibid.; p. 44

[493] ibid.

[494] SGARD, Jacques, quoted from: VIGNY, Annette: Jacques Sgard. Paysagiste & Urbaniste. Liège 1995; p. 52

[495] cf. ASL Dossier 01.04.9963

[496] cf. Anthos, issue 2/1975

[497] Technikum Winterthur (publ.): Laborgebäude Technikum Winterthur. Winterthur 1974; p. 5; ASL Dossier 01.05.003

[498] MATHYS, Heini: "Freiraumgestaltung zum neuen Laborgebäude des Technikums in Winterthur" in: Anthos, issue 2/1975; p. 3

[499] ibid.

[500] WALCH, Walter in an official remark dated 22 December1975

[501] cf. ASL Dossier 01.02.027

[502] cf. ASL Dossier 01.04.749

[503] STEINER, Emil in conversation with the author in spring 1998

[504] cf. ASL Dossier 01.03.024

[505] cf. p. 124

[506] CRAMER, Ernst in a manuscript dated 22 January 1979; ASL Dossier 01.03.024

[507] cf. ASL Dossier 01.04.749

[508] cf. ASL Dossier 01.05.007

[509] The author thanks Emil Steiner and Dr. Georg Steiner for important information about the history of this project

[510] STEINER, Georg in conversation with the author in summer 1998

[511] cf. ASL Dossiers 01.04.411, 01.01.034, 01.01.010, 01.02.032 and 01.02.004

[512] cf. ASL Dossiers 01.01.30 and 01.04.760

[513] cf. ASL Dossier 01.01.29

[514] cf. Aktennotiz Umgebung Bau 324 Sisseln, Besprechung Dr. Schett/ Dr. Hofer/Dr. Steiner vom 23.9.76; ASL Dossier 01.03.003

[515] The author thanks Dr. Georg Steiner
       for essential information about the history
       of this project.

[516] CRAMER, Ernst quoted from
       STEINER, Georg in conversation
       with the author in summer 1998

[517] cf. "The Zurich Cantonal Horticultural
       Show, ZÜGA 1933"; p. 23

[518] STEINER, Georg in conversation
       with the author in summer 1998

[519] in the Archiv für Schweizer Land-
       schaftsarchitektur in Rapperswil

[520] ERIKSSON, Christofer in conversation
       with the author in March 1998

[521] cf. CRAMER, Ernst: "Projekt für
       ein Friedhofgebäude in Gränichen/AG"
       in: Anthos, issue 4/1976; p. 37

[522] cf. p. 195

[523] cf. minutes of Gränichen
       council meeting dated 12 April 1976

[524] cf. ASL Dossier 01.04.761

[525] cf. ASL Dossiers 01.01. 032 and
       01.01.035

[526] CRAMER, Ernst: "Gedanken
       zum Thema Friedhof", lecture manu-
       script dated 16 February 1967 in
       ASL Dossier 01.03.008

[527] The author gained essential
       information on the history of this project
       from a conversation with Herr Gasser
       in summer 1999.

[528] cf. page 58

[529] The estate changed hands
       in summer 1999.

[530] The author gained essential
       information on the background to
       this project from a conversation with
       Emil Steiner in winter 2000.

[531] BAUMANN, Albert: "Die Solothurner
       Gärten im 17., 18. und 19. Jahrhundert" in:
       Gartenbaublatt, issue 49/1961; p. 1091

[532] ibid.

[533] cf. ASL Dossier 01.05.019

[534] cf. ASL Dossier 01.02.057

[535] cf. ASL Dossier 01.01.011

[536] ibid.

[537] cf. ASL Dossier 01.02.056

[538] cf. ASL Dossier 01.01.011

[539] Peter Latz confirms that landscape ar-
       chitecture is at least two decades behind
       compared with art and architecture. LATZ,
       Peter in an interview in: WEILACHER, Udo:
       Between Landscape Architecture and Land
       Art. Basel-Berlin- Boston 1996; p. 130

[540] BARTH, Hans Jakob: "Unruhe und
       Selbstkritik" in: Anthos, issue 2/1987;
       p. 12

[541] ALTHERR, Jürg/LASSERRE,
       Olivier/ZULAUF, Rainer/NOSEDA, Irma:
       "Freiräume" in: Werk, Bauen + Wohnen,
       issue 9/2000; p. 47

[542] cf. KIENAST, Dieter: "Sehnsucht
       nach dem Paradies" in: Hochparterre,
       issue 7/1990; pp. 46–50; and: KIENAST,
       Dieter: "Ohne Leitbild" in: Garten +
       Landschaft, issue 11/1986; pp. 34–38

[543] KIENAST, Dieter quoted from:
       WEILACHER, Udo: Between Landscape
       Architecture and Land Art. Basel-
       Berlin-Boston 1996; p. 142

[544] cf. Anthos, issue 2/1987

[545] cf. page 201

[546] cf. WEILACHER, Udo: "A new
       language in the landscape" in: ibid.: Be-
       tween Landscape Architecture and Land
       Art. Basel-Berlin-Boston 1996; p. 9

[547] MC HARG, Ian: Design with Nature.
       New York 1969

[548] KIENAST, Dieter: "Sehnsucht
       nach dem Paradies" in: Hochparterre,
       issue 7/1990; p. 49;

[549] ibid.; p. 144

[550] AMMANN, Gustav: "Rückschau
       auf die 'ZÜGA'" in: Gartenkunst, 46, 1933;
       pp. 169–171

[551] quoted from: letter from Hans Fischli
       to Ernst Cramer dated 26 August 1959;
       ASL Dossier 01.03.013; cf. page 115

[552] cf. page 119

[553] CRAMER, Ernst quoted from:
       Anthos, issue 2/1987; p. 23

[554] cf. NEMITZ, Barbara: Trans Plant.
       Living Vegetation in Contemporary Art.
       Stuttgart 2000

[555] cf. CRAMER, Ernst: "Gedanken zum
       Thema Friedhof", lecture manuscript dated
       16 February 1967 in ASL Dossier 01.03.008

[556] cf. TOPOS, issue 33/2000

[557] SMITH, Peter F.: Architecture
       and the Human Dimension. London 1979

[558] ENZENSBERGER, Hans Magnus:
       "Reminiszenzen an den Überfluß" in:
       DER SPIEGEL 51/1996, p. 117

[559] ibid., p. 118

[560] CRAMER, Ernst: "Gedanken zum
       Thema Friedhof", lecture manuscript dated
       16 February 1967 in ASL Dossier 01.03.008

[561] KIENAST, Dieter: "Sehnsucht
       nach dem Paradies" in: Hochparterre,
       issue 7/1990; p. 48

BIOGRAPHY

1898
Ernst Friedrich Cramer born in Zurich
on 7 December
1905–1913
Primary and secondary school in Zurich
1913
Started as an apprentice draughtsman
at the Zurich gasworks
1914–1917
Apprentice gardener at the
Froebels Erben horticultural business
in Zurich under Gustav Ammann
1918–1922
Travels as a journeyman and work
in various horticultural firms in Switzerland:
at the Ranft tree nursery in Basel and with
Henry Correvon in Geneva; in Germany and in
France (Savoye and Paris)
1922–1923
Attended Oeschberg Horticultural College
in Koppingen; taught by Albert Baumann
1924–1929
Work for horticultural firms
in Winterthur and in the Schaffhausen
municipal gardening department
1925
Married Anna Russenberger of Winterthur
1929
Took over a horticultural business in Zurich.
Planned and constructed private gardens
from 1929
Taught at the horticultural colleges
in Zurich, Horgen, Wetzikon
1932
Birth of daughter Susanna
1938
Built up his own gardening business and tree
nursery in Suhr with Ernst Racheter (gardener)
1939–1951
Worked with Willi Neukom (gardener)
from 1942
Horticultural businesses in Suhr
and Bellach, also for a time in Ticino
1942–1946
Worked with Albert Zulauf (gardener)
1942–1950
Worked with Ernst Surbeck (gardener)
1943
Death of wife Anna Cramer-Russenberger
after a long illness
1944
Married Gertrud Bürki
1944–1980
Member of the Swiss Werkbund SWB

1944–1948
Worked with Adolf Dubs
(horticultural technician)
1945
Founded Cramer & Surbeck,
Gartenarchitekten, based in Zürich
1946–1951
Worked with Hans Jakob Barth (gardener)
1947
Founded the Manni – Cramer & Surbeck
branch in Cadempino near Lugano with
Arnoldo Manni (gardener with his own
horticultural business)
1947/48
Birth of sons Thomas and Hans-Ulrich
1949–1956
Worked with Wolf Hunziker
(herbaceous gardener)
1950
Cramer & Surbeck split up
1950–1973
Worked with Karl Pappa (gardener)
1955–1963
Worked with Heinz Rimensberger (gardener)
1958–1970
Worked with Fritz Dové (gardener)
1960
First major journey to Brazil, and
from then on other journeys in Europe
and Asia, especially Japan
1963–1964
President of the editoral board of the Swiss
professional magazine *Anthos*
1963–1980
Member of the Arbeitsgemeinschaft
für Friedhof und Denkmal (Cemetery and
Monument Study Group) in Kassel
1964–1970
Worked with Christofer Bengt Eriksson
(graduate landscape architect)
1972
Closed the Zurich and Suhr branches;
moved the planning office to Rüschlikon
1972–1980
Taught at the Athenaeum Ecole d'Architecture
in Lausanne (private college of architecture,
interior design and garden architecture)
from 1975
One-man office in Rüschlikon
1980
Died in Rüschlikon
1985
Ernst Cramer's estate handed over to the
Archiv für die Schweizer Gartenarchitektur und
Landschaftsplanung (now: Archiv für Schweizer
Landschaftsarchitektur) in Rapperswil

CATALOGUE OF PROJECTS

Gertrud Cramer's commitment is the first reason why the drawn and photographic evidence of Ernst Cramer's projects, roughly 1400 of them, has not disappeared without trace. With support from the landscape architect Stefan Rotzler, she first had the plans in her husband's estate examined, then handed over about 5000 plans, 10,000 photographs and various models, notes and professional magazines to the Archiv für Schweizer Landschaftsarchitektur in 1985; this was founded in 1982, under the name of the "Stiftung Archiv für die Schweizer Gartenarchitektur und Landschaftsplanung", based in Rapperswil. About 400 plans from Ernst Cramer's estate are officially classified as missing. Many sets of plans are no longer organized as they originally were because of uncoordinated research in the past. But ultimately there are also many undated and unidentified planning documents because of the lack of labelling for which Ernst Cramer himself is responsible.

The author's years of computer-supported analysis and expert classification of the estate, with the assistance of the archive in Rapperswil (curator: Annemarie Bucher), the Archives de la Construction Moderne at the Federal Institute of Technology in Lausanne and the chair of landscape architecture at the ETH Zurich means that it is now possible to search the material under a variety of headings like: place of origin, nature and scope of projects, date of origin, nature and number of available documents, participating artists and architects and other project participants. A complex relational database gives access to all the information on the individual projects available to date.

Reconstructed models on a scale of 1:75 of the "Poet's Garden", the "Theatre Garden" and the "Postplatz in Vaduz" have been prepared at the ETH Zurich according to the author's instructions. It was only possible to understand the character of Ernst Cramer's work and to write the present book after numerous interviews with contemporary witnesses, collecting additional plans and illustrations, visiting a number of surviving projects in Switzerland and adjacent countries and also an excursion to Brazil.

All the projects in italics in the following list of works are described in this book or mentioned in the context of other project descriptions. These projects were mainly selected on the basis of the importance Ernst Cramer himself ascribed to them within his œuvre. This evaluation was supported by analysis of numerous publications by and about Ernst Cramer in the contemporary professional press and through conversation with former colleagues and project partners. The completeness, variety, nature and scope of the available information played an additional role in the choice of the projects described and interpreted. Even so both the nature and the fate of many projects by Ernst Cramer are still obscure.

1933
Private garden for Vogel-Sulzer in Itschnach, 1933–1952 (cf. p. 26)
Pool Garden at the Zurich Cantonal Horticultural Show, ZÜGA 1933 in Zurich (cf. p. 25)

1934
Private garden for Schoeller, Walter in Erlenbach, 1934–1937 (cf. p. 31)

1935
Competition for lake shore design in Zurich

1936
Private garden for Bianca in Zollikon, 1936–1937 (cf. p. 31)

1937
Private garden for Brändli, Sidney, Dr. in Aarau
Private garden for Lauer, Dr. in Thalwil
Private garden for Schmid, Fritz, manufacturer, in Suhr
Private garden for Siegrist, Rudolf, Dr., state councillor, in Aarau
Private garden for Staub-Graf, Dr. in Oberhofen

1938
First Church of Christ Scientist in Zurich, 1938–1939 (cf. p. 31)
Private garden for Fischer, H., Direktor, in Aarau
Park of the Königsfelden tuberculosis ward

1939
Private garden for Bircher, senior teacher, in Aarau
Fountain for the Sonnenberg gardens in Hirslanden, Zurich
Private garden for Honegger, H.C. in Jona, 1939–1942
Private garden for Schälchlin, Dr. in Küsnacht
Hospital Garden at the Swiss National Exhibition 1939 in Zurich (cf. p. 35)
Private garden for Sulzer-Binet, Dr. in Geneva

1940
Paths for Haus Iona in Jona
Hotel-Restaurant for Merz, Albert in Gebenstorf

1941
Private garden for Andretto in Zurich
Private garden for Aurorastrasse in Zurich
Private garden for Braendli in Zurich
Private garden for Lang, Erich, manufacturer, in Reiden, 1941–1944
Summerhouse for Maurer, F. in Olten
Private garden for Vogt, R. in Locarno Monti, 1941–1948 (cf. p. 132)
Private garden for Zinsli, Direktor, in Sevelen

1942

Autumn in Bloom horticultural show in Zurich,
Kongresszentrum (cf. p. 41)
Private garden for Forrer-Sulzer, Dr. in Moscia
near Ascona, 1942–1948 (cf. p. 44)
Private garden for a country house near Windisch

1943

Private garden for a holiday home near Villars-sur-Fontenais
Private garden for Hafter, Dr. in Zurich
Private garden for Kägi, Walter Emil, Direktor in Vitznau (cf. p. 43)
Landis Private garden (country house) in Minusio (cf. p. 46)
Summerhouse for Romegialli in Enge, Zurich
Open space design for Zollikerberg estate in Zurich, 1943–1944
Private garden for Vorster in Basel

1944

Private garden for Egli, M. in Küsnacht
Fiera Lugano horticultural show in Lugano, 1944–1950 (cf. p. 58)
Private garden for Gunzinger, Direktor in Welschenrohr, 1944–1948
Private garden for Model, Elsa in Weinfelden, 1944–1945
Aegerten primary school in Wiedikon, Zurich
Sulzer cemetery, family tomb, 1944–1945
Open space design for Dachslernstrasse estate in Zurich
Open space design for Hürststrasse estate in Affoltern
Open space design for Rehalpstrasse estate in Zurich
Open space design for Überlandstrasse/Glattstegweg estate
in Zurich, 1944–1947
Open space design for Wasserwerkstrasse estate in Zurich,
1944–1950 (cf. p. 53)

1945

Private garden for B. on Lago Maggiore
Private garden for F. in Bonfol
Roof garden for Fankhauser in Solothurn
Suhr memorial fountain in Suhr
Private garden (villa) for Göhner, Ernst in Morcote,
1945–1948 (cf. p. 48)
Private garden for Rümbeli, Dr. med. in Agnuzzo
Private garden for S. in Wildegg
Private garden for Schmidt-Brandon in Ascona
Open space design for Riedgrabenweg/Wallisellenstrasse estate in
Oerlikon, Zurich, 1945–1946
Open space design for Vetterliweg estate in Altstetten, Zurich
Private garden (remodelling) for Zollikerstrasse 229 in Zurich
Aarau cemetery, 1946–1951

1946

Competition for a cemetery in Herrliberg
Competition for a cemetery and crematorium in Aarau
Cantonal hospital and children's hospital in Aarau, 1946–1957
Private garden for Kraft-Utzinger, A. in Schaffhausen
Private garden for Schindler, Ernst, architect, in Zurich (cf. p. 145)

1947

A.G.A. Aargauische Gartenbau-Ausstellung 1947 in Aarau (cf. p. 63)
Private garden for Bourgeoise, D., Mlle. in Mendrisio
Private garden for single-family house in Höngg, Zurich
Private garden for Graf, manufacturer, in Benken
Private garden for Granella, V. in Wurenlingen
Private garden for Greuter in Aarau
Private garden for Haeny, W., businessman, in Aarau
Private garden for Hügi, Dr. in Aarau
Private garden for Hunziker, E., cantonal engineer, in Aarau
Knüsli, E. horticultural show in Höngg, Zurich
Open spaces for the City of Zurich's new sewage treatment plant,
service building in Opfikon, Zurich
Open spaces (remodelling) for the Oboussier estate
casino buildings in Aarau, 1947–1950

Primary and secondary schools in Rüti, 1947–1949
Hotel/Restaurant Rathausgarten (extension) in Aarau
Private garden for Resinelli, Augusto in Gudo
Private garden for Roth-Spetzmann, M. in Binningen
Private garden for Rubli Mattenberger in Aarau
Private garden (country house) for Schäfer, A., Direktor, Dr.
in Zollikon
Summerhouse proposal for Schild, H., Dr. med. in Aarau
School in Döttingen, 1947–1949
Zelgli school in Aarau
Courtyard design for Schweizerisches Vereinssortiment Olten,
1947–1948
Private garden for Sperisen, O., architect, in Solothurn
Private garden for Tschupp-Wyder, A., engineer, in Wetzikon
Open space design for Baugenossenschaft Nünenen estate in Thun
Open space design for Hünibach estate in Thun
Open space design for Imfeldstrasse estate in Zurich
Open space design for In der Telli estate in Aarau, 1947–1948
Open space design for Rotfluhstrasse/Wirbelweg estate in Zollikon
Open space design for Sperletweg estate (phase 1) in Zurich
Private garden for Vock, Ch. H. in Wohlen, 1947–1959
Open space design for residential and commercial building,
children's playground in Zurich (?)
1947 Zurich Cantonal Agriculture and Trade Exhibition, ZÜKA 1947
in Zurich (cf. p. 60)

1948

New design for the Aare embankment in Aarau
Summerhouse for Buzzi, R., Direktor in Ascona
Private garden for Cosandier, A., Direktor in Solothurn
Private garden for Egger, Prof. in Zurich
Private garden for Fehlmann, C., Dr., pharmacist, in Aarau
Private garden for Fehlmann, D., manufacturer, in Schöftland
Grounds for window factory in Rothrist, 1948–1949
Private garden for Frei, P., Dr. (Nyon) in Prangins
Private garden for Hagmann, Otto in Genoa, 1948–1950
Private garden for Hegner, Wolfgang E. in Feldmeilen (cf. p. 65)
Private garden for Hofmann, W.H. in Zollikon
Kleeweid kindergarten in Leimbach, Zurich
Private garden for Kronauer in Thalwil
Open spaces (front garden) for Suhrsee lecture hall in Sursee
Private garden for Lüthi in Meilen
Private garden for Meyer in Wöschnau
Private garden for Oetterli in Solothurn
Church/vicarage in Wipkingen, Zurich
Roof garden for Roth, Peter, A.G. (watch and clock factory)
in Lyss (cf. p. 65)
Private garden for Rütti-Lack in Solothurn
Grounds for Schaffner AG, new building
in Schönenwerd, 1948–1951
Private garden for Schärer, M. in Rupperswil, 1948–1949
Private garden for Schenker, W. in Schönenwerd
Private garden for Schmid in Zurich
Private garden for Scholz, E. in Zollikon
Suburban school in Solothurn, 1948–1949
Private garden (holiday home) for Schweizer,
Arth., Dr. in Pontresina
Private garden for Spälti, A., Dr. in Küsnacht (cf. p. 66)
Grounds for Sunlight Olten, forecourt
Private garden for Thenisch, Dr. in Oberentfelden
Open spaces outside the transformer station in Rieterplatz in Zurich
Open spaces for "Rainacker" estate in Rekingen,
1948–1949 (cf. p. 180)
Open space design for Baugenossenschaft Reppisch estate
in Birmensdorf
Open space design for Schaffhauserstrasse estate
in Seebach, Zurich
Design for the banks of the factory canal in Aarau
Private garden for Widmer, Ed. in Gränichen
Private garden for Wolfensberger, Otto F. in Wabern near Bern
Garage Wysslig-Bolliger, E. in Buchs
Private garden for Wyssling, E. in Buchs
Private garden (alteration) for Zondler, P., Dr. in Hirslanden, Zurich

1949

Grounds for AEW office building in Aarau, 1949–1954
Private garden (weekend house) for Bechtler, W., Dr. in Freienbach
Private garden for Beetscher, Dr. iur. in Zofingen
Private garden (alteration) for Blumer, H. in Seebach, Zurich
Grounds (packaging factory) for Dimmler, Carl Egon in Zofingen
Private garden for Edelmann, A.E., Dr. in Wollishofen, Zurich
Private garden (alteration/terrace) for Fehlmann-Gradmann
in Zofingen
Private garden for Fretz, Max, Dr. in Aarau
Private garden for Frey, X., Dr., veterinary surgeon,
in Döttingen, 1949–1950
Cemetery (remodelling) in Bannwill, 1949–1967
Competition for a cemetery in Oftringen
Cemetery in Schöftland
Private garden for Grimm, Albert, Direktor in Küsnacht
Confectionary and tearoom Gruner, Max in Suhr
Private garden for Guggisberg, Fr. in Thun
Private garden for Huber, A., Dr. med. dent. in Sins
Private garden for Kocher, S., Direktor in Solothurn
Private garden for Lutz in Zuchwil
"Im Gut" primary school in Wiedikon, Zurich, 1949–1950 (cf. p. 69)
Primary school in Uster, 1949–1950
Rosengartenweg cemetery (?) (alteration) in Aarau
Private garden (filling station) for Schaffner, Martin in Suhr
School in Buchs, 1949–1951
Rüti school in Zurich (cf. p. 69)
Open spaces for seminary in Wettingen
Open space design for "Sunnmatt" estate in Thun
Open space design for Bühlacker estate in Buchs (cf. p. 55)
Open space design for Winterthurerstrasse estate in Zurich
Private garden (holiday home) for Von Arx, Hans in Nottwil
Open spaces for Wohlfahrtshaus Omega in Solothurn
Private garden for Zendralli, Ugo, Dr. in Roveredo

1950

Private garden for Bärtschi, Hans in Schönenwerd, 1950–1951
Private garden for Belser, Th., Dr. in Klosters
Private garden for Brüderlin, K., works manager, in Gelterkinden
Casino garden in Aarau
Private garden for Diethelm, W. in Zumikon
Private garden for Dimmler-Ringier, Carl Egon in Zofingen
Grounds for Dispensaire Antituberculeux in Pruntrut (Porrentruy)
Private garden for Ferrazzini-Pagani, Sig. Ing. in Torre
Competition for a cemetery in Turbenthal
Cemetery in Turbenthal, 1950–1956
Private garden for Guglielmetti, Giulio, Dr. in Mendrisio
Private garden for Härdy, Jakob in Oberentfelden
Private garden for Hauri in Oberentfelden
Grounds for Immobilien AG in Olten
Private garden for Käser, E. in Aarau
"Im Sunneberg" kindergarten in Thalwil
Church in Wetzikon
Private garden for Niederer, M., businessman, in Aarau
"Dorf" primary school in Suhr (cf. p. 71)
Private garden for Renold, Dr. in Aarau
Private garden for Roth, Frl. in Muhen, 1950–1951
Private garden for Schibler, Urban in Aarau
Office building in Bellach
School in Breitenbach
Gönhard school in Aarau
School in Grenchen
Private garden for Stampfli, Oskar, Dr., state councillor, in
Solothurn
Open space design for ASIG estate, Glattalstrasse in Seebach,
Zurich
Open space design for Baslerstrasse estate in Olten
Open space for Bellerivestrasse estate in Zurich (cf. p. 55)
Open spaces for Schmockergut in Steffisburg (cf. p. 55)
Open space design for Wallisellen-, Saatlenstrasse estate,

2nd phase, in Oerlikon, Zurich, 1950–1951
University of Zurich, Faculty of Medicine
Private garden for Wittmer-Bless, Franz in Binningen
Private garden for Wyss-Roth, Otto in Herzogenbuchsee
Private garden for Bodmer-Abegg, Annie, Dr. in Riesbach, Zurich,
1951–1960 (cf. p. 83)

1951

Private garden for Bonomo, W. in Meilen
Private garden for Bühler, René, Dr. in Uzwil
Private garden for Cramer, Charles Dr. in Vaduz (cf. p. 180)
Private garden for Eberhard, Rud., works manager, in Suhr
Cemetery in Fehraltorf, 1951–1952
Private garden for Fürrer, Rud. H. in Zollikon
Private garden for Hartmann, Dr. in Solothurn
Private garden for Hindenberger, Dr., secondary school teacher,
in Unter-Erlinsbach
Private garden for Hollenweger in Wangen near Dübendorf
Private garden for Hug, Alfred, manufacturer, in Herzogenbuchsee
Private garden for Ingold, E. in Herzogenbuchsee
Kindergarten in Oberrieden
Vicarage in Gränichen, 1951–1952 (cf. p. 241)
Schönenwerd school, playground and playing fields, 1951–1953
Municipal park in Baslerstrasse in Olten
Open spaces (embankment planting and inn)
for Wägithal reservoir (?)
Private garden for Sudan, A. in Olten
Private garden for Truninger, E. in Aarau
Open spaces for Genferstrasse estate in Enge, Zurich
Open space design for Russacker estate in Dietikon
"Um 1900" exhibition in Zurich with Willy Guhl,
1951–1952 (cf. p. 74)
Private garden for Von Däniken, Walter F. in Schönenwerd
Private garden for Wartmann, R., engineer, in Brugg

1952

Private garden for Amsler, Ad. in Aarau
Grounds for Ebauches, watch and clock factory (extension)
in Bettlach, 1952–1958
Grounds for ESWA, Ernst+Co (new factory) in Stansstad
Competition for Meisenhard cemetery in Olten
Cemetery (extension) in Wangen, 1952–1955
Private garden for Grüebler, Hugo, Dr. in Küsnacht, 1952–1953
Grounds for Gunzinger Frères S.A., watch and clock factory,
in Welschenrohr
"Don Bosco" Italian church in Zurich
Private garden for Koch in Aarau
Balmberg spa in Balm near Günsberg
Private garden for Lehner, Max, manufacturer, in Gränichen
Lay preachers' house in Bremgarten
"In der Oberwiesen" primary school in Frauenfeld
School in Schöftland
Secondary school in Brüttisellen, 1952–1953
Private garden for Wirth von Muralt in Hirslanden, Zurich
Private garden for Amsler-Merz, E. in Aarau, 1953–1954 (cf. p. 137)

1953

Private garden for Angst in Herrliberg
Fountain near Kölliker bakery in Thalwil
Private garden for Buffat, Paul and Aubert, H., Mlle. in Le Lieu
Grounds for Eternit AG in Niederurnen, 1953–1955 (cf. p. 75)
Open space design for Fretz und Co. (shoe factory and
residential complex) in Aarau
Private garden for Frey, H. in Wangen near Olten
Meisenhard cemetery in Olten
Cemetery in Sins
Private garden for Künzli, P., Dr. in Solothurn
Vicarage in St. Niklaus
Private garden for Rüegger, Paul in Zofingen, 1953–1972
School in Sins
School in Weisslingen
Station square in Fehraltdorf
Dancing and park complex in Thun, 1953–1957 (cf. p. 75)
Open space design for Starrkirchstrasse estate in Olten

1954

Am Baschligplatz private garden, residential building in Zurich
Private garden for Ammann in Oberentfelden
Garden café for Hotel/Restaurant Café Stern in Muri
Chessex-Kürsteiner cemetery, family tomb in Schaffhausen
Private garden for Hess, E., carossier, in Solothurn
Zürcher Oberland secondary school in Wetzikon, 1954–1957
Private garden for König in Erlinsbach
Private garden for Marti, Hanspeter in Bettlach
Bettlach school in Bettlach, 1954–1960
Laupersdorf school (new building) in Laupersdorf
Open space design for Bachstrasse estate in Aarau
Private garden (garage drive) for Vogelsang, W.
in Albisrieden, Zurich

1955

"Im Untermoos" primary school in Altstetten, Zurich (cf. p. 83)
Private garden for Allemann, H., Dr. in Montagnola
Private garden for doctor's house in Muhen
Station square in Luterbach, 1955–1957
Private garden (Haus Stutzera) for Dietschi, Max in Wengen
Private garden (alteration) for Faltz, J. S., Direktor in Zurich
Cemetery in Oftringen, 1955–1960
Private garden for Hänssler, C. in Küsnacht
Catholic church in Oberwil-Zug, 1955–1956
Private garden for Künzel, Max in Buchs
Private garden for Lehner-Klein in Gränichen
Bernarda Female Teachers' Seminary in Menzingen,
1955–1959 (cf. p. 86)
Square design in Rikon
Apfelbaumstrasse primary school in Oerlikon, Zurich
Private garden for Roth-Ott, E., Dr. in Schönenwerd
School in Risch
Private garden for Schwyter, A., pharmacist, in Schöftland
Private garden for Suter in Oberfrick
Gymnasium in Erlinsbach
Open space design for Bellariastrasse estate in Zurich
Open space design for Bombachstrasse estate in Höngg, Zurich
Open space design for cooperative housing association estate
in Langendorf

1956

Private garden for Am Bohlgutsch (block of three flats)
in Zug, 1956–1957 (cf. p. 92)
Private garden for Erne, J. in Olten
Cemetery in Bellach, 1956–1957
Competition for Eichbühl cemetery in Altstetten,
Zurich, 1956–1958 (cf. p. 99)
Cemetery (extension) in Pfäffikon, 1956–1971
Private garden for Hürlimann in Holderbank
Interbau Berlin 1957/Hansaviertel, 1956–1961 (cf. p. 94)
Private garden for Keller, A. in Luterbach
Private garden for Meyer, Dr. in Baden
Private garden for Müller in Suhr
Garden restaurant for Restaurant Schachen in Aarau
Grounds for Riwisa AG in Hägglingen, 1956–1968 (cf. p. 83)
Densbüren school in Densbüren
School in Gränichen, 1956–1958
School in Unterägeri, 1956–1957

1957

Private garden for Bikle, W. (row houses) in Küttigen
Private garden (Gimmenen country house) for Brunner, Andreas, C.,
Dr. iur. in Oberwil, 1957–1958 (cf. p. 100)
Private garden for Heiniger-Moser, Hans in Aarau
Competition for Hotel Darius in Teheran (cf. p. 99)
Private garden for Keller, Eugen in Aarau
Hauriweg church hall in Wollishofen, Zurich
Mülizelg clinic

Private garden for country house in Bünishofen (?)
Private garden for Pusich, B. in Suhr
Private garden for 7 Scheuchzerstrasse in Zurich, 1957–1958
Private garden (country house) for Schoch-Bockhorn, Alice
in Zollikon (cf. p. 149)
"Im Feld" primary school in Wetzikon, 1957–1967 (cf. p. 99)
School in Rudolfstetten, 1957–1959
School and playing fields in Lengnau, 1957–1972
Open spaces for terraced buildings in Zug,
1957–1960 (cf. p. 101)
Stable extension for Wittmer, E., farmer, in Oberrieden
Private garden for Zollinger, H., Dr. in Herrliberg

1958

Private garden for Bodmer, David, Dr.
in Hombrechtikon, 1958–1960
Private garden for De Simoni, Dr. in Langendorf, Soleure
Private garden for Forrer, B. in Zollikon
Cemetery in Dänikon, 1958–1964
Roof garden for Graben in Aarau
Private garden for Trüb-Weber, Hans in Aarau, 1958–1964
Open space design for "Goldern" estate in Aarau, 1958–1968
Open space design for Gestacu P. & Co. estate in Biel
Open space design for Letzigraben-Langgrutstrasse estate in
Zurich, 1958–1960
Open space design for the home of Senn, Otto, architect,
in Zofingen (cf. p. 98)
Open space design for an estate in Wettingen
Open space design for "Zum Fallenden Brunnenhof"
estate in Zurich
Goldbrunnenplatz waiting rooms in Zurich, 1958–1959
Grounds for Widmer, book printers, in Bellach
Private garden for Zuellig, Dr., Schloss Meienberg,
in Jona, 1958–1977

1959

Competition for "Blözen" cemetery in Pratteln,
1959–1962 (cf. p. 120)
Private garden for Fröhlich, H. in Kilchberg
"Poet's Garden", First Swiss Horticultural ShowG|59
in Zurich (cf. p. 106)
Private garden for Hagander-Schneider, Julius
in Basel, 1959–1962
Oberer Friesenberg Jewish cemetery (2nd phase)
in Wiedikon, Zurich
Grounds for JCF Jura Zementfabriken,
(office building) in Aarau, 1959–1961
Vicarage for the Catholic Congregation in Zug
Church in Bettlach
Private garden for Luterbacher, F., Direktor in Zumikon
Neue Bäumliterrasse and Hangfussweg
in Winterthur, 1959–1962
Obertorplatz in Bremgarten
Private garden for Rodel-Moser, R. in Schafisheim (?)
Private garden for Schaad, W. in Wiedikon, Zurich
School in Aesch
School in Baar, 1959–1960
School in Kleinlützel
School in Rupperswil
Open space design for "Brumela" estate in Olten
Open space design for "Sonnmatte" estate in Zofingen
Open space design for Waldpark estate in Oftringen

1960

Private garden for Brack, W. in Aarau
Private garden for Fischer, B. in Zollikerberg
Private garden for Frey-Wiedemann in Aarau
Cemetery in Gränichen, 1960–1968 (cf. p. 241)
Private garden for Hochstrasser in Moscia (cf. p. 132)
Private garden (country house) for Ilgen, Dr. in Zug, 1960–1961
Private garden for Kistler, Robert in Zug
Private garden for Lang, E.C. in Brione, 1960–1961

Private garden for Lerf, Dr. in Küttigen
Private garden for Proebster, W.T., Dr. in Oberrieden
Buchlern school, 1960–1962
Looren school in Witikon, Zurich, 1960–1971 (cf. p. 184)
Playing fields in Bremgarten
Private garden for Stutz, W., Direktor, in Aarau, 1960–1961
Private garden for Thoma, Jean Ulrich, Dr. in Zug
Grounds for U.S. Industrial Chemicals in Baar
Open space design for "Tannstein" estate in Thalwil, 1960–1961
Open space design for Glärnischstrasse estate in Rüschlikon, 1960–1961
Open space design for Heuel estate in Thalwil
Open space design for Wilerfeld estate in Olten, 1960–1963 (cf. p. 144)
Private garden for Zimmermann, Charles in Erlenbach

1961

Old people's home in Suhr
Private garden for Burchard, E. in Schaan
Private garden for Flury, Max in Baden
Private garden for Geiser, Hans in Aarau (cf. p. 136)
Cemetery (extension) in Thalwil, 1961–1966
Futapass cemetery, German military cemetery on the Futa pass, 1961–1967 (cf. p. 126)
Private garden for Henrici, Peter, Prof. Dr. in Rüschlikon, 1961–1962
Private garden for Pesch, Dr. in Riesbach, Zurich, 1961–1963
Post office and community centre square in Urdorf
Private garden for Rothenhäusler in Thalwil
Private garden for Rüegger, E. in Altstetten, Zurich
Private garden for Schmidlin, Josef, architect, in Aarau (cf. p. 136)
School in Bremgarten
School in Wohlen
Private garden for Spirig, Hugo, Dr. in Starrkirch-Wil, 1961–1964 (cf. p. 134)
Playing fields in Urdorf
Open spaces Terra del Sole residence in Ascona, 1961–1962 (cf. p. 132)
Private garden for Treichler, Roman, Direktor in Baar
Gymnasium (new building) in Davos
Open space design "Grüzefeld" estate in Winterthur-Bode, 1961–1974 (cf. p. 180)
Open space design for Baukonsortium estate in Strengelbach
Open space design for Obere Rötelstrasse estate in Zug
Open space design for Sulzbergstrasse estate in Wettingen
Private garden for Villa Bel Riposo in Luzern

1962

Private garden for De Dominicis, Fausto, Dr.-Ing. in Monza
Private garden for Dosenbach, C. in Zug, 1962–1966
Private garden for Dürst in Leihmatt Oberwil
Private garden for Dürst, Georg, Dr. in Ronco sopra Ascona
Private garden for Eichenberger & Gachnang in Thalwil, 1962–1963
Grounds for Finbox (new factory building) in Rickenbach
Private garden for Gloor, B. in Umiken
Private garden (pool) for Heiniger-Moser, Hans in Aarau
Private garden (villa) for Hischmann, R. in Brione sopra Minusio, 1962–1976 (cf. p. 132)
Private garden for Hofmann, E., Direktor in Thalwil
"Theatre Garden", International Horticultural Show IGA 1963 in Hamburg, 1962–1963 (cf. p. 152)
"In der Rüti" site modelling, infil in Thalwil
Intra-Häuser/Intrapolis project study with Walter Jonas, 1962–1967 (cf. p. 142)
Private garden for König, M., Dr.-Ing. in Zollikon, 1962–1963
Private garden for Lüem-Hungerbühler, W., manufacturer, in Lenzburg, 1962–1963
Looren secondary school building in Maur, 1962–1968 (cf. p. 185)
Private garden for Pfenninger, Peter in Interlaken
Primary school in Zollikerberg, 1962–1963

Private garden for Reinmann in Zollikon
Private garden (alteration) for Rohr, W. in Zofingen
Private garden for Simmen-Schwyzer, H. in Brugg
Urban square (AEW) in Aarau, 1962–1970 (cf. p. 190)
Open space design for "Tobelhus" estate in Zumikon, 1962–1971
Open spaces for Badenerstrasse estate in Aussersihl, Zurich, 1962–1965 (cf. p. 149)
Open space design for Sihlbau estate in Gattikon
Private garden for Vitali in Thalwil
Grounds for Wartmann & Cie AG in Brugg

1963

Private garden for Ackersteinstrasse in Zurich
Private garden (villa) for Ambrosoli in Ascona
Private garden for Bein, Hugo, Prof. Dr. med. in Oberwil, 1963–1967
Brack cemetery, family tomb in Aarau, 1963–1964
Private garden for Bruderer, Dr. in Fluntern, Zurich
Grounds for Frawa AG in Zollikon, 1963–1964
Private garden (swimming pool) for Gmür, P., Dr., in Fluntern, Zurich, 1963–1965
Private garden for Hauserstrasse 16 in Hirslanden, Zurich
Private garden for Heeb-Späni, Xavier in Davos
Grounds for Humbel in Obermeilen
Private garden for Huntzeler, R. in Niederrohrdorf, 1963–1964
Grounds for Inter-Hamol SA in Venegono-Varese
Kindergarten in Birmensdorf, 1963–1964
Schürmatt children's home in Zetzwil, 1963–1966
Monastery of St. Joseph in Solothurn
Private garden for Langhard, H., Direktor in Meilen
Private garden for Merz, Albert in Gebenstorf
Private garden for Meyer, E., Direktor in Meilen
Grounds for Migros in Urdorf
Private garden for Regenass in Tennwil, 1963–1965
Private garden for Schärer-Jauquet, J. in Erlenbach
School in Eugen-Huber Strasse (extension) in Zurich
Secondary school in Thalwil, 1963–1964
Private garden for Seyffer, R. in Fluntern, Zurich
Open space design for "Im Hof" estate in Klosters-Platz
Open space design for Brändle-Meierhofer estate in Thalwil, 1963–1964
Open space design for Farlifangstrasse estate in Zumikon
Open space design for Gabarell AG estate in Thalwil
Private garden for Wälty, H. in Schöftland
Wildi family tomb/tomb inscription

1964

Private garden for Bertschinger, Max in Lenzburg
Private garden for Boesch, Walter in Niederrohrdorf
Private garden for Forster-Geret, Willy in St. Gallen
Cemetery in Oberrieden
Grounds for Gerber, Ch. (new factory building) in Horgen
Grounds for Greiner Electronic AG (new building) in Langenthal, 1964–1965
Private garden for Hochstrasser, A. in Lenzburg
Private garden for Klaus in Uerikon, 1964–1967
Mahler family tomb in Thalwil
Private garden for Meienhofer, H. in Güttingen
Private garden for Rentsch, Gertrud and Fritz
Grounds for Schäppi, E. & Co (new factory building) in Horgen
"Doeltschi" school in Zurich
Dintikon school (school yard) in Dintikon
Square design for Sulzer, high-rise office building 222 in Winterthur, 1964–1966 (cf. p. 168)
Open space design for "Bodenmatt" estate in Ennethorw (?), 1964–1965
Grounds for office building in Rupperswil, 1964–1966
Private garden for Vogel, Tom H. in Nyon, 1964–1965
Private garden (country house) for Voney, F., in Russikon
Private garden for Wassmer in Aarau
Grounds for Weidmann AG, dyers, in Thalwil, 1964–1965
Private garden for Weinberg, Rolf, E. in Hirslanden, Zurich, 1964–1968

1965

Private garden for Bachmann, E., Dr. in Aarau
Private garden for Bongiovanni/Cescon, E. in Castelnuovo-Rangone
Private garden ("Casa Ebelin Bucerius") for Bucerius, Gerd, Dr.
in Brione (cf. p. 164)
Private garden for Burchard, H. in Hombrechtikon, 1965–1966
Grounds for CIBA Photochemie AG Fribourg research centre in Marly
Private garden for Erné, H. in Aarau
Competition for Grenchen cemetery (extension)
Cemetery in Hirzel, 1965–1973
Cemetery in Hütten, 1965–1967
Cemetery in Kreuzlingen ("Vibrato"), 1965–1969
Competition for Uetliberg cemetery in Wiedikon, Zurich
Private garden for Gemuseus, A. Walter, Direktor in Thalwil
Private garden for Greiner, Rudolf in Langenthal
Open space design for Grossholz, Leo in Uitikon, 1965–1966
Private garden for Klemperer + Meyer in Herrliberg
Private garden for Landolt, Dr. in Thalwil
Private garden for Lüchinger, H.G., Dr. in Wettswil
Private garden for Mayer-Zbinden, H. in Solothurn
Private garden for Meister, H.R., jeweller, in Zollikon, 1965–1967
Private garden for Merz, R. in Wollishofen, Zurich
Private garden for Prina, Aldo in Starrkirch near Olten
Private garden for Rentsch, Fritz in Wengen (cf. p. 162)
District school in Suhr
Roof garden for Olten town hall, 1965–1968 (cf. p. 177)
Open spaces for "Im Sand" barracks in Schönbühl, 1965–1966
Open space design for "Im Keimler" estate in Urdorf, 1965–1966
Private garden for Urben in Wettingen
Private garden for Urben-Bugmann, J. in Döttingen, 1965–1966
Private garden (swimming pool/bath-house)
for Vock, Dr. in Binningen, 1965–1966
Private garden for Zimmermann, J. in Mägenwil

1966

Open space design for Am Hohentwiel Rationeller Wohnungsbau
estate for Alu Suisse in Singen, 1966–1967
Open space design for atrium estate in Edlibach
Horticultural show "Blumenparadies" racecourse
in Oerlikon, Zurich
Private garden (country house) for Bommer, Paul E. in Uitikon
Private garden for Bugmann, Richard Hans in Döttingen
Grounds for CIBA AG in Basel, 1966–1967
Frauenfeld indoor and outdoor swimming pools
in Frauenfeld, 1966–1973 (cf. p. 188/189)
Private garden for Heiniger, Fritz, general agent,
in Unterentfelden, 1966–1967 (cf. p. 209)
Private garden (screen wall) for Heiniger-Moser, Hans in Aarau
Private garden for Heizmann, Erich, Dipl.-Ing. in Auenstein
Private garden for Hemmeler, H., Dr. iur. in Aarau, 1966–1967
Private garden (alteration) for Hobi, C., Dr. in Risch, 1966–1967
Private garden for Kats, Nico in Küttigen, 1966–1968
Goldern kindergarten (double kindergarten) in Aarau
Kindergarten for the Roman Catholic congregation in Trimbach
Private garden for Kurt, Max in Aarwangen
Private garden (barbecue) for Meyer-Borel, F. in Herrliberg
Private garden (villa) for Neeff in Galliate near Varese
"Säli" primary school in Olten, 1966–1967
Private garden for Schneider, H., architect, in Aarau
Landenhof school for the hard of hearing
in Unterentfelden, 1966–1968
Open space design for social housing estate in Cham, 1966–1967
Open space design for Devo & Witoga estate in Turgi-Wil
Open space design for Goldackerweg estate in Zurich, 1966–1967
Open space design for Landenhof estate in Zug
Open space design for Ruetihof estate in Zug
Open space design for Rütistrasse estate in Adliswil

Open space design for Stockmatt, Vogelmatt, Aegelmatt estate
in Pratteln, 1966–1967
Private garden (summerhouses) for Uiker + Baldesberger
in Hurdnerwäldli/Hurden
Private garden for Weber, H. in Menzingen
Private garden for Zehnder-Arn, H. J. in Gränichen
Private garden for Zeier, Max in Weisslingen

1967

"Bifarg" old people's home in Wohlen, 1967–1968
J. H. Ernst-Stiftung old people's home in Wollishofen,
Zurich, 1967–1969
Private garden for Beckmann, Joseph in Minusio-Brione,
1967–1969
Private garden for Bosshard, W. in Wetzikon
Private garden for Brunner, Albert in Biel-Benken, 1967–1968
Private garden for Buri-Amiet, Rolf in Küttigen
Private garden for Filate, J. in Döttingen
Private garden for Fischlin, E. in Wilen near Sarnen
Competition "Hinderneuwis" cemetery
in Volketswil (cf. p. 192)
Weinfelden cemetery, 1967–1968
Private garden for Götschi-Holenstein, G. in Ins
Private garden for Haas, Emil J. in Forch, 1967–1968
Holiday home for Heiniger-Moser, Hans in Weggis
Private garden for Hilfiker, E. und Büchi, Hch. in Stäfa
Private garden for Humboldstrasse
"Im Tobel" kindergarten in Meilen
Private garden for Lüthy, P. in Schöftland
Car-park (Devo?) in Basel
Private garden for Rentsch, Willi in Aarburg
Private garden for Schellenberg, F. in Uitikon
Competition for sports centre in Dübendorf
Grounds for Trutmann, K. (cement factory) in Regensdorf,
1967–1968
Open space design for Hünenberg estate in Cham
Open space design for Neudorf estate in Heimiswil

1968

Grounds for AEW Immobilien in Aarau, 1968–1969
Private garden for Andermatt, P. in Allenwinden
Private garden for Barth, Robert, Dr. iur. in Rothrist
Private garden for Bernauer, J.G. in Zug, 1968–1969
Bruderholz hospital Basel in Bottmingen,
1968–1972 (cf. p. 195)
Grounds for CIBA offices and factory in Monthey, 1968–1972
Private garden for Di Gallo, A. in St. Niklausen
Private garden for Fleckenstein, A. in Rüschlikon
Home of Gass, Ernst in Wettswil
Patriziale golf club in Ascona
Geiselweid indoor and outdoor swimming pools in Winterthur
Private garden for Häni, G. in Wohlen
Private garden for Hirt, J. in Urdorf
Open spaces for Catholic union in Thalwil, 1968–1969
Open spaces for Töss church hall in Winterthur (cf. p. 212)
Private garden for Leimgrübler, E., Dr. in Urdorf
Private garden for Mann, H. in Baden-Baden, 1968–1969
Open spaces for university cafeteria and
Rechberg gardens in Zurich
Private garden for Meyer, architect, in Binz near Maur
Private garden for Schürmann, Richard, Dr. oec.
in Zug, 1968–1974
Swimming baths in Würenlos
Trägerhard sports and recreation centre in Wettingen
Aubrücke gymnasium and playing fields in Zurich, 1968–1970
Open space design for Enikerfeld estate in Cham
Open space design for Gallis, Baumgarten estate
in Urdorf, 1968–1970
Open space design for Imm. Faustina Nord SPA estate
in Pregnana/Milanese
Open space design for Salvenmatt estate in Baar

Open space design for Schützenmatte estate
in Solothurn, 1968–1970
*Open space design for Im Surinam estate
in Basel, 1968–1970 (cf. p. 210)*
Private garden for Vogel, A., Dr. in Männedorf
Private garden for Völling, P. in Unterkulm
Private garden for Widmer, Alfred, architect,
in Waldegg-Uitikon

1969

Private garden for Buhofer, A. in Steinhausen
Private garden for Fischer, Georg in Zollikon
Transit terrace for Basel-Mulhouse airport in Basel
Competition for recreation area in Kloten, 1969–1970
Private garden for Fritz, Adolf in Brione
sopra Minusio, 1969–1971
Private garden for Kappeler in Frauenfeld
Restaurant Le Dezaley (conversion) in Zurich
Indoor swimming pool for Sager, K., in Dürrenäsch
Private garden for Säuberli-Kühn, W. in Suhr
School in Schwerzenbach, 1969–1970
Private garden for Somary, Wolfgang in Forch
Private garden for Triebold, Eddie R. in Mumpf
Private garden for Troesch, H.A., Dr.-Ing. in Unterengstringen
Open space design for Devo AG estate in Basel, 1969–1970
*Open space design for Heuried estate in Wiedikon, Zurich,
1969–1970 (cf. p. 213)*
*Open space design for Homberg am Niederrhein (Germany),
1969–1974 (cf. p. 215)*
Square by office building in Pratteln
Private garden for Wertheimer, H.R. in Kilchberg

1970

Grounds for BASF in Ludwigshafen/Rhein
Grounds for Bogorad, S. & Co. (conversion)
in Wiedikon, Zurich
Roof garden for Brunner, Dr. in Thalwil
Private garden for Burckardt, J.P. in Oberrieden
Bürgerspital in Basel, 1970–1971
Private garden for Chilacher in Uitikon
Grounds for CIBA factory school in Basel
Private garden for Devile, R. in Zumikon, 1970–1971
Private garden for Dirilgen, N. in Männedorf
Open spaces for Freihof Höngg in Höngg, Zurich
Cemetery and church in Fehraltorf, 1970–1972
Cemetery in Greifensee
Report on Viennese cemeteries (cf. p. 194)
Private garden for Henauer, R. in Thalwil
Private garden (alteration) for Miller, O.L.
Private garden for Rizzi, M., Dr. med. in Zollikon
Private garden for Sager-Acker, M. in Gränichen
"Geisshübel" school in Zollikofen, 1970–1973
"Im Moos" school in Rüschlikon, 1970–1978
Private garden for Simmen, Frl. in Aarau
Trägerhard sports and recreation centre (realization)
in Wettingen, 1970–1974
Private garden for Studer, Dr. in Bellikon
Open spaces for Aberenrain estate (row houses) in Baar
Open space design for Erlinsbacherstrasse estate in Aarau
Open space design for Fustlig estate in Olten
Open space design for Seehalde estate in Thalwil
Site modelling "Im oberen Boden" in Höngg, Zurich
Private garden for Walty-Beer, K. in Schöftland
Private garden for Wicki, F., Dr.
Grounds for Wipf AG Verpackungen (factory) in Volketswil

1971

Old people's home, indoor and outdoor swimming pools
in Wallisellen
Square by office building in Basel
Private garden for Businger-Stutz, H. in Küttigen
Jury for Karlsplatz in Vienna

Kindergarten in Schaanwald, 1971–1972
Private garden for Rüegger, W. in Zofingen
Seefeldstrasse street design in Zurich
Summerhouse for Spohr in Wollishofen, Zurich
*Square design for Winterthur Technical College
(southern extension) in Winterthur, 1971–1978 (cf. p. 220)*
Girls' secondary school in Riesbach, 1971–1972
Open space design for "In der Au" estate in Therwil
*Open space design for Büelen estate in Wädenswil,
1971–1977 (cf. p. 218)*
Open space design for Mühlehof estate in Ebikon
Open space design for Schönbühl estate in Lucerne, 1971–1974
Open space design for Sternen, Park- und Waldsiedlung estate in
Birmensdorf
Open space design for Zelglistrasse estate in Olten
Wasser-Erdbaulabor in Zurich (?), 1971–1972

1972

Private garden for Casa Serenella, Orselina in Locarno
*Private garden for Gasser, Aldo in Sonvico near Lugano,
1972–1978 (cf. p. 245)*
Private garden for Guhl & Scheibler in Aesch
Postplatz in Vaduz, 1972–1978 (cf. p. 224)
Open space design for "Trompete" estate in Wetzikon, 1972–1973
Open space design for Mattenacker in Maur

1973

Grounds for Bucherer, commercial building in Schönbühl
Open spaces for Hotel Hilton in Basel, 1973–1974
Hospital in Thalwil

1974

Grounds for Aubrugg power station in Oerlikon, Zurich
Private garden for Matt, Egon in Mauren
Private garden for Müller (?)
Grounds for Roche AG in Sisseln, 1974–1978 (cf. p. 230)

1975

Secondary school in Balzers, 1975–1977
Open space design for "Im Grund" estate in Olten

1976

Private garden for Bernasconi, Marcel in Olten, 1976–1977
Competition for a cemetery in Witikon, Zurich
Private garden for Hunziker-Fretz, S. in Küttigen
Piazza Battaglia in Lugano (?), 1976–1977

1977

Study City of Trees
Competition for ETH Lausanne, artistic design
Four courtyards in Ecublens
Paradeplatz, study The Mad Flowers in Zurich
Private garden for Rentsch, Fritz in Schönenwerd
*Design for holiday resort in Zibashar (Iran),
1977–1978 (cf. p. 238)*

1978

Roof garden for Von Lick in Zurich

1979

Grounds for Guggenbühl, office building in Zollikon
Grounds/fountain for Kuhn, Heinrich, Metallwarenfabrik AG,
in Rikon, 1978–1979
*Private garden for Metzner in Solothurn, 1979–1980
(cf. p. 250)*
Private garden for Rentsch, Fritz in Muri
Private garden for Schmidheiny, Stephan
in Hurden, 1979–1980

Private garden for Kühling, P. in Baden

Private garden for Kuny-Scherer, H.

Private garden for Kunz in Therwil

Street design (extension) for Küttigerstrasse

Private garden for Im Grüt country house in Meilen

Private garden for Landis, Dr. in Zug (?)

Private garden for Lang, A., manufacturer, in Pruntrut (Porrentruy)

Private garden (pergola) for Leemann in Riesbach, Zurich

Leutholdplatz in Biberist

Garden wall for Linka, C. in Olten

Private garden for Locher, Dr. in Dietikon-Wiesental

Home and offices for Löwen in Glattbrugg

Private garden for Lüthy, Dr. in Seengen

Grounds for Matman und Co.

Grounds for Mauch, E. in Bremgarten

Private garden for Maurhofer, A. in Aarau

Private garden for Mauser, Dr. in Zollikerberg

Private garden for Meier in Zuchwil

Private garden for Meier und Häusler in Basel

Private garden for Meier, Emil

Private garden for Meier, Leo in Zurich

Private garden for Merz, W. in Rombach

Studio extension for Mettler, E. in Zollikon

Private garden for Meyer in Solothurn

Private garden for Meyer, Dr. in Würenlos

Private garden for Meyer in Uerikon (?)

Grounds for Migros in Buchs (?)

Private garden for Moning, B. in Bettlach

Private garden for Moning-Vögeli, W., mayor, in Bettlach

Horticultural show for Morlet in Zurich

Private garden for Mühlebach in Zurich

Private garden for Müller, cantonal forester, in Baden

Private garden for Müller v. Blumencron, Dr. in Thalwil

Private garden for Müller, Dr. in Meilen

Private garden for Müller, J. in Trimbach

Residential area at Murimoos in Muri

Open spaces for new post office building in Birrwil

Private garden for Niederöst in Olten

Private garden for Oehler in Aarau

Waid public park in Wipkingen, Zurich

Private garden for Pauli in Aarau

Open spaces for Peters, architect, in Solothurn

Private garden for Pfiffner, Dr. in Aarau

Private garden for Pfister

Convalescent home in Muri

Private garden for Philbur in Vaduz

Private garden for Plüss-Keimer, F. in Schönenwerd

Private garden for Poma, A. in Biel

Private garden for Portmann, Dr. in Erlinsbach

Private garden for Pulfer-Conzett, H. in Samedan

Private garden for Pümpin, Marg. E.

Private garden for Rahm-Gerber, E., Direktor in Aarau

Private garden for Ramser, Dr. in Aarau

Private garden for Régis, Jean in Aarau

Private garden for Renold-Wuest, Jakob ((Ort))

Private garden for Rentsch, W. in Witikon, Zurich

Private garden (alteration) for Rey, Prof. in Aarau

Private garden for Rieben, Pierre in Peseux

Private garden for Riesen, Fritz, engineer, in Rüschlikon

Private garden for Rimli, E., Dr. ((Ort))

Private garden for Ritschadr ((sp.?)) in Rüschlikon

Private garden for Rogat in Le Lieu (?)

Garage for Rohr, O. in Suhr

Private garden for Rölli, Dr., veterinary surgeon, in Schönenwerd

Private garden (front garden) for Roth, ((gestorben?)) Dr. in Aarau

Private garden for Roth, O. in Uster

Private garden for Rüedi, A. in Zollikon

Private garden for Rüetschi in Brugg (?)

Private garden for Rütschi in Frick (?)

Private garden for Sager in Dürrenäsch

Private garden for Sammet, Dr. in Küsnacht

Private garden for Schatzmann, Dr. in Schöftland

Private garden for Schelbert, G., Dr. in Forch-Wassberg

Private garden for Schenker, H. in Aarau

Private garden for Scherg, Geschwister, Hotel Loewer, in Aarau

Private garden for Scherrer, J. in Schönenwerd

Private garden for Schifferli in Bellach (?)

Private garden for Schmid, Rud. in Buchs

Private garden for Schmid-Burkhalter, H. in Langendorf

Private garden for Schmid-Kubli, E., Dipl.-Ing. in Aarau

Private garden (holiday home) for Schmidt-Walther, André in Ein-
siedeln

Private garden for Schobel, P., Dr. in Basel

Summerhouse for Schoeller in Erlenbach

Private garden for Schoul-Eichenberg in Kilchberg

Private garden for Schuler, Hans in Herrliberg

Langenhard school in Rikon

School in Neuheim

Utogrund school in Zurich

Private garden for Schulthess, engineer, in Niederlenz

Open spaces for Schütz in Solothurn

Private garden (remodelling) for Schützenmatte in Zofingen

Private garden for Schwager in Thalwil

Lake shore in Thalwil

Private garden for Sidler, Dr. in Matzendorf

Private garden for Sonnenbergstrasse in Hirslanden, Zurich

Oftringen playing fields

Competition for municipal gardens in Winterthur ("Suzi")

Private garden for Stähelin, Dr. in Herrliberg

Private garden for Staub-Gronner in Zurich

Private garden for Steinegger ((Ort))

Private garden for Stockar in Erlenbach

Private garden for Stoeckli-Bay, Dr. in Yverdon

Private garden for Stolz in Peseux (?)

Private garden for Storz, Dr. in Rombach

Street square (paving) in Luzern

Private garden for Straumann, U., Dr. in Basel

Private garden for Streule, F. ((Ort))

Private garden for Studer, Herm., teacher, in Bellach

Private garden for Studer-Borer, Oskar in Rohr

Private garden for Stutz-Müller in Aarau (?)

Private garden for Sutter in Gränichen

Summerhouse for Syz, Max in Zurich

Open spaces terraced housing estate in Klingnau

Private garden (country house) for Thommen, Max in Tecknau

Open spaces for veterinary clinic in Aarau

Private garden for Truninger, E.G. in Erlenbach

House for Truninger-Schmid, Hans in Oberstrass, Zurich

Private garden for Tuchschmid, K. in Aarau

Open space/renovation "Im Hüsli" estate in Leimbach

Open space design for "Steinhalde" estate in Zurich

Open space design for "Tierpark" estate in Langnau

Open space design for Coop. "Rione Madonetta" estate in Lugano

Open space design for Enzenbühlstrasse estate in Zurich

Open space design for Guggach-Buchegg-Zeppelinstrasse
estate in Zurich

Open space design for an estate in Hinwil (?)

Open space design for Hirsig estate in Richterswil(?)

Open space design for Hungerberg estate in Aarau

Open space design for Laupersdorf estate (terraced housing)
in Laupersdorf

Open space design for Oberle estate in Aarau

Open space design for Parkweg estate in Buchs

Open space design for Seestrasse/Thomas Scherrstrasse estate
in Küsnacht

Open space design for Selzach estate (apartment house) in Selzach

Open space design for Türlihausstrasse estate (apartment house)
in Solothurn

Open space design for Waisenhausstrasse
estate (apartment house)

Open space design for Winkelacker estate in Dulliken
Open space design for Witikonerstrasse estate in Zurich
Private garden for Venzin in Niederglatt
Private garden for Villinger, Dr. in Schaffhausen
Vogel-Sulzer family tomb ((Ort))
Private garden for Vogt in Cologny
Private garden for Von Arx, Hans in Olten
Private garden for Von Arx-Kalt in Solothurn
Private garden for Von Riedemann, Velladini in Lugano
Private garden for Von Sänger in Thalwil
Private garden for Walther, J. in Aarau
Private garden for Wartmann, Rud., Direktor,
Obergrüt country house in Brugg
Summerhouse for Waser, Bruno in Fluntern, Zurich
Private garden for Wehrli, A., Dipl.-Ing. in Erlenbach
Private garden for Wehrli in Aarau
Private garden for Werder, E. in Aarau
Private garden for Wernle, Jos. in Küttigen
Private garden for Wernli in Rombach
Private garden for Wetter, Dr., federal councillor
Private garden for Wetzel in Baden (?)
Private garden for Wick-Isler, Alfred, engineer, in Muttenz
Private garden for Widmer, E., building firm, in Suhr
Private garden for Wild in Buchs (?)
Private garden for Wildbolz, U., architect, in Zollikon
Private garden for Willy, Franz in Triengen
Grounds for Winkler, Kaspar & Co in Zurich
Private garden for Wittmer in Oberstrass, Zurich
Private garden for Wolfermann-Nägeli, Hans in Witikon, Zurich
Private garden for Wydler, P., Dr. in Kilchberg
Grounds for Wynentalbahn, office building ((Ort?))
Private garden for Wyss, Franz Jos., Dr. in Zurich
Private garden for Wyss, H.A., Dr. in Küsnacht
Grounds for Yesudian, S.R., office building in Zurich
Private garden for Zimmerli, Dr. iur. in Aarau
Private garden for Zingg-Hunziker, Fr.,*
chartered accountant, in Aarau
Open spaces for civil defence centre in Zurich
Private garden for Zoppi in Bissone
Horticultural show for Zubler, Direktor in Sursee
Private garden for Zuccoli, Dr. in Bissone
Private garden for Zürrer, Th. in Zollikon
Private garden for Zwipfer in Aarau

ADORNO, Theodor W.: Ohne Leitbild. Frankfurt 1969

AESCHBACHER, Hans: Hans Aeschbacher. Neuchatel 1959

AESCHLIMANN, Max: "Das Projekt Wasser- werkstraße der Baugenossenschaft des eidgenössischen Personals Zürich" in: Das Wohnen, issue 12/1944; pages 211–213

ALLINGER, Gustav: Das Hohelied von Gartenkunst und Gartenbau. 150 Jahre Gartenbau-Ausstellungen in Deutsch- land. Berlin, Hamburg 1963

ALLINGER, Gustav: "Grosse und kleine Gärten auf der Internationalen Garten- bau-Ausstellung 1963 in Hamburg" in: Deutsche Gärtnerbörse, offprint, issue 40,42,44/1963; pages 1–14

ALTHERR, Jürg/LASSERRE, Olivier/ ZULAUF, Rainer/NOSEDA, Irma: "Freiräume" in: Werk, Bauen + Wohnen, issue 9/2000; pages 44–47

ALVERDES, W.: "Grüne Woche Berlin 1957" in: Garten und Landschaft, issue 2/1957; pages 74–75

AMMANN, Gustav: "Alles fliesst (Heraklit)" in: Garten und Landschaft, issue 1/1953; pages 4–5

AMMANN, Gustav: "Alte Bindungen – Neue Verbindungen" in: Gartenschönheit, issue 1/1933; pages 22–23

AMMANN, Gustav: "Aus dem Garten eines Pflanzenfreundes" in: Gartenschönheit, issue 4/1935; pages 80–81

AMMANN, Gustav: "Aus den Gärten von Versailles und Trianon" in: Die Garten- kunst, issue 8/1912; pages 129–133

AMMANN, Gustav: "Aus den Gärten von Versailles und Trianon" in: Die Garten- kunst, issue 9/1912; pages 113–117

AMMANN, Gustav: "Aus einem alten Schweizer Garten" in: Die Gartenkunst, issue 11/1912; pages 175–176

AMMANN, Gustav: "Begleitworte zu den Arbeiten von Otto Froebels Erben, Zürich" in: Das Werk, issue 4/1919; pages 52–64

AMMANN, Gustav: Blühende Gärten. Landscape Gardens. Jardins en fleurs. Erlenbach, Zurich 1955

AMMANN, Gustav: "Blumenterrassen" in: Gartenschönheit, issue 7/1929; pages 256–257

AMMANN, Gustav: "Das Landschaftsbild und die Dringlichkeit seiner Pflege und Gestaltung" in: Schweizerische Bau- zeitung (Sonderheft Landschaftsgestal- tung), issue 15/1941; pages 172–173

AMMANN, Gustav: "Das Raumgesicht" in: Die Gartenkunst, issue 6/1929; pages 83–84

AMMANN, Gustav: "Der Garten – Ein Rückblick und Ausblick" in: Das Werk, issue 4/1919; pages 49–52

AMMANN, Gustav: "Der Gartenbau" in: Meili, Armin: Schweizerische Landes- ausstellung 1939 Zürich. Volume 1, Zurich 1940; pages 639–655

AMMANN, Gustav: "Der Zoologische Garten – ein ungelöstes Problem" in: Die Gartenkunst, issue 12/1912; pages 190–191

AMMANN, Gustav: "Die Entwicklung der Gartengestaltung" in: Garten und Land- schaft, issue 4/1951; pages 1–2

AMMANN, Gustav: "Die Gärten der Schweizer. Landesausstellung 1939" in: Schweizerische Bauzeitung, issue 18/1939; pages 213–217

AMMANN, Gustav: "Die Gestaltung der Landschaft bei Meliorationen" in: Plan. Schweizerische Zeitschrift für Landes-, Regional- und Ortsplanung, issue 3/1944; pages 63–64

AMMANN, Gustav: "Ein Berner Land- hausgarten" in: Gartenschönheit, issue 4/1938; pages 132–134

AMMANN, Gustav: "Erinnerungen an Schloss Bremgarten" in: Das Werk, issue 9/1923; pages 121–132

AMMANN, Gustav: "Friedhofsgestaltung und Landschaftsbild" in: Schweizerische Bauzeitung, special issue on landscape design, issue 15/1941; pages 170–171

AMMANN, Gustav: "Garten und Landschaft" in: Werk, issue 9/1943; pages 285–288

AMMANN, Gustav: "Gestaltungsprobleme in Garten und Landschaft" in: Die Garten- kunst, issue 54/1941; pages 99–101

AMMANN, Gustav: "Ist das 'Natürliche' ein Form-Ersatz?" in: Schweizer Garten, issue 2/1945; pages 33–38

AMMANN, Gustav: "Kleinarchitektur und Plastik im Hausgarten" in: Schweizer Garten, issue 10/1948; pages 289–294

AMMANN, Gustav: "Mensch, Bauwerk und Pflanze im Garten" in: Das Werk, issue 6/1926; pages 181–189

AMMANN, Gustav: "Neue Sondergärten" in: Die Gartenkunst, issue 5/1913; pages 57–59

AMMANN, Gustav: "Neuerungen bei öffentlichen Parkanlagen" in: Die Gartenkunst, issue 27/1914; pages 184–189

AMMANN, Gustav: "Planschbecken" in: Gartenschönheit, issue 5/1936; pages 106–107

AMMANN, Gustav: "Schloß Benrath und seine Gärten" in: Die Gartenkunst, issue 11/1911; pages 197–203

AMMANN, Gustav: "Sollen wir die Form ganz zertrümmern?" in: Die Gartenkunst, issue 39/1926; pages 81–85

AMMANN, Gustav: "South Kensington Garden" in: Die Gartenkunst, issue 15/1913; page 221

AMMANN, Gustav: "Stiller Gartenwinkel" in: Gartenschönheit, issue 6/1939; page 226

AMMANN, Gustav: "Vom Gartenhaus" in: Die Gartenkunst, issue 21/1912; pages 333–335

AMMANN, Gustav: "'ZÜGA' Die Zürcher Gartenbau-Ausstellung 1933. Die Garten- anlagen" in: Schweizerische Bauzeitung, issue 10/1933; pages 120–124

AMMANN, Gustav: "Zum Friedhofproblem" in: Werk, issue 3/1947; pages 70–73

AMMANN, Gustav: "Zum Jubiläum des Bundes Schweizer Gartengestalter (BSG)" in: Das ideale Heim, Winterthur 1950; pages 307–318

AMMANN, Gustav/EGENDER, Karl/MÜLLER, Wilhelm: "Rückschau auf die 'ZÜGA'. Zürcher Gartenbau-Ausstellung. 24. Juni bis 17. September 1933" in: Die Garten- kunst, issue 46/1933; pages 165–172

AMMANN, Gustav/HAUSZER, Karl Th./ MÜLLER, J. F.: "Natur und Gestaltung" in: Garten und Landschaft, issue 9/1954; pages 20–22

AMMANN, Peter: "Zürichs Stadtspital auf der Waid" in: Schweizer Garten + Wohnkultur, issue 5/1959; pages 120–121

ANGEL: "Ausstellungen im Laufe des Jahres 1949" in: Schweizer Garten, issue 11/1949; pages 325–326

ARIOLI, Richard: "Die Grünanlagen der Expo 1964" in: Anthos, issue 3/1964; pages 34–36

ARIOLI, Richard: "Die Mitwirkung der Künste in der Garten- und Landschaftsplanung – Thema des zweiten internationalen Gartenkunstkongresses in Madrid vom 20. bis 24. Sept. 1950" in: Schweizer Garten, issue 10/1950; pages 317–325

ARIOLI, Richard: "IFLA news. Kongress der IFLA in Japan" in: Anthos, issue 2/1964; pages 39–41

ARIOLI, Richard: "IFLA news. Kongress der IFLA in Japan" in: Anthos, issue 3/1964; pages 32–33

ARIOLI, Richard: "Japanische Gärten" in: Anthos, issue 3/1964; pages 11–16

ARIOLI, Richard: "Nationengärten?" in: Anthos, issue 1/1965; pages 29–31

ARIOLI, Richard: "Schweizerische Lan- desausstellung Lausanne 1964" in: Anthos, issue 2/1964; pages 42–43

B. H.: "Zu den Arbeiten von Richard J. Neutra" in: Werk, issue 12/1956; pages 269–270

BARDI, Pietro Maria: Lembranca de Le Corbusier: Athenas, Italia, Brasil. Sao Paulo 1984

BARTH, Hans Jakob: "Betonplatten im Garten?" in: Garten und Landschaft, issue 1/1953; pages 8–11

BARTH, Hans Jakob: "Gärten in der Schweiz" in: Garten und Landschaft, issue 4/1954; page 22

BARTH, Hans Jakob: "Gärten wie Blumensträusse" in: Anthos, issue 1/1987; pages 5–9

BARTH, Hans Jakob: "… in der Schweiz" in: Garten und Landschaft, issue 4/1955; page 6

BARTH, Hans Jakob: "Unruhe und Selbst- kritik" in: Anthos, issue 1/1987; page 12

BAUMANN, Albert: "Die Entstehung der Garten- und Kulturanlagen an der Garten- bauschule Oeschberg" in: Schweizer Garten, issue 10/1940; pages 291–299

BAUMANN, Albert: "Die Solothurner Gärten im 17., 18. und 19. Jahrhundert" in: Garten- baublatt, issue 49/1961; page 1091

BAUMANN, Albert: Neues Planen und Gestalten für Haus und Garten, Friedhof und Landschaft. Münsingen 1953

BAUMANN, Ernst: Lebende Gärten. Pflanze, Holz und Stein als Verbindungselemente zur Naturlandschaft. Munich, Zurich 1980

BAUMGARTNER, U. J.: "Neubauten des Technikums Winterthur" in: Schweizer Journal. Zeitschrift für öffentlichen Bau und Industrie, issue 12/1979; pages 49–50

BAUR, Hermann: "Ueber die Beziehungen von Haus und Garten" in: Werk, issue 9/1943; pages 289–291

Bezirksamt Tiergarten von Berlin/Abt. Bau- und Wohnungswesen/Naturschutz- und Grünflächenamt (publ.): Das Hansa- viertel 1957 – 1993. Konzepte Bedeutung Probleme. Berlin 1995

BILL, Jakob: Max Bill: Die unendliche Schleife 1935–1995 und die Einflächner. Bern 2000

BILL, Max: "Die mathematische Denkweise in der Kunst unserer Zeit" in: Werk, issue 2/1949; pages 86–91

BILL, Max: "Neue Pflanzenbehälter und Sitzgelegenheiten. Bericht über die Resultate aus einem Wettbewerb" in: Eternit im Hoch- und Tiefbau, issue 52/1959; pages 903–907

BILL, Max: "Schönheit aus Funktion und als Funktion" in: Werk, issue 8/1949; pages 272–283

BILL, Max: Wiederaufbau. Dokumente über Zerstörungen, Planungen, Kon- struktionen. Erlenbach, Zurich 1945

BOESIGER, W.: "Der Dachgarten als er- weiterte Wohnfläche" in: Bauen + Wohnen, issue 10/1950; pages 1–9

BOESIGER, W. (ed.): Richard Neutra. 1961–66. Buildings and Projects. Réalisations et Projets. Bauten und Projekte. Zurich 1966

BOURNOT, Helmut: "Die Gärtnerische Hallenschau der 'Grünen Woche Berlin 1954'" in: Garten und Landschaft, issue 2/1954; page 22

BOURNOT, Helmut: "Koordinierung und Gesamtplanung der Grünflächen im Hansaviertel Berlin" in: Garten und Landschaft, issue 10/1957; pages 256–266

BROGLE, Theodor: "Der Qualitäts- und Formgedanke in der schweizerischen Industrie" in: Werk, issue 8/1949; pages 259–260

BRUNNER-KLINGENSPOR, E.: "Blumen-Landi G/59 in Zürich eröffnet!" in: Schweizerisches Gartenbau-Blatt, issue 17/1959; pages 447–448

BUCHER, Annemarie/JAQUET, Martine (ed.): Des floralies aux jardins d'art. Un siecle d'expositions de paysagisme en Suisse. Lausanne 2000

Bund Schweizer Landschaftsarchitekten und Landschaftsarchitektinnen BSLA, Regionalgruppe Zürich (publ.): Gute Gärten – Gestaltete Freiräume in der Region Zürich. Zurich 1995

Bundesamt für Kultur (publ.): Minimal Tradition. Bern 1996

BURCKHARDT, Lucius: "Kritik der sechziger Jahre" in: Werk/Œuvre, issue 12/1973; pages 1588–1594

BURCKHARDT, Lucius: "Neues aus Intropia" in: Werk-Chronik, issue 7/1964; pages 143–146

BURCKHARDT, Lucius: "Richard Neutra. 1892–1970" in: Werk, issue 6/1970; page 360

CAROL, Hans/WERNER, Max: Städte – wie wir sie wünschen. Ein Vorschlag zur Gestaltung schweizerischer Großstadtgebiete, dargestellt am Beispiel von Stadt und Kanton Zürich. Zurich 1949

CATTANEO, Claudio: "Wohnungsbau zwischen 'Neuem Bauen' und 'Heimatstil'" in: Kunsthaus Zürich (publ.): Dreissiger Jahre Schweiz. Ein Jahrzehnt im Widerspruch. Zurich 1981; pages 172–179

CHADWICK, George F.: The Park and the Town. Public Landscape in the 19th and 20th Centuries. London 1966

CHURCH, Thomas: Gardens are for People. New York 1955

CRAMER, Ernst: "Das heutige Gestalten (Richtlinien für den Bauherrn)" in: unknown; pages 240–242

CRAMER, Ernst: "Die Pflanze macht den Garten!" in: Das ideale Heim, issue 9/1953; pages 361–368

CRAMER, Ernst: "Friedhof Pratteln/Friedhof im Zürcher Oberland" in: Garten und Landschaft, issue 11/1969; pages 344–346

CRAMER, Ernst: "Gärten, Landschaft und Bauliches. Eine kleine Bildreportage aus Arbeiten von E. Cramer, Gartenarchitekt B.S.G., Zürich" in: Schweizer Garten, issue 12/1943; pages 57–63

CRAMER, Ernst: "Gärtnerische Planungen" in: Schweizer Garten, issue 2/1953; pages 41–48

CRAMER, Ernst: "Neuer Dorffriedhof in der Schweiz" in: Garten und Landschaft, issue 11/1969; pages 366–367

CRAMER, Ernst: "Pflanze + Plan" in: Schweizer Garten, issue 2/1954; pages 50–53

CRAMER, Ernst: "Stadtplatz in Aarau/Schweiz" in: Garten und Landschaft, issue 8/1970; pages 259–262

CRAMER, Ernst: "Cover" in: Garten und Landschaft, issue 8/1963; page 250

CRAMER, Ernst: "Cover" in: Schweizer Garten, issue 11/1942; no page

CRAMER, Ernst: "Cover" in: Schweizer Garten, issue 11/1940; no page

CRAMER, Ernst: "Cover" in: Schweizer Garten, issue 12/1942; no page

CRAMER, Ernst: "Cover" in: Schweizer Garten, issue 12/1943; no page

CRAMER, Ernst: "Wir betrachten die Gartenbilder …" in: Schweizer Garten, issue 7/1937; page 221

CRAMER, Ernst: "Wir betrachten die Gartenbilder …" in: Schweizer Garten, issue 8/1937; pages 227–233

CRAMER, Ernst: "Wo stehen wir heute im Gartenbau?" in: Werk, issue 3/1946; pages 85–88

CRAMER, Ernst/EBERLE, K.: "Wettbewerb für einen Zentralfriedhof in Kreuzlingen" in: Anthos, issue 3/1969; page 88

CRAMER, Ernst/M-R: "Einflüsse japanischer Gartenkultur" in: Das ideale Heim, issue 9/1960; pages 371–378

CRAMER, Ernst/MAURER, F.: "Garten des Poeten" in: Anthos, issue 1/1968; pages 26–27

CRAMER, Ernst/SURBECK, Ernst: "no title" in: Schweizer Garten, issue 10/1948; pages 295–299

CRAMER, Ernst/SURBECK, Ernst: "Cover" in: Schweizer Garten, issue 4/1948; no page

CRAMER/JARAY/PAILLARD: "Siedlung 'Rainacker' in Rekingen (Aargau)" in: Werk, issue 12/1949; pages 391–400

CROWE, Sylvia: The Landscape of Power. London 1958

CURJEL, Hans: "Piet Mondrian. Kunsthaus, 22. Mai bis Anfang Juli" in: Werk-Chronik, issue 5/1955; pages 132–134

CURJEL, Hans: "Um 1900. Aus der Ausstellung im Kunstgewerbemuseum Zürich, Juni/September 1952" in: Werk, issue 12/1952; pages 403–407

DÄUMEL, Gerd: "Beton im Garten" in: Schweizer Garten + Wohnkultur, issue 6/1962; pages 128–129

DAGUERRE, Mercedes: Birkhäuser Architectural Guide Switzerland. 20th century. Basel, Berlin, Boston 1997

DAHRENDORF, Ralf: Liberal und unabhängig. Gerd Bucerius und seine Zeit. Munich 2000

Denver Art Museum (publ.): Herbert Bayer. Collection and Archive at the Denver Art Museum. Seattle, London 1998

Direktion der öffentlichen Bauten des Kantons Zürich (publ.): Siedlungs- und Baudenkmäler im Kanton Zürich. Stäfa 1993

DOLF-BONEKÄMPER, Gabi: Das Hansaviertel. Internationale Nachkriegsmoderne in Berlin. Berlin 1999

DOVÈ, Fritz: "Soldatenfriedhof Futa-Pass" in: Anthos, issue 4/1966; pages 28–31

DOVÈ, Fritz: "Soldatenfriedhof Futa-Pass/Italien" in: Garten und Landschaft, issue 11/1969; pages 353–354

DUNINGTON-GRUBB, H. B.: "Modernism arrives in the Garden – To Stay?" in: Landscape Architecture. A Quarterly Magazine, issue 4/1942; pages 156–157

DURTH, Werner/GUTSCHOW, Niels: Architektur und Städtebau der Fünfziger Jahre. Schriftenreihe des Deutschen Nationalkomitees für Denkmalschutz. Volume 33. Bonn 1987

ECKBO, Garrett: Landscape for Living. New York 1950

ECO, Umberto: The open work. Massachusetts 1989

ECO, Umberto: La struttura assente. Milano 1968

EGENDER, Karl: "Gärten im 'Heimatstil'. Kleine Betrachtung zur Ausstellung 'Blühender Herbst'" in: Schweizer Garten, issue 10/1942; pages 275–276

EGENDER, Karl/MÜLLER, Wilhelm: "'ZÜGA' Die Zürcher Gartenbau-Austellung 1933" in: Schweizerische Bauzeitung, issue 10/1933; pages 115–120

EGGER, Alois: "Das neue Stadthaus Olten" in: Schweizer Journal, Zeitschrift für öffentlichen Bau und Industrie, issue 5/1967; pages 33–37

ELIOVSON, Sima: The gardens of Roberto Burle Marx. Portland 1991

ENZENSBERGER, Hans Magnus: "Reminiszenzen an den Überfluß" in: DER SPIEGEL, issue 51/1996; page 117

EPPRECHT, Hans: "Gustav Ammann und sein Wirken" in: Werk, issue 8/1956; pages 238–244

ERB, Ad.: "Aus der Vorgeschichte und Gründung der Gartenbauschule Oeschberg" in: Schweizer Garten, issue 10/1940; pages 290–291

ERNI, Peter: Die gute Form. Eine Aktion des Schweizerischen Werkbundes. Dokumentation und Interpretation. Baden 1983

EXNER, Hermann/NEUTRA, Dione (ed.): Richard und Dion Neutra. Pflanzen Wasser Steine Licht. Berlin, Hamburg 1974

Fachbereich Stadt- und Landschaftsplanung der Gesamthochschule Kassel (publ.): Leberecht Migge. 1881–1935. Gartenkultur des 20. Jahrhunderts. Kassel 1981

FILS, Alexander: Brasilia. Moderne Architektur in Brasilien. Düsseldorf 1988

FILS, Alexander (ed.): Oscar Niemeyer. Selbstdarstellung, Kritiken, Œuvre. Düsseldorf 1982

Finanzamt der Stadt Zürich (publ.): 50 Jahre Wohnungspolitik der Stadt Zürich. 1907–1957. Zurich 1957

FISCHBACHER/DRÖGE: Gartenhöfe. Schriftenreihe der Deutschen Gesellschaft für Gartenkunst und Landschaftspflege, no. 6. Munich 1966

FISCHLI, Hans: "Max Bill zum 60. Geburtstag" in: SWB-Kommentare, issue 9/1969; pages 125–127

FLEMING, John/HONOUR, Hugh/PEVSNER, Nikolaus: The Penguin Dictionary of Architecture and Landscape Architecture. London, New York 1998

FRAMPTON, Kenneth: Modern Architecture. London 1980

FRANKEL, Felice/JOHNSON, Jory: Modern Landscape Architecture. New York 1991

FRIEDRICH, Theo: "Wettbewerb des Arbeitskreises junger Gartenarchitekten: Öffentlicher Garten am Wilhaditurm in Bremen" in: Garten und Landschaft, issue 1/1956; pages 10–11

FRISCH, Max: "Cum grano salis. Eine kleine Glosse zur schweizerischen Architektur" in: Werk, issue 10/1953; pages 325–329

FRISCH, Max: Dienstbüchlein. Frankfurt 1970

FRISCHKNECHT, Walter: "G | 59 im Spiegel der Zeit" in: Anthos, issue 1/2000; pages 8–13

GATZ, Konrad/THIERRY, Jehan (eds.): Baudetails in Gärten und Anlagen. Munich 1966

GERSTER, Georg: "Vom Himmel geschaut" in: Werk/Œuvre, issue 11/1974; pages 1317–1321

GERSTNER, Karl: Kalte Kunst? – zum Standort der heutigen Malerei. Teufen 1957

GERTZ, Ulrich: Plastik der Gegenwart. Kunst unserer Zeit. Volume 8. Berlin 1953

GIEDION, Sigfried: Befreites Wohnen. Zurich 1929

GIEDION, Sigfried: "Brasilien und die heutige Architektur" in: Werk, issue 8/1953; pages 238–256

GIEDION-WELCKER, Carola: Plastik des XX. Jahrhunderts. Volumen- und Raumgestaltung. Zurich 1955

GLEININGER-NEUMANN, Andrea: "Walter Jonas" in: Klotz, Heinrich (ed.): Vision der Moderne. Das Prinzip Konstruktion. Munich 1986; pages 166–171

GLEININGER-NEUMANN, Andrea: "Yona Friedman" in: Klotz, Heinrich (ed.): Vision der Moderne. Das Prinzip Konstruktion. Munich 1986; pages 130–137

GLINZ, Max/ARNET, Edwin (eds.): Offizieller Katalog – 1. Schweizerische Gartenbau-Ausstellung Zürich 1959. 25. April – 11. Oktober. Zurich 1959

GÖDERITZ, Johannes/RAINER, Roland/HOFFMANN, Hubert: Die gegliederte und aufgelockerte Stadt. Tübingen 1957

GOLLWITZER, Gerda: "In Berlin 1957" in: Garten und Landschaft, issue 10/1957; pages 253–254

GOLLWITZER, Gerda (ed.): Kinderspielplätze. Publications of the Deutsche Gesellschaft für Gartenkunst und Landschaftspflege, no. 2. Munich 1957

GOLLWITZER, Gerda (ed.): Schulen im Grün. Publications of the Deutsche Gesellschaft für Gartenkunst und Landschaftspflege, no. 1. Munich 1957

GOLLWITZER, Gerda/NEUKOM, Willi: "Gärten am See. Zu den Gärten des linken Ufers. Zu den Gärten des rechten Ufers" in: Garten und Landschaft, issue 8/1959; pages 225–235

GOLLWITZER, Gerda/WIRSING, Werner: Dachflächen bewohnt, belebt, bepflanzt. Munich 1971

GOTHEIN, Marie Luise: Geschichte der Gartenkunst. Volumes 1 und 2. Jena 1926

GRAMENZ, Gisela: "Beton macht den Garten wohnlich" in: Schöner Wohnen, issue 2/1967; pages 197–205

GRAMENZ, Gisela: "Notizen von einem Streifzug durch die IGA 63" in: Schöner Wohnen, issue 7/1963; pages 92–101

GREBE, Reinhard: "Die Gärten der Nationen auf der IGA 63 in Hamburg" in: Die neue Landschaft, issue 9/1963; page 265

GREENBERG, Clement: The collected essays and criticism. Chicago 1986 ff.

GREENBERG, Clement: "Sculpture in Our Time" in: Arts Magazine, issue 10/1958; pages 22–25

GRÖNING, Gerd/WOLSCHKE-BULMANN, Joachim: Grüne Biographien. Biographisches Handbuch zur Landschaftsarchitektur des 20. Jahrhunderts in Deutschland. Berlin 1997

GROSS, Roland: "1. Schweizerische Gartenbau-Ausstellung 1959 in Zürich" in: Werk, issue 10/1959; pages 343–350

HÄSLER, Alfred A.: Einer muss es tun. Leben und Werk Ernst Göhners. Frauenfeld, Stuttgart 1981

HAGEN, Petra: Städtebau im Kreuzverhör. Max Frisch zum Städtebau der fünfziger Jahre. Baden 1986

HAIST, Marketa: Achtundzwanzig Männer brauchen einen neuen Anzug. Die internationalen Gärten auf der Internationalen Gartenbau-Ausstellung 1963 in Hamburg. (Ph. D. Thesis). Karlsruhe 1994

HAIST, Marketa: "Achtundzwanzig Männer brauchen einen neuen Anzug. Die internationalen Gärten auf der Internationalen Gartenbau-Ausstellung 1963 in Hamburg" in: Die Gartenkunst, issue 2/1996; pages 252–314

HAMMERBACHER, Herta: "Plattenbelag am Hansaplatz, Berlin" in: Garten und Landschaft, issue 11/1957; page 100

HANISCH, Karl Heinz: "Gärten auf der IGA 63" in: Pflanze und Garten, issue 8/1963; pages 196–198

HANSEN, Anne/KRÄUCHI, Men: Zürichs grüne Inseln … unterwegs in 75 Gärten und Parks. Zurich 1997

HARBERS, Guido: Der Wohngarten. Seine Raum- und Bauelemente. Munich 1933

HARTSUYKER, Enrico: "Urbane Plastiken. Zum Schaffen von Mary Viera" in: Werk, issue 10/1968; pages 669–673

HESSE, Jeanne: "Eine Grünanlage in der Großstadt, fünf Jahre nach der IGA" in: Werk-Chronik, issue 12/1968; pages 838–839

HESSE, Jeanne: "Hamburg IGA 63. Internationale Gartenbauausstellung Aprilbis Oktober" in: Werk-Chronik, issue 6/1963; pages 137–138

HESSE, Jeanne: "Neutra im Tessin" in: Werk, issue 9/1967; pages 549–555

HEYER, Hans-Rudolf: Historische Gärten der Schweiz. Die Entwicklung vom Mittelalter bis zur Gegenwart. Bern 1980

Hochbauamt der Stadt Zürich (publ.): Der soziale Wohnungsbau und seine Förderung im Zürich 1942–45. Zurich 1946

HOFFMANN, Herbert (ed.): Garten und Haus. Die schönsten deutschen und ausländischen Wohngärten und ihre Einbauten. Stuttgart 1939

HOLZHAUSEN, Klaus: "Die Qualität der Aussenräume 'La Grande Borne'" in: Anthos, issue 3/1974; pages 8–13

HÜBOTTER, W. et. al.: "Gartenarchitekten planen im Hansaviertel" in: Garten und Landschaft, issue 10/1957; pages 260–266

HUNT, John Dixon: Greater Perfections. The Practice of Garden Theory. London 2000

IMBERT, Dorothée: The modernist garden in France. New Haven, London 1993

Internationale Bauausstellung Berlin GmbH (publ.): Interbau Berlin 1957. Amtlicher Katalog der Internationalen Bauausstellung Berlin 1957. Berlin 1957

JONAS, Walter: Das Intra-Haus. Vision einer Stadt. Zurich 1962

JONAS, Walter: "Das Trichterhaus – Vorschlag zu einer Massensiedlung" in: Bauen + Wohnen, issue 3/1962; pages 133–136

JORAY, Marcel: Le Béton dans l'Art Contemporain. Neuchâtel 1977

JOST, Karl: Hans Fischli – Architekt, Maler, Bildhauer (1909–1989). Zurich 1992

KAHN, Louis I.: "Order and Form" in: Perspecta, The Yale Architectural Journal, issue 3/1955; pages 59–63

Kantonale Gartenbauschule Oeschberg: Jubiläumsschrift 1920 – 1995. 75 Jahre Kantonale Gartenbauschule Oeschberg. Koppigen 1995

Kantonale Gartenbauschule Oeschberg: Parkpflegewerk und Dokumentation der Parkanlagen. Koppigen 1997

KASSLER, Elizabeth B.: Modern gardens and the Landscape. New York 1964

KIENAST, Dieter: "Die Sehnsucht nach dem Paradies" in: Hochparterre, issue 7/1990; pages 46–50

KIENAST, Dieter: "Ohne Leitbild" in: Garten und Landschaft, issue 11/1986; pages 34–38

KIENER, Alfred: "Betonelemente in einem Wohngarten" in: Anthos, issue 2/1966; page 4

KIENER, Alfred: "Betonscheiben in einem Park" in: Anthos, issue 2/1966; page 1

KIENER, Alfred: "Ferienhaus in Wengen/Schweiz" in: Anthos, issue 2/1966; page 8

KIENER, Alfred: "Wohngarten in Aarau" in: Anthos, issue 3/1966; pages 14–17

KIENER, Alfred: "Wohnhaus in Brione TI" in: Anthos, issue 2/1966; page 9

KIRSCHSTEIN, Claudia: "Interpretationsversuch der Gärten zweier zeitgenössischer Landschaftsarchitekten" in: Anthos, issue 1/1983; pages 31–39

KLOTZ, Heinrich: "Konstruktion und Utopie" in: Klotz, Heinrich (ed.): Vision der Moderne. Das Prinzip Konstruktion. Munich 1986; pages 116–117

KLOTZ, Heinrich (ed.): Vision der Moderne. Das Prinzip Konstruktion. Munich 1986

KOCH, Michael: Städtebau in der Schweiz 1800–1990. Entwicklungslinien, Einflüsse und Stationen. Zurich 1991

KOCH, Michael/SOMANDIN, Mathias/SÜSSTRUNK, Christian: Kommunaler und genossenschaftlicher Wohnungsbau in Zürich. Ein Inventar der durch die Stadt geförderten Wohnbauten 1907–1989. Zurich 1989

KRAMER, Peter: "Hallen- und Freibad Frauenfeld" in: Schweizer Journal. Zeitschrift für öffentlichen Bau und Industrie, issue 12/1973; page 43

KÜBLER, Christof: "Expo 64" in: Kunst + Architektur, issue 1/1994; page 11

KUENZLE, Creed: "Brasilia, eine Hauptstadt im Bau" in: Werk, issue 7/1959; pages 259–262

Kunsthaus Zürich (publ.): Dreissiger Jahre Schweiz. Ein Jahrzehnt im Widerspruch. Zurich 1981

KUNZ, Heinrich/GÖTTI, Oskar: "Laborgebäude Technikum Winterthur" in: Schweizerische Bauzeitung, issue 44/1974; pages 1008–1011

LE CORBUSIER: "La guerre de cent ans" in: Werk, issue 1/1944; pages 1–2

LEDER, Klaus: "5. Kongreß der Internationalen Föderation der Landschaftsarchitekten IFLA in Zürich" in: Werk-Chronik, issue 11/1956; pages 219–220

LEDER, Klaus: "Plastik im Garten" in: Schweizer Garten, issue 10/1948; pages 299–310

LEDER, Walter: "Blühend grüne Landi!" in: Schweizer Garten, issue 9/1939; pages 273–281

LEDER, Walter: "Gärten und Pflanzen in der Schweiz" in: Garten und Landschaft, issue 4/1953; pages 22–23

LEDER, Walter: "Vom Zusammenhang der öffentlichen und privaten Grünflächen" in: Werk, issue 5/1951; pages 130–132

LEHR: "Hausgartenwettbewerb des Arbeitskreises junger Gartenarchitekten" in: Garten und Landschaft, issue 7/1954; pages 16–17

LEROY, Louis G.: Natur ausschalten – Natur einschalten. Stuttgart 1973

Lions Club Meilen (publ.): Hans Fischli 1909–1989. Meilen 1990

LOGIE, Gordon: "Swiss landscape exhibition" in: The Architectural Review, issue 755/1960; pages 67–70

LOHSE, R. P.: "'From Le Corbusier to Niemeyer: 1929 – 1949'. The Museum of Modern Art, New York." in: Bauen + Wohnen, issue 6/1949; page 58

LUCHSINGER, Christoph (ed.): Hans Hofmann. Vom Neuen Bauen zur Neuen Baukunst. Dokumente zur modernen Schweizer Architektur. Zurich 1985

MAAß, Harry: Der Garten – Dein Arzt. Fort mit den Gartensorgen. Frankfurt an der Oder 1927

MAAß, Harry: Gartentechnik und Gartenkunst. Nordhausen 1931

MAI, Ekkehard/SCHIRMBER, Gisela: Denkmal – Zeichen – Monument. Skulptur im öffentlichen Raum heute. Munich 1989

MATHESON, John (ed.): Arnold Zürcher. Verona 1993

MATHYS, Heini: "50 Jahre BSG/FSAP" in: Anthos, issue 3/4/1975; pages 2–7

MATHYS, Heini: "Andere gärtnerische Sehenswürdigkeiten in der Ausstellungsstadt" in: Schweizer Garten + Wohnkultur, issue 5/1959; pages 118–119

MATHYS, Heini: "Bedeutung und Aufgabe des Gartens in unserer Zeit" in: Schweizer Garten + Wohnkultur, issue 2/1962; pages 21–22

MATHYS, Heini: "Begegnung mit Werken von Uli Schoop" in: Schweizer Garten + Wohnkultur, issue 8/1960; pages 167–169

MATHYS, Heini: "Das gärtnerische Ereignis des kommenden Jahres" in: Schweizer Garten + Wohnkultur, issue 1/1959; page 22

MATHYS, Heini: "Der Garten des Poeten" in: Schweizer Garten + Wohnkultur, issue 7/1959; pages 153–154

MATHYS, Heini: "Der japanische Garten am Sitz der UNESCO in Paris" in: Schweizer Garten + Wohnkultur, issue 8/1960; pages 169–171

MATHYS, Heini: "Der Platz als Freiraumplastik" in: Anthos, issue 2/1979; pages 17–19

MATHYS, Heini: "Die Ausbildung im Technikum Rapperswil/SG hat begonnen" in: Anthos, issue 4/1972; page 38

MATHYS, Heini: "Die kritische Spalte. Bodenskulptur kontra Pflanzengrün" in: Anthos, issue 2/1975; pages 27–28

MATHYS, Heini: "Dorfplatz in Schwerzenbach/ZH" in: Anthos, issue 4/1971; pages 20–21

MATHYS, Heini: "Ernst Cramer 80jährig" in: Anthos, issue 4/1978; pages 32–33

MATHYS, Heini: "Freiraumgestaltung zum neuen Laborgebäude des Technikums in Winterthur" in: Anthos, issue 2/1975; pages 2–5

MATHYS, Heini: "G | 59 – Eine neue Gartenwelt am Zürichsee" in: Schweizer Garten + Wohnkultur, issue 5/1959; pages 107–117

MATHYS, Heini: "Leitbilder die noch heute gelten" in: Anthos, issue 3/1972; pages 20–23

MATHYS, Heini: "Pausenplatz zum Schulhaus Looren in Witikon/ZH" in: Anthos, issue 4/1971; pages 22–23

MATHYS, Heini: "Projekt für ein Friedhofgebäude in Gränichen/Aargau" in: Anthos, issue 4/1976; pages 37–38

MATHYS, Heini: "Rückblick auf den Wettbewerb für den Friedhof 'Hinderneuwis' in Volketswil" in: Anthos, issue 4/1969; pages 34–38

MATHYS, Heini: "Schweizerische Gartenarchitektur im 20. Jahrhundert. Rückblick und Versuch einer Standortbestimmung. Zum 10jährigen Bestehen von 'anthos'" in: Anthos, issue 3/1972; pages 1–19

MATHYS, Heini: "Stadtsanierung in einem Ballungsgebiet" in: Anthos, issue 4/1972; pages 8–9

MATHYS, Heini: "Stilprobleme im Garten" in: Schweizer Garten + Wohnkultur, issue 2/1960; pages 19–20

MATHYS, Heini: "Vom Kunsterlebnis im Garten" in: Schweizer Garten + Wohnkultur, issue 8/1960; pages 165–166

MATHYS, Heini: "Vom steinigen Garten zum Steingarten" in: Schweizer Garten + Wohnkultur, issue 7/1963; pages 141–143

MATHYS, Heini: "Vor der Eröffnung der G | 59" in: Schweizer Garten + Wohnkultur, issue 4/1959; page 103

MATHYS, Heini: "Was bringt die Gartenbau-Ausstellung?" in: Schweizer Garten + Wohnkultur, issue 3/1959; page 80

MATHYS, Heini: "Wege und Stege an der G | 59" in: Schweizer Garten + Wohnkultur, issue 9/1959; pages 199–201

MATHYS, Heini: "Weltgarten-Panorama in Hamburg. Zur Internationalen Gartenbau-Ausstellung IGA 63 in Hamburg (26. April bis 13. Oktober)" in: Schweizer Garten + Wohnkultur, issue 9/1963; pages 191–194

MATHYS, Heini: "Wesen und Aufgabe einer Gartenschau" in: Schweizer Garten + Wohnkultur, issue 5/1959; pages 105–106

MATHYS,Heini: "Wohngarten in Aarau" in: Anthos, issue 3/1971; pages 14–17

MATHYS, Heini: "Zum Thema unseres Sonderheftes Architekturbezogenes Grün" in: Anthos, issue 2/1975; page 1

MATHYS, Heini: "Zum Thema unseres Herbstheftes: Paris" in: Anthos, issue 3/1974; page 1

MATTERN, Hermann: Gärten und Gartenlandschaften. Stuttgart 1960

MATTERN, Hermann (ed.): Die Wohnlandschaft. Stuttgart 1950

MAURER, Bruno: "'Eternitgerecht' Bauen" in: Archithese, issue 5/1993; pages 24–31

MAURER, G.: "Die neue Einheit von Haus und Garten" in: Das ideale Heim, Winterthur 1948; pages 462–467

MAURER, G.: "Vier Gartenräume" in: Das ideale Heim, issue 10/1947; pages 359–362

MC HARG, Ian: Design with Nature. New York 1969

MEDICI-MALL, Katharina: Im Durcheinandertal der Stile. Architektur und Kunst im Urteil von Peter Meyer (1894–1984). Basel, Boston, Berlin 1998

MEDICI-MALL, Katharina: "Trotz alledem und alledem modern" in: Der Architekt, issue 1/1996; pages 37–39

MEILI, Armin: Bauliche Sanierung von Hotels und Kurorten. Schlussbericht. Erlenbach, Zurich 1945

MEILI, Armin: Schweizerische Landesausstellung 1939 Zürich. Zurich 1940

MERTENS, Gebrüder: "Der Garten zu den drei Türmen" in: Schweizerische Bauzeitung, issue 18/1939; pages 211–212

MERTENS, Oskar: "Formprobleme der heutigen Gartengestaltung" in: Das Werk, issue 9/1941; pages 244–246

MERTENS, Oskar: "Formprobleme der heutigen Gartengestaltung" in: Schweizer Garten, issue 11/1942; pages 297–300

MERTENS, Oskar: "Gedanken über die Gartenkunst von heute" in: Das Werk, issue 9/1923; pages 211–224

MERTENS, Oskar: "Neuzeitliche Gartengestaltung" in: Das ideale Heim, Winterthur 1943; pages 241–252

MERTENS, Oskar: "Ueber Gartenkunst" in: Das Werk, issue 5/1916; pages 65–80

MERTENS, Walter: "Der Bund Schweizerischer Gartengestalter (B.S.G.) zeigt Arbeiten seiner Mitglieder" in: Schweizer Garten, special issue, issue 7/1939; pages 195–221

MESEURE, Anna/TSCHANZ, Martin/WANG, Wilfried (eds.): Architektur im 20. Jahrhundert. Schweiz. Frankfurt/Main 1998

MEYER, Gisbert et al.: "Landhaus bei Windisch, Ferienhaus bei Villars-sur-Fontenais im Jura, Ferienhaus bei Cugnasco im Tessin" in: Werk, issue 8/1947; pages 248–255

MEYER, Peter: "Baugesetz und Gärten. Zum Entwurf eines neuen Baugesetzes für den Kanton Zürich" in: Das Werk, issue 4/1930; pages 122–127

MEYER, Peter: "Die Architektur der Landesausstellung – kritische Besprechung" in: Das Werk, special issue VII on the Schweizerischen Landesausstellung, issue 11/1939; pages 320–352

MEYER, Peter: "Die Gärten der Landesausstellung" in: Meili, Armin: Schweizerische Landesausstellung 1939 Zürich. Volume 2. Zurich 1940; pages 613–615

MEYER, Peter: "Die Gärten der Schweizerischen Landesausstellung, Zürich 1939" in: Das Werk, special issue on the III. Internationalen Gartenbau-Kongress, issue 7/1939; pages 193–223

MEYER, Peter: "Einleitung zu 'Neue Gärten'" in: Baumann, Ernst: Neue Gärten. Zurich 1955; pages 6–9

MEYER, Peter: "Garten, Landschaft, Architektur" in: Schweizerische Bauzeitung, issue 18/1939; pages 203–211

MEYER, Peter: "Planen, Bauen und Wohnen" in: Meili, Armin: Schweizerische Landesausstellung 1939 Zürich. Volume 2, Zurich 1940; pages 61–69

MEYER, Peter: "Schweizerische Landesausstellung" in: Das Werk, issue 5/1939; pages 129–185

MEYER, Peter: "ZÜKA" in: Schweizerische Bauzeitung, issue 39/1947; pages 537–540

MEYER, Peter: "Zürcher Gartenbauausstellung Züga, 24. Juni bis 17. September 1933" in: Das Werk, issue 7/1933; pages 193–212

MIGGE, Leberecht: "Der technische Gartentypus unserer Zeit" in: Gartenschönheit, issue 6201927; pages 36–37

MÜLLER/BANDI: "Sport- und Erholungszentrum Trägerhard in Wettingen" in: Schweizer Journal. Zeitschrift für öffentlichen Bau und Industrie, issue 5–6/1974; page 58

Museum für Gestaltung Zürich, Kunstgewerbemuseum (publ.): Willy Guhl – Gestalter und Lehrer. Reihe Schweizer Design-Pioniere 2. Zurich 1985

MUTHESIUS, Hermann: Landhaus und Garten. Munich 1907

NEUKOM, Willi: "Erste Schweizerische Gartenbauausstellung in Zürich 1959" in: Bauen + Wohnen, issue 7/1958; page 248

NEUKOM, Willi: "Gartenvariationen" in: Bauen + Wohnen, issue 3/1956; pages 101–104

NEUKOM, Willi: "Neue Gärten und Gartenprojekte" in: Bauen + Wohnen, issue 3/1957; pages 101–108

NEUTRA, Richard: Auftrag für morgen. Hamburg 1962; Life and shape. The autobiography of Richard Neutra. 1962

NEUTRA, Richard: Wenn wir weiterleben wollen … Erfahrungen und Forderungen eines Architekten. Hamburg 1954; Survival through design. New York and London 1954

OERI, Georgine: "Über das 'Natürliche' als Formersatz" in: Werk, issue 1/1945; pages 9–10

OESTERLEN, Dieter: Dieter Oesterlen. Bauten und Texte 1946–1991. Tübingen, Berlin 1992

OPPENHEIM, Roy: "Die Schweiz an der Sigma II (14.–19. November 1966)" in: Werk-Chronik, issue 1/1967; pages 42–44

OPPENHEIM, Roy: "Montreal und das Trichterhaus" in: Werk-Chronik, issue 11/1967; pages 747–748

PAILLARD, Claude: "Ueberbauung 'Grüzefeld' in Winterthur" in: Werk, issue 10/1968; pages 654–658

PAILLARD, Claude: "Ueberbauung 'Grüzefeld' in Winterthur" in: Werk, issue 3/1965; page 104

PAILLARD, Claude: "Überbauung Grüzefeld, Winterthur" in: Schweizer Journal, Zeitschrift für öffentlichen Bau und Industrie, issue 8/1967; pages 28–29

PECHÊRE, René: "Um einen neuen Gartenstil" in: Garten und Landschaft, issue 6/1957; pages 154–155

PERSITZ, Alexandre/VALEIX, Danielle: "Berlin 1957 – Bâtiments divers" in: L'architecture d'aujourd'hui, issue 75/1957

PETIT, Jean: Niemeyer, poète d'architecture. Lugano 1995

Pressestelle der Internationalen Bauausstellung Berlin 1957: "Grünflächen im neuen Hansaviertel" in: Garten und Landschaft, issue 3/1956; pages 84–85

PRO.PLAN-ING. AG: "Die Neubauten der Roche AG in Sisseln" in: Schweizer Journal. Zeitschrift für öffentlichen Bau und Industrie, issue 5/1978; page 43

R. G.: "Das Säli-Schulhaus in Olten" in: Schweizerische Bauzeitung, issue 2201970; pages 486–491

R. G.: "Gartenarchitektur und Landschaftsplanung" in: Schweizerische Bauzeitung, issue 18/1975; page 255

R. G.: "Wettbewerb für die künstlerische Gestaltung beim Schulhaus 'Im Moos' in Rüschlikon" in: Schweizerische Bauzeitung, issue 2201970; pages 484–486

RAALTE, D.: "400 Jahre Universität Leiden und ihr Clusius-Garten" in: Der Gartenbau, issue 25/1975; page 983

REICH, Alfred: "Entwicklung zu klaren Formen?" in: Garten und Landschaft, issue 1/1962; pages 14–16

REICH, Alfred: "Zürich und Basel – Garten und Landschaft. Fachliche Reiseeindrücke aus der Schweiz" in: Garten und Landschaft, issue 8/1950; pages 6–12

REICHOW, Hans Bernhard: Organische Baukunst, volume II. Braunschweig, Berlin, Hamburg 1949

REICHOW, Hans Bernhard: Organische Stadtbaukunst. Von der Grossstadt zur Stadtlandschaft. Braunschweig, Berlin, Hamburg 1948

RIEGE, Th.: Der Wiederaufbau des Berliner Hansaviertels im Rahmen der Internationalen Bauausstellung 1957. Dissertation. Berlin 1987

RITTER, Marco: "Wohnungen der Industrie" in: Schweizer Journal, Zeitschrift für öffentlichen Bau und Industrie, issue 2/1970; pages 59–60

ROETHLISBERGER, H.: "Von den Gärten der schweizerischen Werkbund-Ausstellung" in: Das Werk, issue 8/1918; pages 117–121

ROSE, James C.: Creative Gardens. New York 1958

ROSSOW, Walter: "Zur Internationalen Bauausstellung" in: Garten und Landschaft, issue 10/1957; pages 254–256

ROTH, Alfred: "Der neue Lehrplan der Architekturabteilung der Eidgenössischen Technischen Hochschule Zürich" in: Werk, issue 8/1961; pages 258–??

ROTH, Alfred: "Die bauende Schweiz, von einem Amerikaner gesehen. Zu dem Buche 'Switzerland Builds' von G. E. Kidder Smith" in: Werk, issue 10/1950; pages 309–311

ROTH, Alfred: "Die gute Form" in: Werk, issue 8/1949; pages 251–258

ROTH, Alfred: "Fünfzig Jahre Schweizerischer Werkbund" in: Werk, issue 3/164; pages 117–120

ROTH, Alfred: "Gustav Ammann: Blühende Gärten/Landscape Gardens/Jardins en fleurs" in: Werk-Chronik, issue 8/1956; pages 158–159

ROTH, Alfred: "Planen und Bauen nach dem Kriege von der Schweiz aus gesehen" in: Werk, issue 1/1944; pages 2–5

ROTH, Alfred: "Zeitgemäße Architekturbetrachtungen. Mit besonderer Berücksichtigung der schweizerischen Situation" in: Werk, issue 3/1951; pages 65–76

ROTH, Alfred: "Zum Kongreß der 'International Federation of Landscape Architects' in Zürich, 20.–26. August 1956" in: Werk, issue 8/1956; page 237

ROTZLER, Stefan: "Ernst Cramer, Landschaftsarchitekt, 1898–1980" in: Anthos, issue 2/1987; page 1

ROTZLER, Willy: Aus dem Tag in die Zeit. Texte zur modernen Kunst. Zurich 1994

ROTZLER, Willy: Konstruktive Konzepte. Eine Geschichte der konstruktiven Kunst vom Kubismus bis heute. Zurich 1977

ROTZLER, Willy: "Kunst im Grünraum. Zur Plastik an der Schweizerischen Gartenbau-Ausstellung Zürich" in: Werk, issue 10/1959; pages 351–356

ROTZLER, Willy: "Plastik im Grünraum" in: Werk, issue 5/1951; pages 149–155

ROTZLER, Willy: "Wohnbau und Grünfläche" in: Werk, issue 3/1950; pages 65–72

ROWE, Colin/SLUTZKY, Robert: Transparency. Basel, Boston, Berlin 1997

RÜEGG, Arthur: "Ideenflüsse" in: Meseure, Anna et al. (ed.): Architektur im 20. Jahrhundert. Schweiz. Frankfurt am Main 1998; pages 67–72

RÜEGG, Arthur (ed.): Das Atelierhaus Max Bill 1932/33: ein Wohn- und Atelierhaus in Zürich-Höngg von Max Bill und Robert Winkler. Sulgen 1997

RÜEGG, Arthur/MARBACH, Ueli: Werkbundsiedlung Neubühl. Zurich 1990

RÜEGG, Arthur/STEINMANN, Martin: "Einrichtungen" in: Archithese, issue 1/1983; pages 34–53

RÜMMELE, Simone: "'Holländereien', 'Baubolschewismus' und 'geistige Landesverteidigung'" in: Meseure, Anna et al. (ed.): Architektur im 20. Jahrhundert. Schweiz. Frankfurt am Main 1998; pages 27–34

RUFFIEUX, Roland: "Dreissiger Jahre oder die Schweiz auf dem Prüfstand" in: Kunsthaus Zürich (publ.): Dreissiger Jahre Schweiz. Ein Jahrzehnt im Widerspruch. Zurich 1981; pages 46–53

RUST, Roland: "2. Internationaler Kongress der Gartengestalter Berlin-Hannover-Essen" in: Schweizer Garten, issue 11/1938; pages 316–319

RUST, Roland: "Erster Internationaler Kongress für Gartenkunst Paris 1937" in: Schweizer Garten, issue 6/1938; pages 174–177

RUTISHAUSER, Max: Die 40er Jahre. Ein dramatisches Jahrzehnt in Bildern. Zofingen 1976

S. V.: "ZÜKA. Zürcher Kantonale Gewerbe-u. Landwirtschafts-Ausstellung 23. August bis 19.Oktober 1947" in: Werk, issue 10/1947; pages 113–114

SACK, Manfred: Richard Neutra: Moderner, Missionar, Natur- und Menschenfreund. Zurich 1992

SCHEIDEGGER, Alfred: "Der Bildhauer Bernhard Luginbühl" in: Werk, 1960; pages 65–68

SCHILLER, Hans: "Ist der Hausgarten auf dem richtigen Weg? Zum Thema: Garten-liebhaber – Gartengestalter" in: Garten-schönheit, issue 10/1940; pages 186–187

SCHINDLER, Ernst: "Individuelle Wohn-häuser – Eigenheim des Architekten in Zürich" in: Werk, issue 6/1949; pages 175–177

SCHMID, Heinrich E.: Walter Jonas. Maler Denker Urbanist. Zurich 1980

SCHMID, Henri: "Die Beherrschung der Weite" in: Das ideale Heim, Winterthur 1944; pages 271–276

SCHMID, Willy: "Der Gartenbau an der 'Züka'" in: Schweizer Garten, issue9/1947; pages 271–275

SCHMID, Willy: "'Züka' Zürcher-kantonale Landwirtschafts- und Gewerbe-Ausstellung" in: Schweizer Garten, issue 6/1947; pages 195–196

SCHMIDT, Georg: "Abstrakte und sur-realistische Kunst in der Schweiz" in: Werk, issue 1/1943; pages 41–45

SCHMIDT, Hans: "Vom Gesicht der Siedlung" in: Werk, volume 30, issue 7/1943; pages 210–215

SCHMON, Leo A.: "Garten- und Landschafts-gestaltung der Neuzeit. Zum inter-nationalen Kongress für Landschafts- und Gartengestaltung" in: Das ideale Heim, issue 7/1956; pages 333–358

SCHMON, Leo A.: Wohn- und Landschafts-gärten. Winterthur 1961

SCHNEIDER, Camillo: "Die Zürcher Garten-bauausstellung (Züga)" in: Gartenschön-heit, issue 10/1933; pages 196–199

SCHOOP, Uli: "Zu meinen Tierplastiken" in: Werk, issue 11/1956; pages 364–365

SCHÜRENBERG, Wilhelm/MÜLLER, Gerhard/MARTINSSON, Gunnar: "Stimmen zum Wettbewerb 'Garten am Wilhaditurm'" in: Garten und Landschaft, issue 6/1956; pages 183–184

SCHWARZ, Hans-Peter: "Die Mythologie des Konstruktiven" in: Klotz, Heinrich (ed.): Vision der Moderne. Das Prinzip Konstruktion. Munich 1986; pages 46–55

SCHWARZ, Urs: Der Naturgarten. Frankfurt 1980

SCHWEIZER, Johannes Erwin: "Der Bund Schweizerischer Gartengestalter (BSG) zeigt neue Arbeiten seiner Mitglieder" in: Schweizer Garten, issue 1/1942; pages 1–30

SCHWEIZER, Johannes Erwin: "Gedanken über Bilder aus neuen Gärten. Arbeiten des Bundes Schweizerischer Gartengestalter, BSG" in: Das ideale Heim, Winterthur 1942; pages 183–198

SCHWEIZER, Johannes Erwin: "III. Inter-nationaler Kongress für Gartenkunst, Zürich 1939" in: Schweizer Garten, issue 9/1939; page 282

SCHWEIZER, Johannes Erwin: "Land-schaftsverbundene Gärten" in: Garten-schönheit, issue 2/1940; pages 46–47

SCHWEIZER, Johannes Erwin, Dr./ STÜCHELI, Werner/KOLLBRUNNER,Paul/ NEUKOM, Willi: "Schweizerische Garten-bau-Ausstellung G | 59 in Zürich" in: Bauen + Wohnen, Chronik, issue 10/1959; pages X 1–7

SCULLY, Vincent jr.: Louis I. Kahn. Makers of contemporary architecture. New York 1962

SEIFERT, Alwin: "Bodenständige Garten-kunst" in: Gartenkunst, issue 43/1930; pages 162–164

SEIFERT, Alwin: "Gedanken über boden-ständige Gartenkunst" in: Gartenkunst, issue 42/1929; page 118 ff.

Senator für Bau- und Wohnungswesen Berlin/Bund Deutscher Architekten BDA (publ.): Interbau Berlin 57. Wiederaufbau Hansaviertel Berlin. Berlin 1957

SGARD, Jacques: "Le 'Jardin sculpté' der 'Floralies 1969' in Paris" in: Anthos, issue 4/1969; pages 39–44

SHEPHEARD, Peter: Modern Gardens. London 1953

SHEPHEARD, Peter/KÜHN, Erich: Grüne Architektur. Neue Gärten aus neun Ländern. Berlin 1959

SIMON, Jacques: "Spiel mit Steinen in der Zürcher Gartenschau G | 59" in: Garten und Landschaft, issue 1/1960; pages 4–5

SMITH, G. E. Kidder: Switzerland builds – its native and modern Architecture. New York, Stockholm 1950

SMITH, G. E. Kidder: The new architecture of Europe. Cleveland, New York 1961

SMITH, Peter F.: Architecture and the Human Dimension. London 1979

SØRENSEN, Carl Theodor: "Der Garten als Sinnbild der Kultur" in: Schweizer Garten + Wohnkultur, issue 2/1962; pages 25–32

SPIES, Werner: Kontinuität. Granit-Monolith von Max Bill. Zumikon, Zurich 1986

STADT Zürich (publ.): Wohnsiedlungen Heuried und Utohof in Zürich-Wiedikon. Zurich 1978

STAHLY, François: "Aspen – ein amerikanisches Kulturzentrum" in: Werk, issue 7/1961; pages 249–251

STEGMANN, Markus: Architektonische Skulptur im 20. Jahrhundert. Tübingen 1995

STEIGER, Peter: "Dem Werkbund eine Chance!" in: SWB-Kommentare, issue 14/1970; pages 121

STEINBRÜCHEL, Franz: "Intrapolis oder der Mut zum Ungewohnten" in: Schmid, Heinrich E.: Walter Jonas. Maler, Denker, Urbanist, Zurich 1980; pages 141–143

STEINER, Dietmar: Architektur Beispiele Eternit. Kulturgeschichte eines Baustoffes. Vienna 1994

STEINER, Emil: "Baum und Plastik im industriellen Raum" in: Der Gartenbau, issue 33/1977; pages 1315–1316

STEINER, Emil: "Begegnung mit Ernst Cramer" in: Anthos, issue 1/1987; pages 13–37

STEINER, Emil: "Das Grün der Siedlung 'Grüzefeld' in Winterthur/Die funk-tionellen Aufgaben städtischer Grünflächen" in: Der Gartenbau, issue 1/1970; pages 11–20

STEINER, Emil: "De la structure intrinsèque à la forme définitive" in: Der Gartenbau, issue 11/1975; pages 381–384

STEINER, Emil: "Der Baum" in: Der Garten-bau, issue 31/1975; pages 1169–1170

STEINER, Emil: "Der Garten in Erwartung neuer Form – Die 'Grün 80' – wie sie ihre Schöpfer sehen" in: Der Gartenbau, issue 15/1980; pages 729–739

STEINER, Emil: "Die Form in der Garten-gestaltung" in: Schweizerisches Garten-bau-Blatt, issue 25/1959; pages 649–650

STEINER, Emil: "Die verschiedenen Gesichter des Jahres 1976" in: Der Garten-bau, issue 1/201976; pages 13–15

STEINER, Emil: "Erster Rundgang durch die Gärten der G | 59" in: Schweizerisches Gartenbau-Blatt, issue 17/1959; pages 648

STEINER, Emil: "Gestaltete Hügel" in: Der Gartenbau, issue 25/1975; pages 981–982

STEINER, Emil: "Vom Leben unter Bäumen und auf Plätzen. Arbeiten der Abteilung Garten und Landschaftsarchitektur am Athenaeum Lausanne" in: Der Gartenbau, issue 3/1977; pages 85–93

STEINER, Emil: "Von der inneren Struktur zum Erscheinen der Form" in: Der Garten-bau, issue 11/1975; pages 377–381

STEINER, Emil: "Zentrumsgestaltung eines Industrieareals" in: Anthos, issue 2/1995; pages 30–31

Stiftung Archiv für Schweizer Garten-architektur und Landschaftsplanung (publ.): Vom Landschaftsgarten zur Garten-landschaft. Gartenkunst zwischen 1880 und 1980 im Archiv für Schweizer Garten-architektur und Landschaftsplanung. Zurich 1996

STÖCKLI, Peter Paul: "20 Jahre 'anthos'" in: Anthos, issue 4/1981; pages 1–6

STUCKY, Fritz: "Landhaus Gimmenen bei Zug" in: Werk, issue 6/1959; pages 200–201

STUCKY, Fritz: "Terrassenhäuser in Zug" in: Werk, issue 2/1961; pages 58–60

STÜCHELI, Werner/KOLLBRUNNER, Paul R.: "Planung und Gestaltung der Hochbauten für die G | 59" in: Eternit im Hoch- und Tief-bau, issue 52/1959; pages 891–896

SURBECK, Ernst: "Den Garten einmal zeichnerisch gesehen" in: Schweizer Garten, issue 1/1945; pages 1–8

SURBECK, Ernst: "Kosten von Garten-anlagen" in: Werk, issue 2/1946; pages 101

SURBECK, Ernst: "Ueber die gärtnerische Gestaltung von Schulhausanlagen" in: Werk, issue 6/1949; pages 216–217

SUTER UND SUTER AG, Basel: "Das Bruder-holzspital – zweites Kantonsspital des Kantons Basel-Landschaft" in: Schweizer Journal. Zeitschrift für öffentlichen Bau und Industrie, issue 1/1974; pages 28–30

SUTER UND SUTER: "Das Sulzer-Hochhaus in Winterthur" in: Schweizer Journal, Zeitschrift für öffentlichen Bau und Indus-trie, issue 2/1967; pages 41–45

TAMURA, Tsayoshi: "Landschaft und Garten in Japan" in: Garten und Land-schaft, issue 10/1964; pages 338–340

TANDY, Clifford R. V. (ed.): Landscape and human life. The impact of landscape architecture upon human activities. Amsterdam 1966

TREIB, Marc (ed.): Modern Landscape Architecture: A critical Review. Cambridge, London 1993

TREIB, Marc/IMBERT, Dorothée: Garrett Eckbo. Modern Landscapes for Living. Berkeley, Los Angeles, London 1997

TRILLITZSCH, Falk: "Auf der Suche nach Gestalt" in: Garten und Landschaft, issue 8/1979; pages 596–601

TUNNARD, Christopher: Gardens in the modern landscape. Westminster 1938

TUNNARD, Christopher: "Modern Gardens for Modern Houses. Reflections on Current Trends in Landscape Architecture" in: Landscape Architecture. A Quarterly Maga-zine, issue 2/1942; pages 57–64

VALENTIEN, Otto: Der Friedhof. Gärtnerische Gestaltung. Bauten. Grabmale. Munich 1953

VALENTIEN, Otto: "Eindrücke der heutigen Schweizer Gartengestaltung" in: Garten und Landschaft, issue 1/1953; pages 15–16

VALENTIEN, Otto: Gärten. Charlottenburg, Berlin 1938

VALENTIEN, Otto: Mauern und Wege im Garten. Schriftenreihe der Deutschen Gesellschaft für Gartenkunst und Land-schaftspflege, no. 3. Munich 1958

VALENTIEN, Otto: Neue Gärten. Ravensburg 1949

VALENTIEN, Otto: "Neues Bauen – Neue Gärten. Der Gartenarchitekt" in: Garten und Landschaft, issue 1/1953; pages 2–3

VALENTIEN, Otto (ed.): Zeitgemässe Wohn-Gärten. Eine Sammlung alter und neuer Hausgärten. Munich 1932

Verein zur Herausgabe des Schweizerischen Künstler-Lexikons (publ.): Künstler-Lexikon der Schweiz, 20. Jahrhundert. Frauenfeld 1958–1967

Verlag Das ideale Heim (publ.): Special issue Wohngarten. Winterthur 1956

VIGNY, Annette: Jacques Sgard paysagiste & urbaniste. Liège 1995

VOLKART, Hans: Schweizer Architektur. Ein Überblick über das schweizerische Bauschaffen der Gegenwart. Ravensburg 1951

VON MOOS, Stanislaus: "Recycling Max Bill" in: Bundesamt für Kultur (publ.): Minimal Tradition. Bern 1996; pages 9–32

VON WYSS, Roland: "'Blühender Herbst'. Garten- und Blumenausstellung im Kongresshaus in Zürich" in: Schweizer Garten, issue 10/1942; pages 273–275

VON WYSS, Roland: "Die Gärten an
    der 'AGA' in Aarau" in: Schweizer Garten,
    issue 10/1947; pages 312–313
VON WYSS, Roland: "Die Gärten an der
    'ZÜKA' in Zürich" in: Schweizer Garten,
    issue 10/1947; pages 303–311
VON WYSS, Roland: "Erschliessung
    von Landschaftsteilen" in: Schweizerische
    Bauzeitung, special issue on landscape de-
    sign, issue 15/1941; pages 171–172
W. R.: "Neue Schweizer Pflanzenbehälter"
    in: Werk, issue 6/1952; pages 192–193
WALKER, Peter: "The practice of landscape
    architecture in the postwar United States"
    in: Treib, Marc (ed.): Modern Landscape
    Architecture: A critical Review. Cambridge,
    London 1993; pages 250–259
WEBER, Hans-Ulrich: "Gedanken zu
    'La Grande Borne' in Grigny" in: Anthos,
    issue 3/1974; pages 2–7
WEILACHER, Udo: "Gartenarchitektur
    als lebendiger Ausdruck Schweizer Zeit-
    geschichte" in: DISP, issue 138/1999;
    pages 13–16
WEILACHER, Udo: "Schweiz:
    Vom Heimatstil zur guten Form" in: TOPOS,
    issue 33/2000; pages 81–89
WEILACHER, Udo: "Vom Zürichsee
    ins Museum of Modern Art" in:
    Basler Magazin, December 2nd,
    issue 48/2000; pages 10–11
WEILACHER, Udo: Between landscape
    architecture and land art.
    Basel, Berlin, Boston 1996
WIDDER, Bernhard: Herbert Bayer.
    Architektur/Skulptur/Landschafts-
    gestaltung. Vienna, New York 2000
WIEGAND, Heinz: Entwicklung des Stadt-
    grüns in Deutschland zwischen 1890
    und 1925 am Beispiel der Arbeiten
    Fritz Enckes. Geschichte des Stadtgrüns.
    Volume II. Berlin, Hanover 1977
WIMMER, Clemens Alexander: Geschichte
    der Gartentheorie. Darmstadt 1989
WISMER, Beat: Mondrians ästhetische
    Utopie. Baden 1985
WREDE, Stuart/ADAMS, William Howard
    (eds.): Denatured Visions. Landscape
    and Culture in the Twentieth Century.
    New York 1991
ZAHN, Leopold: "Ein geometrischer Garten
    an der Riviera" in: Gartenschönheit,
    issue 6/1929; pages 222–223
ZBINDEN, Pierre: "Die erste Schwei-
    zerische Gartenanbau-Ausstellung" in:
    Eternit im Hoch- und Tiefbau,
    issue 52/1959; page 890
ZELTNER, Hans M.: "Moderne Schweizer
    Wohngärten" in: Das ideale Heim,
    Winterthur 1940; pages 29–36
ZELTNER, Hans M.: "Neuzeitliche Wohn-
    bauten. Architekten Richner & Anliker,
    Aarau. Gartenanlagen: E. Cramer, Garten-
    bau, Zürich" in: Das ideale Heim,
    Winterthur 1937; pages 279–290
Zentrum für Kunstausstellungen der DDR
    (publ.): Max Bill. Weimar 1988
ZEVI, Bruno: "Ein Gartenarchitekt in den
    Tropen. Aus dem Schaffen von Roberto
    Burle Marx" in: Garten und Landschaft,
    issue 10/1958; pages 261–263

No author

"Arbeiten von Mitgliedern des Bundes
    Schweizer Gartenarchitekten BSG" in:
    Bauen + Wohnen, issue 10/1951;
    pages 27–33
"Atriumhäuser auf der Interbau Berlin 1957"
    in: Bauen + Wohnen, issue 7/1958;
    pages 224–226
"Büro-Hochhaus Gebrüder Sulzer,
    Winterthur" in: Bauen + Wohnen,
    issue 8/1966; pages 294–302
"Die neue Kantonsschule in Wetzikon"
    in: Werk, issue 4/1959; pages 121–125
"Ein Berghaus von Neutra" in: Das ideale
    Heim, issue 12/1970; pages 10–21
"Eindrücke junger Weihenstephaner Garten-
    gestalter in der Schweiz" in: Garten und
    Landschaft, issue 8/1951; pages 8–10
"Einfamilienhaus in Oberwil ZG" in: Werk,
    issue 8/1965; pages 294–295
"Friedhof in Pratteln" in: Werk-Chronik,
    issue 10/1959; pages 206–207
"Friedhof-Erweiterung Aarau" in: Werk,
    issue 3/1947; page 84
"Fürst Pücklers Tumulus im Park zu Branitz"
    in: Garten und Landschaft, issue 2/1958;
    page 35
"Garten in schöner Landschaft" in: Das
    ideale Heim, issue 11/1957; pages 445–451
"Grünanlage am Lehrerinnenseminar in
    Menzingen/Schweiz" in: Garten und Land-
    schaft, issue 9/1959; pages 267–269
"Haus mit 3 Wohnungen in Zug" in: Bauen +
    Wohnen, issue 1/1957; pages 14–17
"Primarschulhaus 'Im Feld', Wetzikon"
    in: Bauen + Wohnen, issue 8/1958;
    pages 320–322
"Rationeller Wohnungs- und Siedlungsbau
    System 'Alusuisse'" in: Werk-Chronik,
    issue 12/1967; pages 818–819
"Raum und Landschaft. Ausschnitte aus
    einem Garten der Firma Cramer & Surbeck,
    Gartenarchitekten, Zürich" in: Das ideale
    Heim, Winterthur 1945; pages 399–404
"Ueberbauung Obere Vorstadt, Aarau/AEW-
    Verwaltungshochhaus, Kantonales
    Gerichtsgebäude, Kantinenrestaurant" in:
    Werk, issue 3/1971; pages 181–183
"Verwaltungsgebäude der Eternit AG in
    Niederurnen" in: Eternit im Hoch- und
    Tiefbau, issue 1/1957; pages 1–8
"Wettbewerb für den Friedhof 'Hin-
    derneuwis'" in: Anthos, issue 4/1969;
    page 37
"Wohnkolonie Wilerfeld, Olten/Wohn-
    kolonie Badenerstrasse, Zürich" in:
    Anthos, issue 4/1964; pages 29–36
"Wohnüberbauung Heuried in Zürich-
    Wiedikon" in: Werk, issue 12/1976;
    pages 828–831
"Zur Grünplanung der Internationalen
    Bauausstellung Berlin 1957" in: Garten und
    Landschaft, issue 3/1957; pages 96–97
"Zwei Bronzeskulpturen von Peter Meister"
    in: Werk, issue 12/1971; page 841

ILLUSTRATION CREDITS

ACKNOWLEDGEMENTS

It would not have been possible to realize this book without the co-operation of numerous experts, friends and contemporaries of Ernst Cramer, and it is well-nigh impossible to thank each one appropriately here. Nevertheless I want to acknowledge the help that some of you have given me expressly.

Many owners of Cramer gardens all over Switzerland were willing to tell me about their experiences with Ernst Cramer, and have also received me with lavish hospitality. I thank them all most cordially, above all Fausto Bizzini, Albert Brunner and his family, Ralph Dimmler, Anne Keller, Fritz and Gertrud Rentsch, Josef Schmidlin and his wife, Günther Senfft and his wife, Tom Vogel and his wife and Eva and Günther Wizemann. Although Ernst Cramer did not design the garden of Florian Bischoff and his parents, their special hospitality made the wonderful evenings in Vevey some of the most pleasant experiences during my weeks of research in the Archives de la Construction Moderne in Lausanne.

For their help I should like to thank the staff in the Lausanne Archives, as well as those responsible in the Schweizerisches Wirtschaftsarchiv in Basel and in the Bettlach AG Ebauches factory company museum in Grenchen. My special thanks go to the Archiv für Schweizer Landschaftsarchitektur in Rapperswil under the presidency of Peter Paul Stöckli, and above all to the responsible archivist, the esteemed art historian Annemarie Bucher, without whose infinite patience, expert advice and unconditional helpfulness it would have been simply impossible to work efficiently on Ernst Cramer's estate.

My intensive contact with Ernst Cramer's former employees and professional colleagues was of inestimable value. Their enthusiasm for the subject and their readiness to report from the personal wealth of experience of past decades was almost boundless. Warmest thanks go to: Sven-Ingvar Andersson, Hans-Kurt Boehlke, the late Ermes Cescon, Fritz Dové, Fred Eicher, Christofer Eriksson, Walter Frischknecht, Wolf Hunziker, Gunnar Martinsson, Max Schoch and Albert Zulauf. The architects and designers who worked successfully with Ernst Cramer were equally enthusiastic about my project. Thanks to you as well: Siegfried Bertschi, Fred Cramer, Rainer Fleischhauer, Alois Egger, Willy Guhl, Bruno Gerosa, Heini Seiberth, Georg Steiner, Franz Steinbrüchel, Fritz Stucky, Hans-Rudolf Suter and Walter Walch. Emil Siegfried Oberholzer proved to be a brilliant connoisseur of the work in Ticino and set up impressive on-site encounters with particular gardens and individuals.

It is to the credit of Stefan Rotzler, who knew and admired Ernst Cramer, and the late Gertrud Cramer to have undertaken a first investigation of the Cramer estate. I would like to sincerely thank Stefan Rotzler for his helpful information, and am grateful to Gertrud Cramer and her children Susanna Schneider-Cramer and Hans-Ulrich Cramer for their kind support.

Emil Steiner, editor of the Schweizerisches Gartenbaublatt for many years and friend of Ernst Cramer, proved to be an outstanding Cramer connoisseur and excellent expert on Swiss garden architecture. Thank you for so readily sharing your wealth of experience with me.

I should also like to thank my friends, colleagues and the assistants at the chair of Landscape Architecture at the ETH Zurich. Its director, Professor Christophe Girot, was generous in granting me the time to bring this publication to a close.

To Andreas Tremp and Professor Chet Volski I am indebted for constructive criticism on the draft manuscript and the English translation of this book. But there is scarcely anyone who knows the entire project as well as Andreas Müller, who yet again amazed and delighted me with his open-mindedness and tireless commitment. Karin Weisener gave the material the right graphic polish, being appropriately persistant and showing a fine sense of the essentials. I am extraordinarily grateful to both of you in contributing to the successful outcome of this project.

But I owe no one more heartfelt thanks than my wife Rita Weilacher.

INDEX

This publication was made possible by the kind support
of the following institutions:

ETH Transfer, Swiss Federal Institute of Technology Zurich
Chair of Landscape Architecture, ETH Zurich
Roche Ltd in Sisseln

AEW Energie AG, Aarau
Cassinelli-Vogel-Foundation, Zurich
Ernst Göhner Foundation, Zurich
Eternit AG, Niederurnen
STEO Foundation, Zurich
City of Zurich

Pro Helvetia Arts Council of Switzerland

Editor:
Andreas Müller, Berlin

Graphic Design:
Karin Weisener, Zurich

English translation:
Michael Robinson, London

Copy-editing of the English edition:
Susanne Schindler, Los Angeles/Berlin

Proofreading of the German edition:
Michael Wachholz, Berlin

Proofreading of the English edition:
Ian Pepper, Berlin

Reproductions:
Bertschi & Messmer, Basel

Printing:
Konkordia, Bühl

Binding:
Spinner GmbH, Ottersweier

This book is also available in a German
language edition (ISBN 3-7643-6568-4).

A CIP catalogue record for this book is available from
the Library of Congress, Washington, D. C., USA

Die Deutsche Bibliothek – CIP-Einheitsaufnahme

Visionary gardens: modern landscapes
by Ernst Cramer / Udo Weilacher. With forewords
by Peter Latz and Arthur Rüegg. – Basel; Berlin;
Boston : Birkhäuser, 2001
   Dt. Ausg. u.d.T.: Visionäre Gärten
   ISBN 3-7643-6567-6

© 2001 Birkhäuser – Publishers for Architecture,
P.O.Box 133, CH-4010 Basel, Switzerland
A member of the BertelsmannSpringer Publishing Group
Printed on acid-free paper produced from chlorine-free pulp. TCF ∞
Printed in Germany
ISBN 3-7643-6567-6

www.birkhauser.ch

9 8 7 6 5 4 3 2 1